D1584384

# Discover
# Florida

Contents ➜

Throughout this book, we use these icons to highlight special recommendations:

 **The Best...**
Lists for everything from bars to wildlife – to make sure you don't miss out

 **Don't Miss**
A must-see – don't go home until you've been there

 Local Knowledge | Local experts reveal their top picks and secret highlights

 **Detour**
Special places a little off the beaten track

 **If you like...**
Lesser-known alternatives to world-famous attractions

These icons help you quickly identify reviews in the text and on the map:

 **Sights**

 **Eating**

 **Drinking**

 **Sleeping**

 **Information**

**This edition written and researched by**
**Adam Karlin**
**Jeff Campbell**
**Jennifer Denniston**

33

1 3 MAY 2017

WITHDRAWN

03872723 - ITEM
...EX COUNTY COUNCIL

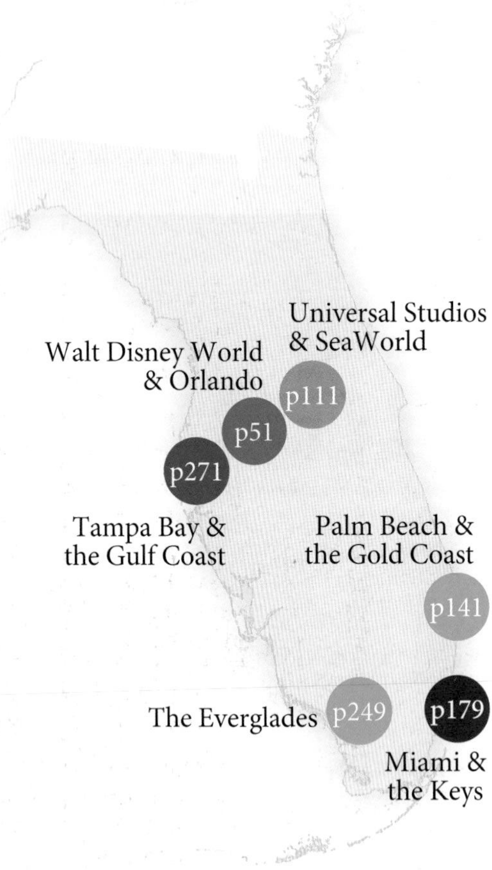
Universal Studios & SeaWorld
p111
Walt Disney World & Orlando
p51
p271
Tampa Bay & the Gulf Coast
Palm Beach & the Gold Coast
p141
The Everglades
p249
p179
Miami & the Keys

## Palm Beach & the Gold Coast



## Miami & the Keys



## Walt Disney



## Universal



## Everglades

# Contents

# Contents

## On the Road

## In Focus

## Survival Guide

# This is Florida

Florida is the USA's playground. Florida is bracken wetlands that melt under soul-searing sunsets. Florida is blue lakes, teal oceans and green rivers cutting a tropical plain into parcels of romantic beauty. Florida is sand like snow. Florida is cities that have dedicated themselves to giving you food, shopping, nightlife and enjoyment. Florida is waiting.

## This state exudes a powerful attraction.
Generation after generation of travelers keeps coming back. Our grandparents had retirement cottages here. Our parents can recall childhood visions of mermaids and manatees and Mickey that their children remember with a similar warm-hearted nostalgia, and want to pass on to the next generation and the next.

## These recollections encapsulate what many deem 'Old Florida.'
But Old Florida sits alongside the new here as the state is constantly pushing itself to reinvent the best in tourism. If you want it, Florida has it, in every color, size and shape.

## There are malls near Fort Myers where you can live out your most lurid consumer fantasies.
Thanks to demand for the local, organic and indigenous, those malls are a few miles from neighborly farmer's markets. There are theme parks galore in Orlando, while in the Everglades to the south and Apalachicola to the north, there are state and national parks where a unique subtropical environment is protected by dedicated citizens settling new frontiers in conservation and environmentalism.

## There are miles of beach in Miami.
And beyond sun and sun, a world class, daring arts district. There are the latest toys and trends of the wealthy in Palm Beach, and a few hours south, simple pleasures and parades dedicated to flights of fantasy in Key West.

## And everywhere you go there is the backbone of Florida: visitors.
They can find anything here, and often, more than what they expected. Get ready to join their satisfied ranks.

> 66
> Florida is the USA's playground
> 99

Lifeguard house at Miami's South Beach (p193).

PHOTOGRAPHER: MCDC/ ISTOCK IMAGES ©

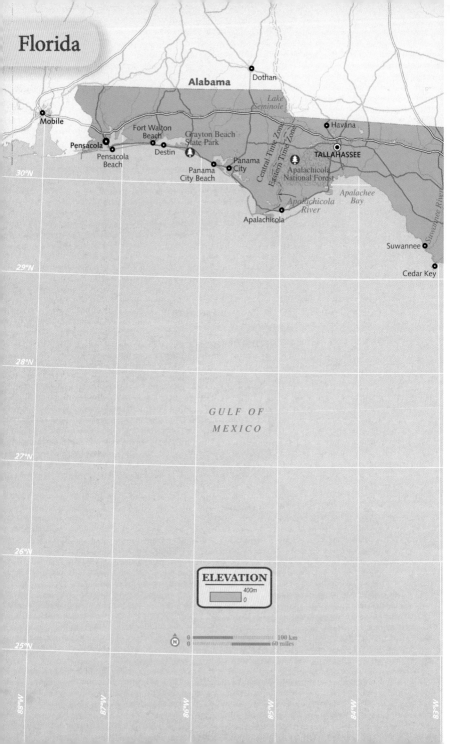

Georgia
Fernandina Beach
Amelia Island
Jacksonville
ATLANTIC OCEAN
St Augustine
Anastasia Island
St John's River
Gainesville
Ocala National Forest
Daytona Beach
Ocala
Canaveral National Seashore
Crystal River
Homosassa Springs
Orlando
Cape Canaveral
Caladesi Island
Cocoa Beach
Melbourne
Lakeland
Florida's Turnpike (toll)
Clearwater
Tampa
St Pete Beach
St Petersburg
Tampa Bay
Fort DeSoto Park
Bradenton
Sarasota
Fort Pierce
Venice
Lake Okeechobee
Palm Beach
Cayo Costa State Park
Fort Myers
Delray Beach
Corkscrew Swamp Sanctuary
Boca Raton
Captiva Island
Sanibel Island
Big Cypress National Preserve
Fort Lauderdale
Alligator Alley
Hollywood Beach
Naples
The Everglades
Miami Beach
Miami
Shark Valley
John Pennekamp Coral Reef State Park
Everglades National Park
Florida City
Flamingo
Florida Bay
Key Largo
Dry Tortugas National Park
Florida Keys
Straits of Florida
Key West
31°N
30°N
29°N
28°N
27°N
25°N
81°W
80°W

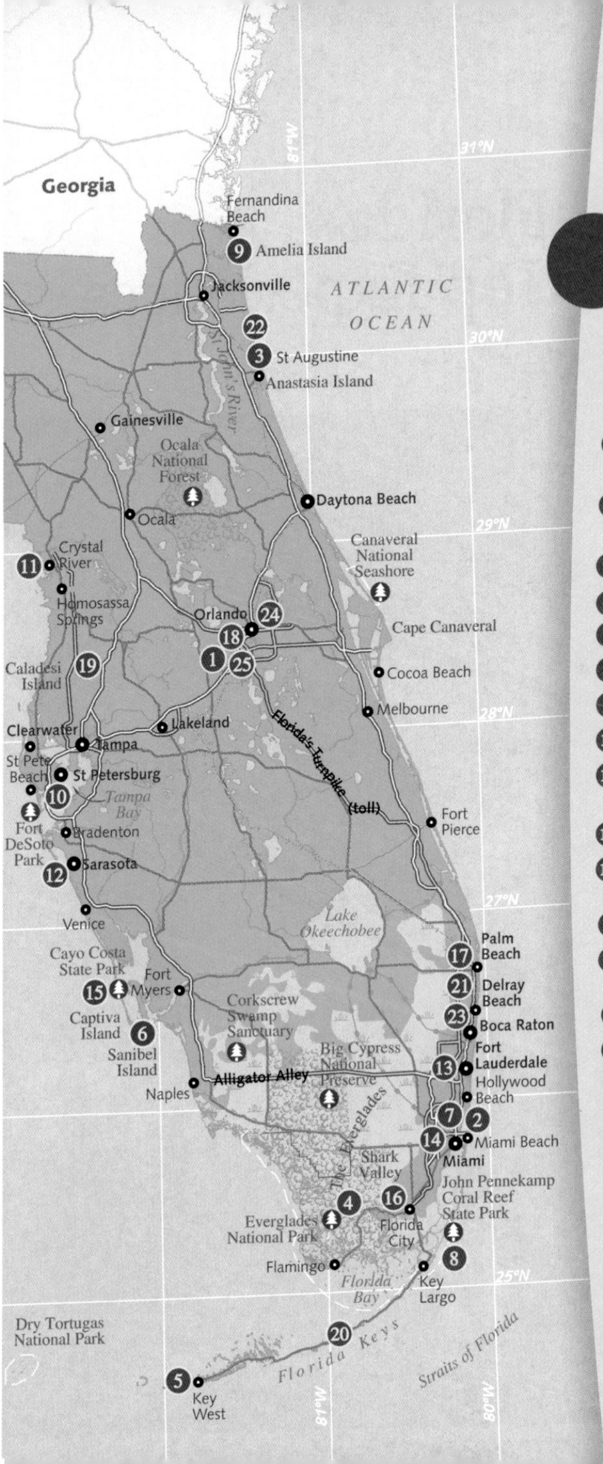

# 25 Top Experiences

1. Walt Disney World
2. Miami Art Deco Historic District
3. Spanish Quarter Museum
4. Wildlife in the Everglades National Park
5. Key West
6. Shelling on Sanibel Island
7. Hollywood Beach
8. Snorkeling in the Keys
9. Amelia Island
10. Salvador Dalí Museum
11. Swimming with Manatees
12. Mote Marine Laboratory
13. Gondola Ride through Fort Lauderdale
14. Miami Art Scene
15. Exploring the Gulf Islands
16. Robert Is Here
17. Shopping in Palm Beach
18. Wizarding World of Harry Potter
19. Weeki Wachee Springs State Park
20. Overseas Hwy Road Trip
21. Blowing Rocks Preserve
22. St Augustine Ghost Tours
23. Morikami Museum & Japanese Gardens
24. Winter Park
25. SeaWorld

# 25 Florida's Top Experiences

# Walt Disney World

Florida's basic reason for being is to function as the world's best playground, and nowhere is this truer than Walt Disney World (p64). Mickey's home is one of the world's original theme parks, the embodiment of imagination and flights of fancy. Children can explore a bright realm that caters to their every need, and adults quickly revert back to childhood. Yes, it gets crowded, but it's the gold standard in all-American fun for a reason. Besides, if you don't go your kids will never, ever forgive you. Expedition Everest (p75)

1

DISNEY ©

## Miami Art Deco Historic District

Art deco isn't just distinctive in Miami. In the Art Deco Historic District (p193), it's definitive. An early 20th-century expression of aesthetic that embodies seemingly contradictory impulses – modernity with nostalgia, streamlining with embellishment, subdued colors and riots of pastel – whatever your take on deco may be, you'll be hard-pressed to find a better concentration of a style that simply screams 'South Florida' outside of Miami and Miami Beach.

## Spanish Quarter Museum

New England and Virginia like to claim they're the oldest parts of America, but the record for a contiguously inhabited city in the continental USA is held by St Augustine. The local Spanish Quarter Museum (p313) covers two acres of grounds and one specific era of history: 1740. Costumed re-enactors go the extra mile by sleeping in scratchy period clothing in camps outside of the complex, so you know you're getting an authentic peek into Florida's – and America's – earliest European roots.

## The Best...
## Theme Parks

**WALT DISNEY WORLD**
The king of all theme parks wears a mouse-eared crown. (p64)

**UNIVERSAL STUDIOS**
A cutting-edge theme park with the most innovative rides. (p122)

**SEAWORLD**
Underwater encounters, killer whales, dolphin shows and oceanic delights abound. (p132)

**BUSCH GARDENS**
Themed around Africa, this park melds wildlife with family fun. (p291)

**WEEKI WACHEE SPRINGS STATE PARK**
The local mermaids are a font of nostalgic Florida romance. (p309)

# The Best...
# Historical Sites

### ART DECO HISTORIC DISTRICT
Miami Beach's art deco district encompasses the best of South Beach. (p193)

### EDISON & FORD WINTER ESTATES
The original snowbird mansions for two American barons of industry. (p300)

### HEMINGWAY HOUSE
Where the great author lived, loved, drank, fought and wrote. (p239)

### INDIAN KEY STATE HISTORIC SITE
Vine-encrusted ruins of a once-inhabited island only accessible by boat. (p233)

### VIZCAYA MANSION
The greatest, grandest and most imaginative of Miami's wedding-cake mansions. (p201)

DOUGLAS STEAKLEY/LONELY PLANET IMAGES ©

## 4 Wildlife in the Everglades National Park

No one can contend with the Sunshine State when it comes to Jurassic-era tropical primeval goodness. At the Royal Palm Visitor Center (p263), peek past trees standing sentinel in wine-dark water, and you'll see great flapping pterodactyl-esque herons, snapping turtles basking under an almost Pleistocene sun, and dozens of alligators. Nature's perfect grinning predator, leathery carnivores found a working design and haven't changed it for millions of years.

CORBIS/TONY ARRUZA ©

## 5 Key West

Here's an island that balances two poles of travel. It's a mangrove-cloaked kingdom where almost anything goes, leading to tolerance of creative types. Yet, Key West is also family friendly, a sunny shelter for folks who want a civilized escape amid stately tropical architecture, excellent dining and innocent (if eccentric) Americana. See both sides of the Key West experience at Mallory Square's daily sunset street festivals (p237).

# Shelling on Sanibel Island

Sanibel Island (p275) has one of the heaviest concentrations of shells in the world. This highlight already sounds like a tongue twister, and just to add some more 'S' sounds, if you visit Sanibel you'll develop the distinctive 'Sanibel stoop' from bending over to inspect little creamy rainbow gems on the sand.

# Hollywood Beach

In Hollywood Beach (p176), there are loads of beautiful people who resemble LA celebrities, and some nights, a few real celebrities strolling about, too. But Hollywood Beach consciously makes an effort to be all accommodating and family friendly. You can shop for a corny souvenir and then run across a gaggle of models heading to the local ice-cream parlor on the boardwalk.

# Snorkeling in the Keys

The continental USA has one coral reef to boast of, and Florida is where it's at. Drive to Key Largo, northernmost of the Florida Keys, and head to John Pennekamp Coral Reef State Park (p231). The trick is getting under the surface of the park – literally. Take a trip from the marina onto and into the water, where you'll find bursts of rainbow-colored fish and water so clear it could be a window. If you don't dive, getting SCUBA-certified here is the capstone of any Florida vacation.

## The Best...
## Beaches

**HOLLYWOOD BEACH**
A bare minimum of attitude, a whole lot of swagger. (p176)

**BAHIA HONDA STATE PARK**
Wild, windswept and wonderful; a perfect slice of the Keys. (p236)

**BOWMAN'S BEACH**
Sparkling sand and family-friendly shelling on quiet Sanibel Island. (p275)

**FORT LAUDERDALE BEACH**
Open views and the Atlantic Ocean combine into a beach exemplar. (p168)

**SOUTH BEACH**
South Beach is sand, celebrities and sexiness sizzling under the sun. (p190)

## Amelia Island

North Florida is part of the Deep South, and one of the more charming reminders of this geographic trivia is Amelia Island (p313). A moss and magnolia draped sea island located just 13 miles south of the Georgia border, Amelia's hub, Fernandina Beach, is as gorgeous a cluster of preserved historical goodness as you'll find between here and the Mason Dixon line. Did we mention cute restaurants and cafes, plenty of Civil War–era history, stately groves of oak trees and gorgeous beaches? Because that's all here, too.

## The Best...
## Outdoors

**SHELLING ON SANIBEL**
Get a suntan, your knees bent and some rare shells. (p275)

**CYCLING MIAMI**
The flat terrain of Miami is perfect for bicycle-bound adventures. (p206)

**PADDLING THE PANHANDLE**
Take a kayak along the waters of Apalachicola National Forest. (p315)

**HIKING IN THE EVERGLADES**
Long hauls and short-jaunt trails prevail in this park. (p260)

**CAYO COSTA STATE PARK**
This semi-isolated island is begging to be explored. (p306)

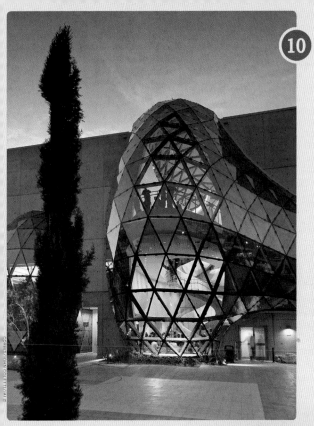

## 10 Salvador Dalí Museum

It's hard to create a museum dedicated to a specific artist. But it's even more difficult to make that museum as clever and creative as the body of said artist's work. And that's where the Salvador Dalí Museum (p295) in St Petersburg, one of the finest modern art museums in Florida, deserves a lot of credit. This innovative experience lures you into Dalí's creative process via architectural tricks (like a contemplation room and sitting garden) on the one hand, and excellent, knowledgeable staff on the other.

## Swimming with Manatees

**11**

The manatee, ponderous icon of the Florida conservation movement, is one of the more interesting species in the world. They're not what you'd call magnificent, or even cute in a conventional sense. But their bulk is immensely endearing – manatees appear kind – and at Crystal River (p310) you can swim a slow, sweet ballet with these gentle giants. The time to come is winter, when hundreds of manatees float their unhurried way into the blue waters of Kings Bay.

## Mote Marine Laboratory

Maybe you don't like aquariums. Maybe you think there's too much flash and not enough science, or the opposite: the science isn't presented in an easily understood way. If either of these criticisms apply to you, or if, on the other hand, you love aquariums, come to the Mote Marine Laboratory (p297) in Sarasota. Part research facility, part aquarium, all educational, and accessible to everyone from scholar to layman, this is one of the finest aquariums in a state that does the genre well.

## Gondola Ride through Fort Lauderdale

If Las Olas Blvd is the heart of Fort Lauderdale, then the hundreds of canals that spread throughout the city are the city's veins and capillaries. The best way to explore South Florida's second city is via gondola (p171). These narrated tours offer nice insight and are a good peek under Lauderdale's skin, although you're welcome to opt for a silent gondola tour for a more romantic experience.

## Miami Art Scene

To me Miami's masterstroke of urban planning has been to use the arts as an engine for city renewal. The move has taken the form of projects like the Adrienne Arsht Center for the Performing Arts and the magnificent New World Center, and marketing the heck out of Midtown Miami, the location of dozens of art galleries and studios. On every weekend of the month you can find arts walks throughout Miami's many neighborhoods (p226), giving you the chance to stroll and peruse paintings, all usually accompanied by a drink. Art Basel, Miami (p45)

## The Best...
# Nightlife Hotspots

**DOWNTOWN/MIDTOWN MIAMI**
The best local hotspots in Miami can be found here. (p225)

**ORLANDO**
Downtown and Greater Orlando have a pumping party scene. (p105)

**YBOR CITY**
Tampa flexes her dancing and entertainment muscles in this district. (p283)

**KEY WEST**
Key West, to put it lightly, really likes to party. (p246)

**MIAMI BEACH**
Beautiful, brash, sexy and celebrity-studded – and yet sometimes, surprisingly down to earth! (p225)

# The Best...
## Culture & Arts

**SALVADOR DALÍ MUSEUM**
Fascinating modern art museum and exploration of one surrealist's life. (p295)

**ADRIENNE ARSHT CENTER FOR THE PERFORMING ARTS**
This wonderful venue bestrides Miami like a set of seashells. (p198)

**MORIKAMI MUSEUM & JAPANESE GARDENS**
Delray Beach's excellent oasis of Japanese arts and aesthetic sensibility. (p162)

**STRAZ CENTER FOR THE PERFORMING ARTS**
Tampa's gem, this is the Gulf Coast's finest theater venue. (p288)

**ORLANDO MUSEUM OF ART**
Once you're done at Disney, absorb fantastic high culture here. (p94)

**15**

## Exploring the Gulf Islands

Florida's Atlantic Coast gets lots of attention from visitors, and rightly so, but the state's Gulf Coast is quintessentially Floridian. Calm, cozy and still like a warm bath, one of the joys of the Gulf Coast – besides considerable wildlife, good beaches and pretty shoreside towns – are its offshore islands. From calm colonies of low-impact seaside developments like Sanibel and Captiva to bubbly hamlets like Siesta Key, to the Zen-induced physical serenity of Cayo Costa (p306), there's a Gulf Coast island made just for you.

PHOTOGRAPHER: LEFT: GETTY/TIM FITZHARRIS © RIGHT: CORBIS/ RICHARD BICKEL ©

## Robert Is Here

We know: why get excited about a farmers' stand? Well, Robert Is Here (for more on the origin of the funny name, see p267) is more than a produce shack. It's a quirky, long-standing emblem of South Florida agriculture and Old Florida eccentricity. It's a petting zoo, a roadside attraction and a place to get some of the best orange juice in the world. Basically, Robert Is Here is an experience, and if you're driving around Homestead, you should be Here, too.

## Shopping in Palm Beach

If you ever waltz into a Grimm's fairy tale and meet the famed emperor who had no clothes, let his highness know he should pop on over to Worth Ave in Palm Beach (p156) to restock his closet. Shopping doesn't get much more aristocratic than this, but you don't need a fat wallet to appreciate Palm Beach (although it helps). Just walking Worth Ave gives a sense of joining, if ever so briefly, the jet set and all the glamour and attitude that world contains.

# Wizarding World of Harry Potter

Florida is where the frontiers of the theme park experience are getting pushed waaay past roller coasters. Enter: the Wizarding World of Harry Potter in Universal Studios (p128). Folks, short of buying a magic broomstick and taking to the Quidditch field, this is as close as you'll come to immersing yourself in Hogwarts. The most jaded theme-park cynics are wowed by the wonder of the Wizarding World, and if you've got any sense of imagination, prepare to have it stimulated to new heights.

## The Best...
## Shopping

**WORTH AVENUE**
The glitziest shopping strip in Florida is a luxury-goods paradise. (p156)

**DESIGN DISTRICT**
Miami's mecca for unique furniture, *objects d'art* and designer homewares. (p227)

**ST ARMAND'S CIRCLE**
More than a mall, St Armand's is Sarasota's social center. (p297)

**KEY WEST**
Look no further for quirky, art-inspired gifts, crafts and souvenirs. (p247)

**CITYPLACE**
West Palm Beach adores its own lovely outdoor shopping mall megaplex. (p157)

## Weeki Wachee Springs State Park

19

We give Florida credit for keeping nostalgic travel romance alive and well. Nostalgia is basically the name of the game at Weeki Wachee Springs (p309), where 'mermaids' have entertained travelers such as Elvis Presley and Esther Williams since 1947. This isn't just impressive underwater ballet (although it is very much that), it's a window into the past and the kitschy sort of attractions that established Florida as America's playground back in the day.

## The Best...
## Food Scenes

**TAMPA**
The capital of the Gulf Coast boasts international-quality restaurants (p285)

**FORT LAUDERDALE**
Lauderdale's food scene trots the globe and showcases local goodness. (p173)

**MIDTOWN MIAMI**
Forget South Beach; locals go here for Miami's best food. (p216)

**KEY WEST**
This little island has some incredibly diverse eating options. (p245)

**ST PETERSBURG**
The Gulf Coast's second city has a sophisticated dining scene. (p292)

## ⑳ Overseas Hwy Road Trip

Traveling around the USA is all about road trips, which we usually associate with mountains, waving grain and other America the Beautiful imagery. But how about a road trip (p236) that traverses over 100 miles of bridges and causeways and pretty mangrove islets, all scattered throughout the twin teal and blue brackets of Florida Bay and the Gulf of Mexico? This is the Overseas Hwy, which connects the Florida Keys to the mainland, and you to all the quirks, characters and sunny sensibilities of Keys life.

CORBIS/GLOWIMAGES ©

## Blowing Rocks Preserve

Blowing Rocks (p170) is a natural wonder: a limestone outcrop perfectly positioned on the state's southeastern Atlantic Coast where water occasionally spews through like a raging geyser. What we really love about this spot is its isolation. Blowing Rocks is far from South Florida's rampant development. Within the protected area of the preserve, you'll find pristine biomes that give you a good feel for the wild heart of the state.

## St Augustine Ghost Tours

St Augustine has been around for almost 500 years and been a haven for conquistadors, smugglers, pirates and (gasp) politicians. For a taste of noir in paradise, get with the folks at St Augustine City Walks (p314). They run fine walking tours of their home that show off plenty of pride, quirks and more than a few spots supposedly haunted by ghosts of St Augustine past.

# Morikami Museum & Japanese Gardens

Delray Beach is not the sort of spot where we expect to find a gateway unto Zen wisdom and Japanese aesthetics, but hey, Florida is full of surprises like that. If you're in the area, do yourself a favor and visit the heart-wrenchingly beautiful Morikami Museum and Japanese Gardens (p162), the best collection of Japanese art in the state and a fine example of landscaping. The history behind the gorgeous gardens is as poignant as the rows of pruned shrubbery and bonsai plants.

## The Best...
## Wildlife

### HOMOSASSA SPRINGS WILDLIFE STATE PARK
A semi-safari of the best of native Florida wildlife. (p308

### EVERGLADES NATIONAL PARK
See gators, waterfowl, snakes and Florida at her most beautiful. (p260)

### JN 'DING' DARLING NATIONAL WILDLIFE REFUGE
A quiet slice of pristine Gulf Coast nature and fauna. (p306)

### JOHN PENNEKAMP CORAL REEF STATE PARK
Get a glimpse of the wildlife that lies beneath Florida's surface. (p231)

### SWIMMING WITH MANATEES
Take a cool, refreshing dip with Florida's own gentle giants. (p310)

## Winter Park

Orlando's theme parks are the main tourism draw in Central Florida, and with good reason. But if you can find the time to take a break from Disney and Universal, we highly recommend a day spent browsing the quiet bookshops and pretty art galleries of Winter Park (p101). This well-kept suburb is a gem, a good spot to while away the day engaging in understated pleasantries, sipping coffee at nice cafes, snacking at excellent restaurants and perusing the latest arts walks and gallery showcases.

## The Best...
## Parks

## 25

# SeaWorld

The most family-friendly, easily accessible route to engaging Florida's fantastic underwater wildlife is SeaWorld (p132). You can watch dolphins (even swim with them), traverse acres of excellent aquarium-style exhibits, feed tropical birds and, of course, watch those killer whales! Discovery Cove and Aquatica are the exceptional, adjacent water parks that will keep kids and adult thrill-seekers soaked and entertained. If you're in the mood, a sleepy stretch on the Lazy River is pretty relaxing...

# Florida's Top Itineraries

# Islands of Adventure to Downtown Disney Theme Park Party

**5 DAYS**

*This Orlando itinerary is tailored to give you time to trip around some of the best theme parks in the world while still giving you a window to enjoy the fine dining, shopping and lifestyle goodness found within said park properties.*

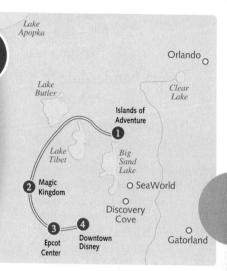

## ① Islands of Adventure (p122)

We'll start this theme-park parade with Florida's most daring park design at Islands of Adventure. Part of Universal Studios, Islands appeals to older children and adults who are kids at heart. The centerpiece of the park is the **Wizarding World of Harry Potter**, at the time of writing the most impressive theme-park experience we've encountered. Have dinner (try the barbeque) at the brilliant **Yellow Dog Eats** in nearby Windermere.

ISLANDS OF ADVENTURE ➲ MAGIC KINGDOM

🚌 **30 minutes** The easiest route between parks is I-4E.

## ② Magic Kingdom (p64)

Move on to the Magic Kingdom, Walt Disney World's foundation stone. **Cinderella's Castle** still graces princess dreams, while the **Pirates of the Caribbean** awaits, along with thrilling **Space Mountain**. Hop on the **monorail**, and have a vintage Americana meal at the **50's Prime Time Cafe** for good-deal Disney dining.

Big Thunder Mountain Railroad (p65) in Walt Disney World.
DISNEY ©

MAGIC KINGDOM ➲ EPCOT CENTER

🚌🚌🚢 **One hour** Connect via monorail, bus or boat through the Transportation & Ticket Center.

## ③ Epcot Center (p70)

Have breakfast at the artsy **White Wolf Café** in Orlando, then head back to the park. Dominated by its geodesic dome, Epcot is an old-school version of what Disney once considered the future to be. The **World Showcase** is also one of the better places to eat in the park. Stick around for the brilliant **Illuminations** light show. If you head back into Orlando, check out the **Ravenous Pig**, a fun, delicious gastropub.

EPCOT CENTER ➲ DOWNTOWN DISNEY

🚌🚌🚢 **One hour** Connect via monorail, bus or boat through the Transportation & Ticket Center.

## ④ Downtown Disney (p80)

An enormous shopping, eating and hotel complex, **Downtown Disney** is where adults can engage in indulgences galore. Dining here is some of the best within the park. If you have time later in the day, leave the park and go swimming at **Typhoon Lagoon**.

**5 DAYS**

# Fort Lauderdale to Jupiter
## Digging Up the Gold Coast

*Southeast Florida is known as the Gold Coast, a tribute to the golden coins left behind by European shipwrecks. Today the title references yellow sands, burnished sunsets and gilt-edged lifestyles of towns like Palm Beach.*

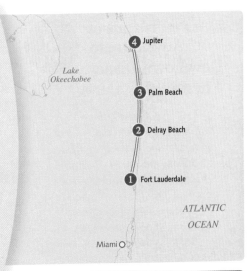

Lake Okeechobee

4 Jupiter

3 Palm Beach

2 Delray Beach

1 Fort Lauderdale

ATLANTIC OCEAN

Miami O

## ① Fort Lauderdale (p168)

South Florida's second city has a wonderful stretch of sand in the form of the **Fort Lauderdale Beach and Promenade**. Have a walk by the water, then get around *on* the water via **gondola** so you can explore Fort Lauderdale's many canals. Make sure you take time to stroll the breezy **Riverwalk** and **Las Olas Riverfront**, and take a tour of the city's lovely harbor on the good ship **Carrie B**.

**FORT LAUDERDALE ➡ DELRAY BEACH**
🚗 **30 minutes** Delray Beach is north of Fort Lauderdale on I-95.

## ② Delray Beach (p162)

Drive north of Fort Lauderdale and pop into Boca Raton to take in the **Gumbo Limbo Nature Center**, a wonderful preserve that includes a sea turtle rehabilitation center. Have lunch and laze the day away in pretty **Mizner Park**. Further north is Delray Beach, home of the **Morikami Museum and Japanese Gardens**, a vale of meditative serenity and *objets d'art* from across Japan. The on-site, acclaimed **Cornell Cafe** serves delicious Japanese cuisine.

**DELRAY BEACH ➡ PALM BEACH**
🚗 **30 minutes** Palm Beach is north of Delray Beach on I-95.

## ③ Palm Beach (p152)

Make sure you stop at **Lake Worth Beach**, the midway point between Delray and Palm Beach, widely considered one of the best beaches in south Florida. You can enjoy half the day here wandering slowly along the seashore. There's excellent Caribbean seafood here at **Sheila's Bahamian Conch & BBQ**. In Palm Beach, marvel at the opulence of the rich and famous in the **Flagler Museum**, on ritzy Ocean Blvd, and along posh **Worth Ave**. The next morning make sure to have some of the best brunch around at the famous **Circle** restaurant at the Breakers Resort.

**PALM BEACH ➡ JUPITER**
🚗 **1 ½ hours** Head north via US 1 or I-95.

## ④ Jupiter (p170)

Just a quick, scenic drive north of Palm Beach, you'll find the attractive beach town of Jupiter, one of Florida's better surfing sites. Nearby you can find the state's version of Old Faithful: the gushing geyser of water at **Blowing Rocks Preserve**. Just north of here is **Hobe Sound National Wildlife Refuge**, where you can find 3½ miles of pristine beach that sea turtles use for nesting in June and July.

Scene at Fort Lauderdale Beach (p168).
ALAMY/NOBLEIMAGES ©

# 10 DAYS

## Tampa to Universal Studios
### From Gulf to Gryffindor

*On this trip we're taking in the arts, culture, kitsch and natural beauty of the Gulf Coast, the becalmed, bathwater-warm alternative to the showy Atlantic Coast, and then turning inland to enjoy the rides and resorts of Universal Studios.*

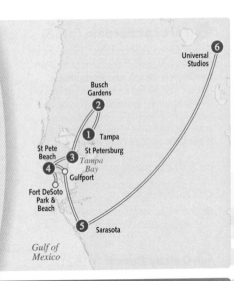

Universal Studios ⑥

Busch Gardens ②

① Tampa

St Pete Beach
St Petersburg

③ *Tampa Bay*

④
Gulfport

Fort DeSoto Park & Beach

⑤ Sarasota

*Gulf of Mexico*

# ① Tampa (p282)

Experience Tampa's family-friendly and cultural sides of the city by taking in the **Lowry Park Zoo** and checking out the **Tampa Museum of Art** – you can do both in a day, with a break for lunch at **Columbia Restaurant**. In the evening, if you're feeling up for cigars and beer (or bright lights), go to Cuban-influenced **Ybor City**.

### TAMPA ● BUSCH GARDENS

🚗**20 minutes** Take I-275 north; Busch Gardens is off exit 50.

# ② Busch Gardens (p291)

A quick drive north of downtown Tampa is **Busch Gardens**, with nine 'African' regions, roller coasters, an open savannah populated by African animals and nearby **Adventure Island** water park. Eating options are OK, but you'll find a better dinner at the **Refinery** in Tampa.

### BUSCH GARDENS ● ST PETERSBURG

🚗**40 minutes** Take I-275 to St Petersburg, 32 miles to the south.

# ③ St Petersburg (p290)

'St Pete' is filled with good culture, good food and good times. Walk around charming historic **Coffee Pot Bayou**, then go forward in time to the ultramodern **Dalí Museum**. During the day have an American-style bistro lunch at **Cassis**.

### ST PETERSBURG ● ST PETE BEACH

🚗**25 minutes** St Pete Beach is nine miles west of downtown St Petersburg. 🚍**45 minutes** Pinellas Suncoast Transit Authority (PSTA) offers a day pass for $4.50.

# ④ St Pete Beach (p294)

**Fort DeSoto Park and Beach** is one of the best beaches on the Gulf Coast. Make a side trip to **Suncoast Bird Sanctuary**, the largest wild bird sanctuary in North America, and **St Pete Beach**, packed with restaurants and bars. Spend the night in the amiable artists' colony of **Gulfport**.

### ST PETERSBURG ● SARASOTA

🚗**45 minutes** Go south of St Petersburg via I-275 and US-301.

# ⑤ Sarasota (p297)

Have Sarasota's best breakfast at the **Broken Egg**, then spend the day at the **Mote Marine Laboratory**, a research center that doubles as a superlative aquarium. In the evening, wander **St Armand's Circle**, an attractive outdoor shopping area.

### SARASOTA ● UNIVERSAL STUDIOS

🚗**2 ½ hours** I-75N from Sarasota, exit 261 to take I-4E toward Orlando.

# ⑥ Universal Studios (p122)

Depart the laidback Gulf Coast for flashy **Universal Studios**. We recommend **Islands of Adventure**, which boasts some of the best rides and themed 'zones' of any Orlando-area park. Make sure to explore the wonderful **Wizarding World of Harry Potter**, where an actual sorting hat assigns you to Hufflepuff, Ravenclaw, Slytherin (boo) or Gryffindor (yay!).

---

The Tampa Museum of Art (p283).
ALAMY/IAN DAGNALL ©

## 10 DAYS

# Miami to Key West
## South Florida's Finest

*You're taking in lots of beauty on this trip: Miami's beautiful people and skyline, Miami Beach's sand and architecture, the ethereal splendor of the Everglades and the funky, quirky good looks of Key West and her sister islands.*

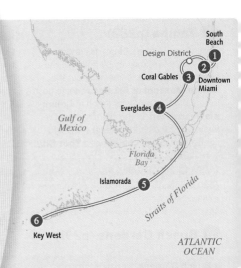

South Beach
Design District
1
Coral Gables 3 2
Downtown Miami
Gulf of Mexico
Everglades 4
Florida Bay
Islamorada 5
6
Key West
Straits of Florida
ATLANTIC OCEAN

# ① South Beach (p193)

Tour the **Art Deco Historic District** and afterwards, pop into the **Wolfsonian-FIU** to learn more about Miami design and architecture. At night, wander up the neon avenue of **Ocean Dr**. When you're worn out from sightseeing, have a delicious Caribbean dinner at Haitian **Tap Tap**.

SOUTH BEACH ❂ DOWNTOWN MIAMI

🚗 **30 minutes** The MacArthur and Venetian causeways connect South Beach to Downtown. 🚌 **30 minutes to one hour** Bus routes A, C, S, M and 120; see www.miamidade.gov/transit for more.

# ② Downtown Miami (p198)

In Downtown Miami, ride the free monorail, the **Metromover**, for a tour of the city skyline. In the evening, head to the **Design District** to sample Miami's best restaurants and nightlife; we recommend the small plates menu at innovative **Michy's**.

DOWNTOWN MIAMI ❂ CORAL GABLES

🚗 **15 to 30 minutes** Located just south of Downtown Miami.

# ③ Coral Gables (p202)

The official heart of Miami's Cuban community is Little Havana; stop by **Maximo Gomez Park** to see old-timers play chess and dominoes. Next door, Coral Gables is full of Mediterranean-style homes, designer shops on **Miracle Mile**, and grand structures like the nearby **Vizcaya Mansion**. Make sure to browse the shelves at **Books and Books**, the best independent book store in Miami.

CORAL GABLES [❂] EVERGLADES

🚗 **One hour** Go south on US 1 or SW 177th Ave/ Krome Ave.

# ④ Everglades (p260)

In this unique wetland you can spot dozens of alligators at the **Royal Palm Visitor Center,** go for a hike along the **Pinelands** trail or watch the sunset from the **Pa-hay-okee Overlook**.

EVERGLADES ❂ ISLAMORADA

🚗 **1 ½ hours** Go south on US 1, which becomes Overseas Hwy in Key Largo. 🚌 **Two to three hours** Commuter buses go from Homestead to the Keys; expect long rides.

# ⑤ Islamorada (p233)

The drive across the Keys is one of the USA's great road trips. In Key Largo, take a glass-bottom boat ride at **John Pennekamp Coral Reef State Park.** Further south in Islamorada, feed the giant fish at **Robbie's Marina**.

ISLAMORADA ❂ KEY WEST

🚗 **Two hours** The drive on the Overseas Hwy is simply gorgeous. 🚌 **Two to three hours** Commuter buses exist, but the schedule is spotty.

# ⑥ Key West (p237)

Check out the **Turtle Hospital** on Marathon. Tiny deer on **Big Pine Key** are on the road to Key West. On Key West, enjoy the evening visiting the fantasy-inspired nightly carnival in **Mallory Sq**.

A scene from Miami's South Beach (p193).
CORBIS/PAUL COLANGELO ©

# 14 DAYS

## Fort Lauderdale to Orlando
## Florida: Coast to Coast

*On this two-week journey we take a loop through Florida, from the Atlantic Coast of south Florida to the tepid serenity of the Gulf Coast to the theme-park paradise of Orlando. Oh, and we're throwing in a gator-inhabited park to add some Jurassic diversity.*

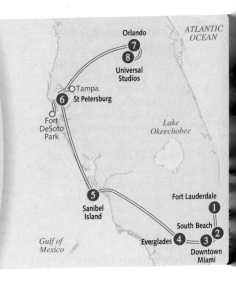

### ❶ Fort Lauderdale (p168)

South Florida's canal-crisscrossed second city has been called the 'Venice of America.' Have a shopping and dining stroll on **Las Olas** and be sure to spend a good chunk of your day wandering the lovely beach **Promenade**.

FORT LAUDERDALE ⬡ SOUTH BEACH

🚗 **45 minutes** I-95S is the quickest way down, but a longer, more scenic route takes in all of Collins Ave.

### ❷ South Beach (p193)

South Beach is simply one of the most beautiful seaside neighborhoods in the country. Take as much in as possible, from the white sands and ocean to the **Art Deco Historic District** to the beautiful people preening on **Lincoln Rd**.

SOUTH BEACH ⬡ DOWNTOWN MIAMI

🚗 **30 minutes** Five causeways link Miami Beach to Miami proper. 🚌 **30 minutes to one hour** Bus routes include A, C, S, M and 120; check www .miamidade.gov/transit.

### ❸ Downtown Miami (p198)

Downtown Miami is bracketed by fascinating **Little Havana**, the heart of the Miami Cuban community, **Wynwood**, and the **Design District**, Miami's official neighborhoods for the arts. Speaking of which, make sure to admire the architecture of the stunning **Adrienne Arsht Center for the Performing Arts**.

DOWNTOWN MIAMI ⬡ EVERGLADES

🚗 **One hour** Take Tamiami Trail/US 41/8th St from Miami to Shark Valley.

### ❹ Everglades(p261)

The Everglades constitute the wild, natural heart of Florida. At **Shark Valley**, you can ride a family-friendly tram, cycle, or walk a flat trail that runs by dozens of alligators and flocks of waterfowl. Check out the photography at the **Clyde Butcher Gallery** on your way out of the park. You can camp in the park, or find good-value lodging in **Everglades City**.

EVERGLADES ⬡ SANIBEL ISLAND

🚗 **Three hours** Take US-41 to Naples, then I-75N to Sanibel.

Whelk shell on the beach at Sanibel Island (p305).
GETTYIMAGES/MARTIN SHIELDS ©

## ⑥ St Petersburg (p290)

Take a detour to check out St Pete's beaches, especially **Fort DeSoto Park**, family friendly and pretty as a postcard. In St Petersburg, avail yourself of fine dining and be sure to visit the Salvador Dalí Museum, an excellent modern arts institution, or catch a show at nearby Tampa's wonderful **Straz Center**.

ST PETERSBURG ➲ ORLANDO

🚗**Two hours** Take I-4E to get to Orlando.

## ⑦ Orlando (p93)

Orlando is much more than theme parks. Wander around the art galleries and cafes of **Winter Park**, and if you want to experience more creativity, go to the extensive, educational **Orlando Museum of Art**. Organic, French fare can be had at cozy **Bikes, Beans & Bordeaux**.

ORLANDO ➲ UNIVERSAL STUDIOS

🚗**20 minutes** Take I-4W to get to Universal Studios

## ⑤ Sanibel Island (p305)

Sanibel Island is a pretty Gulf Island connected to the Florida mainland by causeway. The development here is low-impact, so you can appreciate the island scenery as you potter around. We recommend driving through the **JN 'Ding' Darling Wildlife Refuge** to connect with Florida's natural beauty, and collecting shells on the white sand beaches – the **shelling** here is considered world class.

SANIBEL ISLAND ➲ ST PETERSBURG

🚗**Three hours** I-75N is the easiest way to get to St Petersburg.

## ⑧ Universal Studios (p122)

You can pick whatever theme park you want to visit in Orlando, but we love Universal Studios for the **Wizarding World of Harry Potter**. Of course, if **Disney World** is more your speed, you should spend time wandering around the nostalgic lanes of the **Magic Kingdom** or the semifuturistic realms of **Epcot Center**.

# Florida Month by Month

## Top Events

 **Carnaval Miami**, March

 **Fantasy Fest**, October

 **SunFest**, May

 **Goombay Festival**, June

 **Gay Days**, June

 January

 **College Football Bowl Games**

On January 1, New Year's Day, Floridians go insane for college football. Major bowls are played in Orlando (Capital One Bowl), Tampa (Outback Bowl) and Jacksonville (Gator Bowl), while Miami's Orange Bowl (January 3) often crowns the collegiate champion.

 February

 **Edison Festival of Light**

For two weeks, Fort Myers celebrates the great inventor Thomas Edison with a block party, concerts and a huge science fair. February 11, Edison's birthday, culminates with an incredible Parade of Light (www .edisonfestival.org).

 **Speed Weeks**

During the first two weeks of February, up to 200,000 folks rev their engines for two major car races – the Rolex 24 Hour Race and Daytona 500 – and party full throttle.

 **Florida State Fair**

Over a century old, Tampa's Florida State Fair is classic Americana: two mid-February weeks of livestock shows, greasy food, loud music and old-fashioned carnival rides.

 **South Beach Wine & Food Festival**

No paper-plate grub-fest, this late-February event is a Food Network–sponsored culinary celebration of food, drink and celebrity chefs (www.sobefest.com).

 **Mardi Gras**

Whether it falls in late February or early March, Fat Tuesday inspires parties statewide. Pensacola Beach is Florida's best.

**(left) March** Baseball spring-training game.
ALAMY//JAMES SCHWABEL ©

# March

### Spring Break

Throughout March to mid-April, Colleges release students for one-week 'spring breaks.' Coeds pack Florida beaches for debaucherous binges – but hey, it's all good fun. The biggies? Panama City Beach, Pensacola, Daytona and Fort Lauderdale.

### Baseball Spring Training

Through March, Florida hosts Major League Baseball's spring training 'Grapefruit League.' Thirteen pro baseball teams train and play exhibition games, drawing fans to the Orlando area, the Tampa Bay area, and the southeast.

### Carnaval Miami

Miami's premiere Latin festival takes over for nine days in early March: there's a Latin drag-queen show, in-line-skate competition, domino tournament, the immense Calle Ocho street festival, Miss Carnaval Miami and more (www.carnavalmiami.com).

### Florida Film Festival

In Winter Park, near Orlando, this March celebration of independent films is fast becoming one of the largest in the southeast.

### Captain Robert Searle's Raid

St Augustine meticulously re-creates Robert Searle's infamous 1668 pillaging of the town in March (p313). Local pirates dress up again in June for Sir Francis Drake's Raid. Volunteers are welcome!

### St Patrick's Day

Ireland's patron saint gets his due across Florida on March 17 (any excuse to drink, right?). Miami turns the greenest.

### Winter Music Conference

For five days in late March, DJs, musicians, promoters and music-industry execs converge on Miami to party, strike deals, listen to new dance music and coo over the latest technology (www.wmcon.com).

# April

### Interstate Mullet Toss

In late April on Perdido Key, near Pensacola, locals are famous for their annual ritual of tossing dead fish over the Florida–Alabama state line. Distance trumps style, but some have lots of style.

# May

### Sea Turtle Nesting

Beginning in May and extending through October, sea turtles nest on Florida beaches; after two months (from mid-summer through fall), hatchling runs see the kids totter back to sea.

### Isle of Eight Flags Shrimp Festival

On May's first weekend, Amelia Island celebrates shrimp, art and pirates, with an invasion and lots of scurvy pirate talk – aaarrrrgh!

### SunFest

Over five days in early May, a quarter million folks gather in West Palm Beach for South Florida's largest waterfront music and arts festival (www.sunfest.com).

### Memorial Day Circuit Party

For late May's Memorial Day weekend, Pensacola becomes one massive three-day gay party, with lots of DJs, dancing and drinking.

# June

### Gay Days

Starting on the first Saturday of June, and going for a week, upwards of 40,000 gays and lesbians descend on the Magic Kingdom and other Orlando theme parks, hotels and clubs. Wear red (www.gaydays.com).

lectable bivalve by hand. Anyone can join the following two-month treasure hunt.

#  August

##  Miami Spice

Miami's restaurants join together in August to offer prix-fixe lunches and dinners in an attempt to draw city residents from their apartments.

#  September

##  Mickey's Not-So-Scary Halloween Party

At Disney World on select evenings over two months (starting in September), kids can trick or treat in the shadow of Cinderella's Castle, with costumed Disney favorites and a Halloween-themed parade.

#  October

## 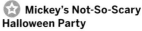 Fantasy Fest

Key West pulls out all the stops for this weeklong costumed extravaganza culminating in Halloween. Everyone's even crazier than usual, and Key West's own Goombay Festival competes for attention the same week.

##  MoonFest

West Palm Beach throws a rockin' block party for Halloween, October 31. Guests are encouraged to come in costume, and dozens of the best local bands play for free.

##  Goombay Festival

In Miami's Coconut Grove, this massive four-day, early-June street party draws over 300,000 to celebrate the city's Bahamian culture with music, dancing and parades; it's one of America's largest black-culture festivals (www.goombayfestivalcoconutgrove.com).

# July

## Fourth of July

America's Independence Day is the cause for parades and fireworks, large and small, across the state. Miami draws the biggest crowd for the best fireworks and laser show.

##  Steinhatchee Scallop Season

The opening day of scallop season in Steinhatchee can draw a thousand folks, who take to the waters to harvest this de-

# November

##  White Party

A raucous gay and lesbian celebration (and HIV/AIDS fundraiser), the White Party is actually a series of parties and nightclub events in Miami Beach and Fort Lauderdale over a week in late November (www.whiteparty.net). And yes, wear white.

##  Tampa Cigar Heritage Festival

Tampa's Ybor City has a long history as the cigar-making capital of the US. That heritage, and the cigars themselves, are celebrated in this one-day festival (www.cigarheritagefestival.com).

##  St Arrrgustine Pirate Gathering

Put on an eye patch and dust off your pirate lingo for this hokey celebration of scurvy dogs and seafaring rascals in St Augustine for three days in mid-November.

 # December

High season begins for South Florida beaches. Manatees arrive in warm-water springs.

##  Art Basel Miami Beach

Very simply, early December sees one of the biggest international art shows in the world, with over 150 art galleries represented and four days of parties (www.artbaselmiamibeach.com).

##  Victorian Christmas Stroll

The landmark 1891 Tampa Bay Hotel (now a museum) celebrates Christmas, Victorian-style, for three weeks in December, with folks in period costume.

## King Mango Strut

Miami's Coconut Grove rings in the New Year with this wacky, freak-alicious, after-Christmas parade, which spoofs current events and local politics (www.kingmangostrut.org).

**Far left: October** Fantasy Fest;
**Left: June** Goombay Festival.

PHOTOGRAPHERS: (FAR LEFT) ALAMY/ PLANETPIX ©; (LEFT) CORBIS/TONY ARRUZA©

# What's New

*For this new edition of Florida, our authors have hunted down the fresh, the transformed, the hot and the happening. These are some of our favorites. For up-to-the-minute recommendations, see lonelyplanet.com/florida.*

## 1 TAMPA
Tampa has transformed its downtown waterfront. Along Riverwalk, major cultural institutions like the Tampa Museum of Art and Glazer Children's Museum have christened dazzling new homes. (p282).

## 2 WIZARDING WORLD OF HARRY POTTER
Expelliarmas, Magic Kingdom! Universal Orlando has cast its spell and conjured the truly magical realm of Hogwarts, Quidditch and the Boy Who Lived. More fizzing whizbies, please (p128).

## 3 SALVADOR DALÍ MUSEUM
In 2011 the Salvador Dalí Museum unveiled its splendid new home, which presents as comprehensive and enlightening a survey of this 20th-century master as you could ever wish for (p295).

## 4 LEGOLAND
Florida's newest theme park, christened in 2011, is based on the cleverest building system ever devised. Rides, shows, recreations of Florida and pirate battles, and oh yes, build-your-own extravaganzas (www.florida.legoland.com).

## 5 PIRATE & TREASURE MUSEUM
In St Augustine, this brand-new museum devoted to all things pirate – stuffed with real treasure chests, gold ingots, maps and cannons – has us wondering: what took so long? (p313)

## 6 KENNEDY SPACE CENTER
In 2011 the US space shuttle program ended, bringing to a close a magnificent 30-year era of watching manned spacecraft lift off from Kennedy, which remains a must-see attraction (p106).

## 7 HOLLYWOOD BEACH HOTEL & HOSTEL
Bright, modern, relaxed and just plain cool, this boutique-y hostel-slash-motel is a welcome budget addition to Hollywood's Venice Beach–like scene (☎ 954-391-9441; www.hollywoodbeachhostel.com; 334 Arizona St, Hollywood; dm from $17, r from $59; ✳ @ 🛜 ).

## 8 SEÑORA MARTINEZ
Michelle Bernstein is one of Miami's culinary stars, and her latest restaurant, Senora Martinez, dishes gourmet Spanish cuisine and cocktails that have created a serious buzz (p220).

## 9 GANSEVOORT SOUTH HOTEL
It's hard to be an upscale boutique hotel in South Beach. So much competition! The Gansevoort delivers understated luxury and a rooftop pool of uncommon perfection (☎ 866-932-6694; www.gansevoortmiamibeach.com; 2377 Collins Ave; r $300-500, ste from $550; P ✳ 🛜 ✕ ).

## 10 EVERGLADES INTERNATIONAL HOSTEL
This is no ordinary hostel but a newly renovated masterpiece, with gorgeous rooms and unforgettable gardens. It's hosteling... with style (p266).

# Get Inspired

## Books

- **Swamplandia!** (2011) Karen Russell's surreal, tragicomic saga of a family of alligator wrestlers.

- **Sick Puppy** (2000) This Carl Hiaasen comedy-tropical-noir novel stars the stupidest Labrador retriever in literature.

- **Continental Drift** (1985) Moving tale by Russell Banks about a blue-collar worker who flees to Florida.

- **The Everglades: River of Grass** (1947) Beautifully written tribute to the Everglades by activist/environmentalist/feminist Marjory Stoneman Douglas.

## Films

- **There's Something About Mary** (1998) Hilarious Farrelly Brothers take on love, Miami and hair gel.

- **Key Largo** (1948) Humphrey Bogart and Lauren Bacall classic.

- **Monster** (2003) Charlize Theron portrays the dark side of the Florida dream.

- **Scarface** (1983) A Cuban gangster goes from rags to riches to... well, trouble.

## Music

- **Primitive Love** (1985) Gloria Estefan puts Cuban-American music on the map.

- **Losing Streak** (1996) Less Than Jake rocks out with ska-punk goodness.

- **Changes in Latitudes, Changes in Attitudes** (1977) Jimmy Buffet's quintessential album.

- **R.O.O.T.S** (2009) Flo Rida's second album is full of massive production and party tracks.

- **Ocean Avenue** (2003) Yellowcard's pop-punk doesn't get any sweeter and/or sadder.

## Websites

- **Tampa Bay News/St Pete Times** (www.tampabay.com) Website for the *St Petersburg Times*, one of the best newspapers in the state.

- **Florida State Parks** (www.floridastateparks.org) Gateway site for Florida state parks.

- **Just Florida** (www.justflorida.org) Exhaustive website on Florida travel.

- **Florida Division of Cultural Affairs** (www.florida-arts.org) Great portal into the local arts scene.

## Short on time?

This list will give you instant insight into the region.

**Read** *Hoot*, by Carl Hiaasen, is a funny, moving tale of growing up and fighting off rapacious land developers – themes the author likes.

**Watch** *The Birdcage*, a Robin Williams classic that captures everything silly and lovable about Florida, especially Miami Beach.

**Listen** Lynyrd Skynyrd's (pronounced *'lĕh-'nérd 'skin-'nérd*) debut is the opus of American Southern (and Florida Swamp) rock and roll.

**Log on** www.visitflorida.com is the state's incredibly comprehensive official tourism portal.

A lookout at the Everglades National Park (p260).
GREG JOHNSTON/LONELY PLANET IMAGES ©

# Need to Know

### Currency
US dollars ($)

### Language
English, also Spanish.

### ATMs
Widely available.

### Credit Cards
Widely accepted.

### Visas
Nationals qualifying for the Visa Waiver Program allowed a 90-day stay sans visa; all others need a visa.

### Cell Phones
Europe and Asia's GSM 900/1800 standard is incompatible with the USA's cell-phone systems.

### Wi-Fi
Common in midrange and top-end hotels, cafes, libraries and malls.

### Internet Access
Common in midrange and top-end hotels. Internet cafes prevalent in towns.

### Driving
Drive on the right; steering wheel is on the left side.

### Tipping
Tipping (15% to 20%) is mandatory. Bartenders, taxi drivers and hotel staff expect small tips (a few dollars).

## When to Go

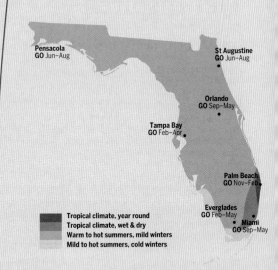

Pensacola
GO Jun–Aug

St Augustine
GO Jun–Aug

Orlando
GO Sep–May

Tampa Bay
GO Feb–Apr

Palm Beach
GO Nov–Feb

Everglades
GO Feb–May

Miami
GO Sep–May

Tropical climate, year round
Tropical climate, wet & dry
Warm to hot summers, mild winters
Mild to hot summers, cold winters

### High Season
(Mar–Aug)
o South Florida beaches peak with Spring Break.

o Panhandle and northern beaches peak in summer.

o Orlando theme parks peak in summer.

### Shoulder
(Feb & Sep)
o In South Florida, February has ideal dry weather, but no Spring Break craziness.

o Northern beaches/theme parks less crowded, still hot.

o Prices drop from peak by 20–30%.

### Low Season
(Oct–Jan)
o Some beach towns virtually close until winter snowbirds arrive.

o Hotel prices can drop from peak by 50%.

o Winter dry season runs November to April.

## Advance Planning

o **Three months before** Start plotting out your overarching itineraries, including routes between major destinations. For good rates, now is the time to book plane tickets and reserve hotel rooms.

o **One month before** Make reservations at high-end restaurants and get car rental (or bus tickets) sorted out.

o **One week before** Check the internet to see if any concerts, plays or other live events are on when you visit.

# Your Daily Budget

### Budget up to $100
- Dorm beds/camping: $20-30
- Supermarket self-catering and cheap eats

### Midrange $150-250
- Budget to midrange hotels: $80-150
- Target theme park and beach shoulder seasons
- Rental car: $40-50 a day, more with insurance

### Top End over $300
- Boutique hotel and Disney World: $200-500
- High-season beach hotel/resort: $250-400
- All-inclusive, four- to seven-day theme-park blowout: $1500-4000

## Exchange Rates

| | | |
|---|---|---|
| Australia | A$1 | $1.03 |
| Canada | C$1 | $0.98 |
| Europe | €1 | $1.38 |
| Japan | Y100 | $1.28 |
| New Zealand | NZ$1 | $0.79 |
| UK | UK£1 | $1.60 |

For current exchange rates see www.xe.com.

# What to Bring
- **Sunscreen** Florida sun is strong and unrelenting, so bring the right sunscreen.
- **Sweater/Sweatshirt** Come winter, it can get nippy at night, even in Miami (plus it gets downright cold in northern Florida).
- **ID** Always bring ID if heading out at night. Florida bouncers rigorously check ID at the door.
- **GPS** A good GPS is invaluable, especially for getting around back roads.

# Arriving in Florida

### Miami International Airport
Metrobus Every 30 minutes 6am-11pm daily; 35 minutes to Miami Beach

Shuttle Vans $20–26

Taxis $38 to South Beach

### Orlando International Airport
Lynx Bus Every 30 minutes 6am-10:30pm daily; 40 minutes downtown, 70 minutes Disney World

Shuttle Vans $20–30

Taxis $33–60. Higher rates to Walt Disney World

### Tampa International Airport
HART Buses Every 15 minutes 5:30am-11:30pm weekdays, every half-hour 7am-8:30pm weekends; 40 minutes to downtown

Shuttle Vans $12–32

Taxis $25

# Getting Around
- **Car** An extensive road network criss-crosses Florida; some major highways have tolls.
- **Bus** Greyhound serves major cities and some midsized towns across the state.
- **Train** Amtrak serves Florida's largest cities.
- **Air** Short hop flights are possible, but expensive.
- **Boat** Ferries connect Key West to Ft Myers and Marco Island.

# Accommodation
- **Boutique Hotels** Smaller, independently owned hotels, many with creative flair.
- **Resorts** Large, sometimes all-inclusive properties with multiple activities on offer.
- **Hotels** Includes larger, business-style and corporate-geared accommodation.
- **B&B** Small properties, often converted homes where (of course) breakfast is included.
- **Hostels** Dorm-style budget rooms,
- **Motels** Budget, usually located near highways.

# Be Forewarned
- **Hurricanes** Official hurricane season lasts from June 1 to November 30.
- **Traffic** Tends to be awful in large Florida cities.
- **Wildlife** Jellyfish are a beach annoyance; gators less so, but never feed them.

# Walt Disney World & Orlando

**Walt Disney World is what happens when innocence meets imagination.** If Florida promises to fulfill your desires, Disney World is your dreams made manifest. Surrounding this movable fantasy feast is Orlando, Theme Park Capital of the World. Then again, if Orlando holds said title, it's because the Theme Park crown is a pair of mouse ears. From nostalgic Magic Kingdom to faux-modern Epcot to glamorous Hollywood Studios, everything in Disney World makes good on the guarantees of childhood: that 'X' marks the spot, the princess will be rescued, true love will triumph and good will beat evil. What accompanies this promise? Illusion and magic and rides, shows and parades, escape from the everyday, the ordinary, the real. Still, when you're ready for the real, explore Orlando's world-class museums and excellent parks – still wonderful, if in the shadow of Cinderella's Castle.

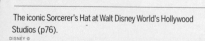

The iconic Sorcerer's Hat at Walt Disney World's Hollywood Studios (p76).
DISNEY ©

51

Main St, USA in the Magic Kingdom (p65).
DISNEY ©

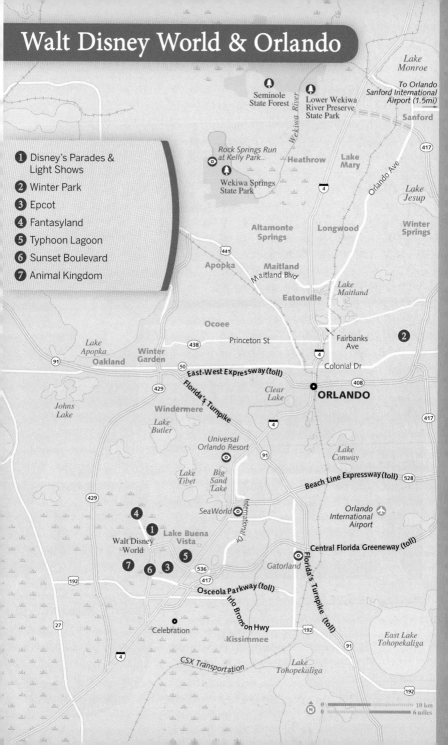

# Walt Disney World & Orlando Highlights

## ① Disney's Parades & Light Shows

In the theme park dedicated to Disney films and the dreams they've inspired, you can see those flights of fancy come alive during daily shows (p73). By day, watch your favorite characters bounce along during the Main Street Electrical Parade and Celebrate a Dream Come True; at night, watch the skies come alive with laser, fireworks and loud noises during Fantasmic! and IllumiNations.

**Need to Know**

**LINES** 30 minutes before opening. **SNACKS** Bring some. **PACING** Let kids set the pace. **DINING** ☎407-939-3463 to book at Disney restaurants. **For more, see p64.**

# Walt Disney World Don't Miss List

DEWAYNE BEVIL, REPORTER, *ORLANDO SENTINEL*

### 1 MAGIC KINGDOM

Don't miss Magic Kingdom, the theme park that changed Florida tourism. Nostalgia and classic attractions dominate, and Disney has upgraded favorites such as Haunted Mansion and the Enchanted Tiki Room, using interactive features to make the standing-in-line routine less tedious. Magic Kingdom is a winner with little princesses, and that is unlikely to change with the major expansion of Fantasyland, set to open in phases beginning in late 2012.

### 2 TOY STORY MIDWAY MANIA

There are always lines outside this ride. Once inside and aboard, guests are effectively shrunk into a video game with characters from the Pixar movies, and rapid-fire virtual carnival games. Most people get off wanting to get on again, so go directly to Toy Story to secure a free FastPass, which allows you to come back at a specific time.

### 3 WILD AFRICA TREK

A behind-the-scenes tour at Disney's Animal Kingdom gives guests unique angles on rhinos and crocodiles, rope bridges and extended quality time on Kilimanjaro Safaris. Only a few dozen folks are allowed each day, so it's $189 per person, on top of regular admission to Animal Kingdom.

### 4 EPCOT INTERNATIONAL FOOD & WINE FESTIVAL

This event in September spotlights global cuisine in kiosks scattered throughout World Showcase. Food is served up tapas-style across six weeks. Locals, even those who normally avoid the tourism corridor, love it! Consider a side trip to La Cava del Tequila, a small tequila bar tucked away in the Mexico pavilion. It's open year-round.

### 5 FIREWORKS

Major pyrotechnics are a nightly event at Walt Disney World. The 'Wishes' show, complete with real-life Tinker Bell flying out of Cinderella Castle, caps off the day at Magic Kingdom, while 'IllumiNations' is the impressive finale at Epcot.

# Winter Park

If you're feeling the need for a break from all the family fun in Walt Disney World, consider spending a day tripping around the pretty suburb of Winter Park (p101). An upscale community with a strong local arts scene, this has plenty of things that make the good life worth living: excellent restaurants, cute cafes and some respectable museums.

**Need to Know**

**CAR** An hour's drive north of the Magic Kingdom. **HOTELS** Laid-back. **VISIT** Visitor center is at 152 W Lyman Ave, ☎407-644-8281. **For more, see p101.**

# Winter Park's Don't Miss List

ALICE MOULTON, WINTER PARK HISTORICAL ASSOCIATION & WINTER PARK SIDEWALK ART FESTIVAL BOARD MEMBER

## 1 THE MORSE MUSEUM

The Charles Hosmer Morse Museum of American Art features the most comprehensive collection of works by Louis Comfort Tiffany in the world. A recent addition to the museum displays stained glass and architectural objects rescued from Tiffany's celebrated Long Island home, Laurelton Hall.

## 2 CORNELL FINE ARTS MUSEUM

The Cornell Fine Arts Museum on the Rollins College campus is home to one of the largest and most distinguished art collections in Florida. The permanent collection includes art by Albert Bierstadt, Alex Katz, John Frederick Kensett, Henri Matisse, Thomas Moran, Pablo Picasso, Ed Ruscha, Tintoretto and Tiepolo, to name a few.

## 3 PARK PLAZA HOTEL

For historic travelers, you can't beat a stay at the Park Plaza Hotel, Winter Park's oldest and only downtown hotel. Originally known as the Hamilton Hotel when it was built in 1922, the hotel has been through major renovations, but retains the retro charm and historic significance of its past.

## 4 SCENIC BOAT TOUR

Nature-lovers won't want to miss the Scenic Boat Tour. The 18-passenger pontoon boat weaves through canals and across three lakes to give visitors a behind-the-scenes look at the lush tropical foliage, wildlife and magnificent lakefront estates of historic Winter Park.

## 5 WINTER PARK SIDEWALK ARTS FESTIVAL

A springtime tradition since 1960, the Winter Park Sidewalk Art Festival (www.wpsaf.org), set amid towering oaks and quaint shops, is a juried fine-arts show that attracts more than 300,000 visitors over three days during the third weekend in March.

# Epcot

If the Magic Kingdom brings fantasy to life, Epcot opts for science fiction and geographic flights of fancy. In Future World the techie-tastic attractions are a Disney-fied glimpse into brave new worlds unlocked by science and exploration. The World Showcase (p73) brings us back to Earth – literally – in the form of (admittedly) clichéd depictions of the global stage, from Moroccan belly dancing to Norwegian Viking longboats.

**3**

## Typhoon Lagoon

**5**

You could drive out to the Atlantic Ocean to catch a surfable wave, or you could just come to Typhoon Lagoon (p79). This impressive water park is filled with slides, lazy rivers and the rest, but its most impressive feature is a gigantic wave pool that generates, every 80 seconds, a swell that would make the cast of *Point Break* proud. Slush Gusher slide, p80

DISNEY ©

## Fantasyland

Fantasyland (p67) is as good as Disney gets when it comes to little kids and their parents. Rides and attractions are gentle and there's a quiet, old-school charm that gives this section of the Magic Kingdom a little more warmth and heart than other parts of the park. That said, you'd be remiss to not check out Mickey's PhilharMagic, a 3-D journey into the heart of the Disney experience.

## Sunset Boulevard

What to do with older kids who are embarrassed to take a pose with Dumbo but aren't independent adolescents yet? Take them to Sunset Boulevard (p77) in Hollywood Studios. The Rock 'n' Roller Coaster and Twilight Zone Tower of Terror provide a bit of a thrill, which should make most kids feel mature enough to leave the Magic Kingdom, but scared enough to still need mom and dad.

## Disney's Animal Kingdom

The Animal Kingdom is great fun. There are roller coasters and Lion King–inspired parades, but you can also spot gorillas and lions on jeep safari or do jungle treks past tigers and real dragons. So while plenty of Disney magic goes on behind the curtains (or bamboo partition) it feels authentically wild at the end of the day too. Kilimanjaro Safaris, p74

# Walt Disney World & Orlando's Best...

## Rides & Attractions

○ **It's a Small World** (p67) This old-school ride brings out the kid in everyone.

○ **Twilight Zone Tower of Terror** (p77) A legitimately scary thrill!

○ **Turtle Talk with Crush** (p72) *Finding Nemo's* Crush leads this awesome interactive experience.

○ **Expedition Everest** (p75) A Nepalese roller coaster of a ride.

○ **Toy Story Midway Mania!** (p77) Another incredible Pixar-based interactive extravaganza.

## Dining

○ **Yellow Dog Eats** (p102) Fine barbecue in a laid-back former general store.

○ **Ravenous Pig** (p101) Eclectic foodie find with new-school American cuisine.

○ **Dessert Lady Café** (p100) Cakes and other sweet treats.

○ **Kouzzina by Cat Cora** (p88) New American fine dining in Disney World.

○ **La Hacienda de San Angel** (p86) Latin flavors infuse this World Showcase favorite.

## Hotels

○ **EO Inn & Spa** (p98) Serene B&B for those seeking crowd escapes.

○ **Courtyard at Lake Lucerne** (p99) Historic inn with art-deco flair.

○ **Disney's Grand Floridian Resort & Spa** (p83) Disney's poshest resort, all Old Florida charm.

○ **Disney's Animal Kingdom Lodge** (p85) Our favorite themed hotel recalls the aesthetic of *The Lion King*.

# Need to Know

## Shows

○ **Finding Nemo: The Musical** (p74) Innovative set and costume design make this the best show at Disney.

○ **IllumiNations** (p70) The Earth's history presented as a flashy light show.

○ **Jammin' Jungle** (p73) Animal puppets and African dancing.

○ **Fantasmic!** (p76) Disney villains take on Mickey Mouse.

○ **Main Street Electrical Parade** (p73) A nostalgic favorite: light show meets parades meets Disney characters.

**Left:** Fireworks above Cinderella's Castle;
**Above:** Primeval World ride (p75)

(LEFT) DISNEY ©; ABOVE) DISNEY ©

## ADVANCE PLANNING

○ **Hotels** If you're planning on staying in Walt Disney World, or visiting the area during any kind of festival, you'll want to book lodging early.

○ **Car rentals** Try to organize at least month in advance; car rentals book fast in Orlando.

○ **Restaurants** The top-end dining places we list, plus themed dining like eating with Disney characters, requires advance reservations.

○ **Babysitters** If you need time to yourself, try to organize a sitter service soon; see www.kidsniteout.com.

○ **Tickets** Get a Fastpass as early as possible in order to bypass Disney's famously long lines.

## RESOURCES

○ **The Orlando Sentinel** The best newspaper covering the region; includes good listings for live shows, arts events, nightlife etc; www.orlandosentinel.com

○ **The Daily Disney** The *Orlando Sentinel*'s eye on Walt Disney World, with peeks into the behind-the-scenes workings of the park; www.orlandosentinel.com/the-daily-disney

○ **All Ears** An unofficial guide to getting around Disney World; allears.net

○ **City of Winter Park** All the information you'll need on Winter Park; www.cityofwinterpark.org

## GETTING AROUND

○ **Car** I-4 is the main highway that runs through Orlando.

○ **Monorail** Three monorail routes intersect the heart of the Disney resort.

○ **Boat** Multiple ferry services link Disney's major subparks and resort areas.

○ **Bus** All areas of Disney World save the Magic Kingdom are connected by bus.

# Walt Disney World & Orlando Itineraries

*You've got a couple kingdoms, 11 nations in Epcot and several dimensions of fantasy. And then there's Orlando: a city that warrants some exploration.*

**4 DAYS**

Wekiwa Springs State Park **9**

West Ivar River

*Lake Apopka*

*Lake Maitland*

Ravenous Pig **9**

Mennello Museum of American Folk Art **7** **8**

Orlando Museum of Art

Yellow Dog Eats **10**

*Clear Lake*

*Lake Butler*

*Lake Tibet*

*Big Sand Lake*

*Lake Conwa*

Magic Kingdom **1 – 6**

Animal Kingdom **1 – 6**

Epcot Center **11**

**7** **8**

Hollywood Studios

---

**MAGIC KINGDOM TO ORLANDO**

## Kids' Quest

This is an itinerary tailored for families with young children (10 or under) who still want to get a little more out of the region than Disney. That said, we'll start in the **(1) Magic Kingdom**, where you should spend your first day wandering from **(2) Fantasyland** to **(3) Adventureland** and everywhere around and in between. If you plan a bit in advance, you should organize **(4) character dining** for your kids. Make sure to catch the **(5) Spectromagic** parade and **(6) Wishes Nighttime Spectacular** fireworks show in the evening.

The next day go to Hollywood Studios; **(7) Pixar Pals Countdown for Fun** showcases familiar characters, while **(8) Toy Story Midway Mania** puts you in the middle of a video game. On your third day, tube around **(9) Wekiwa Springs State Park** in Orlando during the day and have dinner at the scrumptious **(10) Yellow Dog Eats**, which boasts a menu even young ones with picky appetites can handle. If you don't think kids will enjoy a day in Orlando, head to **(11) Epcot Center**: there's plenty more Disney.

**Top Left:** The classic It's a Small World ride (p67);
**Top Right:** Expedition Everest ride (p75).
(TOP LEFT) DISNEY ©; (TOP RIGHT) DISNEY ©

**3 DAYS**

## ANIMAL KINGDOM TO WINTER PARK

# Older Kids & Adults

The title says it all, right? This itinerary caters to parents traveling with preteens or teenagers, or those without children in tow. We start this trip in **(1) Animal Kingdom**, which feels apart from Disney both physically and atmospherically. There are still rides, of course; **(2) Expedition Everest** is a great roller coaster that ought to keep your toes curled in excitement, but the focus here is (duh) animal encounters. So walk past tigers and (Komodo) dragons on the **(3) Maharajah Jungle Trek** and drive on a fun ride-meets-zoo-meets-safari trip via **(4) Kilimanjaro**

**Safari**. If you book in advance, get the ultimate animal by embarking on the **(5) Wild Africa Trek**. Also, don't miss **(6) Finding Nemo: the Musical**; it's a fun theatrical experience with giant puppets, goofy voice acting and lots of color.

The next day, go to Orlando and Winter Park for a change of pace. If you don't have kids, visit the **(7) Mennello Museum of American Folk Art**; if you do, the **(8) Orlando Museum of Art** has more exhibits for young ones. Spend the rest of your day in Winter Park enjoying shopping and cafe culture, and make sure to finish the day with dinner at the excellent **(9) Ravenous Pig**.

# Discover Walt Disney World & Orlando

## WALT DISNEY WORLD

Minutes before the Magic Kingdom opens, Alice in Wonderland, Cinderella, Donald Duck and others stand where all can see them, sing 'Zippidee Doo Dah' and throw sparkly Mickey Mouse confetti into the crowds. They dash off on an open-windowed train, the gates open, and children, adults, honeymooners, grandparents and everyone in between enter the park, some strolling, others dashing down the impeccably clean Main Street toward Cinderella's Castle. That iconic image is as American as the Grand Canyon, a place as loaded with myth and promises of hope as the Statue of Liberty. If only for these few minutes, this is indeed the Happiest Place on Earth.

Yes, there will be seemingly endless lines. You'll get back to the hotel exhausted and aching, and swear next time you'll take a real vacation... Until those last minutes before you fall asleep. You see your child's face staring adoringly at Winnie the Pooh, or reaching out to grab the Donald Duck that pops out from the 3-D movie. And it's OK.

That vacation can wait.

 **Sights**

Walt Disney World covers over 40 sq miles, and includes four separate theme parks and two water parks, all connected by a complicated system of monorail, boat and bus and intersected by highways and roads.

## Magic Kingdom

When most people think of Walt Disney World, they're thinking of the Magic

The Tree of Life landmark (p74).
DISNEY ©

Kingdom (Map p66). This is Disney of commercials, Disney of princesses and pirates, Disney of dreams come true and Tinker Bell, quintessential old-school Disney with classic rides like It's a Small World and Space Mountain. Each land is listed below, in rough geographic order from the park entrance.

## MAIN STREET, USA                    Landmark
Fashioned after Walt's hometown of Marceline, Missouri, bustling Main Street USA is best experienced with an aimless meander. Peruse the miniature dioramas of Peter Pan and Snow White in the street windows, pop in to catch the black-and-white movie reels of old Disney cartoons and browse the hundreds of thousands of must-have Disney souvenirs.

## ADVENTURELAND                    Rides, Shows
Adventure Disney style means pirates and jungles, magic carpets and tree houses, whimsical and silly representations of the exotic locales from storybooks and imagination. Don't miss **Pirates of the Caribbean** – the slow-moving indoor boat tour through the dark and shadowy world of pirates remains one of the most popular at Disney, but there's no FastPass so lines can quickly get very long. Drunken pirates sing pirate songs, sleep among the pigs and sneer over their empty whiskey bottles, but unless you're scared of the dark or growling pirates, it's a giggle not a scream. And that Jack Sparrow looks so incredibly lifelike that you'll swear it's Johnny Depp himself! The silliness continues at **Jungle Cruise (FastPass)**, but this time the captain takes you past fake crocodiles, elephants and monkeys, all the while throwing out the cheesiest jokes in all of Disney World.

Kids love flying around and around, up and down on **Magic Carpets of Alladin**, and its popularity rivals Dumbo, but skip the slow train of folks climbing 116 steps at **Swiss Family Treehouse**, a replica tree house of the shipwrecked family from the book and movie The Swiss Family Robinson. Iago, the scurrilous parrot from Disney's Aladdin, and Zazu, the bossy hornbill from The Lion King, sing and crack jokes at the **Enchanted Tiki Room**, a two-bit attraction that enjoys curious cult attraction.

## FRONTIERLAND                    Rides, Shows
This is Disney's answer to the Wild West. **Splash Mountain (FastPass)**, based on the movie Song of the South, depicts the misadventures of Brer Rabbit, Brer Bear and Brer Fox, complete with chatty frogs, singing ducks and other critters. The 40mph drop into the river makes for one of the biggest thrills in the park, and you will get very wet!

With no steep drops or loop-dee-loops, mild **Big Thunder Mountain Railroad (FastPass)** coaster is a great choice for little ones. The 'wildest ride in the wilderness' takes you through the desert mountain and a cave of bats, past cacti and hot-spring geysers.

Dubbed by many as a peaceful escape, **Tom Sawyer Island** is a disappointment. This was originally designed for California's Disneyland in 1955, and in its day, when Disney was smaller and children's expectations were lower, it was a place for adventure. Today, people mill about, not sure what to do and wondering why they waited so long in line to take a boat out here. Some kids may enjoy exploring Injun Joe's Cave and the rustic (at best) playground, but most seem as puzzled as the adults.

In the odd and strangely dated **Country Bear Jamboree**, stuffed bears emerge from the stage and sing corny country songs.

## LIBERTY SQUARE                    Rides, Shows
The ramblin' 19th-century mansion houses **Haunted Mansion**, another classic favorite low on thrill and high on silly fun and the only real ride in Liberty Sq. Cruise slowly past the haunted dining room, where apparitions dance across the stony floor, but beware of those hitchhiking ghosts – don't be surprised if they jump into your car uninvited! While mostly it's lighthearted ghosty goofiness, kids may be frightened by spooky preride dramatics where everyone gathers in a small room with strange elongated paintings on

# Walt Disney World

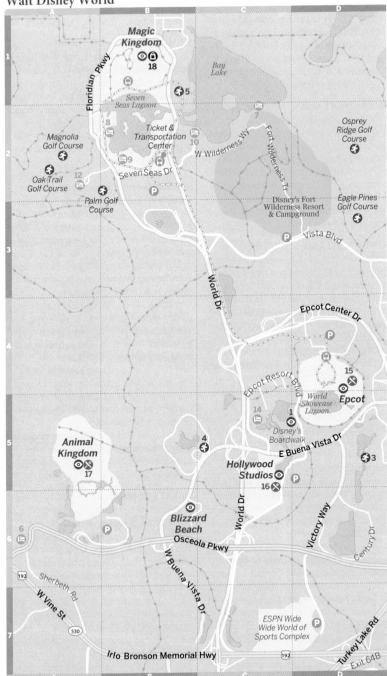

the wall and an eerie voice warns guests that there are no doors, no windows and no escape. All sorts of presidential memorabilia decorate the waiting area of the **Hall of Presidents**. Folks are herded into a theater to watch a super-patriotic flick on US history, ending with every US president before you on stage.

A paddle-wheel **Liberty Belle Riverboat** toots around Tom Sawyer Island on an underwater track.

**FANTASYLAND**          Rides, Shows
Quintessential Disney, Fantasyland is the highlight of any Disney trip for both the eight-and-under crowd and grown-ups looking for a nostalgic taste of classic Disney, though tweens too cool for fairy tales and teens looking for thrills may turn up their noses. Look for big changes here as Disney plans a major overhaul with a new Snow White and the Seven Dwarfs roller coaster and expanded opportunities to mingle with princesses. Check www. disneyworld.disney.go.com for updated information.

Without a doubt the best 3-D show in Disney, **Mickey's PhilharMagic (FastPass)** takes Donald Duck on a whimsical adventure through classic Disney songs and movies. Ride with him through the streets of Morocco on Aladdin's carpet and feel the champagne on your face when it pops open during *Beauty and the Beast*'s 'Be Our Guest'. Fun, silly and lighthearted, this is Disney at its best.

**It's a Small World**, a sweet boat trip around the globe, has captivated children since the song and ride debuted at the 1964 New York World's Fair. Small boats gently glide through country after country, each decked out floor to ceiling with elaborate and charmingly dated sets and inhabited by hundreds of animated dolls dressed in clothes appropriate to their country. They sing 'It's a Small World' as they dance and play in their native environments. While snide comments about how the song sticks irritatingly in your head for weeks have become a Disney cliché, there's something poignantly endearing, almost

# Walt Disney World

melancholy, in this simple ride. Little ones love it and the wait is rarely longer than 10 minutes.

Board a pirate ship and fly through fog and stars over London to Never Never Land on **Peter Pan's Flight (FastPass)**, take a sweet journey through the Hundred Acre Wood on the **Many Adventures of Winnie the Pooh (FastPass)** and ride through *Snow White and the Seven Dwarfs* on **Snow White's Scary Adventures**. While all three are delightful, some children may be afraid of the dark and the pirates on Peter Pan, and the Snow White ride is more about the scary witch than the sweet, animal-

loving girl. Rumor has it that once the Seven Dwarfs roller coaster is up and running, Snow White's Scary Adventures will close. At **Dumbo the Flying Elephant**, toddlers love jumping on a Dumbo and riding slowly around and around, up and down, and thrill at the chance to control how high they go. Lines here can be unbelievably long and slow, and the ride is incredibly short – hit this when the park gates open.

Wait until your last meal is well digested before venturing out on the **Mad Tea Party**, especially if you think your kids have it in for you. It's a basic spinning ride, and you and others in the teacup decide just how much you'll be twirling.

**Dream Along with Mickey** is a high-octane musical performance that brings the villains, princesses, Mickey and Donald to the steps of Cinderella's Castle for dancing and dramatic twists. See the *Times Guide* for show times.

The gilded **Cinderella's Golden Carousel** has plenty of horses, so lines rarely get too long or too slow.

Meet *Tangled*'s Rapunzel and Flynn Ryder at the little stone grotto of **Fairytale Garden**, and keep an eye out for Cinderella and her stepsisters, Mary Poppins, Alice in Wonderland and other favorites throughout Fantasyland.

**TOMORROWLAND**                Rides, Shows

**Space Mountain (FastPass)** hurtles you through the darkness of outer space. This indoor roller coaster is the most popular ride in the Magic Kingdom, so come first thing and, if the line is already excruciating, get a FastPass.

**Monsters, Inc Laugh Floor** picks up where the movie left off – monsters are no longer interested in harnessing screams but instead they must capture human laughter. This hilarious interactive movie, different every time

and incorporating audience members projected on the big screen, is all about trying to make you laugh and it's very silly in the very best sense of the word.

A cross between a ride and a video game, **Buzz Lightyear's Space Ranger Spin (FastPass)** puts you inside the spin-off video game for *Toy Story II*. Cruise along and let loose with your laser cannon at almost anything that moves and see how many points you can rack up. Speed Racer fantasies come to life when kids can put the pedal to the metal on grand-prix-style cars around the huge figure-eight track at **Tomorrowland Indy Speedway**. The cars themselves are affixed to the track and you don't control the steering. Note that kids must be 52in tall to 'drive' on their own, which pretty much eliminates this ride's target audience. Strangely, plenty of childless adults wait in long lines to squish into a car for what can best be described as a 'poke' around a track. **Astro Orbiter** is a revolving rocket ride with nice views of Tomorrowland, and the **Tomorrowland Transit Authority** people mover makes a great break from the chaos of the park. The best time to ride this is when it's really hot or at night, when the area is lit up like a futuristic neon city.

# FastPass

A FastPass is a free paper ticket that allows you to return to an attraction during a designated time window, thereby jumping the mind-numbingly long lines and hopping right on. This is the lowdown: if a ride has a FastPass option (noted next to each attraction description on the park map and within this chapter), there will be automated ticket machines at the ride entrance. Swipe your park ticket and out pops your FastPass with your return time. Return to the ride within the designated time frame, show your paper FastPass ticket at the FastPass line, and zip right onto the ride with no more than a 15-minute wait. The catch? Check the bottom of your FastPass to find out when you are eligible to swipe your card for another FastPass – the crowd level determines whether or not you can get a second one before your allocated time to use the first one, and you are never allowed more than two at a time. FastPasses for the most popular attractions can run out by midday, and don't be surprised if your return time isn't for upwards of five hours from the time you get your pass. If you really want to see something, get your FastPass as soon as possible.

### ⓘ Getting There & Around

The only direct way to get to Magic Kingdom is by boat or monorail from the Magic Kingdom resorts of Disney's Grand Floridian, Disney's Grand Polynesian Resort, Disney's Contemporary Resort, Disney's Fort Wilderness Resort or Disney's Wilderness Lodge, or by 600-passenger ferry or monorail from the Transportation & Ticket Center. There is no parking, so if you drive, you have to park at the Transportation & Ticket Center and then take the monorail or the ferry to the park.

With its massive parking lot and endless lines for bus shuttles, the Transportation & Ticket Center, however, can be unbearable. Instead, consider hopping the monorail or water launch to Disney's Contemporary Resort, Disney's Grand Floridian or Disney's Polynesian Resort, and then taking a cab to your hotel; in the morning, do the reverse.

### Epcot

With no roller coasters screeching overhead, no parades, no water rides, and plenty of greenery, things here run a bit slower, with a bit less va-voom, than in the rest of Walt Disney World. Slow down and enjoy. Smell the incense in Morocco, listen to the Beatles in the UK, sip miso in Japan – then rocket into the future.

**FUTURE WORLD**                    Rides, Shows

Epcot's only two thrill rides are immediately left from the main entrance.

*MISSION: SPACE (FASTPASS)*
You're strapped into a tiny four-person spaceship cockpit and launched into space. While this is not a high-speed ride, the special effects can be nauseating and the dire warnings are enough to scare away even the most steel-bellied folk. There are two options, one with less intensity than the other.

*TEST TRACK (FASTPASS)*
The rather disturbing shtick for this is that that you are a living crash-test dummy. Ride a General Motors car through heat, cold, speed, braking and crash tests – at one point a huge semi with blinding lights heads right for you,

**Left:** Princess Room at the World of Disney store; **Below:** Cinderella's Castle.
(LEFT) DISNEY ©; (BELOW) DISNEY ©

its horn blaring. When testing the acceleration, the car speeds up to 60mph within a very short distance, and while it's fast and fun, there are few turns and no ups and downs like a roller coaster. If you don't have a FastPass, take the line for solitary riders. At the exit, climb around a Hummer, a Saab convertible and other models, talk to a GM representative, and pick up that perfect Disney souvenir, a T-shirt with a pink-sequin Hummer.

*ELLEN'S ENERGY ADVENTURE*
This 45-minute ride is arguably the oddest ride in all of Orlando, perhaps in the entire state of Florida. It begins with a movie during which Ellen DeGeneres dreams that she is playing *Jeopardy!* with Jamie Lee Curtis. Determined to outsmart her know-it-all opponent, Ellen joins Bill Nye the Science Guy on a trip through history to learn about energy sources. At this point, you enter a 96-passenger vehicle and lurch slowly through the darkness into the Cretaceous period (the root of to-

day's fossil fuels). Giant dinosaurs stomp about menacingly and, in one particularly surreal display, a mannequin Ellen battles a ferocious one. After this jaunt through dinosaur-land, the movie preaches wind energy, hydro-energy and other alternative fuel sources, and concludes with Ellen's *Jeopardy!* victory. The whole thing is just very weird.

*SPACESHIP EARTH*
Inside the giant golf ball landmark at the park's entrance is Spaceship Earth, a strange, kitschy slow-moving ride through time that enjoys a cult following.

*SEAS WITH NEMO & FRIENDS PAVILION*
Kids under 10 won't want to miss the two Nemo-themed attractions inside this pavilion. Board a clamshell at the **Seas with Nemo & Friends**, and gently wind through the ocean looking for Nemo. It follows in the footprints of Disney rides like Winnie the Pooh and Peter Pan, where

## Down Time: Magic Kingdom

The covered waterside pavilion in the rose garden just off the bridge to the right of Cinderella's Castle makes a perfect place to pull out those goldfish snacks you brought along and take a quiet rest. Pictured but not labeled on Walt Disney World's Magic Kingdom map, look for this quiet treasure on your way into Tomorrowland.

you ride through the story, and though it may lack the old-school creative energy of those classics, kids love it. From here, head to **Turtle Talk with Crush**, an Epcot highlight. We don't know how they do it, but hey, that's the Disney magic. A small blue room with a large movie screen holds about 10 rows of benches with sitting room for kids in front. Crush talks to the children staring up at him, interacting with and taking questions from the 'dude in the dark-blue shell' and cracking jokes about how sea grass gives him the bubbles. Dory shows up and gets squished against the screen by the whale. It's a fantastic and funny interactive show.

*SOARIN' (FASTPASS)*
Simulates hang gliding over California. Soar up and down, hover and accelerate as the giant screen in front of you takes you over citrus groves, golf courses, mountains, coasts, rivers and cities and, finally, into the fireworks over Cinderella's Castle at Disney Lane. You smell the oranges and your feet almost touch those surfers below. While not at all scary in terms of speed or special effects, folks with agoraphobia may feel a bit uneasy. You'll want to hit this as soon as you get to Epcot, as it's one of the best rides at Disney for everyone from toddlers to grandpas. Lines can be excruciating, and FastPasses either run out quickly or have return times upwards from five hours. When you finally do get to the front of the line, ask for a front-row seat. Otherwise, feet dangling in front of you can ruin the effect.

*LIVING WITH THE LAND (FASTPASS)*
A boat ride past laboratory-like greenhouses. A narrator talks about growing food in and under water, which is actually more interesting than it may sound. Look for vegetables grown into Disney shapes.

Soarin' Lands ride at Epcot (p70).
DISNEY ©

*THE CIRCLE OF LIFE*
This short film, featuring Simba and his buddies from *The Lion King,* addresses the fragile relationship between the environment and the creatures that live within it.

**WORLD SHOWCASE**
Rides, Shows
Who needs the hassle of a passport and jet lag when you can travel the world right here at Walt Disney World? Watch belly dancing in Morocco and buy personally engraved bottles of perfume in France before settling down to watch fireworks about world peace and harmony. Disney was right. It truly is a small world after all. Sure, this is quite a sanitized and stereotypical vision of the world, but so what? This is, after all, a theme park. The featured countries from left to right around the water are Mexico, Norway, China, Germany, Italy, the USA (The American Adventure), Japan, Morocco, France, the UK and Canada.

*GRAN FIESTA TOUR STARRING THE THREE CABALLEROS*
A boat takes you through Mexico with Donald Duck and his comrades from the 1994 Disney film *The Three Caballeros*.

*MAELSTROM (FASTPASS)*
Tucked away in the Norway pavilion, this cute little boat ride meanders past Vikings, trolls and waterfalls. Skip the film put out by a Norway tourism company.

*REFLECTIONS OF CHINA*
A 20-minute film screened on a 360-degree screen focuses on China's stunning landscape and exotic cities.

*AMERICAN ADVENTURE*
Benjamin Franklin and Mark Twain host a cacophony of audio-animatronic figures in this very simplified interpretation of US history. You'll be taken from

## If You Like...
## Parades, Fireworks & Light Shows

These are Disney's parades and nighttime spectaculars.

1 **CELEBRATE A DREAM COME TRUE (PARADE, MAGIC KINGDOM, 3PM)**
Elaborate floats from classic Disney.

2 **MAIN STREET ELECTRICAL PARADE (PARADE, MAGIC KINGDOM)**
Floats made of thousands of twinkling lights.

3 **SPECTROMAGIC (PARADE, MAGIC KINGDOM)**
Night version of Celebrate a Dream Come True.

4 **FANTASMIC! (LIGHT SHOW, HOLLYWOOD STUDIOS)**
Mickey faces Disney's assembled dark side.

5 **WISHES NIGHTTIME SPECTACULAR (FIREWORKS, MAGIC KINGDOM)**
Jiminy Cricket narrates this display over Cinderella's Castle.

6 **ILLUMINATIONS (LIGHT SHOW, EPCOT)**
Fiery interpretation of earth's history.

7 **PIXAR PALS COUNTDOWN TO FUN (PARADE, HOLLYWOOD STUDIOS, 3PM)**
For fans of contemporary hits.

8 **JAMMIN' JUNGLE (PARADE, ANIMAL KINGDOM, 3PM)**
Huge animal puppets and African dancing.

the time of the Pilgrims to Charles Lindbergh, and from Susan B Anthony to Magic Johnson.

*IMPRESSIONS DE FRANCE*
Spectacularly beautiful 18-minute film, screened in an air-conditioned sit-down

# Finding Nemo – The Musical

Arguably the best show at Walt Disney World, this sophisticated theater performance wows children and adults alike. The show is directed by Peter Brosius, artistic director of the Children's Theater Company of Minneapolis, and the spectacular puppets were created by Michael Curry, who helped design the puppets for Broadway's *The Lion King*. The music is fun, the acting is phenomenal, and narrative structure follows the vision and spirit of the movie. Make a lunch reservation for the Tusker House buffet between 1pm and 1:45pm and you'll be given reserved seating to the 3:15 performance, thus avoiding the lines. There's no extra fee, but be sure to ask when you make your lunch reservation. Oddly, Disney doesn't clump the Nemo-themed attractions in one park: Turtle Talk with Crush and the Seas with Nemo & Friends, both a Disney highlight for little ones, are in Epcot.

theater, celebrates France's natural countryside.

*O'CANADA*
Martin Short dispels the myth of Canada as the place of 24-hour snow, and showcases the beauty of the country. The 10-minute film screens in a 360-degree theater

## ⓘ Getting There & Around

A pleasant, well-lit paved waterfront path or boat shuttle connects Epcot to Hollywood Studios, Disney's Boardwalk and the following Epcot resorts: Walt Disney World Swan & Dolphin, Disney's Yacht Club and Disney's Beach Club, and Disney's Boardwalk Inn. The monorail runs a direct line between Epcot and the Transportation & Ticket Center; from there, catch a monorail or ferry to Magic Kingdom. Disney buses depart from outside Epcot to Disney resorts, Hollywood Studios and Animal Kingdom.

Within the park, a boat shuttles folks to and from Morocco and Germany from two boat docks at Showcase Plaza, just outside Future World.

## Animal Kingdom

Set apart from the rest of Disney both in miles and in tone, Animal Kingdom (Map p66) attempts to blend theme park and zoo, carnival and African safari, all stirred together with a healthy dose of Disney

characters, storytelling and transformative magic.

**OASIS**                                              Zoo
Lovely gardens hide all kinds of cool critters, including a giant anteater, but it's best to move along to other attractions before the lines get too long. Pause to enjoy on your way out.

**DISCOVERY ISLAND**            Rides, Shows
This is the park's hub, and like Cinderella's Castle at Magic Kingdom, Spaceship Earth at Epcot and the Sorcerer's Hat at Hollywood Studios, the huge, ornate **Tree of Life** serves as the best landmark for orienting yourself in Animal Kingdom. It's 14 stories tall, holds more than 100,000 nylon leaves, and has over 325 animal images carved into its trunk.

The 3-D **It's Tough to Be a Bug! (FastPass)** is more than a movie, with periods of darkness, dry-ice and flashing lights. It's a lot of fun, but if your kids are terrified of darkness or creepy crawlies keep them out of this extravaganza. Even though it's very cute much of the time, you will definitely hear children crying by the end.

**AFRICA**                                         Rides, Zoo
With live animals and that Disney touch, **Kilimanjaro Safaris (FastPass)** gives just about any zoo in the country some

healthy competition! Board a rickety jeep and ride through the African Sahara. But beware. Just as you're barreling down rutted roads, past zebras, lions and more, the driver gets word that poachers are on the loose! Local law enforcement can't do it alone, so you've got to help, but, oh no! The bridge that's been causing so much trouble seems worse today and it might just give out on you. Unless your kids are frightened of lions, there's nothing scary here at all.

Pass gorillas, hippos, a great bat display and a hive of naked mole rats on the lush **Pagani Forest Exploration Trail**. Nothing more than you'd find in any zoo, but those mole rats sure are cute.

### ASIA                                 Rides, Shows

If you're looking for thrills, **Expedition Everest (FastPass)** won't disappoint. Wait (and wait, and wait) in a reconstructed Nepalese village, made to make you feel that you are indeed about to take a train to the top of Mt Everest. A mini-museum focusing on the mountain's climbers also contains copious evidence of a mysterious mountain creature, but you pay no attention as you board the steam train. It's only as you climb, up and up and up into the glaciers, that you begin to worry. Like so much of Disney the ride is as much about the narrative shtick and set design as the ride itself. This is a roller coaster. It goes backwards, it plummets at high speeds, it zooms around turns, with eerie hints (and more) of that Yeti.

**Kali River Rapids**, the park's second thrill ride (and there are only two), starts out pleasant enough, as you drift free-form on a circular 12-person raft through bamboo, rainforests and temple ruins. But this ain't no float trip – be prepared for rapids, sharp turns and other surprises.

Owls and peregrine falcons dazzle audiences at **Flights of Wonder**, a live bird show. It's got some cheesy dialogue, but the animals are spectacular as they zoom around over your head. Afterwards you can approach the trainers and their birds to ask questions and take photos.

Walk past Bengal tigers, huge fruit bats and Komodo dragons on the **Maharajah Jungle Trek**, a self-guided path past habitats designed to look like Angkor Wat.

### DINOLAND USA                          Games, Rides

This strange carnival-like area seems more like a local fair in rural Midwest America than part of Disney's magic, and it's a bit odd to plop the garish plastic dinosaurs of Dinoland right along with the live animals of Asia and Africa. Everything is oh-so-cleverly tied into the dinosaur theme. Buy fast-food snacks at 'Trilo-Bite' or at 'Restaurantosaurus' and play the usual midway games at **Fossil Fun Games**. The kids' coaster at **Primeval**

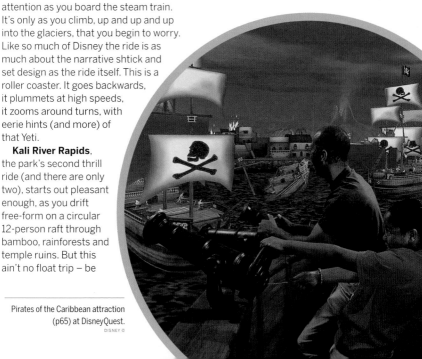

Pirates of the Caribbean attraction (p65) at DisneyQuest.
DISNEY ©

**Whirl (FastPass)** is a particularly whirly-twirly good time, but it's not superbarfy like the teacup ride in Magic Kingdom. The coaster on the left is identical to the one on the right. If you're looking for bigger thrills, head to **Dinosaur (FastPass)**. It takes you back in time to the Cretaceous period, where you've got to rescue a huge and scary dinosaur specimen before a meteor hits... This is definitely not for little kids, unless yours is tough as nails.

### WILD AFRICA TREK                    Tour
( 407-939-8687; $189) Only available to a limited number of guests (and you must be over the age of eight), the Wild Africa Trek is potentially the ultimate Animal Kingdom adventure. Guests are taken on a sort of behind the scenes peek-cum-private safari across the African savannah and on a swaying rope bridge that traverses water teeming with Nile crocodiles and hippos. There's no better wildlife viewing opportunities within the park, but you need to book early.

### RAFIKI'S PLANET WATCH                Zoo
The **Wildlife Express Train** you take to get here might just be the best part of this Disney enigma. The **Habitat Habit** features a few adorable, fist-sized tamarinds, and the **Affection Section** is a pleasant enough petting zoo with sheep and goats. Veterinarians care for sick and injured animals at the **Conservation Station**, the park's veterinary and conservation headquarters, and sometimes they have animal interactions.

### ⓘ Getting There & Away
Disney buses stop at Animal Kingdom, but note the ride here can be up to 45 minutes, maybe longer. There is parking just outside the park gates.

## Hollywood Studios
Hollywood Studios (Map p66) offers none of the nostalgic charm of Magic Kingdom, the sophisticated delights of Epcot or the kitschy fun of Animal Kingdom. It's meant to conjure the heydays of Hollywood, with a replica of Graumann's Chinese Theatre and Hollywood Brown Derby, but most of the attractions find

Splash Mountain ride (p65).

DISNEY ©

their inspiration from unabashed 21st-century energy.

The 122ft Sorcerer's Hat serves as the park's primary focal point. Make a right onto Sunset Blvd to hit the roller coasters, the Beauty and the Beast show and Fantasmic (a nighttime spectacular), and left towards New York for the movie-based attractions, primarily in the form of shows and movies.

**SUNSET BOULEVARD**    Rides, Shows

Two of Disney's most talked about rides are conveniently located right next to each other. At **Rock 'n' Roller Coaster Starring Aerosmith (FastPass)** the shtick is that you're hurrying off in a limo to catch the Aerosmith concert. 'Dude (Looks Like a Lady)' cranks through head-rest speakers as the coaster twists and turns in darkness, but there are no steep drops that send your belly through your mouth. Some claim this is one of the best rides in Disney, but just as many say it's high on hoopla and short on thrill.

Follow the screams to the **Twilight Zone Tower of Terror (FastPass)**, one of the best thrills at any Disney park. The preride spiel explains how the building, once a bustling Hollywood hotel, came to be so ramshackle and empty, and then, Rod Serling invites you into...The Twilight Zone. Enter an elevator and slowly climb up through the eerie old hotel, past the lurking ghosts. Clatter, clatter, clatter, until suddenly and without warning the elevator free falls. Clatter up, crash down, again and again, all in total darkness. Every ride is different.

Both the Rock 'n' Roller Coaster and Tower of Terror are hugely popular – get a FastPass for the coaster first thing in the morning, and then hop into the line for the tower; alternatively, take advantage of the single-rider line for Rock 'n' Roller Coaster.

The simple and sweet outdoor theater performance of **Beauty and the Beast – Live on Stage** follows the storyline, incorporates the classic songs, and doesn't fall back on any special effects or crazy shenanigans. It's a rock-solid hit with the Disney-princess-loving crowd.

## Down Time: Nature Trails

Short trails around Discovery Island lead to quiet spots along the water, where a handful of benches make a great place to relax with a snack. Keep your eye out for animals like tortoises and lemurs in and around the water.

**PIXAR PLACE, ANIMATION COURTYARD AND MICKEY AVENUE**    Rides, Shows

At **Toy Story Midway Mania! (FastPass)**, one of Disney's newest attractions, folks don 3-D glasses and shoot their way through midway games trying to score points. FastPasses are usually gone within three hours of the park opening.

Beautifully executed but disappointingly short, **Voyage of the Little Mermaid (FastPass)** is an indoor live performance. Black lighting creates utter darkness so that the fluorescent sea critters (handled by puppeteers swathed in black) pop out in a brilliant flash of color. Bubbles descend from the ceiling to complete the underwater effect, and Ariel croons classic songs from the film. Unfortunately huge narrative holes confuse even the most die-hard of *Little Mermaid* fans. We meet Ariel under the sea with her fish friends, we see her make a deal with the nefarious Sea Witch and then, next scene, Ariel is happily married to the prince!

Familiar faces from the Playhouse Disney TV channel, including Mickey and Winnie the Pooh, sing and dance at the 20-minute **Playhouse Disney – Live on Stage**. With carpeted floor seating and plenty of interactive action; it's a favorite with toddlers.

When Hollywood Studios opened as MGM Studios in 1989, the park served as a working studio, and you could watch animation artists at work at the **Magic of Disney Animation**. Animation for modern

# Best of Hollywood Studios

Within hours of the park opening, FastPass return times for Tower of Terror and Rock 'n' Roller Coaster can be after dark, so get to the park when the gates open and turn right at the Sorcerer's Hat. Immediately pick up a FastPass to one, and get in line for the other.

**Twilight Zone Tower of Terror** Elevator free fall through a haunted hotel, this is classic Disney thrills.

**Rock 'n' Roller Coaster** Indoor roller coaster and one of the most popular at any park.

**Beauty and the Beast – Live on Stage** Outdoor stage show of the princess tale.

**Voyage of the Little Mermaid** Charming black light live performance, but frustratingly short.

**Toy Story Mania!** Ride-through video game.

**Pixar Pals Countdown to Fun parade** Pixar characters dance through the streets.

**Sci-Fi Dine-In Theater** Burgers and glow-in-the-dark drinks served drive-in movie style (p88).

**50's Prime Time Café** Disney theme dining at its absolute best (p87).

classics like *Beauty and the Beast, The Lion King* and *Alladin* were drawn here. Today, however, this attraction has been reduced to a short film about the animation process, usually featuring the latest Disney movie. Skip the show and head to the interactive exhibits at the end, where you'll also find original celluloids from Disney films.

**HOLLYWOOD BOULEVARD AND ECHO LAKE**  Rides, Shows
Cruise slowly past animatronic stars of some of the world's most beloved movies, including *The Wizard of Oz, Casablanca* and *Raiders of the Lost Ark,* on the **Great Movie Ride**. Yes, it's strikingly dated, but that's part of the charm.

At **American Idol**, preselected contestants (see www.disneyworld .disney.go.com for details on how to audition) compete several times daily, belting out their best for the audience members to judge – winners compete in the end-of-the-day finale. At the **Indiana Jones Epic Stunt Spectacular**

**(FastPass)**, performed in a huge outdoor theater, professional stunt people show the audience how stunts are created. Indiana Jones falls into a vat of steam and fire, is chased by a boulder and leaps out of tall buildings. Audience volunteers, chosen about a half-hour before each show, don costumes to become extras in the Cairo market scene.

## 🛈 Getting There & Away

A paved waterfront walkway or a boat shuttle connects Hollywood Studios to Disney's Boardwalk and the following Epcot resorts: Walt Disney World Swan & Dolphin, Disney's Yacht Club and Disney's Beach Club, and Disney's Boardwalk Inn. Disney buses provide transportation to other parks and hotels, sometimes requiring a transfer.

## Typhoon Lagoon & Blizzard Beach

In addition to the four theme parks, Disney boasts two distinctly themed water parks. Of the two, Blizzard Beach boasts the better thrills and speed, but Typhoon Lagoon has the far superior wave pool, a fantastic lazy river and tots' play area, and plenty of room to splash on the beach.

## TYPHOON LAGOON     Water Park
(Map p66; ☎407-560-4141; adult/child 3-9 $49/43 or incl in Water Park Fun & More ticket; ☺call for hours) Perhaps the most beautiful water park in the country, Typhoon Lagoon boasts an abundance of palm trees, a zero-entry pool with a white sandy beach, and the best **wave pool** in Orlando. Twice the size of a football field, the pool generates a massive 10ft wave every 90 seconds.

First you hear the low rumble as the wave is generated, then the ripples of delighted anticipatory squeals as swimmers see the wave approach, and finally the laughing and screams of joy as everyone dives into and rides the wave. Again and again. And the best part is this: no line. A few islands along the lagoon's shore break the waves and create a calm, shallow inlet for tots.

The center point of the park is **Mt Mayday**. You can't miss it: look for a wrecked shrimp boat on its peak. Several slides emanate from the peak, including the ultrasteep crazy-fast **Humunga Kowabunga** and **Mayday Falls**, where you zip down a winding slide on an inner tube. For more relaxing thrills, float through dense rainforest, rocky gorges and tropical flowers on **Castaway Creek**. The aptly named **Ketchakiddee Creek** attracts the little ones with a leaky tugboat, bubbly fountains, warm-water pools and family-friendly slides.

Typhoon Lagoon has two particularly unique attractions that set it apart from the other water parks. First is the **Crush 'n' Gusher** water coaster, a combination log flume and roller coaster with jets of water that propel your tube up snaking hills and then down through dark tunnels. The second is **Shark Reef**, where you can jump in and snorkel (free rentals) for an up-close look at rays, sharks and tropical fish. Sounds cool, but be warned that the water is very cold, you're not allowed to leave the surface or kick your feet, and the sharks are tiny and hang out down at the bottom.

To spend more time with the fishes, take the **Supplied Air Snorkeling (SAS) Adventure** (per 30min $20), which uses a regulator like in scuba diving; sign up at Hammer Head Fred's Dive Shop.

## BLIZZARD BEACH     Water Park
(Map p66; ☎407-560-3400; adult/child 3-9 $49/43 or incl in Water Park Fun & More ticket; ☺call for hours) Though the newer of Disney's two water parks, Blizzard Beach is the 1980s Vegas Strip hotel to Typhoon Lagoon's Bellagio. At its center sits the snowcapped **Mt Gushmore**, from which the waterslides burst forth. You can choose several options for your descent, but because the wooden-bench chairlift

Crush 'n' Gusher at the Typhoon Lagoon.
DISNEY ©

that transports riders to the top rarely works you'll have to first huff it up before you can zoom down. But don't worry – the lines are usually so long you'll have plenty of time to catch your breath on the way up!

The fastest and craziest ride down is **Summit Plummet**, with a 12-story drop; alternatively, try the slightly less intense **Slush Gusher** or race your friends down the eight-lane **Toboggan Racer**.

## ⓘ Information

Swimsuits with buckles or metal parts aren't allowed on most of the rides. Hours vary by day and by season; call the individual parks for current hours. From October through March, only one Disney water park is open at a time. Disney's two water parks are included in the price of a Water Park Fun & More ticket.

## ⓘ Getting There & Away

Disney buses stop at both Typhoon Lagoon and Blizzard Beach, and there is complimentary self-parking at both parks.

## Disney's Boardwalk

Far less harried and crowded than Downtown Disney, the very small Disney's Boardwalk (Map p66) area across from Epcot and along Crescent Lake echoes waterfront boardwalks of turn-of-the-century New England seaside resorts. On Thursday to Saturday evening street performers like magicians, jugglers and musicians give a festive vibe. Pick up a doughnut or cute little Mickey Mouse cakes at the bakery and toot around on a two-passenger surrey-with-the-fringe-on-top bike.

For drinking and entertainment options at Disney's Boardwalk, see p89.

## ⓘ Information

Public areas at Disney's Boardwalk are open from 8am to 2am.

## ⓘ Getting There & Away

A well-lit paved walking path and small boats connect Disney's Boardwalk to Epcot and Hollywood Studios, as well as to the following Epcot resorts: Walt Disney World Swan & Dolphin and Disney's Yacht Club and Disney's Beach Club. Disney buses stop at the Boardwalk Resort, a low-lying clapboard hotel at the center of the boardwalk.

## Downtown Disney

Stretching along the water, Downtown Disney (Map p66) is an outdoor mall that lures tourists with three districts of shops, restaurants, music venues and more shops: **West Side** is home to a multiplex dine-in theater and the stage show Cirque du Soleil La Nouba, **Marketplace** features the largest Disney store in the world, and **Pleasure Island**

MGM Studio entrance at the Magic of Disney Animation (p78).
JJM STOCK PHOTOGRAPHY/ALAMY©

# Animation Academy

In this day of Photoshop and computer-driven animation, it's hard to imagine the painstaking process behind classic Disney animation. Try your hand at drawing a Disney character at Hollywood Studio's **Animation Academy**, a short course hosted by a Disney animator. There are about 40 drafting tables, equipped with paper and pencil, and your drawing may be one of the best souvenirs of the trip! Classes start at 10:30am and are held every half-hour at the Magic of Disney Animation.

has several restaurants, bars and clubs. There's a Disney-styled party atmosphere here, particularly on the weekends, with folks walking around sipping margaritas from paper cups, street performers dancing on stilts and parents pushing strollers loaded down with Disney shopping bags. For details on select stores, see p89; for table-service restaurants that take advanced reservations, see p88. For drinking and entertainment options, see p89.

Disney is in the midst of completely overhauling Downtown Disney, and in 2013 Pleasure Island will reopen as **Hyperion Wharf**. Call ☏ 407-827-2281 or check www.disneyworld.disney.go.com for updated information.

## ℹ Information

Public areas at Downtown Disney are open from 8am to 2am.

## ℹ Getting There & Around

Downtown Disney is accessible by boat from Downtown Disney resorts and by bus from everywhere else. There is complimentary self-parking, but no direct Disney transportation to any of the theme parks. You can walk from one end of Downtown Disney to the other, or catch a boat shuttle that stops at each district.

## Activities

Disney offers a dizzying array of recreational activities, many based at Disney

hotels and none requiring park admission. Call Walt Disney World Recreation (☏ 407-939-7529) for reservations and details on everything from water-skiing lessons to bike rental; for general information on activities aT Walt Disney World, check www.disneyworld.disney .go.com.

### Biking

Trails along the shores of Disney's lagoons and past woods, resorts and golf courses make for some lovely family-friendly biking, and several Disney hotels rent two-wheel bikes (hour $9, day $18) and old-fashioned surreys ($22 per half-hour).

**Fort Wilderness Bike Barn**   Bicycle Rental
(Map p66; ☏ 407-824-2742; Fort Wilderness Resort & Campground)

**Barefoot Bay Marina**   Bicycle Rental
(Map p66; ☏ 407-934-2850; Disney's Caribbean Beach Resort)

**Surrey Bikes at the Boardwalk**   Bicycle Rental
(Map p66; ☏ 407-560-8754; Disney's Boardwalk)

**Disney's Coronado Springs Resort**   Bicycle Rental
(Map p66; ☏ 407-939-1000; Disney's Coronado Springs Resort)

### Horseback Riding

Carriage rides are also available at Disney's Port Orleans Resort.

# Meeting Disney Characters

Folks of all ages pay a lot of money and spend a lot of time in line to get their photo taken with Winnie the Pooh, Snow White, Donald Duck and other Disney favorites. Note that any character experiences in the resort hotels do *not* require theme-park tickets.

## FREE MEETINGS

In addition to permanent character greeting locations in Epcot and Animal Kingdom, look on individual maps for the pointing white finger and check the *Times Guide* for details. Each theme park has specific places where characters hang out, and you can simply hop in line to meet them and have your photo taken. Not all parks, however, have the same characters. Mickey, Minnie, Pluto, Donald and Goofy are everywhere, but Pixar characters are at Hollywood Studios, which is also where you're most likely to find any new folk, and your best bet to catch a princess is at Magic Kingdom.

## CHARACTER DINING

Make reservations up to six months (yes, six!) either online or by calling **Walt Disney World Dining** (☎407-939-3463) for any of the many character-dining meals in the theme parks and resort hotels. Disney's Grand Floridian Resort features a buffet breakfast with Winnie the Pooh, Mary Poppins and Alice in Wonderland, as well as lunch, tea or dinner with the princesses; there's a jam-packed breakfast and dinner with Goofy and pals at Chef Mickey's in Disney's Contemporary Resort; and the 100-Acre-Wood folk come to Magic Kingdom's Crystal Palace for three meals a day. Probably the most coveted seat is **Cinderella's Royal Table (adult $33-45, child $24-28)** inside Cinderella's Castle at Magic Kingdom. Cinderella greets guests and sits for a formal portrait (included in the price), and a sit-down meal with the princesses is served upstairs. Note that character meals are not fine-dining experiences, nor are they intimate affairs – they can be rather loud and chaotic. Characters rotate around the room, stopping for a minute or so at each table to pose for a photograph and sign autograph books.

**Fort Tri-Circle-D Ranch**  Horseback Riding
(Map p66; ☎407-824-2832; Disney's Fort Wilderness Resort & Campground) Has guided trail, pony and carriage rides.

## Water Sports

More than 10 Disney hotels rent kayaks, canoes, jet skis and pontoons, among other things.

**SAMMY DUVALL'S WATERSPORTS CENTRE**  Water Sports
(Map p66; ☎407-939-0754; www.sammyduvall.com; Disney's Contemporary Resort, 4600 N World Dr; water skiing, tubing & wakeboarding incl instructors for up to 5 people for 2hr $165; ☺10am-5pm) Zip around Seven Seas Lagoon and Bay Lake, in the shadow of Magic Kingdom. This centre rents boats and equipment and offers lessons. It also offers fishing cruises and parasailing.

# Sleeping

Disney resort hotels are divided according to location, and Disney-provided transportation to *that* location is indicated in the hotel details below. Prices vary drastically according to season, and there are 20 (!) different seasons; plus, deluxe resorts can have upwards of 10 different 'room types.' Prices given here are for value/peak weekends; note that weekdays will be a bit less.

In a category all its own, **Shades of Green Resort** (Map p66; ✆407-824-3400; www.shadesofgreen.org; 1950 W Magnolia Palm Dr, Lake Buena Vista; r $90-150, ste $250-275; ❋❅; bus transportation) sits within Walt Disney World but is owned by the Armed Forces Recreation Center. Only active and retired members of the US Armed Services (including National Guard) and their widows and widowers can stay here, and rates are divided into three categories determined according to rank.

## Magic Kingdom

The number-one advantage to staying at one of these hotels on Bay Lake is that they are one easy monorail or boat ride from Magic Kingdom – you can get to classic Disney with no need for transfers.

### DISNEY'S FORT WILDERNESS RESORT & CAMPGROUND    Campground $
(Map p66; ✆407-824-2900; campsites value $51-82, peak $80-118, cabins value/peak $300/405; ❋ ⧳ ❅ ♦; boat transportation) Located in a huge shaded natural preserve, Fort Wilderness caters to kids and families with hayrides, fishing and nightly campfire sing-alongs. Cabins sleep up to six and are hardly rustic, with cable TV and full kitchens, and while cars aren't allowed within the gates, you can rent a golf cart to toot around in. Campsites have partial or full hookups. Staff keep a strict eye on after-hours noise, the grounds are meticulously maintained, and there's a wonderfully casual and friendly state-park-like tone to the entire resort. Boats depart regularly to Magic Kingdom, and buses service the rest of Disney.

### DISNEY'S GRAND FLORIDIAN RESORT & SPA    Resort $$$
(Map p66; ✆407-824-3000; r value $495-820, peak $655-1075, ste value $1235-2345, peak $1600-2944; ❋ ⧳ ❅ ♦; boat & monorail transportation) Just one easy monorail stop

Children eating Mickey Mouse ice-cream bars.

DISNEY ©

# If You Like...
# Dinner Theater

The park's three **dinner shows** (☎407-939-3463; adult $57-65, child $28-34) sell out early, so make your reservation for these up to 180 days in advance; you can cancel up to 48 hours in advance with no penalty.

**1 HOOP-DEE-DOO MUSICAL REVUE**
(Map p66) Nineteenth-century vaudeville show at Disney's Fort Wilderness Resort, with ribs delivered to your table in metal buckets, corny jokes, and the audience singing along to 'Hokey Pokey' and 'My Darling Clementine.' This is one of Disney's longest-running shows and great fun, once you grab your washboard and get into the spirit of it all.

**2 SPIRIT OF ALOHA SHOW**
(Map p66) Lots of yelling and pounding on drums while hula-clad men and women leap around stage, dance and play with fire in this South Pacific–style luau at Disney's Polynesian Resort.

**3 MICKEY'S BACKYARD BARBECUE**
(Map p66) The only dinner theater with Disney characters; expect country-and-western singin', ho-down style stompin', fried chicken and goofy Mickey antics at this Disney favorite at Disney's Fort Wilderness Resort.

from Magic Kingdom, the Grand Floridian rides on its reputation as the grandest, most elegant property in Disney World, and it does indeed exude a welcomed calm and charm. The four-story lobby, with a grand piano, formal seating areas and huge flower arrangements, has all the accoutrements of Old Florida class and style, but at its heart this is Disney. Sparkling princesses ballroom-dance across the oriental rugs, exhausted children sit entranced by classic Disney cartoons and babies cry. In contrast to the massive ferries from the Transportation & Ticket Center, small wooden boats shuttle folks back and forth to Magic Kingdom.

**DISNEY'S WILDERNESS LODGE** Resort $$$
(Map p66; ☎407-824-3200; r value $260-435, peak $425-605, ste value $435-995, peak $640-1405; ❄️ 📶 🏊 👪; boat transportation) The handsome lobby's low-lit tepee chandeliers, hand-carved totem pole and dramatic 80ft fireplace echo national-park lodges of America's ole West. Though it's meant to feel as if you're in John Muir country, with its wooded surrounds and hidden lagoon-side location, the fake geyser and singing waiters in the lobby restaurant dispel the illusion mighty quick.

**DISNEY'S POLYNESIAN RESORT** Resort $$$
(Map p66; ☎407-824-2000; r value $435-750, peak 585-985, ste value $710-2335, peak $930-3000; ❄️ 📶 🏊 👪; boat & monorail transportation) With faux-bamboo decor, a jungle motif in the lobby, and coconut-shell cups and shell necklaces in the store, you just may think you're in the South Pacific. The rounded lagoon-side pool features a slide, a zero entrance perfect for little ones and an excellent view of Cinderella's Castle.

## Epcot

One of the best parts about this cluster of hotels is their easy access to restaurants and entertainment in Epcot, Hollywood Studios and Disney's Boardwalk.

**DISNEY'S BOARDWALK INN** Resort $$$
(Map p66; ☎407-939-5100; r value $370-655, peak $515-845, 1- & 2-bedroom cottages & suites value $720-2295, peak $900-2830; ❄️ 📶 🏊 👪; boat & foot transportation) This resort embodies the seaside charm of Atlantic City in its heyday, with a waterfront the color of saltwater taffy, tandem bicycles with candy-striped awnings, and a splintery boardwalk. The lovely lobby features sea-green walls, hardwood floors and soft floral vintage seating areas. Elegant rooms have a terrace or balcony. The resort is divided into two sections, the Inn and the Villas; the Inn, with cute picket-fenced suites, quiet pools and plenty of grass, is far nicer and subdued. Accommodations range from rooms sleeping up

to five, to two-bedroom cottages sleeping up to nine.

### WALT DISNEY WORLD SWAN & DOLPHIN RESORTS    Resort $$$

(Map p66; 📞888-828-8850, 407-934-3000; www.swandolphin.com; r $140-380; ❄️ 📶 🏊 ♿; boat & foot transportation) These two high-rise hotels, which face each other on Disney property and share a gym and pool facilities, are actually owned by Westin and Sheraton respectively, and there's a distinct toned-down Disney feel here. The cushy feather beds at the Dolphin arguably offer the best night's sleep in Disney, and there's a full-size lap pool along the lagoon. Character breakfasts and other Disney perks, including Disney transportation and extra Magic Hours (where a theme park opens early and closes late for guests at Disney hotels only), are available at both. These are the only non-Disney hotels next to a theme park, and online and last-minute deals can save literally hundreds of dollars.

## Animal Kingdom

To get from these hotels to Epcot, Hollywood Studios, Animal Kingdom, Downtown Disney and Disney's Boardwalk, you must take a bus (or drive), and to get to Magic Kingdom you'll need to take a bus and then a monorail or boat.

### DISNEY'S ANIMAL KINGDOM LODGE    Resort $$$

(Map p66; 📞407-938-3000; r value $285-425, peak $425-580, ste value $800-2420, peak $1070-2960; ❄️ 📶 🏊 ♿; bus transportation only) With an abutting 33-acre savannah parading a who's who of Noah's Ark past hotel windows and balconies, park rangers standing ready to answer questions about the wildlife, a distinctly tribal decor and African-inspired food served at the recommended restaurants, this resort suc-

ceeds better than any other in creating a themed environment. Ask about intimate tours through the animal park and storytelling and singing around the fire. If you want to see giraffes and ostriches out your room window, you'll have to reserve the more expensive savannah-view rooms, but anyone can enjoy animals from the deck out back. Even if you're not staying here, swing by for a drink after an afternoon at Animal Kingdom.

## Eating

Table-service restaurants, listed below according to location, accept 'priority seating' reservations up to 180 days in advance unless otherwise noted. Call Disney Dining at 📞407-939-3463 or go to www.disneyworld.disney.go.com to peruse menus and make reservations.

Interior of the Dessert Lady Café (p100).
FREE PRESS PHOTO

## Magic Kingdom

Three of the five table-service restaurants here are buffet, and none is anything to recommend. You're better off bringing something into the park or hopping the monorail to Epcot or a Magic Kingdom resort hotel.

## Epcot

Eating at Epcot is as much about the experience as the food, and many of the restaurants go overboard to create an atmosphere characteristic of their country.

### LA HACIENDA DE
### SAN ANGEL                        Mexican $$

(Map p66; Mexico; mains $23-30; ⊘4pm-park closing; 👫) Authentic Mexican rather than Tex Mex, this Epcot newcomer features corn tortillas made daily, mango and chipotle salsas and on-the-rocks margaritas ranging from rose-infused Rosita to a classic with cactus lemongrass salt on the rim. Or stick to the basics with a flight of tequila. Massive windows face the lagoon, perfect for watching IllumiNations.

### ROSE & CROWN                     English $$

(Map p66; UK; mains $13-21; ⊘11am-park closing; 👫) Housed in a classic British pub, this little spot serves up ploughman's lunch, steak, fish & chips and a tasty vegetable curry. Wash it down with Bass on tap and head across the path for a garden concert of the Fab Four, or settle on the patio for the nightly light show IllumiNations.

### BISTRO DE PARIS                   French $$$

(Map p66; France; mains $29-43; ⊘11am-park closing; 👫) The most upscale option in the park, and one of the few with a dress code, this elegant 2nd-floor restaurant, decorated in muted earth tones and self-consciously fancy, serves upmarket French food. A multicourse meal with wine pairings costs $89 ($59 without wine), an excellent choice for an upscale Disney experience, and if you're lucky you can score a window seat, with lovely views of the lagoon. There is no children's menu.

**Left:** Swimmer at the Wekiwa Springs State Park (p97);
**Below:** Yummy cake at the Dessert Lady Café (p100).

(LEFT) ALAMY/CARRIE GARCIA ©; (BELOW) FREE PRESS PHOTO

**BIERGARTEN**    German $$
(Map p66; Germany; buffet lunch
adult/child $20/11, dinner $27/13; ⏱11am-
park closing; 👫) Satisfy a hearty appetite
with traditional German foods (don't
miss the pretzel bread) and a massive
stein of cold brew. The restaurant inte-
rior is made to look like an old German
village, with cobblestone, trees and a
Bavarian oompah band in the evening.

**RESTAURANT
MARRAKESH**    Mediterranean $$$
(Map p66; Morocco; mains $21-36; ⏱11am-park
closing; 👫) Sparkling belly dancers shimmer and shake past the massive pillars
and around the tables of the Sultan's
Palace, magnificently decorated with mo-
saic tiles, rich velvets and sparkling gold.
While the lamb kebabs, vegetable cous-
cous and other basics are disappointing,
the windowless elegance is a fun escape
from the searing sun, and kids love to join
in the dancing.

## Animal Kingdom
**YAK AND YETI**    Asian $$
(Map p66; Asia; mains $14-29; ⏱11am-park
closing; 👫) Sharing the name of Kath-
mandu's most exclusive digs in the real
Nepal and serving pan-fried noodles,
pot stickers, and tempura, this getaway
at the base of Mt Everest is a welcome
respite from burgers and chicken
nuggets. With a little imagination, the
vaguely Nepalese-infused decor and the
icy Tsing Tao transports you from Disney
to the Himalayas. And yes, chilled sake is
technically Japanese, but hey, it's close
enough to Nepal's traditional Raksi,
right? An adjacent quick-service option
serves beer and basics.

## Hollywood Studios
**50'S PRIME TIME CAFÉ**    American $$
(Map p66; Echo Lake; mains $13-21; ⏱11am-
park closing; 👫) Step into a quintessential
1950s home for a home-cooked meal,

87

# Specialty Dining

In addition to character meals (p82), check www.disneyworld.disney.go.com for specialty dining offerings ranging from a private safari followed by an African dinner to dessert and reserved seating for Magic Kingdom's Wishes Nighttime Spectacular. One of the most popular is chatting with the folk behind Disney magic at **Dine with a Disney Imagineer** ( ☎ 407-939-3463; Hollywood Brown Derby, Hollywood Studios; adult/child 3-9 $70/35; ⏱ 11:30am).

including Grandma's Chicken Pot Pie, Aunt Liz's Golden Fried Chicken and Mom's Old-Fashioned Pot Roast, served up on a Formica tabletop. Waitresses in pink plaid-and-white aprons banter playfully and admonish folks who don't finish their meals and put their elbows on the table with a sassy 'shame, shame, shame.'

**SCI-FI DINE-IN THEATER**    American $$
(Map p66; Commissary Lane; mains $11-21; ⏱ 11am-park closing; 🛗) A 'drive-in' where you eat in abbreviated Cadillacs and watch classic sci-fi flicks. It's dark in here, and the sky twinkles with stars.

## Disney's Boardwalk

**KOUZZINA BY CAT CORA**    Greek $$
(Map p66; mains $15-35; ⏱ 7-10:30am & 5-10:30pm; 🛗) Though it can be very loud and hectic, with an open kitchen and high ceilings, Kouzzina boasts an interesting menu and pleasant waterfront location, is a great place for a breakfast of blueberry orange pancakes and chicken sausage before walking to Hollywood Studios. Top off a classic Mediterranean dinner with some chilled Ouzo or a flight of Greek wine.

## Downtown Disney

**PARADISO 37**    South American $$
(Map p66; ☎ 407-934-3700; mains $15-25; ⏱ 11:30am-11pm Sun-Thu, to midnight Fri & Sat; 🛗) This waterfront newcomer claims to represent 37 countries of North, South and Central America. A tequila-themed chandelier hangs from the ceiling, and there are 37 kinds of tequila, a 2nd-floor wine bar, pages of specialty drinks and

live music on the weekend. Familyfriendly, with an excellent 'little tykes' menu (with tacos, grilled chicken and a 'triple stack pb & j'), although the mood becomes decidedly barlike as the night progresses. Call directly for reservations, as it often has more flexibility and openings than Disney Dining.

## Resort Hotels

**JIKO**    African $$$
(Map p66; Disney's Animal Kingdom Lodge; mains $24-35; ⏱ 5-10pm; 🛗) Excellent food, with plenty of grains, vegetables and creative twists, a tiny bar and rich African surrounds make this a Disney favorite for both quality and theming. For a less expensive option, enjoy an appetizer (the Taste of Africa features various dips and crackers) at the bar. Swing by for dinner, or at least a cocktail, after a day at Animal Kingdom. You can relax with a glass of wine on the hotel's back deck, alongside the giraffes and other African beasts.

**'OHANA**    Kebab $$
(Map p66; Disney's Polynesian Resort; mains $15-30; ⏱ character breakfast 7:30-11am, dinner 4:30-10pm; 🛗) The Polynesian's signature restaurant evokes a South Pacific feel with rock-art graphics of lizards, octopuses and other animals on the ceiling, a huge oak-burning grill cooking up massive kebabs of meat, and demonstrations of hula and limbo dancing, coconut racing and other Polynesian-themed shenanigans. Kids jump from their seats to join in the fun. The only thing on the menu is the all-you-can-eat family-style

kebabs and veggies, slid off skewers directly onto the giant woklike platters on the table.

##  Drinking & Entertainment

Disney has enough drinking and entertainment options to keep you busy with something different every night of the week for a month straight. Downtown Disney and the much smaller Disney's Boardwalk are Walt Disney World's designated shopping, drinking and entertainment districts, but you'll find bars and sometimes live music at most Disney resorts and within the theme parks. Magic Kingdom is the only place that does not sell alcohol.

**BELLE VUE ROOM** Bar
(Map p66; Disney's Boardwalk; ☺5pm-midnight) On the 2nd floor of Disney's Boardwalk Resort, this is an excellent place for a quiet drink. It's more like a sitting room than a bar: you can relax and play a board game, listen to classic radio shows like *Lone Ranger,* or simply take your drink to a rocking chair on the balcony and watch the comings and goings along Disney's Boardwalk.

**CIRQUE DUSOLEIL LA NOUBA** Performing Arts
(Map p66; ☎407-939-7600; www.cirquedusoleil.com; Downtown Disney's West Side; adult $76-132, child 3-9 $61-105; ☺6pm & 9pm Tue-Sat) This mind-blowing acrobatic extravaganza is one of the best shows at Disney. See p108 for details.

**HOUSE OF BLUES**
Live Music
(Map p66; ☎407-934-2583; www.houseofblues.com;

Downtown Disney; ☺11:30am-11pm Mon-Thu & Sun, to 1:30am Fri & Sat) Though you can swing by for some good ol' Southern cooking, the real reason to come to this national chain is the music. On Sundays, the **Gospel Brunch** (adult/child 3-9 $34/18; ☺10:30am & 1pm Sun) features rockin' gospel with a buffet breakfast.

**JELLYROLLS** Live Music
(Map p66; Disney's Boardwalk; admission $10; ☺7pm-2am) Comedians tickle the keys of dueling pianos and encourage the audience to partake in musical silliness.

##  Shopping

Most stores are thematically oriented, so after the Winnie the Pooh ride you'll find lots of Winnie the Pooh stuff, and after the Indiana Jones ride you'll find, well, an Indiana Jones fedora, of course.

Call **Walt Disney World Merchandise Guest Services** (☎407-363-6200, 877-560-6477; www.disneyparks.com/store) with any questions about shopping at Disney,

Snorkeling in the Shark Reef (p79) at Typhoon Lagoon.
DISNEY ©

including details on returning and exchanging items.

### BIBBIDEE BOBBIDEE BOUTIQUE
Children

(Map p66) Inside Cinderella's Castle, fairy godmothers finalize your kid's transformation from shorts and T-shirt to bedazzling princess with fanciful hairstyling and makeup. Girls three and older can choose from the coach (hair and makeup, from $49), the crown (hair, makeup and nails, from $50) or the castle package (hair, makeup, nails, costume and photograph, $190). For boys, there's the Knight Package (hair, a sword and a shield, $15). Call ☎407-939-7895 for reservations. For just a plain trim, perhaps with some spiky green hair or a pink updo and Disney sequins ($10 to $20), go to the Harmony Barber Shop on Main Street, just as you walk into the Magic Kingdom. There's a second boutique in Downtown Disney.

### ONCE UPON A TOY
Children

(Map p66; Downtown Disney; ⏰9am-11pm) Design a personalized My Little Pony, build your own light saber and create your own tiara at one of the best toy stores anywhere. You'll find old-school classics like Mr Potato Head and Lincoln Logs, board games, action figures, stuffed animals and more.

### LEGO IMAGINATION CENTER
Children

(Downtown Disney; ⏰9am-11pm) Outside there are life-size Lego creations; inside, tables to create your own masterpieces and a wall of individually priced Lego pieces. The center is in the midst of a complete overhaul that promises even more Lego delights.

### RIDEMAKERZ
Children

(Downtown Disney; ⏰9am-11pm) Select from hundreds of options to build your own customized model or remote-control car or truck, and then test it on the store's indoor track. Disney claims that that there are more than 649 million possible combinations of wheels, bodies, accessories etc. Even if you don't want to shell out the bucks to make one of your own, check out the eight full-size cars on display and watch other folks play with their creations.

### World of Disney
Souvenirs

(Downtown Disney; ⏰9am-11pm) With room after room of Disney everything, this massive store is ideal for all things Disney.

Soarin' Lands attraction at Epcot (p70).

DISNEY ©

# Victoria & Albert's: No-Kids-Allowed Dining

When Disney announced that children under 10 would no longer be allowed at Victoria & Albert's (Map p66), crème de la crème of Orlando's dining scene, headlines roared with news of Disney's ban on children and the internet gaggle was nothing short of horrified indignation. But with almost 100 other restaurants to choose from, families should have no problem finding alternatives to this three-hour, seven-course dinner ($125 per person, wine pairing costs an additional $60). Indulge yourself with exquisite food and top-notch service in the Victorian-inspired decor of earthy creams. Along with Cinderella's Table, this place, located inside the Disney's Grand Floridian Resort, books up months in advance; make reservations at ☎407-939-3463 the morning of the 180th day before you want to dine.

## ⓘ Information

### Child Care

Baby-care centers are located in every park. They're air-conditioned, packed with toys, and some run Disney cartoons. You can purchase diapers, formula, baby powder and over-the-counter medicine. Walt Disney World uses Kid's Nite Out (☎800-696-8105; www.kidsniteout .com; per hr $14-21.50, depending on number of children) for private babysitting either in the hotel or in the parks. There is a four-hour minimum and a $10 travel fee is charged.

Several Disney resorts offer drop-off children's activity centers ($11.50 per hour per child including dinner; two-hour minimum) for children aged three to 12, with organized activities, toys, art supplies, meals and a Disney movie to end the evening. You do not have to be a guest at the hotel to use the centers.

Camp Dolphin (☎407-934-3000; Walt Disney World Dolphin Resort; ⏱5:30pm-midnight)

Cub's Den (☎407-824-1083; Disney's Wilderness Lodge; ⏱4:30pm-midnight)

Mouseketeer Club (☎407-824-1000; Disney's Grand Floridian Resort; ⏱4:30pm-midnight)

Never Land Club (☎407-824-1639; Disney's Polynesian Resort; ⏱4pm-midnight)

Sandcastle Club (☎407-939-3463; Disneys Yacht Club Resort; ⏱4:30pm-midnight)

Simba's Clubhouse (☎407-938-4785; Disney's Animal Kingdom Lodge; ⏱4:30pm-midnight)

### Kennels

With the exception of select campsites at Disney's Fort Wilderness Resort & Campground, pets are not allowed anywhere at WDW. Best Friends Pet Care at Walt Disney World (☎877-493-9738; 2510 Bonnet Creek Pkwy; ⏱1hr before WDW parks open to 1hr after closing) offers overnight boarding and day care for dogs, cats and 'pocket pets.' Rates vary based on your pet; call for details.

### Medical Services

Medical facilities are located within each theme park and at both Disney water parks; see park maps for locations.

### Park Hours

Theme park hours change not only by season, but day to day within any given month. Generally, parks open at 8 or 9am and close sometime between 6 and 10pm. At Walt Disney World, one of the four theme parks stays open or closes late for guests of Walt Disney World hotels only – these 'Magic Hours' are a perk of staying at a Disney hotel.

### Parking

If you're staying at a Disney resort, parking at all the parks is free; otherwise, it costs $14 per day. You will find parking lots outside the gates of all the parks except for Magic Kingdom; if you're driving to Magic Kingdom, you have to park at

# Help, I Lost My Ticket

Each person must use their own ticket, identified at theme-park gates by finger-print scan, so if you lose it, you're screwed. If, however, you photocopy or photograph the back of your ticket (the side with the magnetic strip), Guest Relations may be able to use this to issue you a new one.

the Transportation & Ticket Center and take a monorail or ferry to the park.

## Stroller Rental

Strollers (single/double per day $15/31; multiday $13/27) are available on a first-come first-serve basis at Magic Kingdom, Epcot, Animal Kingdom, Hollywood Studios and Downtown Disney, and you can also purchase umbrella strollers (folding strollers). There is no stroller rental at Disney's two water parks, Disney's Boardwalk or at the resort hotels.

## Tourist Information

Guest Services is located at the entrance to each theme and water park, with maps and general information.

Any time you call Disney, you'll be prompted to give all kinds of information they use for customer research. Keep pressing '0' – just cut them off mid-sentence – and you'll get a real human being.
**Disney Dining** (407-939-3463) Dinner reservations, including dinner shows, up to 180 days in advance.

**UK Guest Information** (from UK 0870 24 24 900, from Florida 407-939-7718)

**Walt Disney World** (407-824-8000, 407-939-6244) Central numbers for all things Disney, including packages, resort, ticket and dining reservations and general questions about hours and scheduled events.

## Travelers with Disabilities

The *Guidebook for Guests with Disabilities*, available at Guest Services at each park and on Disney's website, has maps and ride-by-ride guides with information on closed captioning and accommodating wheelchairs and seeing-eye dogs. On many rides, folks in wheelchairs will be waved to the front of the line. You can borrow braille guides and audiotape guides from Guest Services and rent wheelchairs ($12) and electronic convenience vehicles (ECV; $50) at each of Disney's theme parks and at Downtown Disney. All chairs are first-come, first-served; reservations are not possible.

Public transportation is wheelchair accessible and select resort hotels offer features and services for guests with disabilities. Call 407-824-4321 or 407-827-5141 for further information. For thorough information on navigating Disney in a wheelchair, go to www.themouseonwheels.com.

## Websites

**AllEars.Net** (www.allears.net) Updated information on attractions, schedules, menus and more.

**DIS** (www.wdwinfo.com) Particularly readable.

**MouseSavers.com** (www.mousesavers.com) Excellent tips for saving at Disney, as well as printable coupons.

**Walt Disney World Resort** (www.disneyworld.disney.go.com) Official Walt Disney World website is incredibly thorough and easy to navigate.

## ⓘ Getting There & Away

See p92 for information on trains, planes and buses to Orlando.
**TO/FROM AIRPORT** If you have no urge to visit Orlando, you can arrange luxury transportation to and from the airport through **Disney's Magical Express** (866-599-0951).
**CAR & MOTORCYCLE** Disney lies 25 minutes' drive south of downtown Orlando. Take I-4 to well-signed exits 64, 65 or 67. At the **Disney Car Care Center** (407-824-0976; 1000 W Car Care Drive, Lake Buena Vista; 7am-7pm Mon-Fri, to 4pm Sat), near the parking exit of Magic Kingdom,

there is a full-service garage and an Alamo car-rental desk. A second Alamo desk is inside the Walt Disney World Dolphin Resort.

**SHUTTLE** Call one day in advance to arrange personalized transport to/from Universal Orlando Resort and SeaWorld with Mears Transportation (☏407-423-5566; www .mearstransportation.com). It costs $19 round-trip per person.

**TAXI** Taxicabs can be found at hotels, theme parks (except for Magic Kingdom, where there is no road access), the Transportation & Ticket Center, ESPN Wide World of Sports and Downtown Disney.

## ℹ Getting Around

The Transportation & Ticket Center operates as the main hub of this system. Note that it can take up to an hour to get from point A to point B using the Disney transportation system, and there is not always a direct route.

**BOAT** Water launches connect Magic Kingdom directly to Disney's Grand Floridian Resort & Spa and Disney's Polynesian Resort; a second route connects Magic Kingdom to Disney's Fort Wilderness Resort & Campground and Disney's Wilderness Lodge; and a third route, utilizing 600-passenger ferries, connects Magic Kingdom to the Transportation & Ticket Center. Boats also connect Epcot and Hollywood Studios to Disney's Boardwalk Inn & Villas Resort, Disney's Yacht Club Resort and Disney's Beach Club Resort, and Walt Disney World Swan & Dolphin Resorts. Finally, boats connect Downtown Disney to Downtown Disney resort hotels.

**BUS** Everything but Magic Kingdom is accessible by bus (city-bus style) from other areas, but not all destinations are directly connected.

**MONORAIL** Three separate monorail routes service select locations within Walt Disney World. The Resort Monorail loops between the Transportation & Ticket Center, Disney's Polynesian Resort, Disney's Grand Floridian Resort & Spa, Magic Kingdom and Disney's Contemporary Resort. A second monorail route connects the Transportation & Ticket Center to Epcot, and a third route connects the Transportation & Ticket Center to Magic Kingdom.

# ORLANDO & AROUND

☏407 / POP 1.8 MILLION

Orlando is both benefactor and victim of its theme parks. Those parks are the main reason people visit the Orlando area, of course, but so many visitors miss out on Orlando itself: pockets of tree-lined neighborhoods, established communities with an entrenched sense of history,

Mennello Museum of American Folk Art (p95).

RICHARD CUMMINS/LONELY PLANET IMAGES ©

a rich performing-arts scene and several fantastic gardens, parks and museums.

#  Sights

## Downtown Orlando

### LAKE EOLA & THORNTON PARK
Neighborhood

(Map p98) A gathering point for the downtown community, Lake Eola makes a pretty, shaded backdrop on a hot day. A flat, paved sidewalk, about 1 mile long, circles the water, a playground sits on its eastern shore and you can toot around the lake on a **swan paddleboat** (per 30min $15). Thornton Park, an admirable example of urban revitalization, borders the lake to the east. Remodeled historic homes line its narrow brick streets, and giant Spanish oaks weave their gnarly branches into natural green canopies. Though it's only a few blocks, and there's a slight sense that the economic slump halted development just as it was hitting its stride, this neighborhood off the tourist track is where you'll find an excellent independent urban hotel, several good restaurants and a handful of neighborhood bars. To get here from downtown Orlando, head east 0.4 miles from Lake Eola's western shore on Central Blvd or Robinson St to Sumerlin Ave, Thornton Park's main drag.

### WELLS' BUILT MUSEUM OF AFRICAN AMERICAN HISTORY AND CULTURE
Museum

(Map p98; www.pastinc.org; 511 W South St; adult/child 4-14/senior $15/2/3; ⏱9am-5pm Mon-Fri) Dr Wells, one of Orlando's first black doctors, came to Orlando in 1917. In 1921 he built a hotel for African Americans barred from Florida's segregated hotels, and soon after he built South Street Casino, an entertainment venue for black entertainers. Together, they became a central icon of the African American music community. This small museum of African American history is housed in the original hotel.

### GALLERY AT AVALON ISLAND
Gallery

(Map p98; www.galleryatavalonisland.com; 39 S Magnolia Ave; ⏱11.30am-6pm Thu-Sat) Housed in the oldest commercial building in Orlando, this gallery features paintings, photography, sculpture and other mediums by local artists. On the third Thursday every month, the gallery hosts free art receptions with live music from six to nine.

## Loch Haven Park

Loch Haven Park (Map p96), with 45 acres of parks, huge shade trees and three lakes, is home to several museums and theaters concentrated within walking distance.

### ORLANDO MUSEUM OF ART
Museum

(☎407-896-4231; www.omart.org; 2416 N Mills Ave; adult/child 6-18 $8/5; ⏱10am-4pm Tue-Fri, from noon Sat & Sun) Founded in 1924, Orlando's grand center for the arts boasts a fantastic collection. The

Alligator at Gatorland (p95).
ALAMY/GENEVIEVE VALLEE ©

DISCOVER WALT DISNEY WORLD & ORLANDO

# Tickets

Walt Disney World tickets are called **Magic Your Way**. The minimal base ticket, which allows access to one theme park for one day, costs adult $90, child three to nine $84. From that, you can add days and options either when you first purchase your ticket or any time within the 14 days after the ticket is first used.

**Multiple Days up to 10** The per-day cost drops 50% if you buy a seven-day or longer base ticket. Multiple-day tickets allow unlimited admission to all four of Disney's theme parks (but not the water parks), so you can go in and out of a theme park as many times as you'd like, *but you can only go to one theme park a day*. They can be used anytime within 14 consecutive days. Adult tickets for 2/3/4/5/6/7/8/9/10 days cost $168/232/243/251/259/267/275/283/291. Tickets for children aged three to 10 cost a bit less.

**Water Park Fun & More** ($56) Includes one admission per day to your choice of Blizzard Beach water park, Typhoon Lagoon water park, DisneyQuest Indoor Interactive Theme Park (at Downtown Disney), ESPN Wide World of Sports and Disney's Oak Trail Golf Course (with reserved tee time). You will be given one pass for each day of your Magic Your Way ticket, and you can use these passes to access whatever you'd like, whenever you'd like.

**No Expiration** Unused days of multiple-day tickets do not expire after 14 days. The price varies from $22 if added on to a two-day ticket, to $67 days if added on to a four-day ticket.

**Park Hopper** ($56) Allows unlimited access to any of the four theme parks during the course of one day, so you can spend the morning at Magic Kingdom, the afternoon at Animal Kingdom and head to Epcot for the evening. The cost is the same regardless of when you add this option and whether you are adding it to a one-day ticket or to a 10-day ticket.

museum provides family guides, runs week-long day-camps and hosts **Art Adventures** ($10; ⊙9:30am 2nd Tue of month). Each session looks at a particular element within the art (eg brushstrokes) and offers hands-on activities for kids. On the first Thursday of every month, **First Thursday** ($10; ⊙6-9pm) celebrates local artists with regional work, live music, a cash wine bar and food from local restaurants.

**MENNELLO MUSEUM OF AMERICAN FOLK ART**      Museum
(www.mennellomuseum.org; 900 E Princeton St; adult/child under 12 $4/free; ⊙10:30am-4:30pm Tue-Sat, from noon Sun) A tiny but excellent lakeside art museum featuring the work of Earl Cunningham, whose brightly colored images, a fusion of pop and folk art, leap off the canvas.

## Greater Orlando

**GATORLAND**      Animal Park
(Map p96; www.gatorland.com; 14501 S Orange Blossom Trail; adult/child 3-12 $23/15; ⊙9am-5pm) With no fancy roller coasters or drenching water rides, this mom-and-pop park harkens back to Old Florida. It's small, it's silly, and it's kitschy with plenty of gators. Allow time to see all the rather tongue-in-cheek shows, charmingly free of special effects, dramatic music and spectacular light design. At the **Jumparoo Show** 10ft-long alligators leap almost entirely out of the water to grab whole chickens from the trainer, and after the **Gator Wrestling Show** you can go on down to get a photo of yourself sitting on a gator. The best is **Upclose Encounters**, where mysterious boxes hold animals the public

95

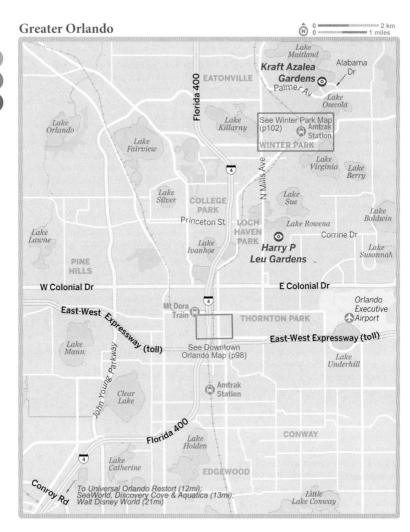

Greater Orlando map showing Eatonville, Kraft Azalea Gardens, Alabama Dr, Palmer Av, Lake Maitland, Lake Osecola, Florida 400, Lake Killarny, See Winter Park Map (p102), Amtrak Station, Winter Park, Lake Orlando, Lake Fairview, Lake Virginia, Lake Berry, Lake Silver, College Park, N Mills Ave, Lake Sue, Lake Baldwin, Princeton St, Loch Haven Park, Lake Rowena, Corrine Dr, Lake Susannah, Lake Lawne, Pine Hills, Lake Ivanhoe, Harry P Leu Gardens, W Colonial Dr, E Colonial Dr, Orlando Executive Airport, East-West Expressway (toll), Mt Dora Train, Thornton Park, John Young Parkway, Lake Mann, See Downtown Orlando Map (p98), Lake Underhill, Clear Lake, Amtrak Station, Florida 400, Lake Holden, Conway, Lake Catherine, Edgewood, Conroy Rd, Little Lake Conway. To Universal Orlando Restort (12mi); SeaWorld, Discovery Cove & Aquatica (13mi); Walt Disney World (21mi)

has sent to the park. The trainers are too scared to open 'em, so they drag audience members down to help. A splintery wooden boardwalk winds past the hundreds of alligators in the **breeding marsh**, and you can buy hot dogs to feed to them.

Sign up in advance for the two-hour **Trainer for a Day (incl park admission $125)** program. After some safety demonstrations you may get to wrestle a gator, feed them chickens and hold one of the adorable babies. Kids must be at least 12 years old to participate, but little ones get a kick just from watching.

**AUDUBON CENTER FOR BIRDS OF PREY** Bird Rehabilitation
( 407-644-0190; 1101 Audubon Way, Maitland; adult/child 3-12 $5/4; 10am-4pm Tue-Sun) Centered at a cool old house and very much off the beaten track, this lovely lakeside rehabilitation center for hawks, bald eagles, screech owls and other talon-toed feathered friends treats nearly 700 birds per year. It's small and low-key,

DISCOVER WALT DISNEY WORLD & ORLANDO  ORLANDO & AROUND

with opportunities to see the birds up close, just hanging out on the trainers' arms, and in aviaries for those unable to return to the wild. A boardwalk leads to a gazebo by the water. The center can be difficult to find; it's located in a residential area along Lake Sybelia in Maitland, immediately north of Winter Park (I-4, exit 88).

**ZORA NEALE HURSTON NATIONAL MUSEUM OF FINE ARTS** Museum (www.zoranealehurstonmuseum.com; 227 E Kennedy Blvd, Eatonville; ☉9am-4pm Mon-Fri, 11am-1pm Sat) Novelist Zora Neale Hurston, a pillar of America's Harlem Renaissance and best known for her novel *Their Eyes Were Watching God,* was born in Eatonville. Changing exhibits of African American artists honor her memory and spirit. The museum is about 5 miles northeast of downtown Winter Park; take Fairbanks Ave west to Orlando Ave, turn right and go 1.6 miles to Lake Ave. Lake Ave turns into Kennedy Blvd.

**WEKIWA SPRINGS STATE PARK** Park (☏407-884-2008; www.floridastateparks.org; 1800 Wekiwa Circle; car $6, RV or tent site $24; ☉8am-6pm) The best way to explore this 42,000- acre park is by paddling along the tranquil waters of the Wekiva River, one of Florida's two federally designated 'Wild and Scenic Rivers.' **Nature Adventures** (☏407-884-4311; www.canoewekiva.com; 2hr $15-20, each additional hour $3) rents kayaks and canoes; arrange at least 24 hours in advance to float the 9 miles to **Katie's Landing** (2-3 people $30-40, child under 6 free; ☉9:30am departure, 3:30pm shuttle return) and hop a shuttle 37 miles back. There's a three-boat minimum, so they'll call to let you know if the minimum has been filled. To really get away, book a riverbank campsite through the state park. Two days and one night, including canoe or kayak, tent, sleeping bags, stoves, lanterns and cooler, costs $132. The park also has 13 miles of wooded hiking trails and a fantastic spring-fed swimming hole.

## Activities

### Biking

Several resorts at Walt Disney World run their own cycling programs, including rentals and trails. One of the prettiest paths is between Disney's Boardwalk and Beach Club resorts – try it on a tandem candy-striped bike. Orlando's bike trails are in flux as the city develops a vast interconnected system of trails. **Outdoor Travels** (www.outdoortravels.com/biking_fl_overview_orlando.php) has descriptions of greater Orlando's bike trails. **Metro Plan Orlando** (www.metroplanorlando) has updated pdf maps.

American Kestrel at Audubon Center for Birds of Prey (p96).

ALAMY/DK©

**DISCOVER WALT DISNEY WORLD & ORLANDO  ORLANDO & AROUND**

### West Orange Trail Bikes & Blades
Biking
( ☎ 407-877-0600; www.orlandobikerental.com; 17914 State Rd 438, Oakland, Florida Turnpike exit 272; bikes hr $6-10, day $30-50, week $99-149; ⏰ 11am-5pm Mon-Fri, 9am-5pm Sat & Sun) There is a $40 delivery/pickup charge, and rates include a car rack.

### Water Sports

**Buena Vista Watersports**  Water Sports
( ☎ 407-239-6939; www.bvwatersports.com; 13245 Lake Bryan Dr; water skiing, tubing & wakeboarding; $145 per hr; ⏰ 9am-6:30pm) Just outside Disney, with similar things for slightly less and a more low-key and bucolic feel. From I-4, take exit 68 (Hwy 535).

 **Sleeping**

Rates outside theme park hubs are lowest from June through September and highest between Christmas and New Year, and in March and April. Prices quoted below are a range during high season. Most hotels offer complimentary shuttles to the theme parks,

### Downtown

**EO INN & SPA**     Boutique Hotel **$$**
( ☎ 407-481-8485; www.eoinn.com; 227 N Eola Dr, Thornton Park; r $139-229; ❄ 🛜 🏊 ) This little hotel sits across the street from the east shore of Lake Eola, blocks from the restaurants and bars of leafy Thornton Park. Soothing beige-and-white rooms

rants and bars in downtown Orlando and Thornton Park. In a better location, this place would be, hands down, a favorite. From downtown, head south one block from South St, turn east on W Anderson St and follow it a couple blocks under the toll road, where it becomes Delaney Ave. The inn is at the end of the road, on Lake Lucerne.

**VERANDA BED & BREAKFAST** B&B $$
( ☎ 407-849-0321; www.theverandabandb.com; 707 E Washington St, Thornton Park; r $109-189, ste $209-269; ❄ 🛜 ☀) Simple and low-key, with several good restaurants and neighborhood bars within blocks. It sits just off Summerlin Ave, about a block east of Lake Eola and two blocks south of Robinson St.

## International Drive (Around Universal Orlando Resort & SeaWorld)

**HILTON GARDEN HOTEL** Motel $$
( ☎ 407-351-2100, 800-327-1366; www.hilton gardenorlando.com; 5877 American Way; r $95-124; ❄ @ 🛜 ☀ 🛏) Handsome rooms with Florida pastels, free internet and parking, a little tiki bar by the pool, and an on-site restaurant, this newly built chain is an excellent midrange option, particularly if you're going to Universal Orlando. It's less than a mile to the parks and though it sits on I-4, it's set apart from the chaos of International Dr.

evoke a sense of serenity that feels miles away from the hustle of the city.

**COURTYARD AT LAKE LUCERNE** B&B $$
( ☎ 407-648-5188, 800-444-5289; www.orlandohistoricinn.com; 211 Lucerne Circle NE; r & ste $99-225; ❄ 🛜 👪) This lovely historic inn (first built in 1883), with its enchanting gardens, romantic fountains, complimentary cocktails and genteel breakfast, strangely sits directly under two highway overpasses. It has art-deco suites, housed in Orlando's first apartment building (c 1946). Suites have small kitchens and plenty of room, and there are handsome antiques on display throughout. Sadly, you can hear the trucks rumbling overhead and it's an ugly, unpleasant walk to the restau-

**HILTON HOMEWOOD SUITES** Motel $$
( ☎ 407-226-0669; http://homewoodsuites1.
hilton.com; 5893 American Way; ste $120-160;
❄ @ 🛜 ⛌ 🛗 ) An all-suite hotel across
from the Hilton Garden Inn that is perfect
for families. Beds are super comfy, suites
are spacious and each one has a fully
equipped kitchen. Fill in your grocery
list when you check in, and they'll do the
shopping for you with no extra fee. There's
complimentary daily breakfast and free
snacks and drinks (including beer) Mon-
day through Thursday, and a warm and
quiet feel at both Hiltons that is lacking at
comparable chain hotels in Orlando.

**WALDORF ASTORIA** Luxury Hotel $$$
(Map p66; ☎ 407-597-5500; www.waldorfastori
aorlando.com; 14200 Bonnet Creek Resort Lane;
r $200-$400, ste $450-560; ❄ @ 🛜 ⛌ 🛗 )
This elegant newcomer doesn't offer the
sheltered-oasis feel of its competitors,
but the quality of its rooms, amenities
and service is impeccable and it's the
closest luxury resort to Disney. The excellent buffet breakfast includes several
stations, and two grandly styled pools
border the golf course. Between the
Guerlain spa and absolutely divine beds,
it's hard to drag yourself to the parks.
Luxury bus shuttle to Disney is complimentary but undependable – it may
make several stops on the way to or from
your destination, stretching what should
be a 15-minute ride closer to an hour and
rendering the benefit of close proximity to
Disney irrelevant. **Hilton Orlando Bonnet
Creek** (www.hilton.com/bonnetcreek, ☎ 407-
597-3600), with a lazy river and pool slide,
shares amenities with the Waldorf, and
rooms and packages are a bit less.

**MONA LISA SUITE HOTEL** Hotel $$
(Map p66; ☎ 407-647-1072, 800-228-7220;
www.monalisasuitehotel.com; 225 Celebration
Pl, Celebration; ste $180-320; ❄ @ 🛜 ⛌ 🛗 )
You can't miss this distinctive round,
stone building floating oddly out of place
next to the hospital, just off I-4 on Hwy
192. Inside, it's stylishly contemporary,
with a circular pool surrounding an

island of palm trees, and earth-toned
suites with fully equipped kitchens. A
golf cart shuttles folks to downtown
Celebration.

#  Eating

Restaurant Row, a half-mile stretch of W
Sand Lake Rd just west of Whole Foods
and inside the strip mall Plaza Venezia, of-
fers a concentration of diverse restaurants
and high-end chains.

## Downtown
### DESSERT LADY CAFÉ Cafe $
(Map p98; ☎ 407-999-5696; www.dessertlady.
com; 120 W Church St; mains $5-10; ⏱ 11:30am-
11pm Tue-Thu, to midnight Fri, 4pm-midnight
Sat) Ask Patti Schmidt how she became
Orlando's first and only Dessert Lady
and she'll tell you that it all started with a
carrot cake. Now enjoy desserts from fruit
cobbler to bourbon pecan pie over a glass
of wine. Rich reds and draping silks give
the tiny interior a bordello atmosphere,
and a bistro menu serves pulled-pork slid-
ers, excellent chicken salad sandwiches,
soups, quiches and salads. A slice of cake
costs as much as the sandwich ($10),
which should tell you something about
that slice of cake!

### SHARI SUSHI Japanese $$
( ☎ 407-420-9420; www.sharisushilounge.
com; 621 E Central Blvd, Thornton Park; mains
$14-24; ⏱ 11am-10pm Tue-Sat, 10am-3pm Sun)
Black and white contemporary minimalist
decor, huge sidewalk windows and excellent sushi.

## International Drive (Around Universal Orlando Resort & SeaWorld)
### THAI THANI Thai $$
(www.thaithani.net; 11025 International Dr;
mains $9-22; ⏱ 11:30am-11pm) Just past the
gates to SeaWorld, Discovery Cove and
Aquatica, this dark little place makes an

ALAMY/M. TIMOTHY O'KEEFE©

# Don't Miss Winter Park

Founded in 1858, this cozy college town concentrates some of Orlando's best-kept secrets.

**Charles Hosmer Morse Museum of American Art** (Map p102; www.morsemuseum.org; 445 N Park Ave; adult/child under 12/student $5/free/1; ⏱9:30am-4pm Tue-Sat, from 1pm Sun, to 8pm Fri Nov-Apr) houses the world's most comprehensive collection of Tiffany lead-glass lamps, windows, jewelry, blown glass, pottery and enamel.

Scattered through the grounds of the stately **Albin Polasek Museum & Sculpture Gardens** (Map p102; www.polasek.org; 633 Osceola Ave; adult/child under 12/senior $5/free/4; ⏱10am-4pm Tue-Sat, from 1pm Sun) are the works of Czech sculptor Albin Polasek. The small yellow villa perched on the shore of Lake Osceola was the artist's home.

The tiny **Cornell Fine Arts Museum** (Map p102; www.rollins.edu/cfam; Rollins College, 1000 Holt Ave; adult/child 2-11 $5/free; ⏱10am-4pm Tue-Fri, noon-5pm Sat & Sun), on the campus of Rollins College, houses an eclectic collection of historic and contemporary art.

Brick walls, clean-lined wood furniture, antiques and luscious white cotton bedding give every room at the historic two-story **Park Plaza Hotel** (Map p102; ☎407-647-1072, 800-228-7220; www.parkplazahotel.com; 307 S Park Ave; r $180-220, ste $260-320; ❄@🛜) a simple elegance.

One of the most talked-about foodie destinations in Orlando, the **Ravenous Pig** (off Map p102; ☎407-628-2333; www.theravenouspig.com; 1234 Orange Ave; mains $14-29; ⏱11:30am-2pm & 5:30-9:30pm Tue-Sat) lives up to its reputation for creative, delicious food. Try the shrimp and grits or lobster taco.

A one-hour **Scenic Boat Tour** (Map p102; www.scenicboattours.com; 1 E Morse Blvd; adult/child 2-11 $8/4; ⏱10am-4pm, every hr) floats through 12 miles of tropical canals and lakes.

To get to Winter Park, take I-4 east to Fairbanks Ave, head east 2 miles to Park Ave and turn left.

## Winter Park

ideal dinner choice after a day of dolphin shows and waterslides. It's friendly, cool and quiet, with gilded Thai decor and traditional Thai seating on the floor. Expect a dramatically watered down spice level, but it's fresh and tasty. There's a second location in Celebration.

**TAVERNA OPA**                                          Greek **$$**
(www.opaorlando.com; Pointe Orlando; mains $12-25; ⏰11am-midnight; ) The waitstaff at this high-ceilinged Greek eatery crush up fresh hummus table-side and serve it with warm pita rather than just plopping down a basket of bread. While it can get kind of crazy at night, when the belly dancer shimmers and shakes from table to table and it isn't unusual for folks to climb onto those solid tables and kick up their heels, the rest of the time it's a pleasant, simple place for solid and tasty Greek classics, including plenty of vegetarian options.

## Greater Orlando

**YELLOW DOG EATS**                          Barbecue **$**
(☎407-296-0609; www.yellowdogeats.com; 1236 Hempel Ave, Windermere; mains $10-20; ⏰11:30am-10pm Mon-Thu, to 11pm Fri, noon-

11pm Sat, 3-8pm Sun; 🖋) Housed in what was once a general store, with a tin roof, an old boys' school locker filled with bottled beer, and an eclectic mix of quirky and dog-inspired decor, this laid-back Orlando gem serves up excellent barbecue. Massive homes, including that of Tiger Woods', have replaced the orange groves that once surrounded the site, and it feels like a drive to get here, but don't be deterred. Menu offerings range from Florida Cracker (pulled pork with Gouda, bacon and fried onions) to the recommended Puppy Love (peanut butter, strawberries, bananas, chocolate shavings, chopped roast peanuts) and excellent Cuban-style black beans. Call in advance for pick-up orders.

Yellow Dog Eats sits about 6 miles northwest of Universal Orlando Resort. Take Turkey Lake Rd (which borders the park on the west) for about a mile and turn left at the T onto Conroy Rd. In 2 miles turn right onto S Apopka Vineland Rd, then left at the church onto Windy Ridge Rd and right onto Hempel Ave.

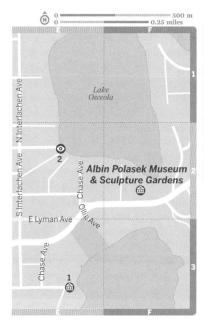

## Winter Park

### ◉ Top Sights
Albin Polasek Museum &
  Sculpture Gardens ..........................F2
Charles Hosmer Morse Museum
  of American Art..............................D1

### ◉ Sights
1 Cornell Fine Arts Museum .................E3
2 Scenic Boat Tour ..............................E2

### Sleeping
3 Park Plaza Hotel ...............................D2

vibe, couches for lounging and bold red walls featuring local art. Try the hot feta dip and delicious quiche, or create your own flatbread concoction. The wine and beer list follows the international cycling season, with French Bordeaux during the Tour de France and so on, and there's weekend live music and cyclists' happy hour specials. From Harry P Leu Gardens, head east on Corrine Dr for 0.6 miles, and look for the tiny strip mall on the right.

**DANDELION
COMMUNITEA CAFÉ**    Vegetarian $
( ☎407-362-1864; http://dandelioncommunitea
.com; 618 N Thornton Ave; mains $5-10; ⏱11am
to 10pm Mon-Sat, to 5pm Sun; ✈) Unabash-
edly crunchy and definitively organic, this pillar of the 'sprouts and tofu, green tea and soy milk' crowd serves up creative and excellent vegetarian fare in a refur-bished old house that invites folks to sit down and hang out. The focus is on Flor-ida-grown produce and locally blended teas, and it is 100% green. If it all sounds too healthy, try a Fluffer Nutter (wheat bread with almond butter, bananas and ricemallow fluff), its nod to junk food. There's an informal fire-pit, tables in the yard, and microbrew beer; check the web-site for details on art openings, poetry readings and live music. From downtown Orlando head north on Magnolia Ave, turn right at E Colonial Dr and then right in 0.7 miles onto Thornton Ave.

**BIKES, BEANS & BORDEAUX**    Café $
(www.b3cafe.com; 3022 Corrine Dr; mains
$6-12; ⏱8am-3pm Tue-Sat, 7am-2pm Sun)
Organic fare with a contemporary cafe

**WHITE WOLF CAFÉ**    Diner $$
(www.whitewolfcafe.com; 1829 N Orange Ave;
mains $14-29; ⏱7am-9pm Mon-Fri, 8am-10pm
Sat, 8am-3pm Sun) Tiffany-styled chande-liers, a massive wooden bar and an ec-lectic mix of antiques offer a welcomed respite from the plethora of chains and themed restaurants that define Orlando eateries. Simple but excellent basics like burgers, pastas and pizzas, as well as stick-to-your-bones breakfasts. From downtown take I-4 exit 85 (Princeton St) and turn right; take the first right onto N Orange Ave and look for White Wolf on the left. Alternatively, head north on Magnolia Ave and right on N Orange.

## 🍷 Drinking

The downtown Orlando drinking scene can be a crazy *Girls Gone Wild* meets Spring Break scene, particularly on the weekends and late at night,

Bars along Church Street in Orlando.

ALAMY/CORBIS FIRST©

Neighborhood bars in Celebration, Winter Park and Thornton Park (which is located just east of downtown Orlando's Lake Eola; listed in the following Downtown section) offer an altogether different vibe, with wine bars, acoustic live music and outdoor cafes sporting water bowls for canine companions.

## Downtown

### LATITUDES                                Bar
(Map p98; www.churchstreetbars.com; 33 W Church St; ⏱4:30pm-2am) Low-key island-inspired rooftop bar with tiki torches and potted palms. It's completely outside, three stories above street level, perfect for balmy Orlando nights. Latitudes is on the 3rd floor of Church Street Bars – look for Chillers on the 1st floor, and there's a microbrewery with pool tables on the 2nd floor.

### BÖSENDORFER LOUNGE            Lounge
(Map p98; ☎407-313-9000; Westin Grand Bohemian, 325 S Orange Ave; ⏱11am-midnight Sun-Wed, to 1am Thu, to 2am Fri & Sat) With zebra-fabric chairs, gilded mirrors, massive black pillars and marble floors, this

hotel bar with a circular bar oozes pomp and elegance. Popular with Orlando residents, who pop on over for an after-work drink, the lounge picks up with live jazz at 7pm. The name stems from the lounge's rare Bösendorfer piano.

### BURTONS                                  Bar
(801 E Washington St, Thornton Park; ⏱noon-2am) A neighborhood corner bar that's been around for almost 70 years. Expect forgettable wine but plenty of cheap cold beer, a jukebox with REM and the like and a couple of pool tables.

## Greater Orlando

### WALLY'S MILLS AVE LIQUORS       Bar
(1001 N Mills Ave; ⏱7:30pm-2am) It's been around since the early '50s, before Orlando became Disney, and while its peeling naked-women wallpaper could use some updating, it wouldn't be Wally's without it. Nothing flashy, nothing loud, just a tiny windowless old-school bar with a jukebox and cheap drinks, as much a dark dive as you'll find anywhere. Wednesday night is $3 microbrews, and the attached package store sells beer, wine and liquor. From

Thornton Park, head north a couple miles on Mills Ave.

 **Entertainment**

**WILL'S PUB**  Live Music
(☎407-898-5070; 1040 N Mills; ⏰4pm-2am Mon-Sat, from 6pm Sun) With $2 Pabst on tap, a permanent layer of smoke hovering over the pool tables, Ms PacMan and pinball and vintage pin-ups on the walls, this is Orlando's less polished music scene. It's an established institution as the spot to catch local and nationally touring indie music. Will's is on Mills Ave, just over a mile north of Thornton Park.

**ENZIAN THEATER**  Cinema
(☎407-629-0054; www.enzian.org; 1300 S Orlando Ave, Maitland; adult/child $7/5, weekend matinees $5; ⏰5pm-midnight Tue-Fri, noon-midnight Sat & Sun; P) The envy of any city or college town, this fantastic clapboard-sided theater screens independent and classic films, and has an excellent on-site restaurant featuring primarily local and organic fare. Have a veggie burger and a beer on the patio underneath the leafy cypress tree, or opt for table service inside the theater. Instead of traditional rows of seats, the theater has tables and comfy chairs. From Friday through Sunday, the Eden Bar serves lunch, with noodles and seafood salad, sandwiches and flatbread, and soup. Everything costs under $10. On the second Thursday of every month, the Enzian teams up with Winter Park to present Popcorn Flicks in the Park (free), a series of classic movies like *Casablanca* screened outdoors...in the park. The Enzian is located in Maitland, just north of Winter Park.

# Gay & Lesbian Orlando

In 1991 Orlando gay activist Doug Swallow and a handful of friends encouraged gays and lesbians to 'wear red and be seen' when visiting the Magic Kingdom. Some 2500 made it. Ever since, an estimated 40,000 to 50,000 red-shirted gay and lesbian visitors descend on Cinderella's Castle on the first Saturday in June. Though it explodes during Gay Days, there is a solid gay and lesbian community in Orlando year-round. Go to www.orlandogaycities.com for a thorough listing and reviews of bars and clubs, events, hotels, bathhouses and more.

**Gay, Lesbian & Bisexual Community Center** (☎407-228-8272; www.glbcc.org; 946 N Mills Ave; ⏰9am-4pm Mon & Thu, to 8pm Tue, Wed & Fri, noon-8pm Sat, noon-5pm Sun) General resource center, with tips on local hot spots and social events.

**Parliament House** (☎407-425-7571; www.parliamenthouse.com; 410 N Orange Blossom Trail; r $60-120, Gay Day $155; 🛜🏊) This legendary gay resort and an Orlando institution sits on Rock Lake and features several clubs and bars, a restaurant and some of the best drag shows south of the Mason-Dixon Line.

**Ritzy Rags** (www.ritzyrags.com; 928 N Mills Ave, Thornton Park; ⏰from 11am Mon-Sat, closing hour varies) Owner and performer Leigh Shannon offers makeup and wardrobe tips for making the most of what you were born with and sells everything a drag queen could want.

**Pulse** (☎407-649-3888; www.pulseorlando.net; 1912 S Orange Ave; $5) Three nightclubs, each with its own distinct vibe but all ultramodern and sleek. Call for directions and hours.

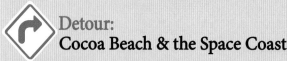

## Detour:
# Cocoa Beach & the Space Coast

Cocoa Beach, an hour east of Orlando, is still a company town for NASA and the air-force base, but these days folks waiting to catch a cruise and surfers looking to party dominate the local scene. The town admirably balances Old Florida attitude with a brash, youthful sexiness that is quintessentially Central Florida. Cocoa Beach, birthplace and home of Kelly Slater, is one of the best spots for surfing in the state.

Three causeways – Hwy 528, Hwy 520 and Hwy 404 – cross the Indian River, Merritt Island and the Banana River to connect Cocoa Beach to the mainland.

**Kennedy Space Center** ( 321-449-4444; www.kennedyspacecenter.com; adult/child 3-11yr $43/33; 9am-6pm), the focal point of American space travel, has a small Visitor Complex that showcases the history and future of US space travel and research, and is the heart of the Kennedy Space Center. Here you'll find replicas of classic rockets and the space shuttle; an hour-long Astronaut Encounter, where a real astronaut fields questions from the audience; the beautiful Astronaut Memorial, which displays photos and names of those who died during shuttle disasters plus IMAX films offering clear explanations of complicated science and cool footage of gravity-free life in space.

The two-hour Kennedy Space Center tour is the only way to see beyond the Visitor Complex without paying for an add-on tour. You'll see an LC 39 Observation Gantry, a 60ft observation tower with views of the twin launch pads and the astronauts' cramped living spaces at the International Space Station Center. Tours depart every 15 minutes from 10am to 2:45pm. Look for the coach buses and long lines to the right when you enter the Visitor Complex.

**Merritt Island National Wildlife Refuge** (www.merrittisland.com; I-95 exit 80; 8am-4.30pm Mon-Fri, 9am-5pm Sat & Sun, closed Sun Apr-Oct) This spectacular 140,000-acre refuge includes brackish marshes, mangrove swamps, pine flatlands and coastal dunes. More than 500 species of wildlife make this their home, including thousands of waterfowl stopping along their north–south migrations, alligators, otters and armadillos.

**Brevard Zoo** (www.brevardzoo.org; 8225 N Wickham Rd, Melbourne; adult/child 2-12yr $13.75/10.25, under 2 free; 9:30am-5pm) Hand feed giraffes and lorikeets, who climb onto your head and arms in their enthusiasm, ride a train past camels and monkeys roaming free, and kayak through 22 acres of wetlands at this jewel of Old Florida zoos. Small, easily navigable, and boasting a great water-play area, this may just outshine the Kennedy Space Center for the under-10 crowd. Take I-95 exit 91 (Wickham Rd) 0.5 miles east.

**Ron Jon Surf School** ( 321-868-1980; www.cocoabeachsurfingschool.com; 3901 N Atlantic Ave, Cocoa Beach; per hr $50-65) offers lessons for everyone from groms (that's surf talk for beginners) to experts, and there are plenty of other schools. For children five to 17.

# 🛍 Shopping

Head to Celebration or Winter Park for pleasant browsing, small-town American style, or to Downtown Disney for shopping on steroids.

**Prime Outlets International**    Mall
(📞407-354-0126; International Dr & I-4; 🕐10am-9pm Mon-Sat, to 6pm Sun) Particularly popular with overseas travelers, this outlet mall offers the usual discount-mall suspects as well as a few surprises, like the ultrachic Barneys.

**Farmers Market Lake Eola**    Market
(off Map p98; Lake Eola; 🕐10am-4pm Sun) Local produce, cheese and handicrafts, live music and a beer and wine garden on the shores of downtown Orlando's Lake Eola.

# ℹ Information

## Medical Services

**Arnold Palmer Hospital for Children** (📞407-649-9111; 1414 Kuhl Ave; 🕐24hr) The city's primary children's hospital. Located just east of I-4 at exit 81 (Kaley Ave).

**Centra Care Walk-In Medical** (📞407-934-2273; www.centracare.org; 12500 S Apopka Vineland Rd/SR 535, Lake Buena Vista; 🕐8am-midnight Mon-Fri, to 8pm Sat & Sun) A walk-in medical center offering adult and pediatric care. Located near Downtown Disney, on SR 535 south of Palm Parkway; see website or call for other locations.

**Doctors on Call Services** (📞407-399-3627; 🕐24hr) House and hotel-room calls to greater Orlando, including Walt Disney World and Universal Orlando Resort, and hotline for regional medical facilities.

# Tourist Information

**Orlando's Official Visitor Center** (📞407-363-5872; www.visitorlando.com; 8723 International Dr; 🕐8:30am-6:30pm) Sells legitimate discount attraction tickets.

## Websites

**Orlando Sentinel** (www.orlandosentinel.com/travel) Travel page of the city paper.

**ReserveOrlando** (www.reserveorlando.com) Central booking agency.

Skyline along Lake Eola (p94), Orlando.

GETTYIMAGES/ZEPHYR PICTURE ©

# On the Stage & Under the Stars

There's more to Orlando than theme parks and techno-club hopping. In addition to the following, Walt Disney World, Universal Orlando Resort and SeaWorld all have an island-inspired luau, Disney offers three dinner shows, and several Disney resorts screen classic Disney films outdoors (free). There's also a free classic movie on the second Thursday of every month in Winter Park.

**Cirque du Soleil La Nouba** (Map p66; ☎407-939-7600; www.cirquedusoleil.com; Downtown Disney; adult $76-132, child 3-9 $61-105; ⏰6 & 9pm Tue-Sat) Disney's best live show features mind-boggling acrobatic feats expertly fused to light, stage and costume design to create a cohesive artistic vision. And of course, there's a Disney twist involving a princess and a frog. This is a small horseshoe theater, with only about 20 rows from the stage to the top, no balcony, and designed by Disney specifically to house La Nouba. There are no bad seats.

**Blue Man Group** (Map p124; ☎407-258-3626; www.universalorlando.com; Universal Orlando Resort CityWalk; adult $59-74, child 3-9 $49-64) Originally an off-Broadway phenomenon in 1991, this high-energy and multisensory fun show features three bald men painted blue engaging in all kinds of craziness involving percussion 'instruments,' paintballs, marshmallows and modern dancing.

**Mad Cow Theatre** (Map p98; ☎407-297-8788; www.madcowtheatre.com; 105 S Magnolia Ave; tickets $18-30) A model of regional theater, with classic and modern performances in downtown space.

**Theatre Downtown** (☎407-841-0083; www.theatredowntown.net; 2113 N Orange Ave; tickets $16-22) Repertory theater featuring original works from local playwrights, regional actors and classic productions. Located two blocks west of Loch Haven Park.

**SAK Comedy Lab** (Map p98; ☎407-648-0001; www.sak.com; 29 S Orange Ave; tickets $15; ⏰9pm shows Tue & Wed) Improv comedy in 200-seat downtown theater; 9pm shows Tuesday and Wednesday cost $3. Reservations recommended. Check the website for other show times.

**John and Rita Lowndes Shakespeare Center** (☎407-447-1700; www.orlandoshakes. org; 812 E Rollins St, Loch Haven Park; tickets $20-35) Set on the shores of Lake Estelle in grassy Loch Haven Park, this lovely theater includes three stages hosting classics like *Pride and Prejudice* and *Beowulf* and excellent children's theater.

**Orlando Repertory Theater** (☎407-896-7365; www.orlandorep.com; 1001 E Princeton St, Loch Haven Park; tickets $10-25) Performances for families and children run primarily in the afternoon or early evening. Shows stretch the gamut of styles and content, including *Anne Frank and Me, Hairspray* and *James and the Giant Peach*.

VisitOrlando (www.visitorlando.com) Orlando Visitors Center.

## ⓘ Getting Around

**TO/FROM THE AIRPORT** Many hotels and motels run complimentary airport shuttles.

Legacy Towncar of Orlando (☎888-939-8227; www.legacytowncar.com) Services both airports; from Sanford International Airport to the Disney area, it's $185 round-trip for a town car (seats four).

**Disney's Magical Express** (☎407-939-6244) If you're staying at a Walt Disney World hotel and are arriving into the Orlando airport (as opposed to Sanford), arrange in advance for complimentary luggage handling and deluxe bus transportation.

**Mears Transportation** (☎407-423-5566; www. mearstransportation.com) Expect to pay $20 to $30 one way to Disney World or Universal Studios areas, a bit less to downtown Orlando and bit more to Winter Park.

**PUBLIC TRANSPORTATION I-Ride Trolley** (www. iridetrolley.com; rides adult/child under 12 $1/ free) Runs along two routes along International Dr from 8am to 10:30pm. Buy one-ride tickets on board (exact change only) or a multiday pass (one-/three-/five-/seven-/14-day pass $3/5/7/9/16) at hotels and stores along I-Drive.

**Lymmo** Free bus service circles downtown Orlando.

## ❶ Getting There & Away

**AIR** Orlando is serviced by two international airports: **Orlando International Airport** (Map p96; www.orlandoairports.net), 12 miles east of downtown Orlando, and the much smaller **Sanford International Airport** (Map p96; www. orlandosanfordairport.com), 30 miles north.

**CAR** Orlando is 285 miles from Miami; the fastest and most direct route is a 4½-hour road trip via the Florida Turnpike. From Tampa it is an easy 60 miles along I-4.

# Universal Studios & SeaWorld

**Universal's got spunk, it's got spirit and it's got attitude.** Universal Orlando Resort is Disney with a dash of hot sauce. Instead of the seven dwarfs, there's the Simpsons. Instead of Donald Duck and Mickey Mouse, there's Spider-Man and Shrek. While Universal can never replace Disney, and it certainly lacks the sentimental charm of Snow White, Peter Pan and Winnie the Pooh, it offers pure, unabashed, adrenaline-pumped, full-speed-ahead fun for the entire family. The Universal Orlando Resort consists of two theme parks – Islands of Adventure, with incredibly designed themed areas and the bulk of the thrill rides, and Universal Studios, with movie-based attractions and shows. Nearby (but separate) SeaWorld offers visitors opportunities to feed stingrays, sea lions and other critters. On top of the leaping dolphins, silly sea lions and splashing whales, SeaWorld is home to two of the biggest thrill rides in Orlando – the Kraken and the Manta.

One Ocean show (p134) featuring killer whales, SeaWorld.
SEAWORLD ©

Hollywood Rip Ride Rockit (p123).
UNIVERSAL ©

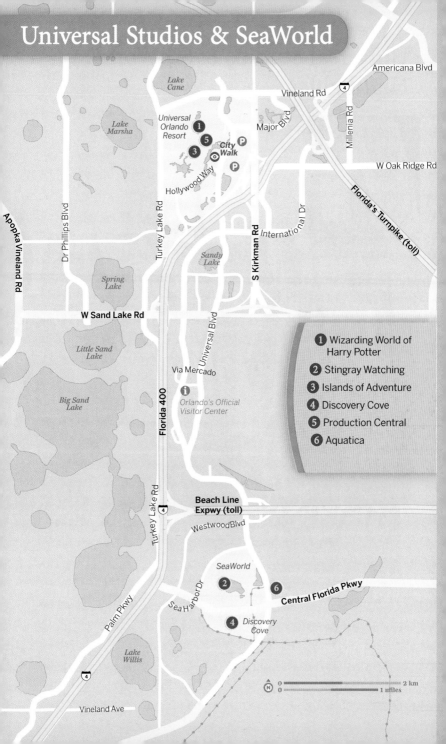

# Universal Studios & SeaWorld

Americana Blvd

Vineland Rd

Lake Cane

Universal Orlando Resort

Major Blvd

Millenia Rd

W Oak Ridge Rd

Lake Marsha

City Walk

Florida's Turnpike (toll)

Hollywood Way

International Dr

S Kirkman Rd

Apopka Vineland Rd

Dr Phillips Blvd

Turkey Lake Rd

Sandy Lake

Spring Lake

W Sand Lake Rd

Universal Blvd

Little Sand Lake

Via Mercado

① Wizarding World of Harry Potter

② Stingray Watching

③ Islands of Adventure

④ Discovery Cove

⑤ Production Central

⑥ Aquatica

Big Sand Lake

Florida 400

Orlando's Official Visitor Center

Beach Line Expwy (toll)

Turkey Lake Rd

Westwood Blvd

SeaWorld

② Central Florida Pkwy

⑥

Palm Pkwy

Sea Harbor Dr

④ Discovery Cove

Lake Willis

Vineland Ave

N  0          2 km
   0      1 miles

# Universal Studios & SeaWorld Highlights

## Wizarding World of Harry Potter

The Wizarding World of Harry Potter (p128) is as close as any of us will get to Harry's universe (or at least, that universe as envisioned by the film franchise). Hogwarts, Hogsmeade, Diagon Alley and other locations from the series are flawlessly recreated here.

### Need to Know

**LINES** Stay at Universal to skip lines at Express Plus rides. **TRANSPORTATION** Shuttles between parks. **RIDES** Universal has more thrill-oriented rides. **For more, see p122 and Map p124.**

# Kelly Timmins Don't Miss List

KELLY TIMMINS, ORLANDO
RESIDENT AND LEAD ADMISSIONS
REPRESENTATIVE AT FULL SAIL
UNIVERSITY.

### 1 INCREDIBLE HULK COASTER
This roller coaster is definitely for thrill-seekers only. After initially strapping in, you are inched forward before taking off on a zero-to-60 incline into tremendous loops and drops. The speed is reminiscent of the strength of the **Hulk** (p122) and as you continue on the ride, the intensity takes your breath away.

### 2 HARRY POTTER & THE FORBIDDEN JOURNEY
The **Forbidden Journey** (p128) is more than a ride; it's an experience. Upon entering the castle, you are surrounded by the world many of us have imagined from *Harry Potter*. The authenticity is present in every detail from Dumbledore's pensieve to the talking sorting hat. The experience is peaked by a fast-paced 'broom ride' through the grounds of Hogwarts, the Forbidden Forest, and the Quidditch pitch.

### 3 HONEYDUKES
This little **shop** (p128) brings the light-hearted, magical world of Harry Potter right into your hands. And stomachs! The shop is filled with candies and chocolates that avid readers of the series will be excited to get their hands on. My top picks are the chocolate frogs (famous wizard card included!) and the jars of chocolate-filled hard candies.

### 4 JURASSIC PARK RIVER ADVENTURE
**Jurassic Park** (p123) has been a classic ride since the '90s. Although it hasn't changed in years, it still stirs up thrills. As you journey on your boat through the forest, you are met with escaped raptors on the prowl. Finally, just when you think you'll fall victim to the jaws of the Tyrannosaurus Rex, you plunge to safety in a massive splash zone.

### 5 REVENGE OF THE MUMMY
This indoor coaster (p125) takes you through an Egyptian tomb as depicted within the movie series. You are met by countless menacing mummies intent on capturing you for sacrifice. At the end you come face-to-face with 'The Mummy,' and a hair-raising end to this fast-paced ride. A nice change up from many other rides and a nice escape from the Florida heat!

115

# Stingray Watching

SeaWorld is all about connecting to the sea, and we love do so at Stingray Lagoon (p135), where visitors of all ages have the chance to hand feed angel-winged stingrays. Nowhere else in the park do you get so close, so literally hands-on, with some very alien, yet beautiful, inhabitants of the ocean. Another place to get close to stingrays is Discovery Cove's Grand Reef. The Grand Reef, p138

## Discovery Cove

Discovery Cove (p138) has top-notch facilities for snorkeling with eagle rays and rainbow clouds of fish. All of this is great, but there's another quality Discovery Cove doesn't trumpet so much: it's relaxing, slow and quiet, which makes it a worthwhile break from Orlando's high energy.

SEA WORLD ©

## Islands of Adventure

UNIVERSAL STUDIOS ©

**3**

There's an experience for everyone in this corner of Universal Studios, from a children's village of Dr. Seuss characters where the Lorax speaks for the trees, to the pages of Marvel comic books brought to whiz-bang-pow life, swinging superheroes and all. (p125)

SEAWORLD ©

**5**

## Production Central

One of the centerpieces of the 'Studios' section of Universal Studios, Production Central (p123) takes you right into the imaginative wonderland of Hollywood filmmaking. There's a few ways this occurs; either via the sensory overload of the Hollywood Rip Ride Rockit roller coaster, or while chasing Princess Fiona with Shrek and Donkey at the Shrek 4-D show.

**6**

## Aquatica

At the time of writing, Aquatica (p137) was the newest water park in Orlando, and it had made quite a splash among the region's many theme parks. For those seeking a bit more action, there's incredibly fast waterslides and inner-tube-esque attractions abounding throughout.

# Universal Studios & SeaWorld's Best…

## Hotels

○ **Portofino Bay Hotel** (p127) Luxurious, Italianate resort situated around a lagoon.

○ **Royal Pacific Resort** (p127) Pacific and Balinese themed, scattered with gardens and tropical flowers.

○ **Hard Rock Hotel** (p127) A bit cheesy, but lots of fun; caters to singles and families.

○ **Veranda Bed & Breakfast** (p99) In Orlando, this peaceful B&B is a nice break from large resorts.

## Rides

○ **Harry Potter & the Forbidden Journey** (p128) Flying broomstick journey through Hogwarts.

○ **Twister...Ride It Out** (p125) Scary attraction puts you in a tornado path.

○ **Incredible Hulk Coaster** (p122) Roller coaster with great ride-narration synchronization.

○ **Amazing Adventures of Spider-Man** (p122) Help Spider-Man battle villains across New York.

○ **SeaVenture** (p138) On this 'ride' you'll venture underwater with a dive mask.

## Animal Encounters

○ **Stingray Lagoon** (p135) Feed stingrays at SeaWorld!

○ **Sharks Deep Dive** (p135) Go shark diving – no scuba experience needed.

○ **Manta Aquarium** (p136) Otherwordly aquarium where you're surrounded by angelic mantas.

○ **Manatees: the Last Generation?** (p135) See these pretty giants get nursed back to health.

○ **Grand Reef** (p138) Shallow tropical reef filled with rainbow clouds of fish.

# Need to Know

## Live Shows

○ **Blue Horizons** (p134) Dolphins, acrobats, lots of lights and good fun.

○ **One Ocean** (p134) The quintessential Shamu Killer Whale show.

○ **Shrek 4-D** (p123) Shrek and Donkey get in your face in this entertaining experience.

○ **Commerson's Dolphin Exhibit** (p137) Great show featuring black-and-white dolphins.

○ **A'Lure the Call of the Ocean** (p134) A surreal circus meets the sea.

**Left:** Pool at a Universal Orlando Resort;
**Above:** Kids and a macaw at Aquatica (p137).
(LEFT) LOEWS RESORT ©; (ABOVE) SEAWORLD ©

## ADVANCE PLANNING

○ **Hotels** Book early to get grand deals and to cut the wait out of many of the parks' lines.

○ **Express Pass** Highly recommended if you want to get the most out of the rides with the least amount of line waiting.

○ **Car Rentals** In Orlando, it's always best to book your rental vehicles as early as possible, especially in high tourist season (November to March).

○ **Sunscreen** If you're going to be outside in the local waterparks, bring plenty of sunblock.

## RESOURCES

○ **Islands of Adventure** An unofficial site devoted to the most ride-heavy portion of Universal Studios: www.islandsofadventure.com.

○ **Sea Inside** This blog for SeaWorld and affiliated parks is a good spot to check for updates: www.seaworldparksblog.com.

○ **Discover Universal** Another unofficial site devoted to the Universal Studios experience: www.discoveruniversal.com.

○ **Theme Park Rangers** The reporting team for *The Orlando Sentinel* gives their insider, and sometimes investigative perspective on the happenings in the region's theme parks: http://blogs.orlandosentinel.com/features_orlando.

## GETTING AROUND

○ **Car** I-4 is your main road for getting between the region's parks.

○ **Boat** Within Universal Studios, water taxis shuttle between the Universal Hotels and CityWalk.

○ **Shuttle** Shuttle services exist between hotels, Universal Studios and in some cases, Walt Disney World.

○ **Walking** All of Universal Studios' parks and hotels are linked by pedestrian walkways.

# Universal Studios & SeaWorld Itineraries

*You're spoiled for choice here. You've got two main parks in Universal Studios, plus three water parks to choose from. So we're gonna show you the best!*

**2 DAYS**

**ISLANDS OF ADVENTURE TO UNIVERSAL STUDIOS**

## The Studio Backlot Tour

This covers the best of the Universal Studios theme parks. Begin in the classic Hollywood backlot of **(1) Universal Studios**, a park dedicated to realizing the magic of the movies. Wander up **(2) Hollywood Boulevard** and ride on attractions that recreate special-effects wonders. Like disaster movies? Get tossed by a tornado and an earthquake in **(3) Twister...Ride It Out** and **(4) Disaster!**, respectively. Into action and adventure? Get your thrills on the **(5) Revenge of the Mummy** roller coaster. Have lunch at **(6) Schwab's Pharmacy**. **(7) Shrek 4-D** is glorious family fun parents and kids will appreciate.

The next morning, head to **(8) Islands of Adventure** early to get to **(9) The Wizarding World of Harry Potter**. This is the Harry Potter universe realized in park form. If you can yank yourself away, head to **(9) Marvel Super Hero Island**. Some of these rides are the best in Orlando, including the twisty, speedy **(10) Incredible Hulk Coaster**. Finish the day with dinner at **(11) Honeydukes**.

**Top Left:** Manta ride (p133) in SeaWorld; **Top Right:** Penguin Encounter (p135) at SeaWorld.

(TOP LEFT) SEA WORLD ©; (TOP RIGHT) SEAWORLD ©

**SEAWORLD TO DISCOVERY COVE**

## Older Kids & Adults

This itinerary takes in three Orlando area water parks. We'll begin in **(1) SeaWorld**, the most classical of the bunch. The big attraction here is the shows, which are world famous, including **(2) One Ocean**, headliner show for the world's most famous orca, Shamu; and **(3) A'lure**, an oddly compelling mix of carnival fantasy and the undersea world. For lunch, dine with the sharks in **(4) Sharks Underwater Grill**. Also make sure to feed the stingrays at **(5) Stingray Lagoon**, chuckle at the flightless birds in their tuxes at **(6) Penguin Encounter** and drop your jaw at **(7) Manta Aquarium**.

The next day head to serene **(8) Discovery Cove**, where you can happily lose an entire day donning a helmet and walking underwater at **(9) SeaVenture**; laze around the **(10) Wind-away River** and gawk at eagle rays at the **(11) Tropical Reef**. With all of that said, the main point of coming here is to relax, so find the pool or tropical lagoon that best suits you and spend your day soaking up some sun and surf. On your final day get back into the ride swing of things: go to **(12) Aquatica** and boat down **(13) Loggerhead Lane**, slip and slide on **(12) HooRoo Run** and have dinner at the **(14) Banana Beach Cookout**.

# Discover Universal Studios & SeaWorld

Walkabout Waters (p137) at Aquatica.
SEAWORLD ©

## UNIVERSAL STUDIOS

 **Sights & Activities**

The main attractions are the rides, movies and shows within Islands of Adventure and Universal Studios theme parks.

### Islands of Adventure

This place (Map p124) is just plain fun. Scream-it-from-the-rooftops, no-holds-barred, laugh-out-loud kind of fun. Superheroes zoom by on motorcycles, roller coasters whiz overhead, and plenty of rides will get you soaked.

**MARVEL SUPER HERO ISLAND** Rides Techno music blares from the fake facades of superhero-covered buildings, the **Incredible Hulk Coaster (Express Plus)** rumbles and roars overhead and superheroes speed through on motorcycles. Bright, loud and fast-moving, Marvel Super Hero Island is sensory overload and a thrill-lover's paradise. Comic-book characters patrol this area, so keep an eye out for your favorites. Don't miss the motion simulator **Amazing Adventures of Spider-Man (Express Plus)**, where super villains rendered in incredible 3D are on the loose, jumping on your car and chasing you around the streets of New York City. At **Dr Doom's Fearfall (Express Plus)**, you're sitting there, strapped, and out of the blue *zoom*, rocket 150ft up in the air and free fall down. **Storm Force Accelatron (Express Plus)** is another barf-o-rama.

**TOON LAGOON**                      Rides

Loud with kids' squeals, with lots of short buildings covered with primary-colored cartoon classics, this sparkly, lighthearted spot aims to transport visitors to the days when lazy weekends included nothing more than watching *Popeye* and the *Rocky and Bullwinkle Show* on a Saturday morning and afternoons spent running under the sprinkler. Most of the attractions here are for kids, but older folks will want to hit **Dudley Do-Right's Ripsaw Falls (Express Plus)**, a classic water ride with a short but steep fall that will get you absolutely soaked.

**JURASSIC PARK**                    Rides

Oddly quiet, with no screams or loud music, no neon colors or hawking vendors, this oasis of palm trees, greenery and ferns takes visitors into the days of dinosaurs. **Jurassic Park River Adventure (Express Plus)**, a water ride with a prehistoric twist, floats you past friendly vegetarian dinosaurs. All seems well and good until, you guessed it, things go wrong and grass-munchin' cuties are replaced with the stuff of nightmares. To escape the looming teeth of the giant T. Rex, you plunge (in darkness) 85ft to the water below. Children will be terrified by the creatures, the dark and the plunge.

**Pteranodon Flyers** floats gently over the lush landscape of Jurassic Park and all its robotic dinosaurs. You must be between 36in and 56in tall to fly. Waits can be upwards of an hour for the 80-second ride, and it's just not worth it. The kids' play area here, enticingly named **Jurassic Park Discovery Center**, is another thing to skip.

**LOST CONTINENT**                   Shows

Magic and myth from across the seas and the pages of fantasy books inspire this mystical corner of the park. Here you'll find dragons and unicorns, psychic readings and fortune-tellers. And don't be startled if that fountain talks to you – yes you, the little girl in blue holding the cotton candy – as you walk past. The **Mystic Fountain** banters sassily, soaking children with his waterspouts when they least expect it and engaging them in silly conversation. And no, no one is hiding with a remote control. This is a talking fountain.

At the **Eighth Voyage of Sinbad Stunt Show (Express Plus)** Sinbad and his sidekick Kabob must rescue Princess Amoura from the terrible Miseria, and of course, Sinbad has to tumble and jump around to do it. There's lots of swashbuckling shenanigans, with corny jokes, the audience warning the clueless Sinbad of lurking danger, and hissing for the bad guys.

**SEUSS LANDING**                    Rides

Anyone who has fallen asleep to the reading of *Green Eggs and Ham* or learned to read with *Sam I Am* knows the world of Dr Seuss: the fanciful creatures, the lyrical names, the rhyming stories. Here, realized in magnificently designed three-dimensional form, is Dr Seuss' imagination. The Lorax guards his Truffula Trees, Thing One and Thing Two make trouble, and creatures from all kinds of Seuss favorites adorn the shops and the rides. Drink Moose Juice or Goose Juice, eat Green Eggs and Ham, and peruse shelves of Dr Seuss books before riding through *The Cat in the Hat* or around and around on an elephant bird from *Horton Hears a Who*. Seuss Landing, one of the best places for little ones in all of Orlando's theme parks, brings the spirit and energy of Dr Seuss' vision to life. So come on in, walk into his world and take a spin on a fish.

## Universal Studios

The silver screen inspired the majority of the rides at this quieter and more peaceful brother to the energy of Islands of Adventure. The park (Map p124) features elaborate New York and San Francisco backdrops, motion-simulator rides and audience-participation shows.

**PRODUCTION CENTRAL**        Shows, Rides

**Hollywood Rip Ride Rockit (Express Plus)**, a multisensory roller coaster, includes 21st-century special effects and Universal's trademark commitment to the interactive experience. You'll Rip up to 65mph, Ride 17 stories above the

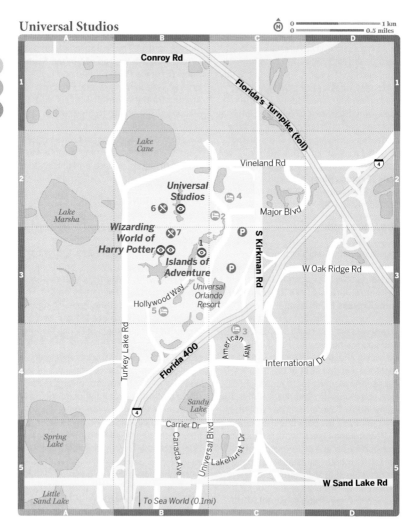

theme park and around a loop-dee-loop, and Rockit to customized music (chosen before you strap in).

Pick up where the movie *Shrek* left off at **Shrek 4-D (Express Plus)**. This 3D movie with 4-D effects sends you zipping along with Shrek and Donkey in a desperate effort to save Princess Fiona from a fierce dragon. And that dragon is indeed fierce – it pops out at you with red eyes, spitting fire into your face. The dragon sneezes and you feel it, and your chair rocks when Shrek and the donkey

chase the dragon. It's a lot of fun, but tiny tots will be scared.

### HOLLYWOOD
### BOULEVARD     Shows, Rides
With glorious 3D 360-degree film footage, live action stunts and 4-D special effects, **Terminator 2: 3-D Battle Across Time (Express Plus)** is complete sensory overload, delicious fun for some, overwhelming and scary for others.

If you're really into horror makeup, **Universal Horror Make-Up Show**

## Universal Studios

**(Express Plus)** may be a little too short and thin on substance. It's humorous, and full of silly antics. Optical illusions could freak out kids if they're not really clear from the get-go that it's not real.

Fans of the famous redhead Lucille Ball will particularly enjoy **Lucy – A Tribute**, a biographical exhibit with *I Love Lucy* clips, costumes, photos and Lucy's letters. Keep an eye out for the loveable redhead herself walking the streets outside.

**NEW YORK** — Shows, Rides

Just waiting in line for **Twister...Ride It Out (Express Plus)** is enough to frighten kids. Several TV screens show film clips from the movie *Twister,* including a child screaming as a tornado makes its way towards her home. Bill Paxton and Helen Hunt, the stars of the movie, talk in grave tones about the dangers of tornados and the perils of working on the film set, and they warn that this attraction will take you into the horror of their filmmaking experience. The attraction itself takes folks into a film set of a rather dilapidated, old-fashioned Midwest America town. There's a drive-in theater and an old gas station. A radio announces a severe storm warning, and slowly you see and feel the storm approach. A tornado develops in the distant sky, and it's coming, closer and closer, louder and louder... Anyone who has felt the fear of living through a real tornado, or children who already wake up scared of them thanks to sirens, hours in the basement and the eerie

blanket of tornado-breeding green skies, should seriously think twice before going to this attraction.

One of the most thrilling coaster rides in Orlando, **Revenge of the Mummy (Express Plus)**, delves into ancient Egyptian catacombs in near pitch black – whatever you do, don't anger Imhotep the mummy or...well, too late for that. Incur his wrath as he flings you past fire, water and more in-your-face special effects.

**WORLD EXPO** — Rides

Can you qualify for the most elite law-enforcement agency in the galaxy? **Men in Black Alien Attack (Express Plus)** gives you the chance to prove it, if you dare. Speed through the streets of New York City and aim your lasers at aliens of every size and description. Your car swings and spins through a danger-laden downtown, and those guys shoot back!

Even if you're not a fan of *The Simpsons,* you won't want to miss **The Simpsons Ride**. This combination ride and 3D film zip you through a Simpsons-inspired adventure with Krusty the Clown and Homer.

**SAN FRANCISCO/AMITY** — Rides, Shows

Take a little boat for a scenic ride through Nantucket harbor on **Jaws (Express Plus)**. But beware. This is Jaws territory, and he just might be lurking below the surface. The captain does his best to keep everyone safe, with various weapons to stave off the great white beast, but it's no

easy task. That shark lurches towards the boat, his huge mouth and sparkling teeth poised for attack, and gas tanks burst into flames.

The premise of **Disaster! (Express Plus)** is that you are the cast of a disaster movie entitled *Mutha Nature*. A fast-talking Hollywood casting agent chooses a handful of folks from the audience, gives the actors directions ('give me terror like Britney Spears is your babysitter'), and each volunteer is filmed for a second or so. Everyone then heads to the 'set' and boards a subway train in the incredibly authentic replica of a San Francisco BART (Bay Area Rapid Transit) station. Suddenly, the big one hits: tracks buckle, the place crumbles and general mayhem ensues. Hint: 65,000 gallons of water are released and recycled every six minutes, but you don't get wet. And yes, you do see the footage of those volunteers.

Beetlejuice, the Werewolf, Dracula, Frankenstein and his Bride rock out in the unbelievably corny and exceptionally loud **Beetlejuice's Graveyard Revue (Express Plus)**, something to skip if time is tight. At **Fear Factor Live (Express Plus)** pre-selected audience members compete to see who can best overcome their greatest fears. Think creepy-crawly bugs and jumps from high places.

### WOODY WOODPECKER'S KIDZONE
Rides, Shows

Rides, shows and a fantastic water-play area for little ones, this rivals Islands of Adventure's Seuss Landing as park favorite of the eight-and-under crowd. Though primarily geared toward little guys, the **Curious George Ball Room**, a giant room of nerf balls and cannons, is fun for all ages.

 **Sleeping**

Universal Orlando Resort boasts three excellent resorts. Generally less expensive than Walt Disney World's deluxe accommodation, they offer far superior service, food, decor, amenities and rooms. For

**Left:** Hollywood Rip Ride Rockit (p123); **Below:** Hard Rock Hotel .

(LEFT) UNIVERSAL STUDIOS ©; (BELOW) LOWES RESORTS ©

reservations and package deals, call ☎888-273-1311.

**PORTOFINO BAY HOTEL**   Resort $$$
(Map p124; ☎407-503-1000; 5601 Universal Blvd; r & ste from $269; ❄@🛜🏊🚻🐾) Sumptuous and elegant, with goose-down duvets, plenty of pillows and chenille throws in the earth-toned rooms, cobblestone streets, and sidewalk cafes around a central lagoon, this resort evokes the charm of seaside Italy. There are three pools, including a family pool, and quiet pools surrounded by grass, palm trees and a peaceful boccie court, the outstanding Mandara Spa and supervised children's activities.

**ROYAL PACIFIC RESORT**   Resort $$$
(Map p124; ☎407-503-3000; 6300 Hollywood Way; r & ste from $325; ❄@🛜🏊🚻🐾) The glass-enclosed Orchid Court, with its reflecting pool, Balinese fountains and carved stone elephants splashing in the water, sits at the center of the airy lobby at this friendly South Pacific-inspired resort. The grounds are lovely, with lots of grass, tropical plantings, flowers, bamboo and palm trees, and the on-site restaurants are excellent (see p129). Unfortunately, the over-the-top, family-friendly pool, with an interactive play area, real sand, volleyball, shuffleboard and Ping-Pong, is loud, chaotic and unsupervised, and rooms tend to be smaller than those at the other two Universal hotels.

**HARD ROCK HOTEL**   Resort $$$
(Map p124; ☎407-503-2000; 5800 Universal Blvd; r & ste from $310; ❄@🛜🏊🚻🐾) From the grand lawn with the massive guitar fountain at its entrance to the shocking black-and-white bathrooms and pumped-in underwater music at the pool, the modern and stylized Hard Rock embodies the pure essence of rock and roll. Families mingle harmoniously alongside a young party crowd, but the loud live band sometimes playing in the lobby and rockin' energy may be overkill for older folk looking for a peaceful getaway.

127

UNIVERSAL STUDIOS ©

# Don't Miss Wizarding World of Harry Potter

The magnificent Wizarding World of Harry Potter in Universal's Islands of Adventure invites muggles into JK Rowling's imagination. Poke along the cobbled streets and impossibly crooked buildings of Hogsmeade, sip frothy Butter Beer, and mail a card via Owl Post, all in the shadow of Hogwarts Caste. The art director and production designer for the films helped to create the most fantastically realized themed experience in Florida.

○ **Harry Potter and the Forbidden Journey** Wind through the corridors of Hogwarts, past talking portraits, Dumbledore's office and other well-known locations. You'll feel the cold chill of Dementors, escape a dragon attack, join a Quidditch match and soar over the castle with Harry, Hermione and Ron.

○ **Dragon Challenge** Gut-churning dueling roller coasters twist and loop, narrowly avoiding each other; inspired by the first task of the Triwizard Tournament in *Harry Potter & the Goblet of Fire*.

○ **Ollivander's Wand Shop** Floor-to-ceiling shelves crammed with dusty wand boxes and a winding staircase set the scene for a 10-minute show that brings to life the iconic scene in which the wand chooses the wizard. Come first thing, as hour-long waits are common.

○ **Flight of the Hippogriff (Express Plus)** Family-friendly coaster passes over Hagrid's Hut; listen for Fang's barks and don't forget to bow to Buckbeak!

○ **Honeydukes** Sweet shop with Bertie Botts Every Flavor Beans, Chocolate Frogs, Rock Cakes and other Harry Potter-inspired goodies.

○ **Owl Post & Owlery** Buy Wizarding World stamps. Send a card postmarked Hogsmeade.

○ **Three Broomsticks & Hog's Head** Tavern with surprisingly good Shepherd's Pie, Pumpkin Juice and Hogs Head Brew.

# Eating

Universal Orlando Resort offers the all-you-can-eat Universal Meal Deal (adult/child under nine, one park on one day $20/10; two parks on one day $24/12), which allows you to eat as much as you'd like from participating restaurants at Islands of Adventure and Universal Studios. It's good only from lunch through dinner.

## Islands of Adventure

**Three Broomsticks**                    English $

(Wizarding World of Harry Potter; mains $11-16; ⊙11am-park closing; 🚹) Fast-food styled British fare inspired by Harry Potter, with Butter Beer, Cornish Pasties and rustic wooden benches. Look out for the growling hog's head at the adjacent Hogs Head Pub.

**Mythos Restaurant**          Mediterranean $

(Map p124; 📞407-224-4012; The Lost Continent; mains $8-15; ⊙11am-5pm; 🚹) Housed in an ornate underwater grotto, this spot offers particularly tasty fare and has some of the best meals at Universal.

## Universal Studios

**FINNEGAN'S BAR & GRILL**          Pub $

(Map p124; 📞407-224-3613; New York; mains $8-20; ⊙11am-park closing; 🚹) An Irish pub with live acoustic music plopped into the streets of New York serves up Cornish pasties and Scotch Eggs, as well as Harp, Bass and Guinness on tap. Try the corned-beef sandwich served on a yummy pretzel roll and warm bread pudding.

**SCHWAB'S PHARMACY**          Ice cream $

(Hollywood Blvd; mains $5-10; ⊙11am-park closing; 🚹) In the '30s two brothers bought what would become a favorite lunch-counter hangout for struggling movie-star wannabes in Hollywood. They say Ava Gardner worked the soda fountain, Harold Arlin composed 'Over the Rainbow' here, and regulars included Marilyn Monroe, Clark Gable and Orson Wells. The original is long gone, but Universal re-created the charm. Grab a sandwich and Ben and Jerry's.

**MEL'S DINER**                    Burgers $

(Hollywood Blvd; mains $6-10; ⊙11am-park closing; 🚹) Classic cars and rockin' bands outside, '50s diner style inside, and you half expect a roller-skating waitress to serve up that burger and fries. This is a fast-food eatery, not much different really than your standard McDonalds, but it's a lot more fun!

## Resort Hotels

Call 📞407-503-3463 for reservations at other sit-down restaurants within the resort hotels.

**ORCHID COURT
SUSHI BAR**                    Japanese $$

(Map p124; Royal Pacific Resort; sushi $4-8, mains $12-20; ⊙11am-11pm; 🚹) Sip on a Cherry Blossom Saketini over sushi and sashimi. Located within the light and airy glass-enclosed lobby of the hotel, with cushioned couches and chairs, this informal restaurant makes a great place to relax.

**EMERIL'S TCHOUP CHOP**          Seafood $$

(Map p124; 📞407-503-2467; Royal Pacific Resort; mains $15-30; ⊙11:30am-2:30pm & 5:30-10pm; 🚹) Excellent island-inspired food, including plenty of seafood and Asian accents, prepared with the freshest ingredients. One of the best sit-down meals at the resort, but unfortunately the service is painfully slow.

**EMACK AND BOLIO'S
MARKETPLACE**                    Ice cream $

(Map p124; Hard Rock Hotel; ice cream $3-8; ⊙6:30am-11pm; 🚹) Originally from Boston, Emack and Bolio ice cream beats all the rest hands down. And of course, only at this bastion of rock and roll will you find Bye Bye Miss American Mud Pie.

# Drinking & Entertainment

**VELVET BAR & LOBBY LOUNGE**          Lounge

(Map p124; 📞407-503-2401; www.hardrocklive.com; Hard Rock Hotel; ⊙5pm-1am) Trendy contemporary-styled bar with zebra-fabric chairs, hardwood floors, floor-to-ceiling windows and excellent martinis. On the last Thursday of the month, the bar hosts Velvet Sessions, a 'rock n' roll cocktail party' with themed drinks, live music and finger food; call for details on other live music events.

**WANTILAN LUAU**　　　Dinner Show
(Map p124; ☎ 407-503-3463; Royal Pacific Resort; adult/child under 12 $60/30; ⏲6pm Tue & Sat May-Aug, call for Sep-Apr showtimes) Pacific Island fire dancers shimmer and shake on stage while guests enjoy a tasty buffet of roast suckling pig, guava-barbecued short ribs and other Polynesian-influenced fare. The Maori warrior's roar can be rather scary and that fire might be a bit close for comfort in the eyes of little ones, but there's a pleasant grassy area next to the open-air dining theater where kids can putz about. The atmosphere is wonderfully casual and, like everything at Universal Orlando, this is simple unabashed silliness and fun. Unlimited mai tais, beer and wine are included in the price.

## ℹ️ Information

### Child Care

Nursing facilities and companion bathrooms are located at the Health Services and First Aid facilities in each park. A baby-bottle icon next to select stores on the park map indicates which stores carry baby supplies (not on display). Each resort has a drop-off child-care center. For private babysitting services, see p91.

### Kennels

**Studio Kennel** (☎ 407-224-9509; per pet per day $10), inside the parking structure, offers day boarding. You must provide food and occasionally return to walk your animal. The three Universal Orlando Resort resorts welcome pets.

### Lost & Found

Inside Guest Services at both parks.
**General** (☎ 407-224-4233)
**Islands of Adventure** (☎ 407-224-4245)
**Universal Studios** (☎ 407-224-4244)

### Medical Services

Each theme park has medical facilities; see park maps for locations.

### Park Hours

Theme park hours change not only by season, but day to day within any given month. Generally, parks open at 8 or 9am and close sometime between 6 and 10pm. Guests at one of the three on-site hotels at Universal Orlando Resort can enter the Wizarding World of Harry Potter inside Islands of Adventure one hour before the park opens.

### Parking

Parking for both theme parks and CityWalk is available inside a giant garage structure (car/RV $11/12); valet parking costs $18.

Scene from Wantilan Luau.
LOEWS RESORTS ©

# Universal for Little Ones

The word on the street says that Universal Orlando Resort is great for teens and adults but doesn't offer much for kids under seven. This is simply not true. No, it doesn't have as much as Walt Disney World and you won't find Disney's nostalgic charm, but Universal Orlando Resort is a master at blending attractions for all ages into one easily digestible and navigable package of fun, fun, fun. Animals from *Madagascar,* Dr Seuss's Grinch, superheroes and other Universal characters make appearances at both Universal Studios and Islands of Adventure, and Cat in the Hat, Spider-Man and Thing One and Thing Two join folks for a **character buffet breakfast** ( ☏ 407-224-4012, diningreservations@ universalorlando.com; Islands of Adventure; adult/child 3-9 $18/12; ☉ 8-10am Sun & Thu) at Confisco Grille. Characters from *Scooby Doo, Shrek* and *Simpsons* swing by restaurants at the three resort hotels on Wednesday, Friday and Saturday nights. CityWalk is very family-friendly, despite its many bars and live music, and the Wantilan Luau (p130) at Portofino Bay Hotel gives folks of all ages a taste of the islands.

## Stroller Rental

Single/double strollers cost $12/16 and are available at Guest Services inside both theme parks.

## Tickets

A one-park one-/two-/three-/four-day ticket costs $82/115/130/140; a one-/two-/three-/four-/seven-day park-to-park ticket costs $112/135/145/150/175. Tickets for children three to nine cost about $10 less. Tickets are good for 14 consecutive days, and multiple-day tickets include admission to paid venues in CityWalk. Universal Orlando Resort participates in the Orlando Flex Ticket.

EXPRESS PLUS This pass allows you to avoid the lines at designated Express Plus rides (identified on the map and also in this book) by flashing your pass at the separate Express Plus line. You can go to any ride, any time you'd like. If you are staying at a Universal resort you automatically receive an Express Plus pass; otherwise, a limited number of passes per day are available online or at the park gate. Prices vary according to season, ranging from $20 to $60 for a one-day/one-park pass, and from $26 to $60 for a one-day/two-park pass. See www .universalorlando.com for details.

DINING PLAN See www.universalorlando .com for details on dining packages at select restaurants throughout Universal Orlando Resort.

WET 'N WILD Package prices include admission to Wet 'n Wild, a water park a few miles away. See www.universalorlando.com for pricing.

## Tourist Information

Guest Services ( ☏ 407-224-6350, 407-224-4233) Located at the entrance to each theme park. Foreign-language maps and brochures and a limited foreign-currency exchange; if you have any problems or questions, go here.

Resort Hotel Reservations ( ☏ 888-273-1311) Room-only reservations.

## Travelers with Disabilities

The free *Rider Safety and Guests With Disabilities* guidebook is available at Guest Services. Rent wheelchairs ($12) and Electric Convenience Vehicles ($40) at the entrance to each park.

**Deaf or Hard of Hearing TDD** ( ☎ 800-447-0672) Information on parks, rooms, entertainment and restaurants.

## ℹ Getting There & Around

See p92 for information on trains, planes and buses to Orlando and p108 for transport to/from the airport.

**BOAT** Water taxis, which leave each point about every 20 minutes, shuttle regularly between the three Universal hotels and CityWalk, just outside the gates of the parks. Service usually begins at 8:30am and ends at 2am.

**CAR** From the I-4, take exit 74B or 75A and follow the signs. From International Drive, turn west at Wet 'n Wild onto Universal Blvd.

**SHUTTLE** Most hotels just outside Universal Studios and along International Drive provide free shuttle service to the Universal Orlando Resort. Call Mears Transportation ( ☎ 407-423-5566; www.mearstransportation.com; round-trip per person $19) one day in advance to arrange personalized shuttle service to Disney.

**WALKING** Universal Orlando's three resort hotels, two theme parks and CityWalk are linked by well-lit and landscaped pedestrian walkways.

# SEAWORLD, DISCOVERY COVE & AQUATICA

SeaWorld is not only a stellar marine-animal facility, but boasts a few knuckle-whitening rides, an excellent kiddie-ride section and a full day's worth of outstanding animal shows. At the idyllic Discovery Cove you can swim with dolphins (but see p238 for arguments for and against the practice), and enjoy the crowd-free atmosphere of a private beach. Aquatica, which opened in 2008, is a rides-oriented water park. The three theme parks, owned by the same parent company and located next to each other, are not a self-contained resort like Walt Disney World and Universal Orlando.

## SeaWorld

Beyond excellent shows, SeaWorld offers opportunities to feed aquatic animals, is pleasantly landscaped with plenty of greenery and flowers, and has decent food. Plus, its home to two of the biggest thrill rides in town.

The beach at Aquatica (p137).

SEAWORLD ©

# Detour:
# CityWalk

Universal Studios and SeaWorld are connected by a pleasantly landscaped pedestrian **mall (Map p124; www.citywalkorlando.com; ☺11am-2am)** lined with themed restaurants, bars, a multiplex movie theater, shops, a carousel and a fountain for kids to play in. Live music and mucho alcohol sums up the entertainment options here and though it can be packed with partying 20-somethings, particularly after the theme parks close, there's a distinct family-friendly vibe. Individual bars charge nightly covers ($5 to $9), or purchase a CityWalk Party Pass ($12, free with multiday theme-park admission) for unlimited all-night club access. For a movie and clubbing, buy the CityWalk Party Pass and Movie Ticket ($15), and for dinner and a movie, purchase the Meal and Movie Deal ($15). Call or stop by **CityWalk Guest Services Ticket Window ( ☏407-224-2691)** or pick them up at any resort. For dinner reservations, call ☏407-224-3663.

○ **Bob Marley – A Tribute to Freedom** Jamaica-inspired food and music.

○ **CityWalk's Rising Star** Karaoke to live music and talent contests.

○ **the groove** Dance club with sleek blue neon walls and blaring music from the '70s and '80s. Look out for select 'teen nights'.

○ **Jimmy Buffet's Margaritaville** Three bars themed around Jimmy Buffet songs, a full menu and live music after 10pm.

○ **Pat O'Brien's** A homogenized slice of New Orleans with Cajun food, that strange Orlando obsession, dueling pianos, and cocktails with a punch.

○ **Red Coconut Club** Live bands, martini bar and rooftop balcony.

○ **Latin Quarter** Latin American flair.

 **Sights & Activities**

For priority seating for rides and shows, consider a SeaWorld VIP Tour (adult/child three to nine $100/75). This seven-hour tour includes premium reserved seating at One Ocean, Clyde and Seamore Take Pirate Island, and Blue Horizons, front-of-the-line access to Manta, Kraken and Journey to Atlantis, lunch, and the chance to feed dolphins, rays, seals and sea lions. Make reservations at www.seaworld.com/orlando or by phone at ☏888-800-5447.

## Rides

Folks with little ones in tow should count on spending a couple of hours at **Shamu's Happy Harbor**, where six eye-candy rides, four stories of nets connected with slides and tunnels and a water-spewing playground delight the under-10 crowd. Ride a dolphin or another creature of the sea on the **Sea Carousel**, spin on **Jazzy Jellies** and board the **Shamu Express** for a gentle coaster thrill.

The two sea-inspired roller coasters at Sea World push the thrill level up a notch with simple design twists. **Kraken**, a whiplash ride of twists, turns, inversion and plunges touted by aficionados as one of the most wicked coasters in Florida and beyond, has no floor so your feet dangle free. On **Manta**, you lie horizontally, face down, several to a row, so that the coaster vaguely resembles a manta ray, and dive and fly through the air in this position, reaching speeds of almost 60mph. Neither of these hard-core coasters is for the faint of heart or weak bellied! SeaWorld's third and last

# SeaWorld

To Universal Studios (0.1mi)

Turkey Lake Rd

🍽 Taverna Opa

**Beach Line Expwy (toll)**

Palm Pkwy

SeaWorld ◎

Aquatica ◎

Central Florida Pkwy

Discovery Cove ◎

Thai Thani 🍽

International Dr

Lake Willis

Vineland Ave

thrill is a water ride. **Journey to Atlantis** begins in darkness, moving gently through an underwater world of neon and fluorescent coral and fish. Things turn macabre when the creepy evil mermaid beckons you into her world and up, up, up you go, clackity-clack, through the steam, before the coaster plunges 60ft into the water.

On **Wild Arctic**, an IMAX movie combines with a simulated ride to take viewers on a helicopter ride to Bas Station. A bad storm front moves in, and the pilot brings you very close to some polar bears before setting down on thin ice. Of course, after hearing an awful rumbling sound, you fall through the ice, and it's touch and go for a while, but... Afterwards, see above- and below-water views of polar bears, walrus and other Arctic life.

For something more leisurely, head to the **Skytower**. Capsules take six minutes to slide up the 400ft pole, slowly rotating for a 360-degree panorama of the area, including points as far away as downtown Orlando.

# Shows

Show are why folks come to SeaWorld, and none of them disappoint. Check www .seaworld.com/orlando for a schedule or look on the park map when you arrive.

### BLUE HORIZONS                    Show
More than a dolphin show, this fantastic extravaganza of light, music, dolphins, birds and acrobats in spectacular costumes tells some sort of story of good and evil. But never mind the details of the narrative, as none of that matters. It's just a good ole show, with lots of splashing and drama.

### CLYDE & SEAMORE TAKE PIRATE ISLAND                    Show
Another must-see, this delightful show stars sea lion, otter and walrus 'comedians.' It's particularly fun for kids, who find its goofy and slapstick humor just hilarious, but also great for the whole family.

### A'LURE THE CALL OF THEOCEAN                    Show
A bit like Cirque du Soleil on a much pared-down level, this unusual 30-minute circus performance combines acrobats, elaborate costumes and a heap of special effects to tell the story of the sea sirens, those mythical creatures who lured Odysseus. The gravity-defying stunts will have you holding your breath.

### ONE OCEAN                    Show
Killer whales are the stars at the newest Shamu show at SeaWorld, and it actually brings tears to some folks' eyes! The first 15 rows – sometimes more – of Shamu Stadium are the 'splash zone,' and both whales and trainers enjoy soaking the crowd with icy seawater.

### Pets Ahoy                    Show
Featuring the talents of cats, birds, rats, potbellied pigs and others, this show tickles little ones' funny bones. Many of the stars were rescued from local animal shelters.

### Reflections                    Show
During the holiday season and in the summer, the park closes with a fireworks and light show over the lagoon.

# Other Attractions

**STINGRAY LAGOON**    Stingray Feeding
Pick up a box of fish ($7) and feed the stingrays any time. Don't get frustrated if the stingrays don't take your fish, as there's a trick: hold the food between your index and middle finger, and place your hand in the water palm-up, with the lil' fishies swaying enticingly in the water. When the rays go by, they vacuum it right up. Pet their backs as they glide past – it feels just like the white of a hard-boiled egg.

**Beluga Interaction Program**    Animal Interaction
(from $99; minimum age 10) There aren't that many places where you can feed and talk (via hand signals) to a beluga whale. Or any whale, for that matter.

**Marine Mammal KeeperExperience**    Animal Interaction
(from $399; minimum age 13) Just what it sounds like: participants join animal trainers working with dolphins, beluga whales and sea lions.

**Sharks Deep Dive**    Diving
(from $59; minimum age 10) Descend in a steel cage into a tank of sandtiger sharks, nurse sharks

and schools of fish. You don't need to know how to scuba dive, thanks to a 'water helmet'.

**Dolphin Cove**    Animal Interaction
Here you can personally feed the dolphins rather than just watch 'em get fed. Feeding times are scheduled regularly throughout the day.

**Pacific Point Preserve**    Animal Watching
California sea lions, fur seals and harbor seals make merry (and plenty of noise).

**Shark Encounter**    Animal Watching
Ride a conveyer belt through a 60ft-long Plexiglas tube surrounded by menacing sharks, rays, barracudas, lionfish and skates.

**Penguin Encounter**    Animal Watching
Watch these silly little birds waddle around, slide into the water, and swim like munchkin torpedoes in tanks made to look like the Arctic, complete with manufactured snow and ice.

**Manatees: The Last Generation?**    Wildlife Sanctuary
The SeaWorld Orlando Animal Rescue Team rescues injured and sick manatees, and you can see the recuperating sweeties here.

**Jewel of the Sea Aquarium**    Aquarium
A well-designed aquarium of brightly colored tropical fish sits next to Journey to Atlantis and

Blue Horizons show (p134) at SeaWorld.

SEAWORLD ©

makes a good spot to keep little ones busy while everyone else is on the ride

### Manta Aquarium
Aquarium

Spectacular floor-to-ceiling tanks with more than 300 graceful rays gliding overhead, the adorably shy Pacific octopus and more.

 ## Tours

Make required reservations for this and a handful of others at www.seaworld.com/orlando or by phone at ☎888-800-5447.

### UP-CLOSE TOURS
Guided Tour

(adult/child 3-9 dolphins $50/30, penguins $40/20, sea lions $40/20) These 45- to 60-minute tours take you up close to penguins, dolphins or sea lions, well worth it if you're particularly enamored with a particular critter. If you're really looking to really personal with a dolphin, however, consider a day at Discovery Cove – an unlimited 14-day pass to SeaWorld is included in the price.

## Eating & Drinking

Eating at SeaWorld is mostly fast food and cafeteria-style options, though there's a pleasant selection of decent healthy alternatives. The park's All Day Dining Meal (adult $30, child three to 10 $15) allows for one main, one side or one dessert, and one nonalchoholic beverage each time you go through the cafeteria line at six eateries in the park.

### Sharks Underwater Grill
Seafood $$

( ☎407-351-3600; mains $9-21; ⊙11am-park closing) Eat among the sharks in an underwater grotto. Cool, dark and particularly fun for kids; the bar is literally a tropical aquarium.

### Voyager's Smokehouse
Barbecue $

(Waterfront; mains $9-15; ⊙11am-park closing) Barbecue and corn on the cob.

### Seafire Inn
Fast Food $

(Waterfront; mains $8-14; ⊙11am-park closing) Serves up a blend of flavors, and it's not unusual to see burgers flipped right next to Mongolian woks.

## Information

KENNELS Air-conditioned and staffed kennels for dogs only are located outside the main entrance of SeaWorld. They are open from park opening until just after park close and cost $15 per day. You must have proof of vaccinations and return to walk your pet.

LOCKERS Can be rented for $7 to $12 daily.

LOST & FOUND Located in Guest Services, at the front entrance.

PARK HOURS The park opens around 9am but park closing hours vary within the year and within the week, ranging from 6pm to 11pm. See www.seaworld.com/orlando for a calendar of daily hours.

Interior of Mythos Restaurant (p129).
UNIVERSAL STUDIOS ©

**PARKING** Costs $14.

**STROLLERS & WHEELCHAIRS** Go to www
.seaworld.com/orlando to reserve strollers
(single/double $13/18), wheelchairs ($12) and
ECVs ($45) in advance, or pick one up first-come
first-serve at the front gate.

**TICKETS** A two-day pass is sold as a 'one day
pass, second day free' and costs $72; be sure to
trade your ticket in for a return ticket when you
leave the park, and you can come back for one
day anytime within seven days at no extra charge.
The Quick Queue Unlimited Pass includes all-day
priority access to Kraken, Manta, Journey to
Atlantis and Wild Arctic and costs an additional
$20 to $35; a Quick Queue One-Time Access
costs a bit less. Unlimited entrance over 14
consecutive days to both SeaWorld and Aquatica
costs $115/107 for adult/children three to nine.
SeaWorld participates in Orlando's Flex Ticket.
Go to www.seaworld.com/orlando for details on
accommodation packages.

**TOURIST INFORMATION** Located in Guest
Services, at the front entrance. Contact SeaWorld
(☎407-351-3600, 888-800-5447; www.seaworld
.com/orlando; 7007 SeaWorld Dr; ⏰from 9am)
for all questions.

##  Getting There & Away

SeaWorld is located at intersection of I-4 and FL
528 at the southern end of International Drive.
From Walt Disney World take I-4 east towards
Orlando to exit 71 and follow the signs; from
Universal Orlando Resort and downtown Orlando,
take I-4 west to exit 72 and follow the signs. Public
buses do not stop at SeaWorld, but a free shuttle
connects SeaWorld to Aquatica.

## Aquatica

Orlando's latest water park has good
food, plenty of tropical greenery, some
cool animals to check out and little of
the narrative shtick that defines Disney
attractions.

## Sights & Activities

Aquatica boasts that the **Dolphin Plunge**
spits you through a glass-enclosed tube
through a tank of Commerson's dolphins,
and it does indeed do this; the problem,
of course, is that perhaps a high-speed

waterslide just isn't the best way to see
dolphins. You zoom through so fast and
the stretch through the tank is so short
that you're lucky if you catch a passing
glance at the black-and-white cuties.
Check 'em out at the **Commerson's
Dolphin Exhibit** instead. Other animal
encounters include rafting **Loggerhead
Lane** through the grotto of tropical fish,
and meeting macaws, anteaters, turtles
and other critters that roam the park
with their trainers. For high-speed thrills,
try the **HooRoo Run**, a blessedly simple
open-aired inner-tube slide, and its enclosed sister ride the **Walhalla Wave**; **Tas-
sie's Twisters**, where you speed around
and around and are then dropped into a
pool below; **Taumata Racer**, the multilane
toboggan run; and **Whanau Way**, a
twisting, enclosed inner-tube slide. Two
lagoon-inspired **Wave Pools**, lined with
white sand and row upon row of beach
chairs, make a good base to hunker down
for the day.

The children's play areas here are
excellent. At **Walkabout Waters**, buckets
of water dump regularly over all kinds of
brightly colored climbing structures and
fountains, while **Kookaburra Cove** offers
tiny slides and shallow water perfect for
toddlers.

##  Eating & Drinking

Food at the park's three restaurants is
better than what you'll find at Orlando's
other water parks, and of course, there's
plenty of cold beer available throughout
the park.

**BANANA BEACH COOKOUT**     Buffet $$
**(all-day pass adult/child 3-9 $16/10)** If you've
built up an appetite from all that slippin'
and slidin', your best option is this all-
you-can-eat cookout. The buffet includes
veggie burgers, barbecue chicken, corn
on the cob, hot dogs and salads. Purchase
tickets at www.aquaticabyseaworld.com
in advance or at the park.

**WaterStone Grill**   Fast-Food $

(mains $6-12; ⏱11am-park closing) Stick-in-your-gut items like cheese-smothered steak sandwiches and Cuban pork as well as a few hearty salads.

**Mango Market**   Fast Food $

(mains $5-13; ⏱park hr) Tasty wood-fired flatbread pizza, grilled-chicken salad, veggie wraps and other grab-and-go options. You can also buy baby food here.

## ℹ Information

**KENNELS** Air-conditioned and staffed kennels for dogs-only are located outside the main entrance of SeaWorld. They are open from park opening until just after park close and cost $15 per day. You must have proof of vaccinations and return to walk your pet.

**PARK HOURS** During Spring Break Aquatica is open 10am to 5pm, with extended hours on weekends and in summer. Go to www .aquaticabyseaworld.com for a calendar that lists day by day hours.

**PARKING** Costs $14.

**STROLLERS & WHEELCHAIRS** Go to www .aquaticabyseaworld.com to reserve a strollers (single/double $13/18), wheelchairs ($12) and ECVs (45) in advance, or pick one up first-come first-serve at the front gate.

**TICKETS** One-day pass costs $42. Unlimited entrance to Aquatica and SeaWorld over 14 consecutive days costs $115/107 for adult/children three to nine. Aquatica participates in Orlando's Flex Ticket.

**TOURIST INFORMATION** Located in Guest Services, at the front entrance. Call ✆866-787-4307 for current park hours and weather-related closings. Contact **Aquatica** (✆407-351-3600, www.aquaticabyseaworld.com; 5800 Water Play Way; ⏱10am-5pm, extended hr on weekends & from Jun-Aug) for all questions.

## ℹ Getting There & Away

Aquatica is located just east of the intersection of I-4 and FL 528, at the southern end of International Drive. A free shuttle connects SeaWorld to Aquatica.

# Discovery Cove

One of the most relaxing places in Orlando, Discovery Cove (✆8am-5:30pm) is luxuriously slow, marvelously lazy and delightfully subdued. You won't find high-speed thrills, fight any crowds or see any princesses. Discovery Cove allows only 1000 guests per day and you must make advance reservations. Once you're in the park, everything from wetsuits to unlimited beer and snacks, from a family portrait to a buffet lunch, is included in the price.

## ◉ Sights & Activities

The most popular reason to come to the park is the 30-minute **Dolphin Swim Experience** (see p238 for arguments for and against the practice). Groups of about 10 gather under a thatched-roof tiki hut, are given a brief orientation and a wet suit and then head into the chilly lagoon with the dolphins. The minimum age for a dolphin swim is six, and children under 12 must be accompanied by a paying adult. For the rest of the day, relax. Wiggle your toes in the sand, pull on your mask and fins and snorkel among tropical rainbow fish and massive spotted eagle rays in the **Tropical Reef**. **Wind-away River**, a shallow and warm lazy river, curves around the entire cove, and an enormous waterfall empties **Serenity Bay**, a tropical swimming lagoon. In 2011 Discovery Cove opened the 2.5 acre **Grand Reef**, a second tropical reef surrounded with paths and bridges and filled with rays, sharks and other sea creatures.

Make reservations in advance to walk along an underwater trail in **SeaVenture** (per person $59; minimum age 10). You'll don a 75-pound 'dive helmet' and join schools of saltwater fish, rays, sharks and other creatures, but don't worry – the more dangerous ones lie behind a glass barrier! The experience is limited to six people at a time, does not require scuba experience, and takes one hour. This attraction wasn't open at the time of writing, but should be open by the time you read this.

## ℹ️ Information

TICKETS All-day Resort Only Package costs $129 to $169 and includes breakfast, lunch, unlimited beer, soda and snacks, snorkel gear, a wet suit, a locker, shower facilities, towels and parking; the Dolphin Swim Package includes the same plus the dolphin interaction experience and costs $169 to $319. Both tickets include unlimited entrance over 14 consecutive days to your choice of SeaWorld, Aquatica or Busch Gardens; for $50 more you can add unlimited entrance to all three parks.

## ℹ️ Getting There & Away

Discovery Cove sits at the intersection of I-4 and FL 528 at the southern end of International Drive.

# Palm Beach & the Gold Coast

**The Gold Coast lives up to its namesake on several levels.** With wealth. Luxury goods. Sunshine. The reflected allure of all of the above. Palm Beach is one of Florida's wealthiest enclaves – enjoy gawking at the castlelike beachfront mansions, but don't rear-end that $350,000 Bentley when parallel parking in front of the Gucci store.

And yet: all that glitters is not gold, and the 'Gold Coast' is more than glitz. Here you'll find an endearing collection of beach towns. From activity-packed, gay- and family-friendly Fort Lauderdale to laid-back Lauderdale-by-the-Sea to rugged Jupiter, you'll find more culture than you can handle.

Numerous natural gems – secluded islands, moss-draped mangrove swamps, wild rivers, empty dunes – will surely satisfy your demands for nonmaterial pleasures. So please, whatever you do, don't skip over this region on your journey from Miami to Disney World.

Aerial view of Breakers resort (p153).
THE BREAKERS PRESS PHOTO ©

A scene of sand, sea and palm trees at Palm Beach (p152).
ALAMY/ MICHAEL WALD ©

# Palm Beach & the Gold Coast

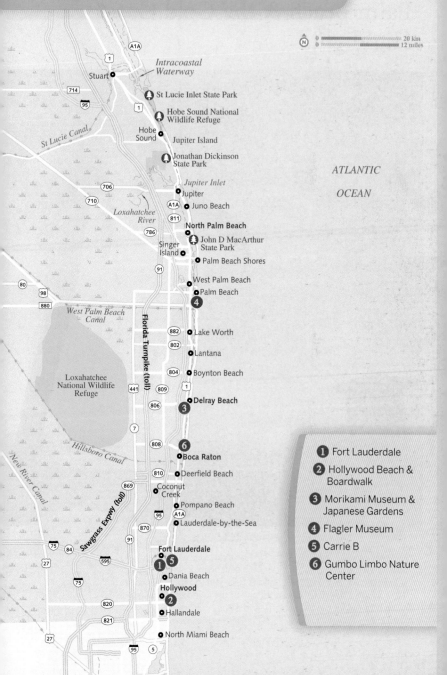

St Lucie Inlet State Park

Hobe Sound National Wildlife Refuge

Jupiter Island

Jonathan Dickinson State Park

Jupiter Inlet
Jupiter
Juno Beach
North Palm Beach
John D MacArthur State Park
Singer Island
Palm Beach Shores
West Palm Beach
Palm Beach

Lake Worth
Lantana
Boynton Beach
Delray Beach
Boca Raton
Deerfield Beach
Coconut Creek
Pompano Beach
Lauderdale-by-the-Sea
Fort Lauderdale
Dania Beach
Hollywood
Hallandale
North Miami Beach

Stuart
Intracoastal Waterway
Hobe Sound
St Lucie Canal
Loxahatchee River
West Palm Beach Canal
Loxahatchee National Wildlife Refuge
Hillsboro Canal
New River Canal
Florida Turnpike (toll)
Sawgrass Expwy (toll)

ATLANTIC OCEAN

0    20 km
0    12 miles

1. Fort Lauderdale
2. Hollywood Beach & Boardwalk
3. Morikami Museum & Japanese Gardens
4. Flagler Museum
5. Carrie B
6. Gumbo Limbo Nature Center

# Palm Beach & the Gold Coast Highlights

## 1

### Fort Lauderdale

Although it's known as South Florida's second city, Fort Lauderdale doesn't deserve to take a backseat to anyone. This town has miles of canals, one of the loveliest beach promenades in the country and a busy cultural scene that will keep foodies, historians and nighthawks happy.

**Need to Know**

**DAY TRIPS** Day-trip to Grand Bahama from here. **BOAT** One of the largest yacht and cruise harbors in the world. **SPRING BREAK** Hits in March. **For more, see p168 and Map p168.**

# Fort Lauderdale Don't Miss List

ANDREA RICHARD IS AN EDITOR, AUTHOR AND NATIVE OF FORT LAUDERDALE.

## 1 BONNETT HOUSE

Bonnet House and gardens (p169) is a historical oasis of art, nature and eclectic architecture. The estate, which boasts rooms portraying different architecture styles, was built in 1920. It sits atop 35 acres of preserved land and gardens composed of Fort Lauderdale's native ecosystem and foreign plants. The owners were both artists who shared a love for animals, nature and of course art.

## 2 LASER WOLF

Excellent Laser Wolf (p174) is operated and owned by natives. The space has a courtyard where indie bands perform, and an extensive menu of craft brews, sake and wine. A 'no jerks' policy caters to Lauderdale's artsy, intellectual folks. Whatever you do, don't dare to utter the word 'hipster' on the premises or you may get a blank stare of indifference; otherwise, the bar boasts a friendly locals crowd.

## 3 HIMMARSHEE NIGHTLIFE DISTRICT

Most nightlife districts in the United States don't offer what Fort Lauderdale's Himmarshee (p174) does: bars that open until 4am and an open-container allowance. Yes, within the confines of Himmarshee, it is legal to bar-hop with an open container.

## 4 LAUDERDALE-BY-THE-SEA/SHIPWRECK SNORKEL TRAIL

Quaint Lauderdale-by-the-Sea (p166) has a code restricting buildings to two stories. Aside from charming restaurants, bars and a sandy beach, what's truly worth visiting about this spot is an artificial reef built to resemble a shipwreck a short distance offshore.

## 5 THE FLORIDIAN

Whether late-night munchies or traditional breakfast cause your hunger pangs, 'The Flo' is there, 24/7. Located on chic Las Olas, The Floridian (p174) is anything but upscale. The neighborhood eatery is ideal for people-watching – oddballs sometimes frequent here late nights.

# Hollywood Beach & Broadwalk

While some beaches are grungy, and some are too up themselves, Hollywood Beach (p176), to quote the Three Bears, is Just Right. There's a boardwalk that gets taken up with party animals, dog walkers, toned bodies and cruising teens and families out for the night.

## Flagler Museum

The original Palm Beach palace is the mansion Henry Flagler, railroad baron and Florida tycoon, gifted to his wife in 1902. To say the house is opulent is to be guilty of gross understatement. Now a museum (p152), the Flagler mansion is representative of both the heights of beaux arts decor and the luxury of old American aristocracy.

ALAMY/MICHAEL WALD ©

## Morikami Museum & Japanese Gardens ③

Delray Beach is not the first name that springs to mind when discussing Japanese aesthetics, but actually, one of the finest stateside collections of arts, crafts and sculpture from Nippon can be found in this town at the Morikami Museum (p162). Make sure to stop in for tea at the on-site Seishin-An teahouse.

ALAMY/AMY STRYCULA ©

ALAMY/JEFF GREENBERG ©

## ⑤ Carrie B

Fort Lauderdale is a city that is rich in canals and yachts. A tour aboard the *Carrie B* (p170), a replica 19th-century riverboat, sheds a little light into both the waterways that intersect Fort Lauderdale and the mind-boggling wealth exhibited by the inhabitants of the huge houses that line said waterways.

## ⑥ Gumbo Limbo Nature Center

Gumbo Limbo sounds like a dance invented in the back bayous of Louisiana to us, but the name actually applies to a singularly fine slice of nature preserve (p164). You can hike on boardwalks between strands of wetland wilderness, and visit a host of oceanic animals, including sea turtles recovering in a rehabilitation center.

# Palm Beach & the Gold Coast's Best...

## Delicious Dining

○ **Circle** (p155) Best brunch around, hands down. Plus: there's a harpsichordist.

○ **Michelle Bernstein's** (p155) Pushing the limits of Floridian cuisine.

○ **Rhythm Cafe** (p159) Bright, bouncy bistro with to-die-for chocolate cake.

○ **Le Tub** (p177) Bathtub flowerpots and burgers shipped from heaven.

○ **Gran Forno** (p173) Affordable, scrumptious Northern Italian cuisine; fantastic value for lunch.

## Natural Beauty

○ **Gumbo Limbo Nature Center** (p164) An awesome environmental education centre.

○ **Blowing Rocks Preserve** (p170) Where waves, wind, tides and erosion combine into something beautiful.

○ **Lion Country Safari** (p161) Admittedly, an artificial environment. But one that lovingly recreates the African bush.

○ **Jonathan Dickinson State Park** (p170) A fine park that catalogs the natural beauty of Central Florida.

## The Beaches

○ **Lake Worth Beach** (p161) Simply one of the finest beaches on the Gold Coast.

○ **Hollywood Beach** (p176) A good combination of natural prettiness and fun activities.

○ **Fort Lauderdale Beach** (p168) The adjacent promenade is an exemplary boardwalk.

○ **Palm Beach Municipal Beach** (p153) Lovely public beach that can get crowded in the high season.

# Need to Know

## Must-see Museums

○ **Museum of Art** (p169) Fort Lauderdale's cultural cornerstone.

○ **Boca Raton Museum of Art** (p173) Impressive collection of European masters.

○ **Morikami Museum & Japanese Gardens** (p162) Japanese masterpieces presented in a tranquil atmosphere.

○ **Flagler Museum** (p152) Lifestyles of the rich and famous (and historical).

○ **Norton Museum of Art** (p156) A West Palm Beach gem for the arts.

### BE FOREWARNED

○ **Dress up** If you're heading out in Palm Beach, try to dress to impress.

○ **Humidity** It can get swampy and steamy in deep summer.

○ **Spring Break** You may want to avoid Fort Lauderdale in Mar–Apr (unless you love partying with college kids).

○ **Hurricanes** They can hit here too, from Jun–Oct.

### GETTING AROUND

○ **Car** I-95 and the Florida Turnpike are the most direct roads between cities, but we recommend getting off the highways.

○ **Bus** Greyhound connects major cities on the Gold Coast.

○ **Train** The Miami Tri-Rail connects to Fort Lauderdale.

○ **Air** For better ticket deals, try booking to any of the cities in this chapter, as they're all fairly close to each other.

### RESOURCES

○ **Palm Beach County Convention & Visitors Bureau** Palm Beach resources, www.palmbeachfl.com.

○ **South Florida Sun-Sentinel** Regional newspaper, www.sun-sentinel.com.

○ **Fort Lauderdale Tourism** Includes information on Broward County, www.sunny.org.

○ **Yachting** Go to www.saltwatertides.com for an excellent searchable database of tide tables.

### ADVANCE PLANNING

○ **Hotels** During major festivals and events hotels can get packed early.

○ **Car rentals** Try to organize a month in advance.

○ **Restaurants** You'll want reservations at the posher places we recommend.

○ **Yachting** Go to www.saltwatertides.com for an excellent searchable database of tide tables.

○ **Arts Calendar** If you want to know what's going on culturally in South Florida, visit www.artscalendar.com

**Left:** Giraffes at the Lion Country Safari (p161);
**Above:** Palm trees in Palm Beach (p152).

(LEFT) LION SAFARI/PRESS PHOTOS ©; (ABOVE) CORBIS/ATLANTIDE PHOTOTRAVEL ©

# Palm Beach & the Gold Coast Itineraries

*They call it the Gold Coast because the beaches shimmer, the sun is radiant and some of the houses are downright palatial. These itineraries will take in all of the above, plus lovely dining and treats for culture vultures*

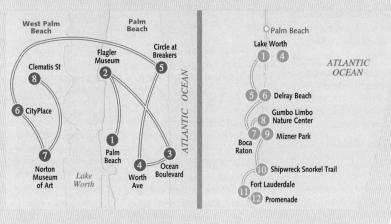

**2 DAYS**

**PALM BEACH TO WEST PALM BEACH**
## The Palm Beaches

We'll wake up in **(1) Palm Beach**, one of the natural nerve centers for this region. When you're here you should check out the opulent homes folks have built up for themselves throughout the year, so we'll start on the historical end of things at the **(2) Flagler Museum**. Built by South Florida founding father Henry Flagler, this museum is a monument to the man's wealth and beaux-arts decor. The on-site museum cafe is good for lunch.

Afterwards head up **(3) Ocean Boulevard** and goggle at the houses of the modern Palm Beach elite. These folks furnish their luxury on shopping streets

like **(4) Worth Avenue**; it's heavy on showy brand names, but that's kinda the point.

The next day head to West Palm Beach, but not before breakfast at the **(5) Circle**. Wander around the shopping and dining district of **(6) CityPlace** before balancing consumerism with a dash of culture at the **(7) Norton Museum of Art** and its attached sculpture garden. Finish your day in the historic revival-cum-dining and nightlife strip that is **(8) Clematis Street.) 10,000 Islands**.

**LAKE WORTH TO HOLLYWOOD BEACH**

## Gold Coast Cruising

Starts in **(1) Lake Worth**, an artsy enclave located just south of the Palm Beaches. The beach here is simply outstanding. When you're done relaxing on it, grab dinner at **(2) Sheila's Bahamian Conch & BBQ** and enjoy a night at the **(3) Havana Hideout** or Lake Worth Playhouse. Alternatively, have dinner at **(4) Michelle Bernstein's**, where you can enjoy Florida's Latin-fusion haute cuisine. The next day, check out the **(5) Morikami Museum & Japanese Gardens** in Delray Beach for taste of Japanese aesthetics. Carry on the theme with lunch at **(6) Lemongrass**. Spend the night in Delray, then go on to **(7) Boca Raton**. In 'Boca'

you're going to take a slight departure from culture and beaches and opt instead for the considerable natural beauty of Florida at the **(8) Gumbo Limbo Nature Center**. When you've finished here, shop and dine in the Spanish villa-esque mall at **(9) Mizner Park**.

On your fourth day drive to Lauderdale-by-the-Sea, where you can experience an underwater, treasure-hunting trail on the **(10) Shipwreck Snorkel Trail**. If you have dinner in acclaimed **(11) Da Campo Osteria** you're already in Fort Lauderdale, where you can finish with a walk on the excellent beach **(12) Promenade**.

# Discover Palm Beach & the Gold Coast

Scene in the Ann Norton Sculpture Garden (163).
ANN NORTON SCULPTURE GARDEN PRESS PHOTO ©

## GOLD COAST

This coastline has a split personality. First, there's slow-going, ocean-fronting Rte 1, a pleasant drive revealing infinite vistas and unspoiled beaches...though occasionally it feels like driving through a high-rise condo-canyon. Second, there's wizened Dixie Hwy, running parallel to Rte 1 but further inland, past dive bars, hole-in-the-wall eateries and diverse, working-class communities. Drive both stretches; each is rich with divergent offerings.

## Palm Beach

✦ 561 / POP 9,600

The third-wealthiest city in America, Palm Beach looks every inch the playground for the rich and famous that it is. Though all the bling may feel a bit intimidating, fear not – much of Palm Beach is within the reach of even the brokest budget traveler.

 **Sights**

**FLAGLER MUSEUM** Museum
(www.flagler.org; 1 Whitehall Way; adult/child $18/10; ⊘10am-5pm Tue-Sat, noon-5pm Sun) The only true museum on Palm Beach is probably the county's most fascinating. Housed in the spectacular 1902 mansion built by Henry Flagler as a gift for his bride, Mary Lily Keenan, the beaux arts–styled Whitehall Mansion is beyond belief. Built in 18 months, the elaborate 55-room palace was the first residential home to feature both a heating system and an air-con system; features pink aluminum-leaf wallpaper (more expensive, at the time, than gold); impresses with a 4750-sq-ft

Grand Hall, the largest single room of any gilded-age private residence; and sports a drool-worthy billiards room. Don't expect many details about Flagler the Railroad Mogul, however, as the emphasis here is on the couple's opulent lifestyle. Gruesome tip: Flagler died as a result of injuries sustained from tumbling down the Grand Staircase, so watch your step.

The **Café des Beaux-Arts** treats you to a full 'Gilded Age-Style' lunch ($36), with finger sandwiches, scones and custom-blended teas. It's served 11:30am to 2:30pm Tuesday to Saturday, noon to 3pm on Sunday. Pinkies out!

### OCEAN BOULEVARD                    Scenic Drive

There are the rich, there are the super-rich, and then there are the denizens of Ocean Blvd. Driving along this seaside stretch of Hwy A1A is an eye-popping lesson in exactly how much money can buy – the road is lined with sprawling estates ranging from faux Greco-Roman temples to pink Spanish-style palaces as big as any hotel. And most of these houses are merely second (or third or fourth) homes for their owners! You may find the view inspirational, or it may make you want to start a proletarian uprising – either way, it's a gorgeous drive complete with impeccably manicured lawns and snatches of cobalt sea visible through the hedgerows.

### PALM BEACH MUNICIPAL
### BEACH                                      Beach

(Ocean Blvd btwn Royal Palm Way & Hammon Ave; ☺sunrise-sunset) One of Palm Beach's two beautiful public beaches, both kept pleasantly seaweed-free by the town. Metered beachfront parking is an absurd $5 per hour – head inland to snag free streetfront parking downtown. This beach can get crowded.

For privacy, head north on S Ocean Blvd and turn left on Barton Ave. There's free two-hour parking near the church before S County Rd and public access to the beach across from Clarke Ave, one block before you turned onto Barton.

# Sleeping

If you're looking for a deal, head west. Palm Beach properties aren't cheap.

### BREAKERS                          Resort $$$

( ☎561-655-6611, 888-273-2537; www.thebreakers.com; 1 S County Rd; r $270-1250, ste $510-5500; ✲@🛜☒) Originally built by Henry Flagler (in 1904 rooms ran $4 per night, including meals), today this 550-room resort sprawls across 140 acres and boasts a staff of 2300 fluent in 56 languages. Just feet from the county's best snorkeling, this palace has two 18-hole golf courses, a mile of semiprivate beach, four pools, two croquet courts and the best brunch around (see p155). For opulence, elegance and old-world charm, there's no other choice. Green Lodging certified.

### OMPHOY                            Resort $$$

( ☎561-540-6440; www.omphoy.com; 2842 S Ocean Blvd; r $220-440; ✲@🛜☒) The first new oceanfront hotel to open in Palm Beach in nearly two decades, the Omphoy debuted in 2010 to the delight of design lovers everywhere. Sleek and moody, all mod wood paneling and smoked glass, it's a hit with a slightly younger crowd of glitterati who find grande dames like the Breakers a bit...old-fashioned. Hip amenities include a yoga studio, a meditation garden and a yummy infinity pool lined with private cabanas. The hotel restaurant, Michelle Bernstein's (see p155), draws foodie pilgrims all the way from Miami.

### COLONY                              Hotel $$$

( ☎561-655-5430; www.thecolonypalmbeach.com; 155 Hammon Ave; r $190-450, ste $250-1100; ✲🛜☒) Like much of Palm Beach, this 90-room hotel recently received a facelift. Super-stylish – as it should be, towering over Worth Ave – the pale-yellow and hunter-green rooms have hosted the likes of President Clinton and Zsa Zsa Gabor. The beach is a block away, which can be tricky, considering how alluring the alfresco poolside court is. A certified Green Lodging.

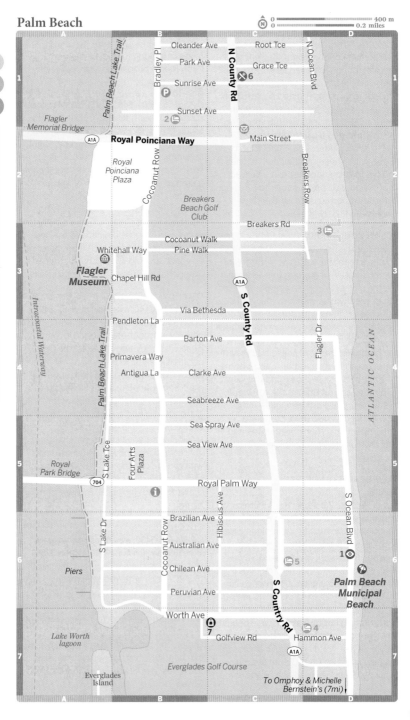

# Palm Beach

**PALM BEACH HISTORIC INN**    B&B **$$**
(📞561-832-4009; www.palmbeachhistoricinn
.com; 365 S County Rd; r $79-279, ste $129-329;
❄🛜) Housed on the 2nd floor of a land-
mark building brimming with character,
this intimate European-style hotel has
well-lit rooms with hardwood floors and
brightly painted walls. Best of all: it's two
blocks to Worth Ave and less than a block
to the beach.

**BRADLEY PARK HOTEL**    Hotel **$$**
(📞561-832-7050; www.bradleyparkhotel.com;
2080 Sunset Ave; r $89-200; ❄🛜) Another
good midrange choice, this hotel has no
lobby to speak of but features plushly
comfortable rooms done up in golds and
neutrals just a short walk from the shops
and restaurants of Royal Poinciana Way.

# Eating

Dining out in Palm Beach is pretty much a
high-end affair, though there is a pleasant
selection of budget bites.

**MICHELLE
BERNSTEIN'S**    Modern American **$$$**
(📞561-540-6440; www.omphoy.com; 2842 S
Ocean Blvd; mains $29-38; ⏱5:30-10pm) Miami
celebrity chef Michelle Bernstein riffs on
Nouvelle Floridian cuisine at this new res-
taurant in the trendy Omphoy hotel, draw-
ing on her own Jewish and Latin American
heritage, and on the rich produce and
seafood offerings of South Florida. Start,
for example, with foie gras and tangerine
compote, move on to shrimp *tiradito* (a
Japanese-Peruvian raw-fish dish), then
dig into a main of local cobia fish with shii-
takes and Spanish ham. If the homemade
donuts are on the dessert menu, we must
insist you order them – you'll thank us
later. There's the odd grumble about slow
service, so come here when you're plenty
relaxed.

**CIRCLE**    American, European **$$$**
(📞561-659-8440, 888-273-2537; www
.thebreakers.com; 1 S County Rd; per person
$90; ⏱11am-2:30pm Sun) Sure, it's steep,
but brunch at the Breakers' storied
restaurant will certainly rank among the
most amazing you'll ever enjoy. Beneath
soaring 30ft frescoed ceilings, surrounded by ocean views and entertained
by a roving harpsichordist, guests begin
their feast at the breakfast bar, featuring
homemade donuts, tropical fruits and
an on-demand omelet chef. Next, swing
through the carving station, past the
cheese table brimming with exotic goat
cheeses and more, and make your way
to the 4ft-tall ice sculpture standing vigil
over the seafood bank overflowing with
tiger shrimp, king-crab legs and mussels.
Hit the hot-foods banquette and as you
weave back to your seat, grab a treat
from the caviar station (featuring both
American sturgeon and salmon). Gorge.
Repeat.

**GREEN'S PHARMACY**    Lunch Counter **$**
(151 N County Rd; mains $4-13; ⏱breakfast &
lunch) This place, housed inside a working
pharmacy, hasn't changed since John F
Kennedy, looking to slip away from the
Secret Service, would stroll across the
mint-green linoleum and grab a bite.
Choose between a table or a stool at
the Formica counter and order from the
paper menu like everyone from the trust-
fund babies slumming it to the college
girls headed to the beach.

#  Shopping

The quarter-mile, palm-tree-lined strip along **Worth Avenue** (www.worth-avenue.com) is Florida's answer to Rodeo Dr. You'll find more than 200 shops, representing every exclusive brand known. Half the shops close for summer, but it's fun to stroll and window-shop (and celeb-spot), whether you want to lay down your plastic or not.

# ⓘ Information

**Chamber of Commerce** (☏561-655-3282; www.palmbeachchamber.com; 400 Royal Palm Way) Excellent maps, racks of pamphlets and several gratis glossy magazines, including *Worth Avenue, Palm Beach Illustrated, Palm Beach Society* and *Vive,* all of which offer convincing arguments for indulgence at every level.

# ⓘ Getting There & Around

**PalmTran** (www.palmtran.org) Bus 41 covers the bulk of the island, from Lantana Rd to Sunrise Ave; transfer to bus 1 at Publix to go north or south along US 1.

# West Palm Beach
☏561 / POP 100,000

West Palm is a groovy place to explore, despite the seemingly never-ending condo construction. It's a community with a surprisingly diverse collection of restaurants, friendly inhabitants (including a strong gay community) and a gorgeous waterway that always seems to reflect the perfect amount of starlight.

# ◎ Sights

**NORTON MUSEUM OF ART**     Museum
(www.norton.org; 1451 S Olive Ave; adult/child $12/5; ⏱10am-5pm Tue-Sat, to 9pm Thu, 11am-5pm Sun) The largest museum in Florida, the Norton opened in 1941 to display the enormous art collection of industrialist Ralph Hubbard Norton and his wife Elizabeth. The Norton's permanent collection of more than 5000 pieces (including

**Left:** There's plenty of shopping in Florida; **Below:** Street scene in West Palm Beach (p156)

(LEFT) ALAMY/JEFF GREENBERG ©; (BELOW) CORBIS/BRANDON KRUSE/ZUMA PRESS ©

works by Matisse, Warhol and O'Keeffe) is displayed alongside important Chinese, pre-Columbian Mexican and US Southwestern artifacts, plus some wonderful contemporary photography and regular traveling exhibitions. Don't miss the Nessel Wing, consisting of an oval atrium, 14 galleries and a colorful crowd-pleaser: a ceiling made from nearly 700 pieces of handblown glass by Dale Chihuly. Lie back on one of the corner couches and get lost in his magical creation.

### CITYPLACE    Shopping, Entertainment

(www.cityplace.com; 701 S Rosemary Ave) This massive outdoor shopping and entertainment center is the crown jewel of West Palm Beach's urban-renewal initiative; locals love telling visitors how this area was formerly filled with crack houses. A mix of boutiques and chain stores, CityPlace is a one-stop destination for diners, moviegoers, trendy-shop shoppers and anyone who wants a reason to take a stroll. Its 600,000 sq ft comprise a slew of stores,

about a dozen restaurants, a 20-screen movie theater, the Harriet Himmel Theater and 570 private residences – not to mention free concerts in the outdoor plaza. Beautiful but vaguely sterile, CityPlace has nevertheless been immensely successful in bringing all types together in one spot, from tourist families looking for fun on a rainy day to clutches of local ladies out for a day of shopping – and everyone in between.

### CLEMATIS STREET    Shopping, Dining

Long before CityPlace came along, there was Clematis St, a hip, bohemian strip bustling with locals doing their shopping, diners looking for a foodie scene, and scads of bar-hoppers come nightfall. In short, this stretch is the most eclectic strip in town – and much of it's also a historic district with a jumbled collection of architecture – Greek Revival, Venetian Revival, Mediterranean Revival and art deco.

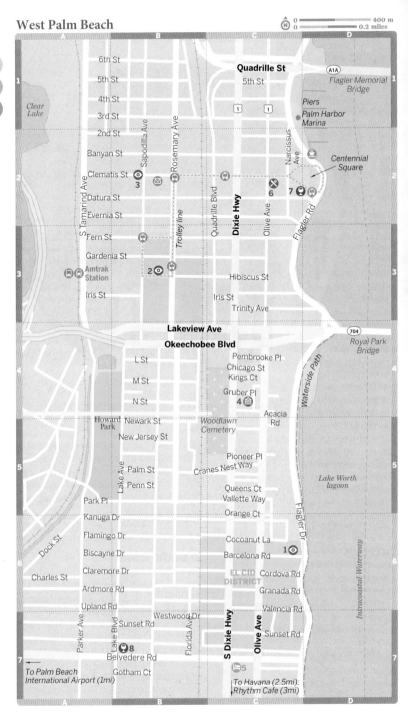

0    400 m
0    0.2 miles

A1A
Flagler Memorial
Bridge

Quadrille St

6th St
5th St
4th St
3rd St
2nd St
Banyan St
Clematis St

5th St

Piers
Palm Harbor
Marina

Centennial
Square

Sapodilla Ave
Rosemary Ave
S Tamarind Ave

Datura St
Evernia St
Fern St
Gardenia St

Quadrille Blvd
Dixie Hwy
Olive Ave
Narcissus Ave
Flagler Rd

Trolley line

Amtrak
Station

Iris St

Hibiscus St

Iris St
Trinity Ave

704
Royal Park
Bridge

Lakeview Ave
Okeechobee Blvd

L St
M St
N St

Pembrooke Pl
Chicago St
Kings Ct
Gruber Pl

Waterside Path

Howard
Park

Newark St
New Jersey St

Woodlawn
Cemetery

Acacia
Rd

Lake Ave

Palm St
Penn St

Pioneer Pl
Cranes Nest Way

Park Pl
Kanuga Dr
Flamingo Dr
Biscayne Dr
Claremore Dr
Ardmore Rd
Upland Rd

Queens Ct
Vallette Way
Orange Ct

Cocoanut La
Barcelona Rd

Lake Worth
lagoon

Dock St

Charles St

EL CID
DISTRICT

Cordova Rd
Granada Rd
Valencia Rd

Flagler Dr

Parker Ave
Lake Blvd
Sunset Rd
Florida Ave
Westwood Dr
S Dixie Hwy
Olive Ave

Belvedere Rd
Gotham Ct

Sunset Rd

Intracoastal Waterway

To Palm Beach
International Airport (1mi)

To Havana (2.5mi);
Rhythm Cafe (3mi)

Clear
Lake

## West Palm Beach

 **Tours**

**PALM BEACH WATER TAXI**    Boat Tours
( ☎ 561-683-8294; www.sailfishmarina.com;
98 Lake Dr, Singer Island) Water taxis run
between downtown West Palm and Singer
Island ($15), as well as to Peanut Island
(round-trip $10), leaving from the Singer
Island. Additionally, the outfit offers guided tours along the Intracoastal, including
90-minute narrated tours of Palm Beach
mansions ($28).

 **Sleeping**

Skip the depressing chain hotels
near the airport and try one of
these cool spots.

**HOTEL BIBA**    Motel $$
( ☎ 561-832-0094; www
.hotelbiba.com; 320 Belvedere
Rd; r winter/summer $129/79;
❄ 🛜 🏊 ) Funky, retro
Hotel Biba has injected
an ordinary motel with
pop-art flair. This groovy
spot has lots going for
it – spare-chic decor in
vibrantly colored rooms;
a leafy little courtyard with

hidden-away pool; and a hip, sexy bar
where you'll find the complimentary con-
tinental breakfast (featuring local Cuban
pastries) in the morning and a thriving
lounge scene at night. A block from the
Intracoastal, the Biba is perched on the
edge of the beautiful El Cid district.

 **Eating**

The food scene here is an eclectic affair –
ethnic eats mixed with quirky spaces and
quaint tearooms – and lots of affordable
options.

**RHYTHM CAFE**    Eclectic $$
( ☎ 561-833-3406; www.rhythmcafe.cc; 3800 S
Dixie Hwy; mains $15-30; ⏰ 5:30-10pm Tue-Sat,
to 9pm Sun) There's no lack of flair at this
colorful, upbeat bistro, in a converted
drugstore in West Palm's antiques district, strung with Christmas lights and
hung with bright, bobbing paper lanterns.
The menu is equally vibrant, bopping happily from goat-cheese pie to 'the best tuna
tartar ever' to pomegranate-infused catch

A boat tour on the 19th century riverboat *Carrie B* (p170).
ALAMY/KENNY WILLIAMS©

**159**

of the day. Dessert's a star – the chocolate butter-cream cake is advertized as 'so good you'll slap your momma!' We don't advise that, but do taste the cake.

### ROCCO'S TACOS & TEQUILA BAR
Mexican $$

(www.roccostacos.com; 224 Clematis St; mains $12-19; ⏰11:30am-11pm Sun & Mon, to midnight Tue & Wed, to 1am Thu-Sat) This saucy Nuevo Mexican restaurant, in the heart of West Palm's Clematis St, is not your typical taqueria. Under the warm twinkle of funky chandeliers enjoy guacamole prepared tableside, fresh-made ceviche, or a range of tacos from pork to mushroom to cactus paddle. And, oh yeah, there are 175 different kinds of tequila to choose from. Just remember the immortal words of George Carlin: one tequila, two tequila, three tequila, floor!

### HAVANA
Cuban $$

(www.havanacubanfood.com; 6801 S Dixie Hwy; dinner mains $12-18; ⏰11am-11pm Sun-Thu, to 1am Fri & Sat) Biting into this Cuban restaurant's tender *ropa vieja* (shredded beef in a spicy sauce) is like stepping into Cuba, c 1955. Added bonus: the walk-up window, serving the full menu, is open round the clock. When you need a pick-me-up, nothing works faster or tastes better than the steaming *café con leche* (coffee with milk) here.

## 🍷 Drinking & Entertainment

Clematis and CityPlace have a revolving door of ultrachic bar-lounges and late-night dance clubs; they're also home to a couple of great, casual, stalwart hangouts.

### ER BRADLEY'S SALOON
Bar, Restaurant

(www.erbradleys.com; 104 S Clematis St) Mostly a restaurant until about 10pm, at which point the music cranks up, the rum starts flowing, and the mixed-age crowd starts grooving on the multiple decks and bar areas. If you find yourself, um, a little peaky in the morning, come right back for 8am steak and eggs! Great views of the Intracoastal make this a nice happy-hour spot as well.

### HG ROOSTERS
Bar

(www.hgroosters.com; 823 Belvedere Rd) A mainstay of West Palm's thriving gay community, this bar has been offering wings, bingo and hot young male dancers since 1984.

Every Thursday from 6pm to 9:30pm, the city shuts down the eastern terminus of Clematis St, rolls in some food carts, arts and crafts vendors, and stages a free outdoor music festival under the stars. The kid- and dog-friendly **Clematis by Night** (www.clematisbynight.net)

Fish tacos at Havana Hideout (p162).
HAVANA HIDEOUT/PRESS PHOTO ©

# Detour:
# Lion Country Safari

A half an hour's drive west of West Palm, you'll find the first cageless drive-through safari in the country: **Lion Country Safari** (www.lioncountrysafari .com; 2003 Lion Country Safari Rd; adult/child $26.50/19.50; 9:30am-5:30pm; ) This incredible animal park puts you in the cage (ie your car) as 900 creatures roam freely, staring at *you*. Equal parts conservation area and safari, the park's 500 acres are home to bison, zebra, white rhinos, chimpanzees and, of course, lions. You tour the safari section in your car (unless it's a convertible; short-term rentals are available), driving slowly, hoping the animals approach the vehicle. The best time to go is when it rains, because the animals are more active when it's cool.

spotlights great local and national acts playing everything from rock to swing. Drink up: proceeds from the beer truck are split between the city and the nonprofit group pouring drinks that night.

On Friday and Saturday, CityPlace hosts **free outdoor concerts** (www .cityplace.com) from 6pm to 10pm in front of the gorgeous CityPlace Fountain.

## ℹ Information

**Visitor centre** (☎800-554-2756; www .palmbeachfl.com; 1555 Palm Beach Lakes Blvd)

## ℹ Getting There & Around

**Palm Beach International Airport** (PBI; ☎561-471-7420; www.pbia.org) The king of medium-sized airports, refreshingly small and hassle-free. PBI is served by most major airlines and car-rental companies.

A cute, convenient and free trolley runs between Clematis St and CityPlace starting at 11am.

# Lake Worth
☎561 / POP 36,000

Billing itself as 'Where the tropics begin', this bohemian community has an artsy vibe and a cool collection of eateries and nightspots.

 **Sights & Activities**

**LAKE WORTH BEACH**     Beach
This stretch of sand is universally agreed to be the finest beach between Fort Lauderdale and Daytona. Surfers come from miles to tame the waves; everyone else comes to enjoy the fine, white sand. If you're looking for a laid-back place to get sunburned – er...to relax on the beach – this is a great place to do it.

## 🍴 Eating

**SHEILA'S BAHAMIAN CONCH & BBQ**     Bahamian $
(US 1 & S 12th Ave; mains $6-13; ⏱11:30am-late) As authentic a Bahamian conch shack as you'll find this side of the Gulf Stream, this concrete bunker hunkers down on a stretch of bare asphalt on the corner of the Dixie Hwy. Smoke pouring from the back chimney attests to the ribs being slow-smoked inside. Order from a window in the wall and sit down at a picnic table to wait. Cracked conch (a battered and fried Caribbean sea snail, which tastes like calamari) is crisp and tender, while sides like collards and plantains taste just like granny's Nassau kitchen. Expect a line at lunch and dinner – sip a cold Bahamas-brewed Kalik beer while you wait.

**COTTAGE**          Fusion $$
(www.thecottagelw.com; 522 Lucerne Ave; mains $7-16; ⏱11am-2am) The prettiest spot in Lake Worth, the Cottage offers multicultural small plates (hummus, sliders, ahi-tuna tartar) and a dynamic bar featuring local and regional microbrews and wines. Dine alfresco under a twinkling canopy, surrounded by thick weeping figs and in sight of the projector screening classic films, or inside by the light of candles and the one-of-a-kind rainbow-splashed stained-glass bar back.

**PELICAN**          Diner, Indian $
(610 Lake Ave; mains $3-10; ⏱6:30am-2pm; ✈) This early-risers' place offers hearty portions of perfectly prepared breakfast, plus a carnival of vegetarian-friendly specials, many with Mediterranean or Middle Eastern flavors (the owners are Pakistani). It also offers divine Indian dinners on Friday from 6pm to 10pm with a range of potent curries and masalas.

# 🍷 Drinking & Entertainment

Nightlife is where Lake Worth shines. It offers an outsized wealth of great bars and music venues.

**HAVANA HIDEOUT**      Bar, Restaurant
(www.havanahideout.com; 509 Lake Ave) The most happening place in town, open-air, palm-fringed Havana has live music most nights, a thoughtful draft-beer selection and an on-site taqueria that fills countless stomachs on Taco Tuesdays, when tacos are $1.50 apiece.

**BAMBOO ROOM**        Live Music
(☎561-585-2583; www.bamboorm.com; 25 S J St) This favorite spot with an intimate roadhouse feel features regional and internationally known blues, rockabilly, alt-country and jam bands, drawing music lovers from miles around.

**LAKE WORTH PLAYHOUSE**      Theater
(☎561-586-6410; www.lakeworthplayhouse.org; 713 Lake Ave; tickets $15-32) Housed in a restored 1924 vaudeville venue, this intimate spot stages classic community theater. The attached Stonzek Studio Theatre screens independent films (tickets $6 to $8).

**LAKE WORTH DRIVE-IN**      Cinema
(☎561-965-4517; 3438 Lake Worth Rd) When was the last time you went to the drive-in?! Screening first-run movies under the stars seven nights a week – drive in, tune in and sit back. Coolers are welcome; dogs are not.

## ℹ️ Information

Chamber of Commerce (☎561-582-4401; www.lwchamber.com; 501 Lake Ave)

## ℹ️ Getting There & Around

The Tri-Rail Station (1703 Lake Worth Rd) is at the intersection of A St. PalmTran bus 61 connects the station to downtown.

# Delray Beach

☎561 / POP 65,000

Delray effortlessly juggles casual seaside vibe, suave urban sophistication and wide-ranging restaurant options.

## ◎ Sights & Activities

**MORIKAMI MUSEUM & JAPANESE GARDENS**    Museum, Garden
(www.morikami.org; 4000 Morikami Park Rd; adult/child $12/7; ⏱10am-5pm Tue-Sun) West of the beach, away from the hub-bub downtown, is this serene cultural landmark. The initial aim of the so-called Yamato settlement was to attract Japanese families to Florida, where they would introduce new and profitable agricultural techniques to the region. There was one big problem when it opened in 1905: only single Japanese men came; the stable families that founders had hoped for were uninterested. The group soon disbanded, though one settler, Sukjei 'George' Morikami, stuck around and planted some gardens.

Today his plantings skirt the edge of the 200-acre property – with more than a mile

NORTON MUSEUM OF ART ©

## Don't Miss **Ann Norton Sculpture Garden**

This serene collection of sculptures is a real West Palm gem. The historic house, verdant grounds and enormous sculptures are all the work of Ralph Norton's second wife, Ann. When creating the garden, she intended to create a soothing environment for the public to relax. She succeeded. After poking through Norton's historic, but simple, antique-filled home, you can wander the grounds and uncover her soaring feats of granite, brick, marble and bronze. Perhaps most awe-inspiring is the 1965 Cluster, a collection of seven burka-clad Islamic women done in pink granite.

### THINGS YOU NEED TO KNOW

www.ansg.org; 253 Barcelona Rd; admission $7; ☺10am-4pm Wed-Sun

of trails – highlighting traditional Japanese landscaping techniques from intricate bonsai to authentic koi-filled ponds, all with monuments favored by Japanese gardeners of various eras. The outstanding Morikami Museum has a collection of 5000 Japanese antiques and objects, including textiles, tea-ceremony items and works of fine art. There are tea ceremonies in the **Seishin-An teahouse (with museum admission $5)** on the third Saturday of the month from October to June.

The museum's **Cornell Cafe (mains $7-10; ☺11am-3pm)**, which, despite its Anglo name, serves neo-Japanese cuisine like sweet-potato tempura, ginger-roasted duck and sushi rolls, is considered one of the best museum restaurants in the country.

### BEACHES                    Beaches

Among the best sandy spits are the **Atlantic Dunes Beach** (1600 Ocean Blvd), with 7 acres of shorefront sporting clean restroom facilities, volleyball courts and picnic areas, and the **public beach** (Ocean Blvd at Atlantic), a hip gathering spot for young locals and visitors, with excellent surf for swimming. Coin-operated parking meters charge $1.25 per hour.

##  Eating

Delray's got one of the area's best eating scenes, with everything from Parisian-style cafes to funky lunch counters to swanky seafood bistros.

**BAMBOO FIRE**  Caribbean $$
(www.bamboofirecafe.com; 149 NE 4th Ave; mains $9-15; ☺6-10:30pm Wed-Thu, to 11:30pm Fri, noon-11:30pm Sat) On a quiet shopping street a few blocks from the main Delray action, this arty little hole-in-the-wall is a cult favorite for authentic Caribbean fare like conch fritters, jerk chicken and oxtail stew. Veggies and vegans will be in tofu heaven – try it curried, grilled or fried.

**LEMONGRASS**  Asian $$
(☎561-247-7077; www.lemongrassasianbistro.com; 420 E Atlantic Ave; mains $8-25; ☺11am-3pm & 5:30-10:30pm Mon-Thu, to 11:30pm Fri & Sat, to 10pm Sun) Buddhist art, soothing earth tones and sleek, calming lines in this modern Asian bistro almost make up for the absolute always-totally-packed franticness of it all. The food, though, is divine; hence, the always-totally-packed franticness. Authentic Thai curries, one-off sushi creations (like Sex on the Moon) and Vietnamese noodles are some of the many offerings here.

## ⓘ Information

**Chamber of Commerce** (☎561-278-0424; www.delraybeach.com; 64 SE 5th Ave) For maps, guides and local advice.

## ⓘ Getting There & Around

Delray Beach is about 20 miles south of West Palm Beach and 45 miles north of Miami on I-95, US Hwy 1 or Hwy A1A.

# Boca Raton

☎561 / POP 86,000

The name Boca Raton may mean 'mouth of the rat', but there's nothing ratty about this proud-to-be-posh coastal town, especially not its alfresco mall, Mizner Park.

## ◎ Sights & Activities

**GUMBO LIMBO NATURE CENTER**  Park
(Map p165; www.gumbolimbo.org; 1801 N Ocean Blvd; admission by donation; ☺9am-4pm Mon-

O Bar at the Omphoy (p153).

MICHELLE BERNSTEIN'S/PRESS PHOTO ©

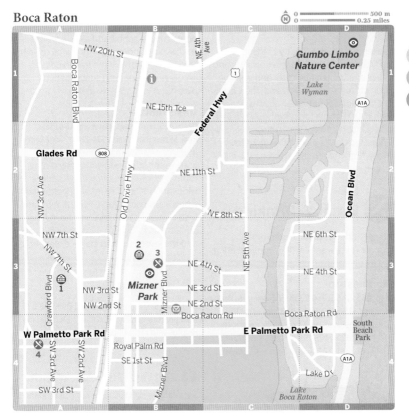

Sat, noon-4pm Sun; 👫) Boca's best asset is not its collection of retail, cultural or culinary treats, but this condo-free stretch of waterfront parkland. The crown jewel of the system is this wild preserve of tropical hammock and dunes ecosystems, a haven for all manner of sea creatures and birds. Dedicated to educating the public about sea turtles and other local fauna, the natural-history displays include fascinating saltwater tanks full of critters – fed with leftover seafood scraps donated by local businesses. The highlight is the brand-new sea-turtle rehabilitation center, which cares for sick and injured turtles, and is open for 90-minute tours at 10am and 1pm Monday through Saturday, and 1pm Sunday.

The preserve also has a number of secluded hikes along elevated boardwalks

## Boca Raton

### ◎ Top Sights

### ◎ Sights

### ✖ Eating

through tropical foliage and along an artificial mangrove wetland, reclaimed using filtered wastewater from the city. A native-flower garden attracts a slew of gemstone-colored butterflies.

### MIZNER PARK · Shopping

(Map p165; www.miznerpark.com) This Spanish-style outdoor shopping mall, bookended on one side by the Boca Raton Museum of Art, has valet parking and a slew of chichi restaurants and upscale chain stores. At the north end, the Count de Hoernle Amphitheater accommodates over 4000 people for symphonies, ballet, rock concerts and other cultural events. Since Boca lacks a cohesive downtown, Mizner Park generally serves as the city's center.

## Eating & Drinking

Mizner Park has a half dozen or so upscale restaurants with outdoor seating and a see-and-be-seen vibe.

### SAPORISSIMO · Italian $$$

(Map p165; ☎561-750-2333; 366 Palmetto Park Rd; mains $15-50; ⏰5:30-10:30pm daily) Its name translates as 'extremely delicious,' and this Italian restaurant is simultaneously romantic and shabby-chic, unlike many of its more frou-frou neighbors. Choose from unusual Tuscan treats – wild boar, truffles, rabbit and elk – or more traditional options such as ravioli or veal. Finish it off with a rustic Italian dessert like *torta della nonna* (custard cake with pine nuts), or apple strudel.

### MAX'S GRILLE · Modern American $$

(Map p165; www.maxsgrille.com; 404 Plaza Real, Mizner Park; mains $14-28; ⏰8am-2am) In Mizner Park, Max's sleek, slightly corporate slate-and-mahogany dining room is always packed with shoppers, wine-sippers and ladies (and gentlemen) who lunch. The likeable 'New American bistro' menu has everything from Asian duck tacos to Cobb salads to skirt steak, and the lovely outdoor bar is excellent for people-watching.

## ℹ Information

**Chamber of Commerce** (☎561-395-4433; www.bocaratonchamber.com; 1800 N Dixie Hwy) Helpful, with racks of pamphlets and the best map in town.

## ℹ Getting There & Around

Boca Raton is about 50 miles north of Miami and sprawls several miles east and west of I-95. You can also get there from points north and south on Hwy A1A or US 1.

**Boca Taxi** (☎561-392-2727; www.bocataxi.com) serves the area. Cabs to the Fort Lauderdale or West Palm airports are $55; the Miami airport is $95.

# Lauderdale-by-the-Sea & Deerfield Beach

☎954 / LAUDERDALE-BY-THE-SEA POP 5900 / DEERFIELD BEACH POP 75,000

Just north of Fort Lauderdale, the high-rises and mega-hotels thin out, giving way to

Sculpture in Mizner Park shopping mall, Boca Raton.
ALAMY/JEFF GREENBERG ©

these two sleepy, family-oriented vacation communities.

##  Sights & Activities

**QUIET WATERS PARK**  Water Park
(401 S Powerline Rd, Deerfield Beach; admission $1.50; ) Hardly quiet, this 430-acre county park rings with the squeals of kids (and grown-ups) enjoying all kinds of wet 'n' wild fun. There's **Splash Adventure** (admission $5), a kiddie water playground with a shallow pool and fountains spraying every which way. Then there's the **Ski Rixen** (www.skirixenusa.com; per hour/day $20/40; ☺10am-7pm Tue-Fri), a super-cool cable water-ski system. Using an innovative cabling system suspended from towers surrounding a half-mile course, water-skiers (and wakeboarders) are pulled over a wake-free watercourse. Obstacles are available for advanced tricksters; otherwise, riders can perfect their water-skiing techniques without the hassle of a boat. For lower-octane adventures, the park has fishing, hiking trails, kayak rental, and a mountain-bike trail.

**BUTTERFLY WORLD**  Butterfly Park
(www.butterflyworld.com; 3600 W Sample Rd, Coconut Creek; adult/child $25/20; ☺9am-5pm Mon-Sat, from 11am Sun; ) The first indoor butterfly park in the US, this is also one of the largest butterfly exhibits anywhere, featuring thousands of live, exotic species, such as the bright-blue morphos or camouflaged owl butterfly. Various exhibits, each highlighting different creatures – from butterflies to hummingbirds – make Butterfly World an excellent place to spend the better part of a day, especially with wide-eyed children or trigger-happy shutterbugs.

##  Eating & Drinking

**DA CAMPO OSTERIA**  Italian $$$
(☎954-226-5002; www.dacamporestaurant.com; 3333 NE 32nd St, Fort Lauderdale; meals $26-45; ☺lunch 11:30am-2:30pm Tue-Sat, dinner 5:30-10pm Mon-Sat) Technically in Fort

Detour:
# Kayaking the Loxahatchee River

One of two federally designated 'Wild and Scenic' rivers in the state, the free-flowing Loxahatchee River, about 23 miles north of downtown West Palm, is home to a wide range of habitats, from tidal marsh riverines and dense mangrove communities to tidal flats and oyster bars. Translated as 'River of Turtles', the coffee-colored river is home to shelled reptiles, as well as herons, ospreys, otters, raccoons, the occasional bobcat – and lots of alligators. For a great day exploring the various aquatic preserves here, no one beats Riverbend Park's **Canoe Outfitters** (☎561-746-7053; www.canoeskayaksflorida.com; 9060 W Indiantown Rd; 2-person canoes/single kayaks $50/40), which provides access to this waterway. This terrific day out is gentle enough to be kid-friendly but eye-popping enough to appeal to the discerning adventurer.

Lauderdale, though much closer to the center of Lauderdale-by-the-Sea, this new spot by celebrity chef Todd English has been drawing no shortage of crowds and buzz, despite its awkward setting in an ugly gray hotel tower at the end of a shoddy commercial strip. Reserve well in advance to enjoy divine house-made pastas and homey-yet-exquisite mains like oxtail ragu and jumbo meatballs. Don't miss the pièce de résistance – homemade mozzarella prepared tableside with your choice of spices and seasonings.

**ARUBA BEACH CAFE**  Caribbean $$
(www.arubabeachcafe.com; 1 Commercial Blvd, Lauderdale-by-the-Sea; mains $10-22; ☺11am-11pm Mon-Sat, 9am-11pm Sun; ) The food

isn't the only reason people flock here (though the conch fritters *are* divine). There's also live music nightly, daily drink specials served from three separate bars and only a bank of sliding glass doors separating you and the beach.

## ⓘ Information

**Deerfield Beach Chamber of Commerce** ( ☎954-427-1050; www.deerfieldchamber.com; 1601 E Hillsboro Blvd)

**Lauderdale-by-the-Sea Chamber of Commerce** ( ☎954-776-1000; www.lbts.com; 4201 Ocean Dr) Info on businesses throughout the area.

## ⓘ Getting There & Around

**Tri-Rail** (www.tri-rail.com) heads north from Fort Lauderdale. If you're driving, try to take A1A (sometimes called Ocean Blvd): the drive's glorious.

## Fort Lauderdale

☎954 / POP 185,000

After years of building a reputation as *the* destination for Spring Break, Fort Lauderdale now angles for a slightly more mature and sophisticated crowd – think martinis rather than tequila shots. There's still plenty of carrying-on within the confines of area bars and nightclubs. But there's also beautiful beaches, a system of Venice-like waterways, an international yachting scene, spiffy new hotels, top-notch restaurants and gay hot spots.

## ⦿ Sights

**FORT LAUDERDALE BEACH & PROMENADE** Beach, Promenade
In the mid-1990s, this promenade received a $26-million renovation, and boy-oh-boy, does it show. A magnet for runners, inline skaters, walkers and cyclists, the wide, brick, palm tree-dotted pathway swoops along the beach, running parallel to A1A. You can also surf at Fort Lauderdale beach.

And what a beach it is, stretching from the southern edge of **South Beach Park** (Map p171), where the cruise ships pass, north 7 miles to Lauderdale-by-the-Sea (see p166). Thirty public-parking facilities

## Fort Lauderdale

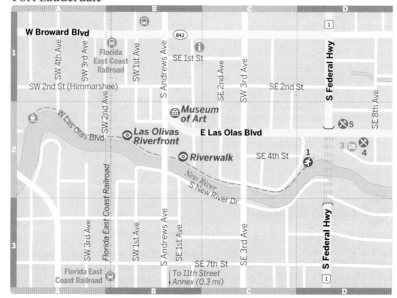

– expect to pay about a buck an hour, if you can find a meter – serve the smooth, white beaches here, recently declared among the nation's cleanest, safest and most accessible. The park's 27.5-acre South Beach is the most family friendly, regularly hosting basketball games, beach-volleyball tourneys and family reunions at the on-site grills and picnic tables. Further north, the stretch across from E Las Olas Blvd is less for recreation and more for, um, sightseeing. Expect olive-skinned, oiled-up saline queens and European guys in banana hammocks strutting their stuff.

### RIVERWALK & LAS OLAS RIVERFRONT    Walk, Shopping

Curving along the New River, the meandering **Riverwalk** (Map p168; www.goriverwalk.com) runs from Stranahan House to the Broward Center for the Performing Arts. Host to culinary tastings and other events, the walk connects a number of sights, restaurants and shops. **Las Olas Riverfront** (Map p168; cnr SW 1st Ave & Las Olas Blvd) is basically a giant alfresco shopping mall with stores, restaurants and live entertainment nightly; it's also the place to catch many river cruises (see p170).

### BONNET HOUSE    Historic Home

(Map p168 ;www.bonnethouse.org; 900 N Birch Rd; adult/child 6-18yr $20/16, grounds only $10; ☺10am-4pm Tue-Sat, 11am-4pm Sun) Hugh Taylor Birch, after being blown ashore in a freak accident in 1893, believed this part of the world was where God wanted him. Subsequently, he purchased 3 miles of beachfront property (for $1 per acre) and developed it. Today, the picturesque Bonnet House stands as a tribute to Birch and features 35 subtropical acres overflowing with native and imported plants, including a vast orchid collection. Seeing the art-filled house requires a guided tour (and 1¼ hours), but you're free to wander the grounds and nature trails on your own.

### MUSEUM OF ART    Museum

(Map p168; www.moafnsu.org; 1 E Las Olas Blvd; adult/child $10/7; ☺11am-6pm, to 8pm Wed, noon-5pm Sun) After vigorously reinventing itself, this curvaceous museum has now become one of Florida's standouts. The impressive permanent collection includes works by Picasso, Matisse, Dalí and Warhol, plus a growing and impressive collection of Cuban, African and South American art. Its temporary exhibitions range freely across time and genre, covering everything from Catholic religious art to 20th-century fashion photography.

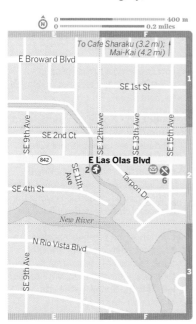

## If You Like...
# Nature Preserves

The Treasure Coast encompasses a series of fine nature and wildlife preserves. A trip out here can give you a real sense of the gentle beauty Florida's Atlantic Coast possessed in its pristine, undeveloped days.

**1** **JOHN D MACARTHUR STATE PARK** (www .macarthurbeach.org; 10900 Jack Nicklaus Dr; admission per vehicle $5; ☾8am-sunset) This state park has one of the best turtle-watching programs around, as loggerhead, green and leatherback turtles nest along the beach in June and July.

**2** **JONATHAN DICKINSON STATE PARK** (16450 SE Federal Hwy; admission per vehicle $6; ☾8am-sunset) There's no ocean access in the park, but its attraction lies in several habitats: pine flatwoods, cypress stands, swamp and increasingly endangered coastal sand-pine scrub.

**3** **HOBE SOUND NATIONAL WILDLIFE REFUGE** (US 1) A 1035-acre federally protected nature sanctuary, Hobe Sound National Wildlife Refuge includes 3½ miles of beach mangroves and sand dunes. In June and July, nighttime turtle-watching walks occur on Tuesday and Thursday (reservations necessary), and birding trips can be arranged through the Hawley Education Center at Blowing Rocks Preserve.

**4** **BLOWING ROCKS PRESERVE** (admission $2; ☾9am-4:30pm) This Jupiter Island preserve encompasses a mile-long limestone outcrop riddled with holes, cracks and fissures; when the tide is high and there's a strong easterly wind (call for conditions), water spews up as if from a geyser. Even when seas are calm, you can hike through four coastal biomes: shifting dune, coastal strand, interior mangrove wetlands and tropical coastal hammock. Finding the refuge is a little tricky, as there's no signage: from US Hwy 1, take Bridge St (708 east) to Hobe Sound. Turn left on Beach St (707). Travel about 3 miles; the refuge is on your right.

 # Activities

**Best Boat Club** (Map p170; ☏954-779-3866; www.fortlauderdaleboatrentals.com; per day from $100) Rents everything from single-engine 21ft Bowriders to luxurious 27ft Crownlines.

**FORT LAUDERDALE PARASAIL** Parasailing (Map p170; ☏954-543-2938; www. ftlauderdaleparasail.com; 1005 Seabreeze Blvd; flights $70-95) If you're curious how mansions along Miracle Mile look from above, sign up for a trip to soar between 600ft and 1000ft above the waves while strapped securely to an enormous smiley-face parachute.

**SEA EXPERIENCE** Boating, Snorkeling (Map p171; ☏954-467-6000; www.seaxp. com/departures.html; 801 Seabreeze Blvd; adult/child $35/21; ☾10:15am & 2:15pm daily; c) Takes guests in a 40ft glass-bottom boat along the Intracoastal into the ocean to snorkel on a natural reef, thriving with marine life, in 10ft to 20ft of water. Also offers scuba trips.

 # Tours

Fort Lauderdale's miles of canals make it one of the top spots in Florida for boat tours.

**CARRIE B** Boat Tours (Map p171; ☏954-768-9920; www.car riebcruises.com; tours adult/child $20/13) Hop aboard this replica 19th-century riverboat for a narrated 90-minute 'lifestyles of the rich and famous' tour of the ginormous mansions along the Intracoastal and New River. Because Florida's infamous 'homestead exemption' law prevents houses from being seized by creditors, some of these homes are used as money shelters for white-collar criminals ('to your left, note the Spanish-style villa of notorious tax evader Richie

# Fort Lauderdale Beach

**Fort Lauderdale Beach**

Hugh Taylor Birch State Recreation Area

E Sunrise Blvd

Bonnet House

Canine Beach

9th Ct

NE 9th St

N Birch Rd

A1A

Intracoastal Waterway

Vistamar St

Belmar St

Auramar St

Terramar St

Windamar St

Viramar St

Riomar St

(N Fort Lauderdale Beach Blvd)

Antioch Ave

Orton Ave

N Birch Rd

Bayshore Dr

Fort Lauderdale Beach

Granada St

Seville St

5

Alhambra St

Sebastian St

6 Castillo St

Valencia St

Cortez St

Poinsettia St

Las Olas Cir

Banyan St 7

E Las Olas Blvd

Seabreeze Blvd

ATLANTIC OCEAN

Intracoastal Waterway

SE 5th St

S Atlantic Blvd

Fort Lauderdale Beach

Bahia Mar Resort & Yacht Center

A1A

4

2

3

Seabreeze Blvd

New River Sound

1

Harbor Dr

McRicherson'). Tours leave at 11am, 1pm and 3pm from Las Olas at SE 5th Ave.

**GONDOLA MAN**     Gondola Rides
(Map p171; ☎877-926-2467; www.gondolaman. com; rides $125) With over 300 miles of navigable inland waterways, Fort Lauderdale is known as 'the Venice of the Americas'. And what do you do in Venice? A gondola tour, of course! Float around the canals as an authentically dressed gondolier narrates the sights (or keeps quiet while you sip champagne – your choice). Rides depart from the canal adjacent to 1109 E Las Olas Blvd.

# Sleeping

The splashiest (and priciest) hotels are found along the beach. Go inland and you'll discover wonderful inns with Old Florida charm/

**PILLARS**     B&B $$$
(Map p171; ☎954-467-9639, 800-800-7666; www.pillarshotel.com; 111 N Birch Rd; r $179-520; P ✳ ✳ 🛜) From the harp in the sitting area to the private balconies to the intimate prearranged dinners for two, this tiny boutique hotel radiates hushed good taste. Sun-soaked rooms, done up in natural fibers and elegant botanical prints, look torn from the pages of *Coastal Living* magazine. It's a block from

FLORIDA DEPARTMENT OF ENVIRONMENTAL PROTECTION ©

## Don't Miss **Whiskey Creek**

Once an important stop for Prohibition-era bootleggers, lush Whiskey Creek (get it?), nestled inside John U Lloyd Beach State Park, is now a kayaking hot spot. The dense mangrove-lined route, roughly 2.5 miles long, is shallow, calm, ideal for beginners and just 15 minutes from downtown Dania. Full Moon Kayak Co runs day trips here and to other local paddling places. No guarantees, but they have spotted manatees.

### THINGS YOU NEED TO KNOW

○ **Full Moon Kayak Co** ☎954-597-3040; www.fullmoonkayak.com; tours from $35; ☉10am-6pm Mon-Sat

○ **John U Lloyd Beach State Park** www.floridastateparks.org/lloydbeach; per vehicle $6; ☉8am-sundown

the beach, half a mile from E Las Olas Blvd and facing one of the best sunsets in town. If you want to get as far away as possible from liquor-fueled beach culture, this is your spot.

**PINEAPPLE POINT**  Guesthouse $$$
(☎888-844-7295; www.pineapplepoint.com; 315 NE 16th Terrace; r $199-279, ste $299-399; P ❄ @ ☎ ≋) Tucked away behind a tall fence in a quiet residential neighborhood, this intimate guesthouse complex caters to a loyal gay male clientele. Suites and

apartments are bright and beachy (with the occasional tasteful erotic photo), all clustered around a handful of pools, hot tubs and tree-shaded sitting areas. Daily happy hours ensure mingling, and the super-friendly staff know all the best restaurants and gay bars in town. Pineapple Point is a few blocks northeast of the main drag of Las Olas, inland from the beach.

**ALHAMBRA BEACH RESORT**  Hotel $$
(Map p171; ☎954-525-7601; 3021 Alhambra St; r $99-200; P ❄ ≋ ☎) Beloved for its

reasonable prices and warm-hearted owners, this charming little 1930s-era inn has modest-but-immaculate rooms and suites painted in cheerful buttercup yellow, and a pleasant pool deck amidst a manicured garden of palms and hibiscus. A gate adds a private feel, though the beach is only half a block away. Scads of return guests mean the place books up quickly!

**RIVERSIDE HOTEL** Hotel $$
(Map p171; ☏954-467-0671, 800-325-3280; www.riversidehotel.com; 620 E Las Olas Blvd; r $143-200; P ❄ @ ⛱ ☎) This 1936 hotel, smack in the middle of downtown and fronted by stately columns, oozes an old-fashioned, Old Florida charm. Save some money by opting for a 'Traditional' room – they're older, and have slightly creaky furniture and odd coffered ceilings, but those features only add character, in our opinion. 'Standard' rooms are plush and classic. The lobby, all Spanish tile and potted ferns, has a stately charm, and the hotel restaurant, the Golden Lyon, is prime for people-watching, with outdoor tables right on Las Olas.

 **Eating**

Fort Lauderdale's got a great food scene; Las Olas Blvd in downtown Fort Lauderdale has the bulk of nicer spots.

**GRAN FORNO** Italian, Bakery $$
(Map p171; www.granforno.com; 1235 E Las Olas Blvd; mains $6-12; ☉7:30am-7pm Tue-Sun) At midday, follow the hordes of business-people to the best lunch spot in downtown Fort Lauderdale. A delightfully old-school Milanese-style bakery and café, Gran Forno ('big oven' in Italian) turns out warm, crusty pastries, bubbling pizzas and fat, golden loaves of ciabatta, which they stuff with ham, roast peppers, pesto and other delicacies, creating some of the area's best sandwiches. Seating is limited – crowd into one of the banquettes in the black-and-white tiled interior, or sip your Peroni under a big red umbrella on the sidewalk. Finish it up with a thimble of hot, strong espresso and a sliver of homemade biscotti.

## If You Like...
## Museums

For a relatively small town, Boca Ration has a surprising amount of excellent museums. They tend to cater to adults and children, and in that vein, we present two exemplars of each genre.

**1 BOCA RATON MUSEUM OF ART** (www.bocamuseum.org; 501 Plaza Real; adult/child $8/4; ☉10am-5pm Tue-Fri, noon-5pm Sat & Sun) In Mizner Park, this elegant museum showcases the minor works of modern masters like Picasso, Chagall and Modigliani, and has a genuinely worthwhile collection of pieces by 20th- and 21st-century American and European painters, sculptors and photographers.

**2 BOCA RATON CHILDREN'S MUSEUM** (www.cmboca.org; 498 Crawford Blvd; admission $5; hnoon-4pm Tue-Sat; c) Housed in the 1925 'Singing Pines' home, one of the oldest wooden structures in town, this children's museum has rooms with various themes, like Oscar's Post Office (where kids can make their own postcards), KidsCent's banking and FACES Multicultural Room (with musical instruments, try-on clothing and crafts from around the world). A major expansion should be finished by the time this book goes to press.

**JOHNNY V'S** Modern American $$$
(Map p171; ☏954-761-7020; 625 E Las Olas Blvd; mains $28-42; ☉11am-3pm daily & 5-11pm Mon-Fri, to midnight Fri & Sat) Despite the vaguely mafioso-sounding name (it's actually named after the chef, Johnny Vinczencz), this perennially popular bistro is Nouvelle American all the way – modern brick-and-slate dining room, menu full of witty takes on regional classics (wild-mushroom 'pancakes' with balsamic 'syrup', braised short ribs with haute onion rings). The late-afternoon happy hour is a daily event among well-heeled Fort Lauderdale-ites.

### FLORIDIAN
Diner $

(Map p171; ☎954-764-3500; www.casablanca cafeonline.com; 1410 E Las Olas; mains around $10; ⏰24hr) This all-day, all-night diner is one of the oldest restaurants in Fort Lauderdale. Given its position near the bars and clubs of Las Olas, it's also one fo the best places in the city for people-watching. The food is as solid as the selection: American and Cuban mains that are as good for dinner as they are for soaking up hangovers if you've been partying.

### 11TH STREET ANNEX
American, Eclectic $

(Off map p171; twouglysisters.com; 14 SW 11th St; lunch mains $9; ⏰11:30am-2pm Mon-Fri) You don't get more off-the-beaten path than this tiny peach cottage, on a residential side street just off busy S Andrews Ave. Inside, Jonny Altobell and Penny Sanfilippo – both culinary-school grads who call themselves 'the two ugly sisters' – serve up whatever strikes their fancy on a given day. Brie mac 'n' cheese, chicken confit, and sour-cream chocolate cake have all made appearances in the past. There's always a veggie option, much of which comes from the cottage's garden.

### CAFE SHARAKU
Asian Fusion $$$

(Off map p171; ☎954-563-2888; www.cafeshar aku.com; 2736 N Federal Hwy; mains $25-32; ⏰11:30am-3pm Tue-Fri, 5:30-10pm Tue-Sun) Local foodies only whisper about this place, unwilling to allow the exquisite little 18-seat bistro to be trampled by the masses. Well, sorry, but the cat's out of the bag: Sharaku is fabulous. Chef Iwao Kaita treats fish with the utmost respect, crafting gem-like plates of miso bass or sesame-crusted salmon. The restaurant is a short drive north of downtown Fort Lauderdale.

##  Drinking & Entertainment

The best variety of bars in Fort Lauderdale can be found in the **Himmarshee Nightlife District** area. These places run the gamut from mellow wine bars to more raucous frat-pack spots. The beach offers plenty of open-air boozing. For gay and lesbian venues, see p176.

### LASER WOLF
Bar

(www.laserwolf.com; 901 Progresso Dr, Suite 101) We don't want to call Laser Wolf sophisticated, but its extensive booze menu and pop-art styling definitely attracts Fort Lauderdale's cerebral set. But they're a cerebral set that *loves* to party, so if this wolf is sophisticated, it knows how to let its hair down.

### ELBO ROOM
Bar

(Map p171; www.elboroom.com; 241 N Fort Lauderdale Beach Blvd) Open since 1938, this dive achieved immortality thanks to the '60s classic 'Where the Boys Are'. Attracts the young, beer-swilling, hip-shaking set.

### MAI-KAI
Dinner Show

(www.maikai.com; 3599 N Federal Hwy) This old-school Polynesian joint is pure kitsch, with Vegas-style dinner shows and froofy tiki cocktails. Mai-Kai is a short drive north of downtown Fort Lauderdale towards Lauderdale-by-the-Sea.

##  Shopping

Fort Lauderdale Beach Blvd has T-shirt shops and sunglass huts, while Las Olas is lined with swanky boutiques and antiques shops.

### SWAP SHOP
Flea Market

(www.floridaswapshop.com; 3291 W Sunrise Blvd; ⏰9am-6pm) Perhaps the most fun shopping in town, the state's biggest flea market has acres of stalls selling everything from underwear to antique cookie jars to pink lawn flamingos, and a carnival atmosphere of mariachi music, hot-dog trucks and a 14-screen drive-in movie theater. The flea market is slightly northwest of downtown.

## ℹ Information

**Convention & Visitors Bureau** (Map p168; ☎954-765-4466; www.sunny.org; 100 E

GETTY IMAGES/ROBERT HOLLAND ©

## Don't Miss **Shipwreck Snorkel Trail**

Head to Datura Ave in Lauderdale-by-the-Sea (it intersects N Ocean Blvd and El Mar Dr), then go east till you hit water. Now head *under* water and you'll find the Shipwreck Snorkel Trail, an artificial reef that has been designed to resemble a sunken Spanish galleon. There are over 300 recorded species of fish here, and the area is regarded as having some of the best underwater wildlife viewing in the Western Atlantic Ocean. With a pair of flippers and a snorkel or some SUBA gear (easily rented by businesses within walking distance of Datura), you can live out your underwater archaeology fantasies; keep an eye out for an authentic anchor and replica cannons.

Broward Blvd, ste 200) Has an excellent array of visitor information about hotels and attractions in the greater Fort Lauderdale region.

### 🟢 Getting There & Away

### Air

Fort Lauderdale-Hollywood International Airport (FLL; ☎954-359-1200; www.fll.net) Easy to reach from I-95 or US 1 and sandwiched about halfway between Lauderdale and Hollywood. From the airport, it's a short 20-minute drive to downtown, or a $20 cab ride.

### Boat

The Port Everglades Authority (www. porteverglades.org) runs the enormous Port Everglades cruise port. From the port, walk to SE 17th St and take bus 40 to the beach or to Broward Central Terminal.

If you're heading to Fort Lauderdale in your own boat (not that unlikely here), head for the Bahia Mar Resort & Yacht Center (Map p171; www.bahiamarhotel.com; 801 Seabreeze Blvd; Fort Lauderdale).

### Train

Tri-Rail (www.tri-rail.com) Runs between Miami and Fort Lauderdale (one way $5, 45 minutes).

## ℹ Getting Around

**Sun Trolley** (www.suntrolley.com; fare $0.50)
Runs between Las Olas and the beaches.

**Broward County Transit** (BCT; www.broward
.org/bct; fare $1.75) operates between downtown,
the beach and Port Everglades.

From **Broward Central Terminal** (101 NW
1st Ave), take bus 11 to upper Fort Lauderdale
Beach and Lauderdale-by-the-Sea; bus 4 to
Port Everglades; and bus 40 to 17th St and the
beaches.

**Water Taxi** (www.watertaxi.com; 651
Seabreeze Blvd; all-day pass adult/child $20/12)
travels the canals and waterways between 17th St
to the south, Atlantic Blvd/Pompano Beach to the
north, the Riverfront to the west and the Atlantic
Ocean to the east.

# Hollywood &
# Dania Beach

☎954/ HOLLYWOOD POP 143,000/DANIA BEACH POP 28,000

Hollywood, a bustling, varied waterfront
town that positions itself as a gateway
to Fort Lauderdale. Dania (dane-ya)
remains a mellow little town, with a
fledgling antiques district and a breezy
fishing pier.

## ◉ Sights & Activities

**HOLLYWOOD BEACH
 & BROADWALK**          Beach, Shopping

Reminiscent of California's famed Venice
Beach, this beach and adjacent promenade teems with scantily clad rollerblad-
ers, fanny pack-wearing tourists and local
families speaking a rainbow of languages.
Standing guard over the walk are tacky
T-shirt shops, ice-cream vendors, snack
shacks and bars. This ain't no snooty
Palm Beach, and that's why it's so much
fun. The Broadwalk itself is a 2.2-mile,
six-person-wide cement path, regularly
clogged with skaters, strollers, and entire
families pedaling enormous group bikes. If
you feel like rolling along it, a dozen or so
Broadwalk vendors rent bikes, rollerblades
and other gear by the hour or the day.

## ✖ Eating & Drinking

Give most of the Broadwalk restaurants
a miss – they're overpriced, overcrowded
and mediocre. There are better eats to be
found along Ocean Dr, or inland in downtown Hollywood.

# Gay & Lesbian Fort Lauderdale

Compared to South Beach, Fort Lauderdale is a little more rainbow-flag
oriented and a little less exclusive. The city is home to several dozen gay bars
and clubs, as many gay guesthouses, and a couple of way-gay residential areas
including **Victoria Park**, the established gay hub just northeast of downtown
Fort Lauderdale, and, a bit further north, **Wilton Manors**, more recently
gay-gentrified and boasting endless nightlife options, including **Bill's Filling
Station** (www.billsfillingstation.com; 2209 Wilton Dr), a friendly 'bear' bar, **Matty's**
(www.mattysonthedrive.com; 2426 Wilton Dr), a low-key neighborhood watering hole,
and **Georgie's Alibi** (www.georgiesalibi.com; 2266 Wilton Dr), which is best for its
Wednesday comedy night with Cashetta, a fabulous female impersonator.

For more information, see www.gayftlauderdale.com and the glossy weekly
rag *Hot Spots* (www.hotspotsmagazine.com).

**LE TUB**     Burgers, American **$$**
(www.theletub.com; 1100 N Ocean Dr, Hollywood; mains $9-27; ☺noon-4am; 📶) Decorated exclusively with flotsam collected over four years of daybreak jogs along Hollywood Beach, this quirky Intracoastal-side institution features multiple tiers of outdoor seating, plus bathtubs and toilet bowls (!) sprouting lush plants. The thing to order here is the sirloin burger – it's bigger than your head (seriously) and is routinely named 'Best in America' by the likes of *GQ*. Expect a wait, both for seating and for cooking time. It's worth it.

### JAXSON'S ICE CREAM PARLOR
Ice Cream **$**
(www.jaxsonsicecream.com; ice cream from $4; 128 S Federal Hwy, Dania; ☺11:30am-11pm, to midnight Fri & Sat; 📶) Originally opened in 1956, this place has 80-plus flavors of homemade ice cream. Come hungry and try one of the signature gourmet concoctions like the meant-to-be-shared Kitchen Sink – several *gallons* of ice cream served in a real kitchen sink!

## ❶ Getting There & Around

An old-fashioned **trolley** travels between downtown Hollywood and the beach from 10am to 10pm Wednesday through Sunday. Fares are $1; bright-colored signs mark the stops.

## Detour:
# The Bahamas

Just 55 miles east of Florida, the Bahamian island of Grand Bahama is close enough for day-trip or overnight cruises. **Discovery Cruise Line** (📞800-259-1579; www.discoverycruiseline.com; trips from $99) does a popular one-day party cruise from the Port Everglades cruise dock, with all-you-can-eat breakfast and dinner buffets, free booze and casino gambling. The trip is about four hours each way, and yes, you need a passport.

Parking at the beach in Hollywood is hellacious – if you can't find on-street parking, try the parking deck on Johnson St.

# Miami & the Keys

You're still technically in the USA. But you're also somewhere... different.

Florida's edge is the state at her most cosmopolitan and endearingly funky. Spanish and Haitian Creole are as common as English. Miami's nickname is the 'Magic City,' as if to underscore that town's shimmering beauty, which stretches from the sexy sand and deco design of South Beach to the Mediterranean mansions of Coral Gables; from the glass skyline of Downtown to quiet, family-friendly beaches on Key Biscayne.

Meanwhile, in Key West, fishermen on brightly painted boats and artists who dress up as gossamer fairies sit on planning committees with doctors and police. And in the other 'Keys' (islands), villages are tucked away, connected by causeway, bridge and boat, not boulevards.

There's a different rhythm in the air here. Listen to the beat of Miami salsa and Keys Caribbean parades, and get ready to dance to it.

Classic American car on Miami's South Beach (p193).
SHUTTERSTOCK/IAN D WALKER ©

# Miami & the Keys

1 Miami Art Deco District

2 Key West

3 Hemingway Home

4 No Name Key

5 Venetian Pool

6 Little Havana

7 Cycling, Overseas Highway

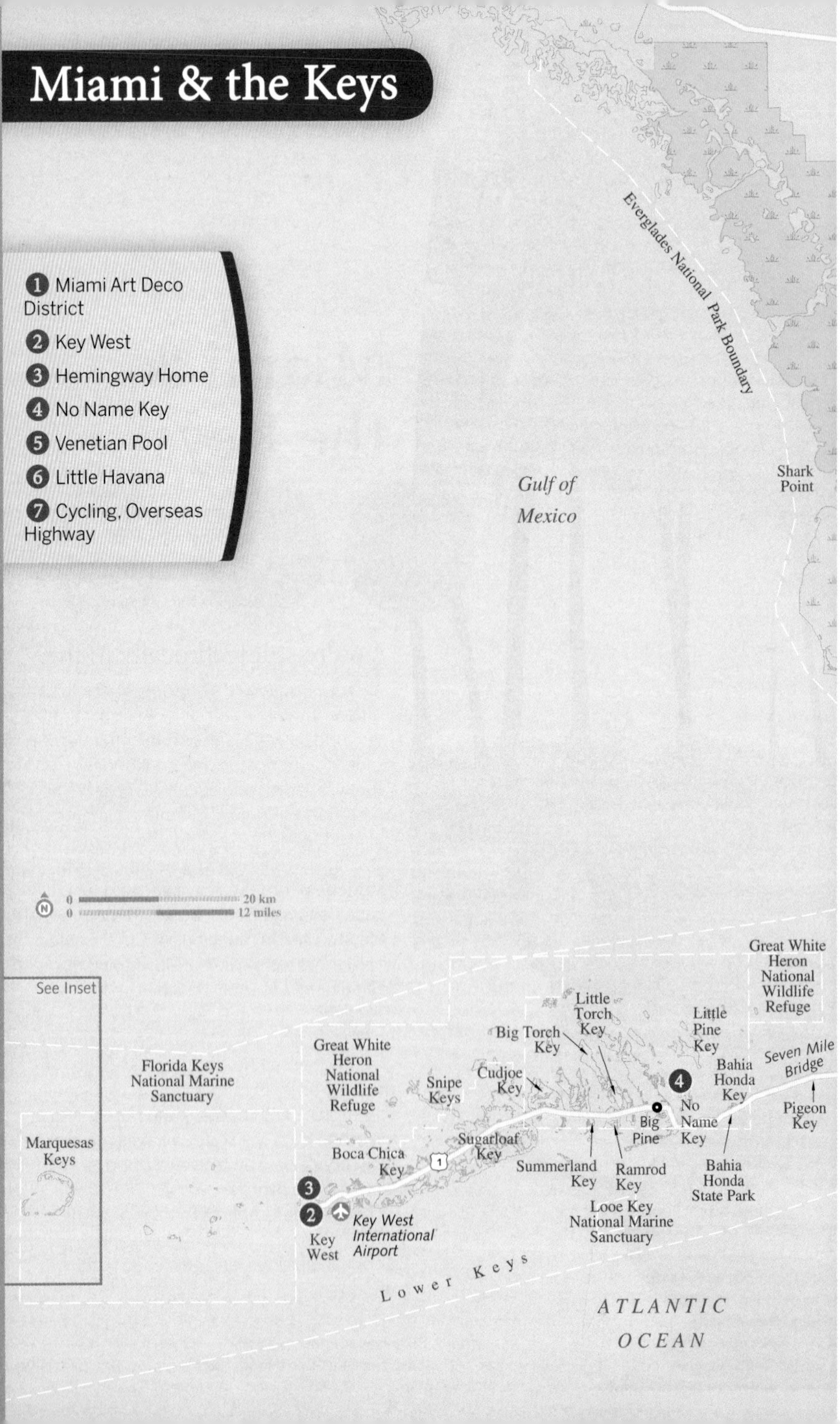

*Gulf of Mexico*

Everglades National Park Boundary

Shark Point

0 ———— 20 km
0 ———— 12 miles

See Inset

Florida Keys National Marine Sanctuary

Marquesas Keys

Great White Heron National Wildlife Refuge

Great White Heron National Wildlife Refuge

Snipe Keys

Boca Chica Key

3

2
Key West

Key West International Airport

Sugarloaf Key

Summerland Key

Cudjoe Key

Big Torch Key

Little Torch Key

Ramrod Key

Looe Key National Marine Sanctuary

Big Pine Key

4
No Name Key

Little Pine Key

Bahia Honda Key

Bahia Honda State Park

Pigeon Key

Seven Mile Bridge

Great White Heron National Wildlife Refuge

*Lower Keys*

*ATLANTIC OCEAN*

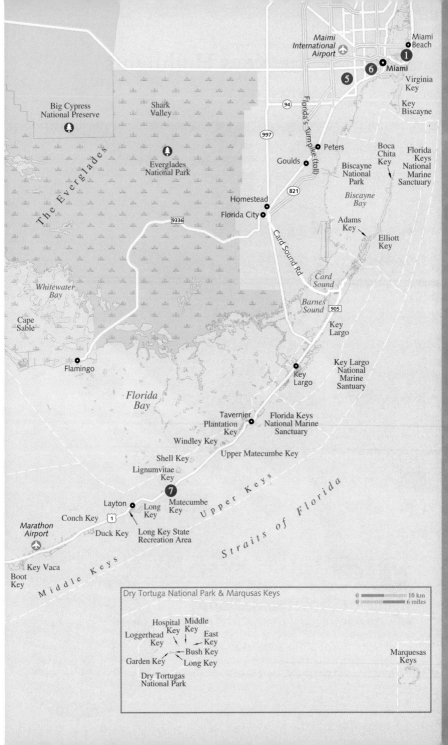

# Miami & the Keys Highlights

## 1 Miami Art Deco Historic District

Mainly concentrated in South Beach, Greater Miami's deco can be found amid hotels, housing projects, restaurants, bars and other assorted buildings. Without a doubt the deco district is the architectural highlight of Miami. The area can easily be explored by foot or on a bicycle.

**Need to Know**
**SIZE** 2.5 miles long. **BEST SHOPPING** Lincoln Rd. **PHOTO OPS** Ocean Ave neon at night. **PUBLIC PARKING** Anywhere with blue 'P' signs. **For more, see p189 and Map p194.**

# Miami Beach Don't Miss List

BY JEFF DONNELLY, PUBLIC
HISTORIAN & TOUR GUIDE, MIAMI
DESIGN & PRESERVATION LEAGUE

## 1 ART DECO WELCOME CENTER

You can try to find things for yourself, or you can go here for information on everything to do and see in the art deco district. **Miami Design & Preservation League** (MDPL) daily walking tours start here. The MDPL website has information about MDPL-sponsored festivals, film and lecture series and exhibitions.

## 2 WOLFSONIAN-FIU MUSEUM

Mickey Wolfson donated his collection of art, artifacts, and day-to-day materials from the 1885–1945 period, when the world slowly became 'modern.' A tour of the Wolfsonian's (p193) permanent and touring exhibits makes an excellent counterpoint to the District's buildings, which document the same transition from romanticism to modernism.

## 3 MAC'S CLUB DEUCE

Don't be put off by Mac's Club Deuce listing in Playboy's *Guide to America's Greatest Bars*. The Deuce (p223), which has been around since 1926 and survived Prohibition, will always resist trendiness. There are other dives, but only the Deuce has interior neon lighting supplied by Michael Mann of *Miami Vice* fame.

## 4 TAP TAP

In Haiti, the jitney buses that navigate the back roads are called tap-taps. Food here (p216) is simple but good, and Haitian art fills tabletops and walls. Many artists were exiles who supported former President Aristede's Lavalas party, and previous owners gave them employment both as waitstaff and artists.

## 5 PARK CENTRAL HOTEL

This 1937 art-deco building was fully restored 50 years later in 1987 at the beginning of the South Beach Renaissance. Listed with the National Trust for Historic Preservation among the Historic Hotels of America, the Park Central preserves and presents the work of both Henry Hohauser and Leonard Horowitz.

# Key West

The western half of the island, also known as Old Town, is the area where you'll likely spend most of your time exploring. There are rows and rows of preserved historical homes, cute cafes and restaurants and enough bars to keep several universities partying for a year.

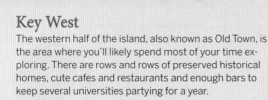

### Need to Know

**POPULATION** 26,000 **SOUTHERMOST POINT** Noncivilian-accessible naval base. **PUBLIC PARKING** Street parking and pay garage. **For more see p189 and Map p242.**

# Key West Don't Miss List

BY JULIET GRAY, KEY WEST CONCH
(NATIVE), BOX OFFICE DIRECTOR, RED
BARN THEATRE

### 1 KEY WEST ON TWO WHEELS
To truly experience Key West like a local, you must ride like a local. Rent a bike (or 'conch cruiser' as locals call it) to really get to know the southernmost city. A car is just not necessary in Key West. There are plenty of bike racks available around town.

### 2 LOUIE'S BACKYARD
For lunch or dinner, make sure to head here for delicious bounty from the sea. Tourists have their sunset celebration at Mallory Square, but locals head to the Afterdeck at Louie's Backyard (p247) to raise a glass to the sun. The drink of choice? An Island Cosmo with homemade pineapple-infused vodka.

### 3 WATCH DOLPHINS
Key West's surrounding waters are reason alone to visit – the entire area is a marine sanctuary. Hop aboard Captain John Baltzell's **Dolphin Watch** (p241) for an intimate trip to go see dolphins up close, then swim with other sea life as you snorkel on a reef far away from the crowds.

### 4 RED BARN THEATRE
'The Barn' (p247) is Key West's longest-running professional theatre. Shows start most nights at 8pm and range from classic musicals to Broadway hits. In addition to local writers and performers, Shel Silverstein, Jimmy Buffett and Tennessee Williams have all made the Barn a part of their cultural experience in Key West.

### 5 THE PORCH
Best place on the island to get craft beer (and root beer!) on tap as well as wine by the glass or bottle. In addition to fabulous libations, also on tap at the Porch (p246) you'll find wine tastings, local art installations, jewelry shows, mustache parties or even a zombie jamboree.

## Hemingway Home

Besides being the digs of one of the masters of 20th-century fiction and the arguably the father of literary modernism, the Hemingway Home (p239) is also a great example of Keys' Caribbean colonial architecture. Note the six-toed cats that wander about, the author's writing desk and the pool that broke Hemingway's bank, where the author famously left behind his 'last penny.'

## 5 Venetian Pool

Appropriately located in Coral Gables, one of the prettiest neighborhoods in Miami, you'll find the Venetian Pool (p203) one of the most impressive public pools in the state. Built out of the remains of a quarry, the pool resembles a sort of fantastic Roman-Renaissance villa, like the major set piece in a classical musical. Bring your swimming outfit, and maybe a toga.

CORBIS/DAVE G. HOUSER ©

ALAMY/MICHAEL VENTURA ©

## No Name Key

**4**

This oddly named island isn't much more than a speck of land, but there's a bizarre sense of reaching the end of the world when you drive out here (No Name is connected to Big Pine Key by a small bridge). Besides being inhabited by small Key Deer, the island is home to the No Name Pub (p237), where you can find some fine beer and pizza.

ALAMY/M. TIMOTHY O'KEEFE ©

**6**

## Little Havana

While it's officially the heart of South Florida's Cuban community, the fact is Latin South Florida extends far beyond the boundaries of Little Havana. With that said, much of the seminal arts, food, social scene and history of Miami's Cubans can be found here. Máximo Gómez Park (p201) is a fantastically atmospheric space where older Caribbean men battle it out on the chess board and dominoes table.

**7**

## Overseas Highway Cycling

The sea salt breeze, the presence of two beautiful bodies of water – one dark blue, the other a shimmering turquoise – a wealth of bridges, mangrove orchards, swaying palmettos and the flat topography of the Keys make the Overseas Hwy (p236) one of the finest places in Florida for getting on board two wheels.

# Miami & the Keys' Best...

## Cultural Encounters

◦ **Wynwood** (p199) Studio central and arts walks.

◦ **New World Center** (p196) Stunning stage and concert hall.

◦ **Studios of Key West** (p240) A collection of the Keys' best studios.

◦ **Adrienne Arsht Center for the Performing Arts** (p198) Miami's premier performing-arts venue.

◦ **Viernes Culturales** (p218) Little Havana's Friday fiesta.

◦ **Bass Museum of Art** (p198) Extensive collection of classical and modern work.

## Foodie Finds

◦ **Key West** (p245) Great food variety on this small island.

◦ **South Beach** (p222) Four-star elegance and tiny cafes.

◦ **Design District** (p220) The best of new Miami cuisine.

◦ **Coral Gables** (p222) A magnet for foodies.

◦ **Little Havana** (p221) Cuban cuisine done right.

◦ **Marathon** (p235) Fresh fish, sea breezes and comfort food.

## When Night Falls...

◦ **Green Parrot** (p246) Key West's locals' hideaway, with crazy art and live music.

◦ **Coconut Grove** (p224) Down-to-earth, student-y scene.

◦ **Design District** (p224) New bars, clubs and concert halls in Miami's fastest-growing 'hood.

◦ **Islamorada** (p233) Beach bars and sunsets.

◦ **South Beach** (p222) Chic clubs, grungy dives and neighborhood pubs.

# Need to Know

## Family-Friendly Fun

● **Bill Baggs Cape Florida State Recreation Area** (p200) Short trails, family-friendly beach and nature center.

● **Key West** (p237) Historic homes and easily walkable shady streets.

● **Miami Children's Museum** (p206) A ton of activities awaits toddlers to tweens.

● **Miami Seaquarium** (p199) Killer whales, dancing dolphins and barking sea lions.

● **Metrozoo** (p203) Playful otters gambol next to mysterious monitor lizards.

### ADVANCE PLANNING

● **Hotels** Book at least a month in advance if visiting during winter, and a week in advance even in low season.

● **Restaurants** Make reservations a week before at pricier places.

● **Excursions** Boat trips, walking tours and the like can usually be booked the day before.

● **Traffic** If driving to the Keys, keep in mind one accident can jam the entire Overseas Highway.

### GETTING AROUND

● **Car** Convenient for distances, but annoying for parking. Book rentals early for the best rates.

● **Bicycle** Highly recommended for Key West and Miami Beach. Other areas are flat, but bicycle infrastructure isn't nearly as well developed.

● **Bus** Miami has a decent city bus system; Key West's is easier to navigate. The Keys are connected to the mainland by commuter buses.

● **Train** The Tri-Rail system connects Miami to its suburbs.

### BE FOREWARNED

● **Traffic** Miami traffic is some of the worst in Florida. If you have a good GPS system, you can use backroads to avoid the inevitable jams on the main highways.

● **Crime** Avoid Overtown and Downtown Miami at night.

● **Sun** Even on cloudy days you can get badly burnt.

● **Language** In much of Miami, especially Little Havana and Downtown, it really helps to know a little Spanish.

**Left:** Colorful lifeguard house on a Miami beach;
**Above:** Art in Miami's Design District (p199).

(LEFT) SHUTTERSTOCK IMAGES/FOTOMAK ©; (ABOVE) ALAMY/JEFF GREENBERG ©

# Miami & the Keys Itineraries

*From the mangrove-fringed beaches of the Florida Keys to the shiny towers of Miami, from dark blue oceans to aquamarine lagoons in Florida Bay, we take in some of the best schedules for exploring South Florida.*

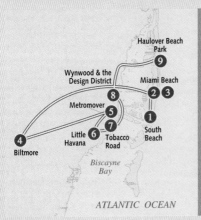

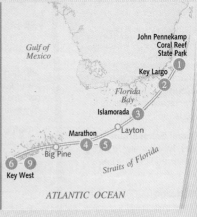

**SOUTH BEACH TO NORTH BEACH**

## Best of Miami

**4 DAYS**

Start your days exploring **(1) South Beach**, making sure to stop by the headquarters of the **(2) Miami Design & Preservation League**, the facades of the hotels on Ocean Dr and the exhibits that put local architecture in context at the **(3) Wolfsonian-FIU Museum**. On your second day in the city, head to Coral Gables to take in the opulence of the **(4) Biltmore** and go shopping along the Miracle Mile; afterwards, enjoying a leisurely drive by some of the finest homes in the city.

On your third day in the city take the **(5) Metromover**, a free commuter train,

around town to get a great view of the Miami skyline. When you're done here you're not far from 8th St, better known as Calle Ocho, in **(6) Little Havana**. At night, have dinner and drinks near the iconic **(7) Tobacco Road**. On the final day of this itinerary, take in some of the fine art galleries of **(8) Wynwood and the Design District**, then relax on the quiet beaches in North Miami Beach. We like **(9) Haulover Beach Park** – just keep in mind one of its beaches is a nude beach!

**KEY LARGO TO KEY WEST**

# The Keys Quest

**3 DAYS**

In Key Largo, spend a day snorkeling, diving or on board a glass-bottom boat at the lovely **(1) John Pennekamp Coral Reef State Park.** For dinner, make sure to have a fish taco at the **(2) Key Largo Conch House.** The next day, drive down to Islamorada, making sure to stop in and feed the giant tarpon fish at **(3) Robbie's Marina.** This is a short drive, so continue to Marathon, where there's excellent lobster reubens at **(4) Keys Fisheries**, and have a walk around the pretty park at **(5) Crane Point.**

On your third day, you'll make the one-hour drive to Key West, admiring the ocean and Florida Bay from the bridges of the Overseas Hwy. In Key West itself, take a tour of the **(6) Hemingway Home** and then spend the rest of your day pottering around the green, leafy avenues and historic homes of Old Town. We advise you to rent a bicycle so you can easily get about the city on two wheels. Make sure to head to **(7) Mallory Square** for the fun sunset celebrations held here nightly, and if the mood takes you, enjoy a night out on raucous **(8) Duvall St** or have an elegant dinner at the lovely **(9) Café Sole.**

Snorkeling in Dry Tortugas National Park (p246).
ALAMY/DANITA DELIMONT ©

# Discover Miami & the Keys

## At a Glance

○ **Miami** (see right) Startling contrasts, sparkling skylines.

○ **Miami Beach** (p193) White sands hug a celebrity-studded shoreline.

○ **The Keys** (p230) A smattering of quirky islands that march to their own beat.

○ **Key West** (p237) A historical, funky fantasy town at the end of the road.

Tightrope walker performing at sunset, Miami.
CORBIS/BOB KRIST ©

## MIAMI

✏ 305 / POP 362,500

Miami is so many things, but to most visitors it's glamour, condensed into urban form.

Well, the archaic definition of 'glamour' is a kind of spell that mystifies a victim. And they call Miami the Magic City. And it is mystifying. In its beauty, certainly: the clack of a model's high heels on Lincoln Rd, the teal sweep of Biscayne Bay, flowing cool into the wide South Florida sky; the blood-orange fire of the sunset setting the Downtown skyline aflame.

Then there's less conventional beauty: a Haitian dance party in the ghetto attended by University of Miami literature students, or a Venezuelan singing Metallica *en español* in a Coral Gables karaoke bar, or the passing *shalom/buenas días* traded between Orthodox Jews and Cuban exiles. Miami is so many things. All glamorous, in every sense of the word. You could spend a fun lifetime trying to escape her spell.

### When to Go

**January to March** Warm and dry, with lots of tourists; snowbirds from the northeast and Europeans.

**April to June** Not as muggy as deep summer, but lusher and greener than winter.

**July to October** Prices plummet, but when it's not as hot as an oven, there are storms: it's hurricane season.

# Sights

Miami's major sights aren't concentrated in one neighborhood; there is something for everyone just about everywhere.

## South Beach

South Beach, the most iconic neighborhood in Greater Miami, encompasses the region south of 21st St in the city of Miami Beach.

### ART DECO HISTORIC DISTRICT
Neighborhood

South Beach's heart is its Art Deco Historic District, from 18th St and south along Ocean Dr and Collins Ave. It's ironic that in a city built on speculative real estate, the main engine of urban renewal was the preservation of a unique architectural heritage. See, all those beautiful hotels, with their tropical-Americana facades, scream 'Miami.' They screamed it so loud when they were preserved they gave this city a brand, and this neighborhood a new lease on life. Back in the day, South Beach was a ghetto of vagrants, druggies and retirees. Then it became one of the largest areas in the USA on the National Register of Historic Places, and then it attracted models, photographers, hoteliers, chefs and...well, today it's a pastel medina of cruisers, Euro-fashionistas, the occasionally glimpsed celebrity, and tourists from Middle America.

Your first stop here should be the **Art Deco Welcome Center** (Map p194; 305-531-3484; 1200 Ocean Dr; 9:30am-7pm daily). You can book some excellent $20 guided walking tours (plus audio and private tours), which are some of the best introductions to the layout and history of South Beach on offer. Tours depart at 10:30am daily, except on Thursday when they leave at 6:30pm. No advance reservations required; just show up and smile. Call ahead for information on walking tours of Lincoln Rd (p193) and Collins Park, the area that encompasses upper South Beach.

### WOLFSONIAN-FIU
Museum

(Map p194; www.wolfsonian.org; 1001 Washington Ave; adult/student, senior & child under 12yr $5/3.50; 11am-9pm Thu, 11am-6pm Fri & Sat, noon-5pm Sun) Visit this excellent design museum early in your stay to put the aesthetics of Miami Beach into fascinating context. It's one thing to see how wealth, leisure and the pursuit of beauty manifests in Miami Beach, it's another to understand the roots and shadings of local artistic movements. By chronicling the interior evolution of everyday life, the Wolfsonian reveals how these trends were architecturally manifested in SoBe's exterior deco. Which reminds us of the Wolfsonian's own noteworthy facade. Remember the Gothic-futurist apartment complex-cum-temple of evil in *Ghostbusters*? Well, this imposing structure, with its grandiose 'frozen fountain' and lion-head-studded grand elevator, could serve as a stand-in for that set.

### LINCOLN ROAD MALL
Road

Calling Lincoln Rd (Map p194) a mall, which many do, is like calling Big Ben a clock: it's technically accurate but misses the point. Yes, you can shop, and shop very well here. But this outdoor pedestrian thoroughfare between Alton Rd and Washington Ave is really about seeing and being seen; there are times when Lincoln feels less like a road and more like a runway. We wouldn't be surprised if you developed a slight crick in your neck from whipping around to check out all the fabulously gorgeous creatures that call 'the road' their natural environment. Carl Fisher, the father of Miami Beach, envisioned the road as a '5th Ave of the South.' Morris Lapidus, one of the founders of the loopy, neo-Baroque Miami–Beach style, designed much of the mall, including several shady overhangs and waterfall structures, traffic barriers that look like the marbles a giant might play with, plus the wonderfully deco **Colony Theatre** and the currently empty **Lincoln Theatre** (541 Lincoln Rd). There's also an excellent **farmers market** ( 9am-6pm Sun) and the **Antique & Collectible Market**

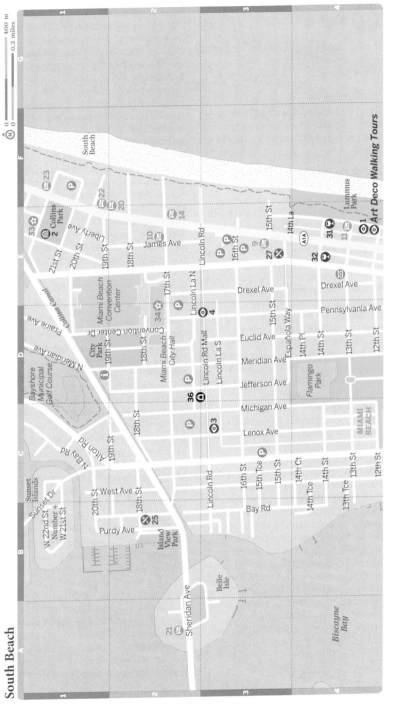

South Beach

0 0
0 0

400 m
0.2 miles

Art Deco Walking Tours

Biscayne Bay

MIAMI BEACH

Belle Isle

Sunset Islands

Bayshore Municipal Golf Course

South Beach

Lummus Park

Flamingo Park

Island View Park

City Park

Miami Beach Convention Center

Collins Park

Miami Beach City Hall

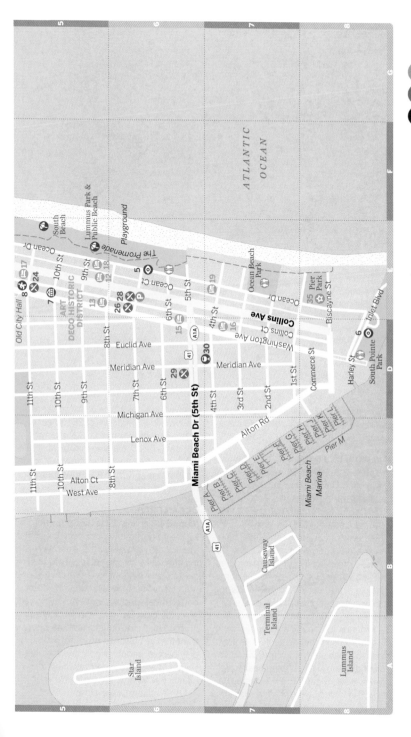

## South Beach

(⏱9am-5pm, every 2nd Sun Oct-May; www.an
tiquecollectiblemarket.com), both held along
Lincoln.

**NEW WORLD CENTER**  Notable Building
(Map p194; ☎305-673-3330; www.nws.edu; 500
17th St) Miami has a penchant for sumptuous performing arts venues. And the New
World Center is certainly competing with
the Arsht Center (p198) for most-
impressive concert hall in the city. The
New World Center, designed by Frank Ge-
hry, rises majestically out of a manicured
lawn just above Lincoln Rd, looking some-
what like a tissue box (note the 'fluttering'
stone waves that pop out of the exterior)
from the year 3000 with a glass facade.
The grounds form a 2½-acre public park;
performances inside the center are projected to those outside via a 7000-sq-ft
projection wall (like you're in the classiest
drive-in movie theater in the universe).
Inside, the folded layers of white walls feel
somewhere between organic and origami.

The venue is the home of the acclaimed
New World Symphony (p226); to get inside you generally need tickets to a show,
but if you call ahead you may be able to
organize a free guided walking tour of the
interior, a program that was just beginning at the time of research.

**OCEAN DRIVE**  Road
(Map p194; Runs from 1st to 11th St) Yar, here
be the belly of the South Beach beast. It's
just a road, right? No, it's the great cruising strip of Miami; an endless parade of
classic cars, testosterone-sweating young
men, peacock-like young women, street
performers, vendors, those guys who yell
unintelligible crap at everyone, celebrities
pretending to be tourists, tourists who
want to play celebrity, beautiful people,
ugly people, people people and the best
ribbon of art deco preservation on the
beach. Say 'Miami.' That image in your
head? Probably Ocean Drive.

**SOUTH POINTE PARK**  Park
(Map p194; 1 Washington Ave; ☺sunrise-10pm)
The very southern tip of Miami Beach has
been converted into a lovely park, replete
with manicured grass for lounging, views
over a remarkably teal and fresh ocean,
a restaurant, a refreshment stand, warm,
scrubbed stone walkways and lots of
folks who want to enjoy the great weather
and views sans the South Beach strutting. That said, we saw two model photo
shoots go off here in under an hour, so it's
not all casual relaxation.

## Northern Miami Beach

Mid-Beach is located around the 40th
streets, while North Beach extends from
70th St and above. Indian Creek waterway
separates the luxury hotels and high-rise
condos from the residential districts in
the west.

**BOARDWALK**  Beach
(Map p200; 21st St to 46th St) What's trendy
in beachwear this season? Seventeenth-
century Polish gabardine coats, appar-
ently. There are plenty of skimpily dressed
hotties on the Mid-Beach boardwalk, but
there are also Orthodox Jews going about
their business in the midst of gay joggers,
strolling tourists and sunbathers. Nearby
are numerous condo buildings occupied
by middle-class Latinos and Jews, who
walk their dogs and play with their kids
here, giving the entire place a laid-back,
real-world vibe that contrasts with the
nonstop glamour of South Beach.

**HAULOVER BEACH PARK**  Park
(www.miamidade.gov/parks/parks/haulover_
park.asp; 10800 Collins Ave; per car $4; ☺sun-
rise-sunset) Where are all those tanned
men in gold chains and speedos going?
That would be the clothing-optional beach
in this 40-acre park hidden by vegetation from condos, highway and prying
eyes. There's more to do here than get
in the buff, though; most of the beach is
'normal' (there's even a dog park) and is
one of the nicer spots for sand in the area
(also note the colorful deco-ish shower
'cones'). The park is located on Collins
Ave about 4.5 miles north of 71st St.

Shopping along Mallory Square (p237), Key West.

ALAMY/INGOLF POMPE 77 ©

197

ALAMY/JEFF GREENBERG ©

# Don't Miss **Bass Museum of Art**

The best art museum in Miami Beach has a playfully futuristic facade, a crisp interplay of lines and bright, white wall space – like an Orthodox church on a space-age Greek isle. All designed, by the way, in 1930 by Russell Pancoast (grandson of John A Collins, who lent his name to Collins Ave). The collection isn't shabby either: permanent highlights range from 16th-century European religious works to northern European and Renaissance paintings. The Bass forms one point of the Collins Park Cultural Center triangle, which also includes the three-story Miami City Ballet and the lovingly inviting Miami Beach Regional Library, which is a great place for free wi-fi.

## THINGS YOU NEED TO KNOW

☏ 305-673-7530 www.bassmuseum.org; 2121 Park Ave; adult/student & senior $8/6; ◷ noon-5pm Wed-Sun

## Downtown Miami

**ADRIENNE ARSHT CENTER FOR THE PERFORMING ARTS** Notable Building
(Map p204; www.arshtcenter.com; 1300 N Biscayne Blvd) The largest performing arts center in Florida (and second largest, by area, in the USA) is Miami's beautiful, beloved baby. It is also a major component of Downtown's urban equivalent of a facelift and several regimens of botox. Designed by Cesar Pelli (the man who brought you Kuala Lumpur's Petronas Towers), the center has two main components: the Ziff Ballet Opera House and Knight Concert Hall, which span both sides of Biscayne Blvd. The venues are connected by a thin, elegant pedestrian bridge, while inside the theaters there's a sense of ocean and land sculpted by wind; the rounded balconies rise up in spirals that resemble a sliced-open seashell. If you have the chance, catch a show here; the interior alone is easily a highlight of any Miami trip.

**METROMOVER** Train

(Map p204; www.miamidade.gov/transit/mover. asp) This elevated, electric monorail is hardly big enough to serve the mass transit needs of the city, and has become something of a tourist attraction. Whatever its virtues as a commuting tool, the Metromover is a really great (and free!) way to see central Miami from a height (which helps, given the skyscraper-canyon nature of Downtown). Because it's gratis, Metromover has a reputation as a hangout for the homeless, but at the time of research a fair few folks were using it to commute as well, a number the media reported was climbing due to the price of gas.

## Wynwood, Design District & Little Haiti

Now rebranded as 'Midtown,' Wynwood and the Design District are Miami's official arts neighborhoods, plus the focal points of new art, food and nightlife in Greater Miami. Little Haiti sits above the Design District.

**LITTLE HAITI
CULTURAL CENTER** Gallery

(Map p208; www.miamigov.com/lhculturalcenter; 212 NE 59th Tce; ◷9am-5pm, open evenings during events) Miami has the largest community of *Ayisyens* (Haitians) in the world outside Haiti, and this is the place to learn about their story. The cultural center is a study in playful island designs and motifs that houses a small but vibrant art gallery, crafts center and activities space – dance classes, drama productions and similar events are held here year-round. The best time to visit is for the **Big Night in Little Haiti** (www.bignightlittlehaiti.com), a street party held on the third Friday of every month from 6pm to 10pm. The celebration is rife with music, mouth-watering Caribbean food and beer, and is one of the safest, easiest ways of accessing the culture of Haiti outside of that island.

**WYNWOOD WALLS** Public Art

(Map p208; www.thewynwoodwalls.com; NW 2nd Ave btwn 25th & 26th St; ◷noon-8pm Wed-Sat) Not a gallery per se, Wynwood Walls is a collection of murals and paintings laid out over an open courtyard in the heart of Wynwood. What's on offer tends to change with the coming and going of major arts events like Art Basel (one of the US's major annual art shows); when we visited the centerpiece was a fantastic portrait of Aung San Suu Kyi by artist Shepard Fairey.

## Key Biscayne

The scenic drive along the Rickenbacker Causeway leads to Key Biscayne, an island just 7 miles long. The road turns into Crandon Blvd, the key's only real main road, which runs to the Cape Florida Lighthouse at the island's southernmost tip.

**MIAMI SEAQUARIUM** Aquarium

(Map p212; www.miamiseaquarium.com; 4400 Rickenbacker Causeway; adult/child $39/30, parking $8; ◷9:30am-6pm, last entry 4:30pm) This 38-acre marine-life park excels in preserving, protecting and educating about aquatic creatures, and was one of the country's first places dedicated to sea life. There are dozens of shows and exhibits, including a tropical reef; the Shark Channel, with feeding presentations; and Discovery Bay, a natural mangrove habitat that serves as a refuge for rehabilitating rescued sea turtles. Check out the Pacific white-sided dolphins or West Indian manatees being nursed back to health; some are released. Frequent shows put gorgeous animals on display, including a massive killer whale, some precious dolphins and sea lions. The Seaquarium's newly opened Dolphin Harbor is an especially fun venue for watching marine mammals play and show off; it also offers swim-with-the-cetacean fun via its Encounter (adult $139, child five to nine years $99), Odyssey ($199) and, for total dolphin lovers only, Trainer for a Day ($495). Note that children under five cannot participate in the Encounter, people under 5ft 2in cannot participate in the Odyssey and children under three cannot enter the observation area. Read about the pros and cons of swimming with dolphins (see p238) before committing to these programs.

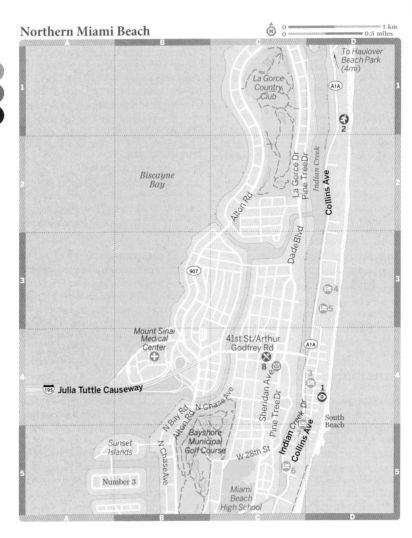

**CRANDON PARK**  Park
(Map p212; www.miamidade.gov/parks/parks/crandon_beach.asp; 6747 Crandon Blvd; per car $5; ☉sunrise-sunset) This 1200-acre park boasts Crandon Park Beach, a glorious but crowded beach that stretches for 3 miles. Much of the park consists of a dense coastal hammock (hardwood forest) and mangrove swamps. Pretty cabanas at the south end of the park can be rented by the day for $37.45. The two-mile-long beach here is clean, uncluttered with tourists, faces a lovely sweep of teal

goodness and is regularly named one of the best beaches in the USA. An on-site nature center hosts educational activities aimed at kids.

**BILL BAGGS CAPE FLORIDA STATE RECREATION AREA**  Park
(Map p212; www.floridastateparks.org/capeflorida; 1200 S Crandon Blvd; per car $8, pedestrian $2; ☉8am-sunset) If you don't make it to the Florida Keys, come to this park for a taste of their unique island ecosystems. The 494-acre space is a tangled clot of

tropical fauna and dark mangroves – look for the 'snorkel' roots that provide air for half-submerged mangrove trees – all interconnected by sandy trails and wooden boardwalks, and surrounded by miles of pale ocean. A concession shack rents kayaks, bikes, rollerblades, beach chairs and umbrellas. The nearby Cape Florida Lighthouse sits at the southern tip of the property.

## Little Havana

Little Havana's main thoroughfare is Calle Ocho (SW 8th St).

### MÁXIMO GÓMEZ PARK                    Park
(Map p219; SW 8th St at SW 15th Ave; ⏰9am-6pm) Little Havana's most evocative reminder of Old Cuba is Máximo Gómez Park, or 'Domino Park,' where the sound of elderly men trash-talking over games of chess is harmonized by the quick clak-clak of slapping dominoes. The jarring backtrack, plus the heavy smell of cigars and a sunrise-bright mural of the 1993 Summit of the Americas, combine to make Máximo Gómez one of the most sensory sites in Miami.

### CUBAN MEMORIALS          Monuments
(Map p219) The two blocks of SW 13th Ave south of Calle Ocho contain a series of monuments to Cuban and Cuban-American heroes, including those that died in the Cuban War of Independence and anti-Castro conflicts. The memorials include the **Eternal Torch in Honor** **of the 2506th Brigade** for the exiles who died during the Bay of Pigs Invasion; a huge **Cuba brass relief** depicting a map of Cuba, dedicated to the 'ideals of people who will never forget the pledge of making their Fatherland free'; a **José Martí memorial**; and a **Madonna statue**, which is supposedly illuminated by a shaft of holy light every afternoon. Bursting out of the island in the center of the boulevard is a massive ceiba tree, revered by followers of Santeria. The tree is an unofficial reminder of the poorer *Marielitos* (those who fled Cuba in the 1980 Mariel Boatlift) and successive waves of desperate-for-work Cubans, many of whom are *santeros* (Santeria practitioners) who have come to Miami since the 1980s.

## Coconut Grove

Coconut Grove, which attracts a mix of old hippies, middle-class and mall-going Miami and college students, unfolds along S Bayshore Dr as it hugs the shoreline.

### VIZCAYA MUSEUM &
### GARDENS                    Notable Building
(www.miamidade.gov/vizcaya; 3251 S Miami Ave; adult/child $12/5; ⏰museum 9:30am-4:30pm Wed-Mon) They call Miami the Magic City, and if it is, this Italian villa, the housing equivalent of a Fabergé egg, is its most fairy-tale-like residence. In 1916, industrialist James Deering started a long and storied Miami tradition by making a ton of money and building some ridiculously grandiose digs. He employed 1000 people (then 10% of the local population) for four years to fulfill his desire for a pad that looked centuries old. He was so obsessed with creating an atmosphere of old money that he had the house stuffed with 15th- to 19th-century furniture, tapestries, paintings and decorative arts; had a monogram fashioned for himself; and even had paintings of fake ancestors commissioned. The 30-acre grounds are full of splendid gardens and Florentine gazebos, and both the house and gardens are used for the display of rotating contemporary-art exhibi-

tions. It's located between Downtown and Coconut Grove, roughly where SW 32nd Rd intersects with Dixie Hwy and S Miami Ave.

## Coral Gables

The lovely city of Coral Gables, filled with Mediterranean-style buildings, is bordered by Calle Ocho to the north, Sunset Dr to the south, Ponce de León Blvd to the east and Red Rd to the west.

**BILTMORE HOTEL**  Notable Building
(www.biltmorehotel.com; 1200 Anastasia Ave) In the most opulent neighborhood of one of the showiest cities in the world, the Biltmore peers down her nose and says, 'hrmph.' It's one of the greatest of the grand hotels of the American Jazz Age, and if this joint were a fictional character from a novel, it'd be, without question, Jay Gatsby. Al Capone had a speakeasy on-site, and the Capone Suite is still haunted by the spirit of Fats Walsh, who was murdered here (for more ghost de-

tails, join in the weekly storytelling in the lobby, 7pm Thursday). Back in the day, imported gondolas transported celebrity guests like Judy Garland and the Vanderbilts around because, of course, there was a private canal system out the back. It's gone now, but the largest hotel pool in the continental USA, which resembles a sultan's water garden from *One Thousand & One Nights,* is still here. The lobby is the real kicker: grand, gorgeous, yet surprisingly not gaudy, it's like a child's fantasy of an Arabian castle crossed with a Medici villa.

**LOWE ART MUSEUM**  Museum
(www.lowemuseum.org; 1301 Stanford Dr; adult/student $10/5; ⏲10am-4pm Tue-Sat, from noon Sun) Your love of the Lowe, located on the campus of the University of Miami, depends on your taste in art. If you're into modern and contemporary works, it's good. If you're into the art and archaeology of cultures from Asia, Africa and the South Pacific, it's great. And if you're

**Left:** The grand, historic Biltmore Hotel (p202), Coral Gables;
**Below:** Sculpture at the Bass Museum of Art (p198).
(LEFT) ALAMY/PHILIPUS ©; (BELOW) ALAMY/GREGORY WRONA ©

into pre-Columbian and Mesoamerican art, it's simply fantastic; the artifacts are stunning and thoughtfully strung out along an easy-to-follow narrative thread. That isn't to discount the lovely permanent collection of Renaissance and baroque art, Western sculpture from the 18th to 20th centuries, and paintings by Gauguin, Picasso and Monet – they're also gorgeous. To get here, look for the entrance to the University of Miami at Stanford Dr off Dixie Hwy.

### VENETIAN POOL Pool

(www.coralgablesvenetianpool.com; 2701 De Soto Blvd; adult/child $11/7.35; ⏱10am-4:30pm; 👪) Just imagine: it's 1923, tons of rock has been quarried for one of the most beautiful neighborhoods in Miami, but now an ugly gash sits in the middle of the village. What to do? How about pump the irregular hole full of water, mosaic and tile up the whole affair, and make it look like a Roman emperor's aquatic playground? Result: one of the few pools listed on the National Register of Historic Places, a wonderland of coral rock caves, cascading waterfalls, a palm-fringed island and Venetian-style moorings. Take a swim and follow in the foot(fin?)steps of stars like Esther Williams and Johnny 'Tarzan' Weissmuller. Opening hours vary depending on the season, so check the website for details.

## Greater Miami – South

### METROZOO Zoo

(www.miamimetrozoo.com; 12400 SW 152nd St; adult/child $16/12; ⏱9:30am-5:30pm, last admission 4pm) Miami's tropical weather makes strolling around the Metrozoo almost feel like a day in the wold. Look for Asian and African elephants, rare and regal Bengal tigers prowling in an evocative Hindu temple, pygmy hippos, Andean condors, a pack of hyenas, cute koalas, colobus monkeys, black rhinoceroses and a pair of Komodo dragons

Downtown Miami

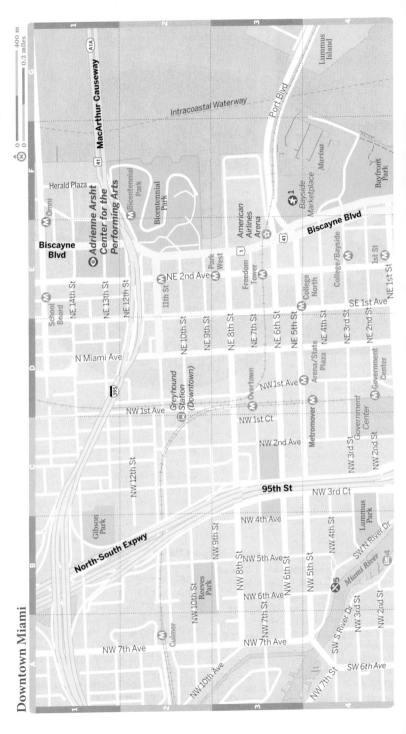

0 0
0 400 m
0 0.2 miles

MacArthur Causeway

Intracoastal Waterway

Herald Plaza

Omni

Adrienne Arsht Center for the Performing Arts

Biscayne Blvd

Bicentennial Park

Lummus Island

Port Blvd

Bayside Marketplace

Marina

Bayfront Park

American Airlines Arena

Biscayne Blvd

College/Bayside

School Board

NE 14th St
NE 13th St
NE 12th St

N Miami Ave

Park West

11th St
NE 2nd Ave

Freedom Tower

College North

SE 1st Ave

1st St

NE 1st St

NE 10th St
NE 9th St
NE 8th St
NE 7th St
NE 6th St
NE 5th St

NE 3rd St
NE 2nd St

Greyhound Station (Downtown)

NW 1st Ave

Overtown

NW 1st Ave

NW 1st Ct

NW 2nd Ave

Arena/State Plaza

NE 4th St

Metromover

Government Center

Government Center

NW 12th St

Gibson Park

North-South Expwy

95th St

NW 3rd Ct

NW 3rd St
NW 2nd St

NW 4th Ave

Lummus Park

NW 9th St

NW 8th St
NW 5th Ave
NW 6th St

NW 5th St

NW 4th St

Miami River

SW N River Dr

NW 3rd St
NW 2nd St

NW 10th St

Reeves Park

NW 6th Ave

SW S River Dr

SW 6th Ave

Culmer

NW 7th Ave

NW 7th Ave

NW 7th St

NW 10th Ave

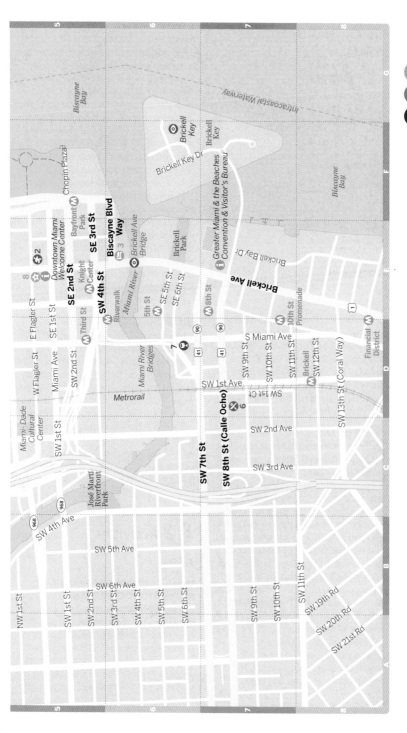

Biscayne Bay

Intracoastal Waterway

Brickell Key

Brickell Key

Brickell Key Dr

Biscayne Bay

Chopin Plaza

Downtown Miami Welcome Center

Bayfront Park

Knight Center

SE 2nd St

SE 3rd St

E Flagler St

SE 1st St

SW 4th St

Biscayne Blvd

Brickell Ave Bridge

Third St

Miami River

Riverwalk

W Flagler St

Miami Ave

SW 2nd St

Brickell Ave Way

Brickell Park

Greater Miami & the Beaches Convention & Visitor's Bureau

Brickell Ave

5th St

SE 5th St

SE 6th St

8th St

Brickell Bay Dr

SW 1st St

SW 1st Ave

Miami River Bridges

Metrorail

S Miami Ave

SW 9th St

SW 10th St

SW 11th St

SW 12th St

Brickell

10th St Promenade

Financial District

SW 13th St (Coral Way)

Miami-Dade Cultural Center

SW 1st St

José Martí Riverfront Park

SW 4th Ave

SW 5th Ave

SW 6th Ave

SW 7th St

SW 8th St (Calle Ocho)

SW 1st Ct

SW 2nd Ave

SW 3rd Ave

NW 1st St

SW 1st St

SW 2nd St

SW 3rd St

SW 4th St

SW 5th St

SW 6th St

SW 9th St

SW 10th St

SW 11th St

SW 19th Rd

SW 20th Rd

SW 21st Rd

205

## Downtown Miami

from Indonesia. Keep your eyes peeled for informative zookeeper talks in front of some exhibits. For a quick overview (and because the zoo is so big), hop on the Safari Monorail; it departs every 20 minutes. There's a glut of grounds tours available, and kids will love feeding the Samburu giraffes ($2).

**JUNGLE ISLAND**  Zoo
(www.jungleisland.com; 1111 Parrot Jungle Trail, off MacArthur Causeway, Watson Island; adult/child/senior $33/25/31; ⊙10am-5pm, to 6pm Sat & Sun) Jungle Island, packed with tropical birds, alligators, orangutans, chimps, lemurs, a (wait for it, *Napoleon Dynamite* fans) liger (a cross between a lion and a tiger) and a Noah's Ark of other animals, is a ton of fun. It's one of those places kids (justifiably) beg to go, so just give up and prepare for some bright-feathered, bird-poopie-scented fun in this artificial, self-contained jungle. The waterfront facility, lushly landscaped and using a minimum of pesticides, is pretty impressive, thanks in part to the flamingos, macaws, cockatoos and other parrots, flying about in outdoor aviaries. The cape penguin colony is especially cute.

**MONKEY JUNGLE**  Zoo
(www.monkeyjungle.com; 14805 SW 216th St; adult/child/senior $30/24/28; ⊙9:30am-5pm, last admission 4pm) The Monkey Jungle brochures have a tag line: 'Where humans are caged and monkeys run free.' And, indeed, you'll be walking through screened-in trails, with primates swinging freely, screeching and chattering all around you. It's incredibly fun, and just a bit odorous, especially on warm days (well, most days). In 1933, animal behaviorist Joseph du Mond released six monkeys into the wild. Today, their descendants live here with orangutans, chimpanzees and lowland gorilla. The big show of the day takes place at feeding time, when crab-eating monkeys and southeast Asian macaques dive into the pool for fruit and other treats. There's also a lovely aviary for clouds of beautiful rescued parrots.

**MIAMI CHILDREN'S MUSEUM**  Museum
(www.miamichildrensmuseum.org; 980 MacArthur Causeway, Watson Island; admission $15; ⊙10am-6pm) This museum, located between South Beach and downtown Miami, isn't exactly a museum. It feels more like an uber-playhouse, with areas for kids to practice all sorts of adult activities – banking and food shopping, caring for pets, reporting scoops as a TV news anchor in a studio, and acting as a local cop or firefighter. Be forewarned: this place is a zoo on rainy days.

# 🏃 Activities

## Biking

**MIAMI-DADE COUNTY PARKS & RECREATION DEPARTMENT**  Cycling
(📞305-755-7800; www.miamidade.gov/parks-masterplan/bike_trails_map.asp) Leads frequent eco-bike tours through parklands and along waterfront paths, and offers a list of traffic-free cycling paths on its website. For less strenuous rides, try the side roads of South Beach or the shady

streets of Coral Gables and Coconut Grove. Some good trails:

**Old Cutler Bike Path** Starts at the end of Sunset Dr in Coral Gables and leads through Coconut Grove to Matheson Hammock Park and Fairchild Tropical Garden.

**Rickenbacker Causeway** This route takes you up and over the bridge to Key Biscayne for an excellent workout combined with gorgeous water views.

**Oleta River State Park** (3400 NE 163rd St) Has a challenging dirt trail with hills for off-road adventures.

## Kayaking & Windsurfing

Kayaking through mangroves, one of the coolest ecosystems on Earth, is magical: all those slender roots kiss the water while the ocean breeze cools your flanks.

**Blue Moon Miami**  Water Sports
( 305-957-3040; www.bluemoonmiami.com) Offers single kayaks ($18 per 1½ hours, $25 per three hours), tandem kayaks ($25.50 per 1½ hours, $40 per three hours) and bike rental ($18 per 1½ hours, $25 per three hours).

**Sailboards Miami**  Water Sports
( 305-361-7245; www.windsurfingmiami.com; 1 Rickenbacker Causeway; per hr s/tandem $15/20) Rents kayaks. You can purchase 10 hours' worth of kayaking for $90. This is also a good spot to rent (and learn how to operate) windsurfing gear (lessons from $35, gear per hour $30).

Also, try these places:

**Haulover Beach Park** (10800 Collins Ave)

**Bill Baggs Cape Florida State Recreation Area** (Map p212; www.floridastateparks.org/capeflorida; 1200 S Crandon Blvd)

## Yoga

All of the following studios offer a large range of classes; bring your own mats.

**Green Monkey Yoga** (Map p208;  305-669-5959; www.greenmonkey.net; 3301 NE 1st Ave, Miami; classes from $20) Midtown.

**Prana Yoga Center** (  305-567-9812; www.pranayogamiami.com; 247 Malaga Ave, Coral Gables; 1/2/5 class pass $18/34/50) In Coral Gables.

**Bikram Yoga Miami Beach** (Map p194; 305-448-3332; www.bikramyogamiami.com; 235 11th St, Miami Beach; one day/week $25/50) South Beach.

Windsurfing in Florida.

ALAMY/BABETTE FRENCH ©

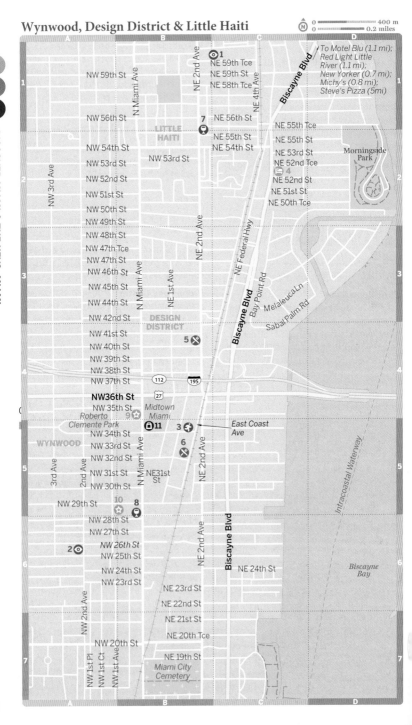

## Wynwood, Design District & Little Haiti

#  Tours

**Art Deco Welcome Center** Walking
(Map p194; ☎ 305-531-3484; 1001 Ocean Dr, South Beach; guided tour per adult/child/senior $20/free/15; ⏱10:30am Fri-Wed, 6:30pm Thu) Tells the stories and history behind the art-deco buildings in South Beach, either with a lively guide from the Miami Design Preservation League, or a well-presented recording and map for self-guided walks (try the guides). Tours last 90 minutes.

**Dr Paul George** Walking
( ☎ 305-375-1621; www.historymiami.org/tours/walking-tours; $25-42) For great historical perspective, call the lively Dr George, a historian for HistoryMiami. George leads several popular tours – including those that focus on Stiltsville, Miami crime, Little Havana and Coral Gables at twilight – between September and late June; hours vary. Dr George also offers private tours by appointment.

**Urban Tour Host** Walking
(Map p204; ☎ 305-416-6868; www.miamiculturaltours.com; 25 SE 2nd Ave, ste 1048; tours from $20) Has a rich program of custom tours that provide face-to-face interaction in all of Miami's neighborhoods. A deluxe city tour includes Coral Gables, South Beach, downtown Miami and Coconut Grove.

#  Sleeping

What sets South Beach apart – what defines it as a travel destination – is the deco district, and the deco district's backbone is hotels. This is one of the largest concentrations of boutique hotels in the country.

## South Beach (1st to 11th Streets)

**PELICAN HOTEL** Boutique Hotel $$$
(Map p194; ☎ 305-673-3373; www.pelicanhotel.com; 826 Ocean Dr; r $225-345, ste from $1500; ✳🕸) When the owners of Diesel jeans purchased the Pelican in 1999, they started scouring garage sales for just the right ingredients to fuel a mad experiment: 30 themed rooms that come off like a fantasy-suite hotel dipped in hip. From the cowboy-hipster chic of 'High Corral, OK Chaparral' to the jungly electric tiger stripes of 'Me Tarzan, You Vain,' all the rooms are completely different (although all have beautiful recycled-oak floors), fun and even come with their own 'suggested soundtrack.'

**HOTEL ST AUGUSTINE** Boutique Hotel $$
(Map p194; ☎ 305-532-0570; www.hotelstaugustine.com; 347 Washington Ave; r $180-280; 🅿✳🕸) Wood that's blonder than Barbie and a crisp-and-clean deco theme combine to create one of SoFi's most elegant

A myriad hotels line Collins Ave, Miami.

CORBIS/RAIMUND KOCH©

yet stunningly modern sleeps. Color schemes blend beige, caramel, white and cream – the sense is the hues are flowing into one eye-smoothing palette. The familiar, warm service is the cherry on top for this hip-and-homey standout, although the soothing lighting and glass showers – that turn into personal steam rooms at the flick of a switch – are pretty appealing too.

### SENSE SOUTH BEACH
Boutique Hotel $$$

(Map p194; ☎ 305-538-5529; www.sensesobe. com; 400 Ocean Dr; r $240-280; P❄🖥🏊🚶) The Sense is fantastically atmospheric – smooth white walls disappearing behind melting blue views of South Beach, wooden paneling arranged around lovely sharp angles that feel inviting, rather than imposing, and rooms that contrast whites and dark grays into straight duochromatic cool. Pop art hangings and slender furnishings round out the Macbook-esque air. The staff are extremely helpful – warm even – which is eminently refreshing.

### LORDS HOTEL
Boutique Hotel $$

(Map p194; ☎ 877-448-4754; www.lordsouth-beach.com; 1120 Collins Ave; r $120-240, ste $330-540; P❄🖥) The epicenter of South Beach's gay scene is this cream puff of a hotel, with rooms decked out in lemony yellow and whites offset by graphic and pop art. A giant polar bear stands to greet you in the lobby, while out the back the boys gather around a pool and prepare to party. As hip as the Lords is, it doesn't affect any attitude; you'll be at ease here, unless you sit the wrong way on the weird studded chairs situated around the bar.

### FASHIONHAUS
Boutique Hotel $$

(Map p194; ☎ 305-673-2550; www.fashion-haushotel.com; 534 Washington Ave; r $130-250 P❄🖥🏊) The Fashionhaus doesn't just sound like a Berlin avant-garde theater – it kinda feels like one, with its smooth geometric furnishings, 48 individualized rooms decked out in original artwork, from abstract expressionism to washed out photography, and its general blending of comfort, technology and design. Popular with Europeans, fashionistas, artists (and

European fashionista artists) and those who just want to emulate that lifestyle.

**CHESTERFIELD HOTEL** Boutique Hotel **$$**
**(Map p194; ☎305-531-5831; www.thechesterfieldhotel.com; 855 Collins Ave; r $140-220, ste $280-520; P ❄ 🛜)** Hip-hop gets jiggy with zebra stripes on the curtains and cushions in the small lobby, which turns into the site of one of the hoppin'-est happy hours on Collins when the sun goes down. Leave a tip for the giant African statue while you're draining that mojito. Rooms mix up dark wood furniture overlaid with bright-white beds and vaguely tropical colors swathed throughout.

**CLINTON HOTEL** Boutique Hotel **$$**
**(Map p194; ☎305-938-4040; www.clintonsouthbeach.com; 825 Washington Ave; r $140-396; P ❄ 🛜 🏊)** Washington Ave is the quietest of the three main drags in SoBe, but the Clinton doesn't mind. This joint knows it would be the hottest girl in the most crowded party, with her blue velveteen banquettes and uber-contemporary metal ceiling fans. The tiny sunporches in the Zen rooms are perfect for breakfast or an evening cocktail.

## South Beach (11th to 23rd Streets)

**THE STANDARD** Boutique Hotel **$$$**
**(☎305-673-1717; www.standardhotels.com/miami; 40 Island Ave; r $170-280, ste from $480; P ❄ 🛜 🏊)** Look for the upside-down 'Standard' sign on the old Lido building on Belle Island (between South Beach and downtown Miami) and you'll find the Standard – which is anything but. This excellent boutique blends hipster funk with South Beach sex, and the result is a '50s motel gone glam. There are organic wooden floors, raised white beds, and gossamer curtains, which open onto a courtyard of earthly delights, including a heated hammam (Turkish bath). The crowd, which feels like the Delano kids with a bit more maturity, gathers to flirt and gawk. Shuttles ferry guests to the Sagamore every 30 minutes, so you're never too isolated from the scene – unless you want to be, and given the grace of this place, we'd totally understand why. Show up on Sunday afternoons for the coolest outdoor bingo/bar/barbecue experience in the city.

**SHORE CLUB** Boutique Hotel **$$$**
**(Map p194; ☎305-695-3100; www.shoreclub.com; 1901 Collins Ave; r $270-470, ste from $1400; P ❄ @ 🏊)** Imagine a Zen ink-brush painting; what's beautiful isn't what's there, but what gets left out. If you could turn that sort of art into a hotel room, it might look like the stripped-down yet serene digs of the Shore Club. Yeah, yeah: it has the 400-thread-count Egyptian cotton sheets, Mexican sandstone floors etc; a lot of hotels in SoBe lay claim to similar luxury lists. What the Shore Club does like no other hotel is arrange these elements into a greater whole that's impressive in its understatement; the aesthetic is compelling because it comes across as an afterthought.

**CARDOZO HOTEL** Boutique Hotel **$$$**
**(Map p194; ☎305-535-6500, 800-782-6500; www.cardozohotel.com; 1300 Ocean Dr; r $220-290, ste $320-460; P ❄ 🛜)** The Cardozo and its neighbor, the Carlyle, were the first deco hotels saved by the Miami Design Preservation League, and in the case of the Cardozo, we think they saved the best first. Owner Gloria Estefan, whose videos are looped on flat-screen mini-TVs in the lobby, likely agrees. It's the combination of the usual contemporary sexiness (white walls, hardwood floors, high-thread-count sheets) and playful embellishments: leopard-print details, handmade furniture and a general sense that, yes, you are cool if you stay here, but you don't have to flaunt it. Oh – remember the 'hair gel' scene in *There's Something About Mary*? Filmed here.

**CADET** Boutique Hotel **$$**
**(Map p194; ☎305-672-6688; www.cadethotel.com; 1701 James Ave; r $170-280, ste $340-530; P ❄ 🛜)** The Cadet wins our award for most creative embellishments in its

# Key Biscayne

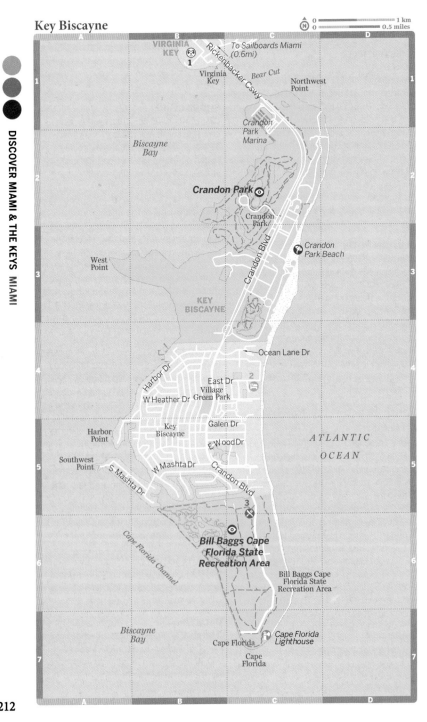

0 _____ 1 km
0 _____ 0.5 miles

VIRGINIA KEY
1
To Sailboards Miami (0.6mi)
Virginia Key
Bear Cut
Rickenbacker Cswy
Northwest Point
Biscayne Bay
Crandon Park Marina
**Crandon Park**
Crandon Park
Crandon Blvd
Crandon Park Beach
West Point
KEY BISCAYNE
Ocean Lane Dr
Harbor Dr
East Dr
Village Green Park
2
W Heather Dr
Key Biscayne
Galen Dr
Harbor Point
E Wood Dr
ATLANTIC OCEAN
Southwest Point
S Mashta Dr
W Mashta Dr
Crandon Blvd
3
**Bill Baggs Cape Florida State Recreation Area**
Cape Florida Channel
Bill Baggs Cape Florida State Recreation Area
Biscayne Bay
Cape Florida Lighthouse
Cape Florida
Cape Florida

rooms. From paper lanterns hanging from ceilings to furry throw rugs; from clamshell designs encapsulating large mirrors to classical Asian furniture and, as always, a great art deco facade, this spot has the aesthetics right. Check out the back, shaded veranda, lifted from a fantasy idea of what a plantation should feel like.

**TOWNHOUSE HOTEL**  Boutique Hotel $$
(Map p194; ☏ 305-534-3800; www.townhouse hotel.com; 150 20th St at Collins Ave; r $145-195, ste from $350; ❄ 🛜 ☻) You'd think the Townhouse was designed by the guy who styled the iPod but no, it was Jonathan Morr and India Mahdavi who fashioned a cool white lobby and igloo-like rooms with random scarlet accents and a breezy, white rooftop lounge. Who needs mints on pillows when the Townhouse provides beach balls?

**W HOTEL**  Resort $$$
(Map p194; ☏ 305-938-3000; www.starwood hotels.com; 2201 Collins Ave; r $460-510, ste $660-1100; P ❄ 🛜 ☻) There's an astounding variety of rooms available at the South Beach outpost of the famous W chain, which brings the whole W-brand mix of luxury, hipness and overblown cool to Miami Beach in a big way. The 'spectacular studios' balance long panels of reflective glass with cool tablets of cippolino marble; the Oasis suite lets in so much light you'd think the sun had risen in your room; the Penthouse may as well be the setting of an MTV video (and given the sort of celebrities who stay here, that assessment might not be far off). The at-

tendant bars, restaurants, clubs and pool built into this complex are some of the most well-regarded on the beach.

**DELANO HOTEL**  Boutique Hotel $$$
(Map p194; ☏ 305-672-2000; www.delano-hotel. com; 1685 Collins Ave; r $380-540, ste $885-1400; P ❄ 🛜 ☻) The Delano opened in the 1990s and immediately started ruling the South Beach roost. If there's a quintessential 'I'm too sexy for this song' South Beach moment, it's when you walk into the Delano's lobby, which has all the excess of an over-budgeted theater set. 'Magic mirrors' in the halls disclose weather info, tide charts and inspirational quotes. The pool area resembles the courtyard of a Disney princess's palace and includes a giant chess set; there are floor-to-ridiculously-high-ceiling curtains in the two-story waterfront rooms; and the bedouin tent cabanas are outfitted with flat-screen TVs. Rooms are almost painfully white and bright, all long, smooth lines, reflective surfaces and sexy, modern, luxurious amenities.

**AQUA HOTEL**  Boutique Hotel $$
(Map p194; ☏ 305-538-4361; www.aquamiami. com; 1530 Collins Ave; r $150-180, ste from $200; P ❄ 🛜 ☻) A front desk made of shiny surfboard sets the mellow tone at this former motel – the old, family kind where the rooms are set around a pool. That old-school vibe barely survives under the soft glare of aqua spotlights and an alfresco lounging area, popular with the mostly gay clientele. The sleekness of the rooms is offset by quirky furniture, like a sumptuous chair made of spotted cowhide.

## Northern Miami Beach

**CIRCA 39**  Boutique Hotel $
(Map p200; ☏ 305-538-3900; www.circa39. com; 3900 Collins Ave; r $90-150; ❄ @ ☻) If you love South Beach style but loathe South Beach attitude, Circa has got your back. The lobby, with its multicolored light board, molded furniture and wacky embellishments, is one of the funkiest in Miami. The hallways are low-lit under sexy red lamps and the icy-blue-and-white rooms are hip enough for the most exclusive scenesters (although c frowns

on folk who act like snobs). Be you a family, a gay person or just someone who loves laid-back fun, this hotel welcomes all. The buy-in-advance web rates are phenomenal – you can find deals here for under $80.

**INDIAN CREEK HOTEL**  Boutique Hotel $
(Map p200; ☏ 305-531-2727; www.indiancre ekhotel.com; 2727 Indian Creek Dr; from r $90; ✳ ❄ 🛜) Get your room key – attached to a plastic alligator – and walk through the old Miami lobby, spruced up with souvenir-stand schlock, to your comfortable, earthy-warm digs. Or wander out to the surprisingly modern pool, where happy, sexy people are ready to have a good time. Mix in friendly staff and an easy stroll to the boardwalk, and you've got a classic boutique hotel.

**RED SOUTH BEACH**  Boutique Hotel $$
(Map p200; ☏ 800-528-0823; www.redsouth beach.com; 3010 Collins Ave; r $130-200; ✳ 🛜 ❄) Red is indeed the name of the game, from the cushions on the sleek

chairs in the lobby to the flashes dancing around the marble pool to deep, blood-crimson headboards and walls wrapping you in warm sexiness in the small but beautiful guest rooms. The Red is excellent value for money and come evening the pool/bar complex is a great place to unwind and meet fellow guests.

**FONTAINEBLEAU**  Resort $$$
(Map p200; ☏ 800-548-8886; www.fontaineb leau.com; 4441 Collins Ave; r $369-461, ste $551-861; 🅿 ✳ 🛜 ❄) The 1200-room Fontainebleau opened in 1954, when it became a celeb-sunning spot. Numerous renovations have added beachside cabanas, seven tennis courts, a grand ballroom, a shopping mall and a fabulous swimming pool. The rooms have a mid-century modern vibe and are surprisingly bright and cheerful – we expected more hard-edged attempts to be cool, but the sunny disposition of these chambers is a welcome surprise.

**Left:** Night scene along Miami's Ocean Drive (p196); **Below:** Dancers at the Calle Ocho Festival in Little Havana (p201).
(LEFT) CORBIS/OCEAN ©; (BELOW) ALAMY/JULIET FERGUSON ©;

### EDEN ROC RENAISSANCE
Resort $$$

(Map p200; ☎305-531-0000, 800-327-8337; www.edenrocmiami.com; 4525 Collins Ave; r from $310, ste from $430; P❄☎☎) The Roc's immense inner lobby draws inspiration from the Rat Pack glory days of Miami Beach cool, and rooms in the New Ocean Tower boast lovely views over the Intracoastal Waterway. All the digs here have smooth, modern embellishments and amenities ranging from mp3 players to HDTV, ergonomic furniture and turn-down service, among others.

## Downtown Miami

### MIAMI RIVER INN
B&B $$

(Map p204; ☎305-325-0045, 800-468-3589; www.miamiriverinn.com; 119 SW South River Dr; r $99-300; P❄☎) Cute mom-and-pop B&Bs stuffed full of antique furniture, pretty-as-lace gardens and a general 'Aw, thanks for breakfast' vibe are comparatively rare in Miami. The River Inn, listed

on the National Register of Historic Places, bucks this trend, with charming New England–style rooms, friendly service and one of the best libraries of Miami literature in the city. In a place where every hotel can feel like a loud experiment in graphic design, this relaxing watercolor invites you onto the back porch.

### EPIC
Hotel $$$

(Map p204; ☎305-424-5226; www.epichotel.com; 270 Biscayne Blvd; r $250-510; P❄☎☎) Epic indeed! This massive Kimpton hotel is one of the more attractive options downtown and it possesses a coolness cred that could match any spot on Miami Beach. Of particular note is the outdoor pool and sun deck, which overlooks a gorgeous sweep of Brickell and the surrounding condo canyons. The rooms are outfitted in designer-chic furnishings and some have similarly beautiful views of greater Miami-Dade. There's an onsite spa and bar that gives this spot a bit of youthful energy that's lacking in other corporate-style Downtown hotels.

## Key Biscayne

### SILVER SANDS BEACH RESORT
Resort $$

(Map p212; ☎305-361-5441; www.silversands beachresort.com; 301 Ocean Dr; r $169-189, cottage $279-349; P ❄ ☲) Silver Sands: aren't you cute, with your one-story, stucco tropical tweeness? How this little, Old Florida–style independent resort has survived amid the corporate competition is beyond us, but it's definitely a warm, homey spot for those seeking some intimate, individual attention – to say nothing of the sunny courtyard, garden area and outdoor pool.

## Coral Gables

### BILTMORE HOTEL
Hotel $$$

(☎305-913-3158, 800-727-1926; www.biltmore hotel.com; 1200 Anastasia Ave; r $240-400, ste from $1200; P ❄ 🛜 ☲ ♿) Though the Biltmore's standard rooms can be small, a stay here is a chance to sleep in one of the great laps of US luxury. The grounds are so palatial it would take a solid week to explore everything the Biltmore has to offer – we highly recommend reading a book in the Romanesque/Arabian Nights opulent lobby, sunning underneath enormous columns and taking a dip in the largest hotel pool in the continental USA.

### HOTEL ST MICHEL
Hotel $$

(☎305-444-1666; www.hotelstmichel.com; 162 Alcazar Ave; r $125-220; P ❄ 🛜 ♿) The Michel is more Metropole than Miami, and we mean that as a compliment. The old-world wooden fixtures, refined sense of tweedy style and dinner-jacket ambience don't get in the way of friendly service. The lovely restaurant and cool bar-lounge are as elegant as the hotel they occupy.

# Eating

Miami is a major immigrant entrepôt and a place that loves showing off its wealth. Thus you get a good mix of cheap ethnic eateries and high-quality top-end cuisine here.

## South Beach (1st to 11th Streets)

### TAP TAP
Haitian $$

(Map p194; ☎305-672-2898; www.taptaprestaurant.com; 819 5th St; mains $9-20; ◷noon-11pm Mon-Thu, to midnight Fri & Sat) In Haiti, tap-taps are brightly colored pickup trucks turned public taxis, and their tropi-psychedelic paint scheme inspires the decor at this excellent Haitian eatery. No Manhattan-style, South Beach Lounge this – here you dine under bright murals of Papa Legba, guardian of the dead, emerging from

The Venetian Pool (p203).
CORBIS/DAVE G. HOUSER ©

CORBIS/MICHELE EVE SANDBERG ©

# Don't Miss Jimbo's

How to describe **Jimbo's** in Virginia Key? This bar...no, shrimp shack...no, smoked fish house...no, 24-hour trailer park bonfire...well, whatever. A series of dilapidated river shacks and a boccie court has been, for decades, its own version of Old Florida. Other flicks filmed here include *Ace Ventura, True Lies* and the cinematic masterpiece, *Porky's 2*. But today the shacks have been claimed as the set pieces.

## THINGS YOU NEED TO KNOW
www.jimbosplace.com; Duck Lake Rd; ☉sunrise-sunset

a Port-au-Prince cemetery. Meals are a happy marriage of West African, French and Caribbean: spicy pumpkin soup, snapper in a scotch bonnet lime sauce, curried goat and charcoal-grilled Turks and Caicos conch. Make sure you try the Mayi Moulen, a signature side of cornmeal smothered in a rich bean sauce – bloody delicious! If you need some liquid courage, shoot some Barbancourt rum, available in several grades (all strong).

**GRAZIE** Italian $$$
(Map p194; ☎305-673-1312; www.grazieital-iancuisine.com; 702 Washington Ave; mains $19-34; ☉noon-3pm Mon-Fri, 6pm-midnight daily) Thanks indeed; Grazie is top class

and comfortably old-school Northern Italian. There's a distinct lack of gorgeous, clueless waitstaff and unwise menu experimentation. Instead there's attentive service, solid and delicious mains, and extremely decent prices given the quality of the dining and high-end nature of the location. The porcini risotto is simple in construction yet deeply complex in execution – one of the best Italian dishes on the beach.

**PUERTO SAGUA** Cuban $
(Map p194; ☎305-673-1115; 700 Collins Ave; mains $6-17; ☉7:30am-2am) There's a secret colony of older working-class Cubans and construction workers hidden among

South Beach's sex-and-flash, and evidently, they eat here (next to a Benetton). Puerto Sagua challenges the US diner with this reminder: Cubans can greasy-spoon with the best of them. Portions of favorites such as *picadillo* (spiced ground beef with rice, beans and plantains) are stupidly enormous. The Cuban coffee here is not for the faint of heart – strong stuff.

### 11TH STREET DINER
Diner $

(Map p194; www.eleventhstreetdiner.com; 1065 Washington Ave; mains $8-15; ⏱24hr) You've seen the art deco landmarks. Now eat in one: a Pullman-car diner trucked down from Wilkes-Barre, Pennsylvania, as sure a slice of Americana as a *Leave it to Beaver* marathon. If you've been drinking all night, we'll split a three-egg omelet with you and the other drunkies at 6am – if there's a diner where you can replicate Edward Hopper's *Nighthawks,* it's here.

## South Beach (11th to 23rd Streets)

### OSTERIA DEL TEATRO
Italian $$

(Map p194; ☎305-538-7850; www.osteriadelteatromiami.com; 1443 Washington Ave; mains $16-31; ⏱6-11pm Mon-Thu, to 1am weekends) There are few things to swear by but the specials board of Osteria, one of the oldest and best Italian restaurants in Greater Miami, ought to be one. When you get here, let the gracious Italian waiters seat you, coddle you and then basically order

for you off the board. They never pick wrong.

### BURGER & BEER JOINT
Burgers $

(Map p194; ☎305-531-1200; www.bnbjoint. com; 450 Lincoln Rd; mains $5.50-9; ⏱11:30am-midnight; ☝) Gourmet burgers. Microbrew beer. Clearly, the folks at B&B did their marketing research. Because who doesn't love both? Oh yes, vegetarians, you're catered to as well; the 'Dear Prudence.' a mix of portobello, red pepper, walnut pesto and zucchini fries will keep herbivores happy. Oh, there's a turkey and stuffing burger with gravy served *between turkey patties,* an ahi tuna burger, a patty of wagyu beef with foie gras...you get the idea. Did we mention the microbrew beer?

## Northern Miami Beach

### STEVE'S PIZZA
Pizza $

(☎305-233-4561; www.stevespizzas.net; 18063 Dixie Hwy; pizzas from $10; ⏱10:30am-11pm, to midnight weekends, 11am-11pm Sun) So many pizza chains compete for the attention of tourists in South Beach, but ask a Miami Beach local where to get the best pizza and they'll tell you about Steve's. This is New York–style pizza, thin crust and handmade with care and good ingredients. New branches of Steve's are opening elsewhere in Miami, all in decidedly non-touristy areas, which preserves that feeling of authenticity.

# Viernes Culturales (Cultural Fridays)

The Little Havana Arts District may not be Wynwood, but it does constitute an energetic little strip of galleries and studios (concentrated on 8th St between SW 15th Ave & SW 17th Ave) that house some of the best Latin American art in Miami. Rather than pop into each gallery, look around and feel pressure to buy, why not visit on the last Friday of each month for **Viernes Culturales** (www.viernesculturales.org). No wine-sipping art walk this; Cultural Fridays in Little Havana are like little carnival seasons, with music, old men in *guayaberas* (Cuban dress shirts) crooning to the stars and more booty-shaking than brie. Although there is also brie, and plenty of time to appreciate local art as all the Little Havana galleries throw open their doors.

# Little Havana

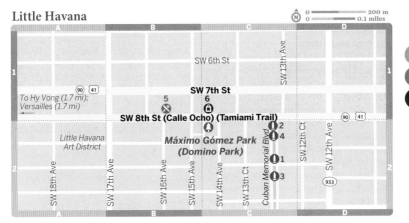

## Little Havana

**◎ Top Sights**

Máximo Gómez Park (Domino
Park) ....................................................C2

**◎ Sights**

1 Cuba Brass Relief ...............................C2
2 Eternal Torch in Honor of the
2506th Brigade..................................C2
3 José Martí Memorial..........................C2
4 Madonna Statue .................................C2

**⊗ Eating**

5 El Cristo ...............................................B1

**⊕ Shopping**

6 Little-Havana-To-Go ..........................C1

---

**ROASTER'S N TOASTERS**     Deli **$**
(Map p200; www.roastersntoasters.com; 525
Arthur Godfrey Rd; mains $8-16; ⊙6:30am-
3:30pm) Miami Beach has one of the
largest Jewish populations in the US,
so people here naturally expect quite a
lot out of their delis. Given the crowds
and the satisfied smiles of (well-fed)
customers, Roasters' n Toasters meets
the demanding standards of its target
demographic. It's all thanks to juicy deli
meat, fresh bread, crispy bagels and
warm *latkes* (potato pancakes). Sliders
(mini-sandwiches) are served on Jewish
challah bread, an innovation that's as
charming as it is tasty.

## Downtown Miami

**LA MOON**     Colombian **$**
(Map p204; www.lamoonrestaurantmiami.com;
144 SW 8th St; meals $6-15) Nothing – and
we're not necessarily saying this in a
good way – soaks up the beer like a
Colombian hot dog topped with eggs
and potato sticks. Or fried pork belly
and pudding. These delicacies are the
preferred food and drink of Miami's 24-
hour party people, and the best place for
this wicked fare is here, within stumbling
distance of bars like Tobacco Rd. To really fit in, order a *refajo:* Colombian beer
(Aguila) with Colombian soda (preferably the red one).

**GARCIA'S**     Seafood **$**
(Map p204; ☏305-375-0765; 398 NW River
Dr; mains $8-18; ⊙11am-9:30pm) Crowds of
Cuban office workers lunch at Garcia's,
which feels more like you're in a smug-
gler's seafood shack than the financial
district. Expect occasionally spotty
service (a bad thing), freshly caught-and-
cooked fish (a good thing) and pleasantly
seedy views of the Miami River.

## Wynwood, Design District & Little Haiti

**SEÑORA MARTINEZ** American $$$

(Map p208; ☎305-424-9079; www.sramartinez. com; 3252 NE 1st Ave; mains $13-30; ☺noon-3pm Tue-Fri, 6-11pm Tue-Thu, to midnight Fri & Sat, to 10pm Sun; ✈) At the time of our research, Señora Martinez was the most exciting top-end restaurant in Miami, pushing the boundaries of experimentation and plain good food. The menu is eclectic, with no one overriding regional influence, besides perhaps Miami, entrepôt that it is. Squid-ink risotto comes with *chimichurri* sauce; roasted bone marrow is scooped out next to pickled onions; duck sausage swims in port wine. The cocktail menu is as exciting as the food; with bartenders mixing up stuff like espresso tequila, fernet and honey, or rum, allspice, cider and maple syrup. Eat up, drink up, revel in your own decadent excess and hit the town.

**SUSTAIN** American $$$

(Map p208; ☎305-424-9079; www.sustain miami.com; 3252 NE 1st Ave; mains $13-30; ☺11:30am-3pm, 5-10:30pm; ✈) Sustain is one of the leading – and more affordable – purveyors of locally sourced, organi-cally grown, raised and caught food in the Miami area. The lovely dining room blends smooth white walls with warm wood paneling and rounded metallic edges. The food is fantastic; try the bright, meltingly textured fish sandwich or fried chicken swimming in creamy kale and barbecued beans. The menu changes with the sea-son. Vegetarians and vegans are always catered to, although carnivores will find plenty to enjoy as well.

## Key Biscayne

**BOATER'S GRILL** Seafood $$

(Map p212; ☎305-361-0080; 1200 S Crandon Blvd; mains $14-34; ☺9am-9pm) Located in Crandon Park, this waterfront restaurant (actually there's water below and all around) feels like a Chesapeake Bay sea house from up north, except the menu is packed with South Florida maritime goodness: stone crabs, mahimahi and lobster paella.

Restaurants along Miami's Ocean Drive (p196).

ALAMY/TRAVEL PICTURES ©

# Detour:
# Turkish Delight

Just because you enjoy a good back rub doesn't mean you need to go to some glitzy spa where they constantly play soft house music on a repetitive loop. Right? Why not head to a favorite 'hot' spot among folks who want a spa experience without the glamor, the **Russian & Turkish Baths** ( ☎305-867-8316; www.russianandturkishbaths.com; 5445 Collins Ave; ☺noon-midnight). Enter this little labyrinth of *banyas* (steam rooms) and there's a plethora of spa choices. You can be casually beaten with oak leaf brooms (for $40) called *venik* in a lava-hot spa (it's actually really relaxing...well, interesting anyway). There's Dead Sea salt and mud exfoliation ($50), plus the on-site cafe serves delicious borscht, blintzes, dark bread with smoked fish and, of course, beer.

## Little Havana

### HY VONG VIETNAMESE
### RESTAURANT
Vietnamese $

( ☎305-446-3674; www.hyvong.com; 3458 SW 8th; mains $7-22; ☺6-11pm Wed-Sun, closed mid-late Aug) In a neighborhood full of exiles from a communist regime, it makes sense to find a Vietnamese restaurant. And it's telling that despite all the great Latin food around, Little Havanans still wait hours for a seat here. Why? Because this great Vietnamese food (with little touches of Florida, like Florida-style mango marinade) combines quality produce with Southeast Asian spice and a penchant for rich flavors inherited from the French colonial past. Just be prepared to wait a long time for your culinary reward. Check the website to learn about Hy Vong's cooking classes. Hy Vong is on 8th St, located about 2 miles west of the heart of Calle Ocho.

### ISLAS CANARIAS
Cuban $

( ☎305-649-0440; 285 NW 27th Ave; mains $8-19; ☺7am-11pm) Islas may not look like much, sitting in a strip mall, but it serves some of the best Cuban in Miami. The *ropa vieja* (shredded beef) is delicious and there are nice Spanish touches on the menu (the owner's father is from the Canary Islands, hence the restaurant's name). Don't pass up the signature homemade chips, especially the ones cut from plantains.

### EL CRISTO
Cuban $

(Map p219; ☎305-643-9992; 1543 SW 8th St; mains $6-18; ☺7am-11pm) A popular hangout among locals, the down-to-earth El Cristo has options from all over the Spanish-speaking world. Lots of people say it's as good as Calle Ocho gets. The menu has daily specials, but the standout is fish – try it fried for a local version of fish 'n' chips, or take away some excellent fish empanadas or *croquettes* (deep-fried in breadcrumbs). The outdoor area is an excellent perch for enjoying 8th St eye candy.

### VERSAILLES
Cuban $

( ☎305-444-0240; 3555 SW 8th St; mains $5-20; ☺8am-2am) Versailles (ver-*sigh*-yay) is an institution, and a lot of younger Cubans will tell you it's an overrated institution. We disagree – the food may not be the best Cuban in Miami, but it's certainly quite good (the ground beef in a gratin sauce is particularly good). And besides, older Cubans and Miami's Latin political elite still love coming here, so you've got a real chance to rub elbows with a who's who of Miami's most prominent Latin citizens. It's located 2 miles west of central Calle Ocho.

## Coconut Grove

### XIXON
Spanish $$

( ☎305-854-9350; 1801 SW 22nd St; tapas $8-15; ☺11am-10pm Mon-Thu, to 11pm Fri & Sat, closed Sun) It takes a lot to stand out in Miami's

# Miami for Children

Well really, it's Florida, folks; your kids will be catered to. Many of the attractions run toward animal experiences, starting with the **Miami Seaquarium** (p199), which boasts a large collection of crocodiles, dolphins and sea lions and a killer whale, most of which perform. Next comes the **Metrozoo** (p203), a 740-acre zoo with plenty of natural habitats (thank you, tropical weather). Should your little ones like colorful animal shows, the outdoors and the smell of animal poo in all its myriad varieties, Miami shall not disappoint. **Monkey Jungle** (p206) acts as a habitat for endangered species and is everything you'd expect: screeching primates, covered pathways and a grand finale show of crab monkeys diving for fruit. **Jungle Island** (p206), on the other hand, tends to entertain with brilliant bird shows. Next door is the new **Miami Children's Museum** (p206), an indoor playland where youngsters can try out the roles of TV anchor, banker and supermarket customer, among others.

crowded tapas-spot stakes. Having a Basque-country butcher-and-baker-turned-hip interior is a good start. Bread that has a crackling crust and a soft center, delicate explosions of *bacalao* (codfish) fritters and the best eels cooked in garlic we've ever eaten secures Xixon's status as a top tapas contender. The *bocadillo* (sandwiches), with their blood-red Serrano ham and salty Manchego cheese, are great picnic fare. This place is a few miles north of the central Coconut Grove area.

## Coral Gables

**EL CARAJO** Spanish $$
( ☏ 305-856-2424; www.elcarajointernation altapasandwines.com; 2465 SW 17th Ave; tapas $3.50-15; ☺ 11:30am-10pm Mon-Thu, 11:30 am-midnight Fri & Sat, 1-8pm Sun) Pass the Penzoil, please. We know it is cool to tuck restaurants into unassuming spots, but the Citgo station on SW 17th Ave? Really? Really. Walk past the motor oil into a Granadan wine cellar and try not to act too fazed. And now the food, which is absolutely incredible: chorizo in cider blends burn, smoke and juice; frittatas are comfortably filling; and *sardinas* and *boquerones*...wow. These sardines and anchovies cooked with a bit of salt and olive oil are dizzyingly delicious. It is tempting to keep El Carajo a secret, but not singing its praises would be lying and we're not

going to lie: if there's one restaurant you shouldn't miss in Miami, it's this one.

**MATSURI** Japanese $
( ☏ 305-663-1615; 5759 Bird Rd; mains $7-20; ☺ 11:30am-2:30pm Tue-Fri, 5:30-10:30pm Tue-Sat) Note the customers here: Matsuri, tucked into a nondescript shopping center, is consistently packed with Japanese people. They don't want scene; they want a taste of home, although many of the diners are actually South American Japanese who order *unagi* (eels) in Spanish. Spicy *toro* (fatty tuna) and scallions, grilled mackerel with natural salt, and an ocean of raw fish are all *oishi* (delicious). The excellent $8 bento lunch makes the rest of the day somewhat disappointing in comparison.

# 🍷 Drinking

Miami has an intense variety of bars to pick from that range from grotty dives to beautiful – but still laid-back – lounges and nightclubs. Not to say you can't spot celebrities if you want to...

## South Beach

**ABRAXAS** Bar
(Map p194; 407 Meridian Ave) Abraxas is open, uncrowded, located in a classical

deco building, serves fantastic beer from around the USA and the world, and has clientele and staff who are the friendly sort, the types who will quickly make friends with a stranger and then keep said stranger entertained and inebriated until closing time. It's tucked away in a residential area; take your traveling friends here and they'll wonder how you ever found it.

### B BAR
Bar

(Map p194; Betsy Hotel, 1440 Ocean Ave) This smallish basement bar, tucked under the Betsy Hotel, has two salient features. One is a crowd of the beautiful, in-the-know SoBe-tastic types you expect at South Beach nightspots. The other is an odd, low-hanging reflective ceiling, built out of a sort of wobbly material that sinks in like soft jello and ripples like a stone in a pond when you touch it. It's a pretty cool thing to witness, especially when all sorts of drunk, beautiful people try to (literally) raise the roof.

### MAC'S CLUB DEUCE BAR
Bar

(Map p194; 222 14th St) The oldest bar in Miami Beach (established in 1926), the Deuce is a real neighborhood bar and hype-free zone. It's just straight-up seediness, which depending on your outlook can be quite refreshing. Plan to see everyone from transgendered ladies to construction workers – some hooking up, some talking rough, all having a good time.

## Northern Miami Beach

### LOU'S BEER GARDEN
Pub

(Map p200; www.lousbeergarden.com; 7337 Harding Ave) We're frankly surprised it took so long for a beer garden to open in Miami. The weather's perfect, right? Nonetheless, this is the first beer garden to open in the Magic City in anyone's memory. Gather around long tables under tropical trees, order a cheese plate or a Kobe beef burger and down pints of Belgian craft ales. What could be better?

## Downtown Miami

### TOBACCO ROAD
Bar

(Map p204; www.tobacco-road.com; 626 S Miami Ave) Miami's oldest bar has been on the scene since the 1920s. These days it's a little touristy, but it has stayed in business for a reason: old wood, blue lights, cigarette smoke and sassy bartenders greet you like a buddy. Cold beers are on tap and decent live acts crank out the blues, jazz and rock. The staff proudly reminds you its liquor license was the first one issued in a city that loves its mojitos. Tobacco Rd has been here since the 1920s when it was a Prohibition-era speakeasy; today it remains a great place to order a drink or listen to live music. Film buffs may recognize it as the place where Kurt Russell has a drink in *The Mean Season* (1985).

Bengal Tiger, Metrozoo (p203), Miami.
MARK NEWMAN/LONELY PLANET IMAGES ©

# If You Like...
# Boutique Motels

That cute little phrase means 'Miami Modern on Biscayne Boulevard.' and refers to the architectural style of buildings on north Biscayne Blvd past 55th Street. Specifically, there are some great roadside motels here with lovely, Rat Pack–era '50s neon beckoning visitors in. This area was neglected for a long time, but today north BiBo is one of Miami's rapidly gentrifying areas, and savvy motel owners are cleaning up their act and looking to attract the hipsters, artists and gay population flocking to the area.

**1 NEW YORKER**
(off Map p208; ☎305-759-5823; www .hotelnewyorkermiami.com; 6500 Biscayne Blvd; r $75-130; P ❄ ⓢ) This hotel has been around since the 1950s and it shows – in a good way. If you could turn a classic Cadillac into a hotel with a modern interior and hipster cred, then bam, there's the New Yorker in a nutshell. Staff are friendly and rooms, done up with pop art, geometric designs and solid colors, would make Andy Warhol proud.

**2 MOTEL BLU**
(off Map p208; ☎877-784-6835; www .motelblumiami.com; 7700 Biscayne Blvd; r $52-150; P ❄ ⓢ ⌚) Situated above Miami's Little River, the Blu may not look like much from the outside, but inside you'll find freshly done-up rooms with a host of modern amenities. Rooms are comfortable and have a soothing lime-and-lemon interior.

**3 MOTEL BIANCO**
(Map p208; ☎305-751-8696; www .motelbianco.com; 5255 Biscayne Blvd; r $80-110; P ❄ ⓢ) The Bianco situates several orange-and-milky-white rooms around a glittery courtyard where coffee is served and guests can get to know each other. Contemporary art designs swirl through the larger rooms and wicker furniture abounds throughout.

## Wynwood, Design District & Little Haiti

**ELECTRIC PICKLE**     Bar
(Map p208; www.electricpicklemiami.com; 2826 N Miami Ave) Miami can work its magic on anyone, even Wynwood's angst-ridden artists and hipsters (Wypsters). Like Cinderella touched by a fairy godmother (or a very good DJ), they become glamorous club kids in this two-story hepcat hot spot. The Pickle is as sexy and gorgeous as Miami gets, but with its modish library and (semi)literati clientele, it's also intelligent enough to hold a conversation...though you should expect it to be a sloppy, fun drunk by midnight.

**CHURCHILL'S**     Pub
(Map p208; www.churchillspub.com; 5501 NE 2nd Ave, Little Haiti) Churchill's is a Brit-owned, East End–style pub in the midst of what could be Port-au-Prince. There's a lot of live music here, mainly punk, indie and more punk – expect a small cover charge if a show is on when you visit. Not insipid modern punk either: think the Ramones meets the Sex Pistols. While everyone's getting their ya-yas off, Haitians are waiting outside to park your car or sidle in and enjoy the gig and a beer with you. Brits, this is the place to watch your sports.

## Coconut Grove
Everything here closes at 3am.

**TAURUS**     Bar
(3540 Main Hwy) The oldest bar in Coconut Grove is a cool mix of wood-paneling, smoky leather chairs, about 100 beers to choose from and a con-vivial vibe – as neighborhood bars go in Miami, this is one of the best.

## Coral Gables
**SEVEN SEAS**     Bar
(2200 SW 57th Ave) Seven Seas is a genuine Miami neighborhood dive, decorated on

One of the many art deco hotels in Miami's South Beach (p209).

DENNIS JOHNSON/LONELY PLANET IMAGES ©

the inside like a nautical theme park and filled with University of Miami students, Cuban workers, gays, straights, lesbians and folks from around the way. The best time to come is on Tuesday, Thursday and Saturday for the best karaoke in Miami – there's plenty of Spanish-language music, which adds some Latin spice.

### THE BAR                                    Bar
(172 Giralda Ave) All in a name, right? Probably the best watering hole in the Gables, The Bar is just what the title says (which is unusual in this neighborhood of extravagant embellishment). If you're in the 'hood on Friday, come here for happy hour (5pm to 8pm), when the young Gables professionals take their ties off and let loose long into the night.

 **Entertainment**

Miami's artistic merits are obvious: homegrown talent, migratory snowbirds bringing the funding and attention of northeastern galleries, and immigrants from across the Americas.

## Clubs

### BARDOT                                    Club
(Map p208; ☎ 305-576-5570; 3456 N Miami Ave) If you can't stand lines and crowds, we recommend visiting Bardot, in Wynwood, on a weekday. This could be said of any club in Miami, but you really should see the interior of Bardot before you leave the city. It's all sexy French vintage posters and furniture seemingly plucked from a private club that serves millionaires by day, and becomes a scene of decadent excess by night. There are a lot of gorgeous Miamians here and we stress: the crowd is local, so while it's a glam scene, it's a much more friendly, laid back one than the ridiculous posturing you might see in South Beach (not that there's no posturing going on). The entrance looks to be on N Miami Ave, but it's actually in a parking lot behind the building (indicated on our map).

225

**NIKKI BEACH MIAMI**  Club

(Map p194; ☎ 305-538-1111; www.nikkibeach.com; 1 Ocean Dr) Get your groove on outdoors, wandering from immaculate gossamer beach cabana to cabana at Nikki's, which feels like an incredibly upscale full-moon party. On Sunday (Sunday?!), starting around 4pm, it's the hottest party in town, as folks clamor to get in and relive whatever it was they did the night before.

## Performing Arts

**GUSMAN CENTER FOR THE
PERFORMING ARTS**  Theater

(Map p204; ☎ 305-374-2444; www.gusmancenter.org; 174 E Flagler St) This elegantly renovated 1920s movie palace services a huge variety of performing arts including film festivals, symphonies, ballets and touring shows. The acoustics are excellent.

### THEATER

**JERRY HERMAN RING THEATRE**  Theater

(☎ 305-284-3355; www.miami.edu/ring; University of Miami, 1321 Miller Dr; tickets $8-15) This University of Miami troupe stages musicals, dramas and comedies, with recent productions including *Falsettos* and *Baby.* Alumni actors include Sylvester Stallone, Steven Bauer, Saundra Santiago and Ray Liotta.

### DANCE

**MIAMI CITY BALLET**  Dance

(Map p194; ☎ 305-929-7000; www.miamicityballet.org; 2200 Liberty Ave, South Beach) Formed in 1985, this troupe is guided by artistic director Edward Villella, who studied under the great George Balanchine at the NYC Ballet. So it's no surprise Balanchine's works dominate the repertoire, with shows held at a lovely three-story headquarters designed by famed local architectural firm Arquitectonica. The facade allows passersby to watch the dancers rehearsing through big picture windows, which makes you feel like you're in a scene from *Fame,* except the weather is better and people don't spontaneously break into song.

### CLASSICAL

**NEW WORLD SYMPHONY**  Orchestra

(Map p194; NWS; ☎ 305-673-3330; www.nws.edu; 500 17th St) Housed in the New World Center (p196) – a funky explosion of cubist lines and geometric curves, fresh white against the blue Miami sky – the acclaimed New World Symphony holds performances from October to May

# Art Walks: the New Clubbing?

It's hipsters gone wild! Or to put it another way: it's free wine! And artsy types, and galleries open till late, and the eye candy of a club, and the drunken momentum of a pub crawl and – best of all – no red ropes. The free Wynwood and Design District Art Walk is one of the best nightlife experiences in Miami. And we're not (just) being cheapskates. The experience of strolling from gallery to gallery ('That piece is *gorgeous*. Pour me another'), perusing the paintings ('No, I don't think there's a bathroom behind the performance artist') and delving into the nuances of aesthetic styles ('The wine's run out? Let's bounce') is as genuinely innovative as...well, the best contemporary art. Just be careful, as a lot of galleries in Wynwood are separated by short drives (the Design District is more walkable). Art Walks take place on the second Saturday of each month, from 7pm to 10pm (some galleries stretch to 11pm); when it's all over, lots of folks repair to Electric Pickle (p224) or Bardot (p225). Visit www.artcircuits.com for information on participating galleries.

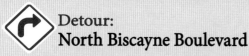

## Detour:
## North Biscayne Boulevard

As North Biscayne Blvd continues to gentrify, better and better restaurants are opening up. Here are some winners from this foodie find:

**Michy's** (off Map p208; 305-759-2001; 6927 Biscayne Blvd; meals $28-43; 6-10:30pm, 5:30-11pm Fri & Sat, Tue-Fri, 5:30-10pm Sun; ) Blue-and-white pop-decor. Organic, locally sourced ingredients. A stylish, fantastical bar where Alice could drink before painting Wonderland red. Welcome to Michelle 'Michy' Bernstein's culinary lovechild – one of the brightest stars in Miami's culinary constellation. The emphasis is on good food and fun. The 'half plates' concept lets you halve an order and mix up delicious gastronomic fare, such as foie gras on corn cakes, chicken pot pie with wild mushrooms, white almond gazpacho, and blue-cheese *croquettes*.

**Red Light Little River** (off Map p208; 305-757-7773; 7700 Biscayne Blvd; mains $14-28; Tue-Thu 6-11pm, to midnight Fri & Sat) New Orleans comfort food gets mixed up with Florida ingredients in this laid-back, excellent-value eatery perched above its namesake, Little River. The result is cuisine both clean and rich; sour oranges with sea scallops and hearty lentils; spicy shrimp grilled-cheese sandwiches; and skirt steak in decadent rosemary and gorgonzola demi-glacé.

DISCOVER MIAMI & THE KEYS MIAMI

(tickets $20 to $70). The deservedly heralded NWS serves as a three- to four-year preparatory program for very talented musicians who have already graduated from prestigious music schools.

#  Shopping

## Art, Furniture & Home Design

**Miami Mid Century**　　　Antiques
(Map p208; 305-572-0558; 3404 N Miami Ave; 10am-7pm) Miami Mid Century has a playful approach to antiques and retro homewares – big sunglasses, old stacks of magazines, cool geometric lamps – sorely lacking in the more snooty shops of the Design District.

## Clothing & Accessories

**C Madeleine's**　　　Vintage
( 305-945-7770; 13702 Biscayne Blvd; 11am-6pm Mon-Sat, noon-5pm Sun) The undisputed queen of vintage Miami, C Madeleine is more than your standard used-clothes

write-off. This is a serious temple to classical style, selling Yves Saint Laurent couture and classic Chanel suits. Come here for the sort of timeless looks that are as beautiful now as when they first appeared on the rack. Located on North Biscayne Blvd about 7.5 miles north of the Design District.

## Gifts

**BOOKS AND BOOKS**　　　Books
(Map p194; 305-442-4408; 265 Aragon Ave St; 10am-11pm, to midnight Fri & Sat) The best indie bookstore in South Florida is a massive emporium of all things literary. Hosts frequent readings and is generally just a fantastic place to hang out. Has other outposts on Lincoln Rd (**305-532-3222; 927 Lincoln Rd**) and the Bal Harbour shops.

**Little-Havana-To-Go**　　　Souvenirs
(Map p219; 305-857-9720; www.littleha vanatogo.com; 1442 SW 8th St) This is Little Havana's official souvenir store, and has some pretty cool items, from Cuban-pride T-shirts to posters, flags, paintings, photo

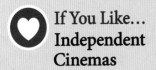

# If You Like...
# Independent Cinemas

Miami has a glut of art-house cinemas showing first-run, independent and foreign films. Here are some of our favorites:

## 1 BILL COSFORD CINEMA
(www.cosfordcinema.com; Memorial Classroom Bldg, University of Miami, University Dr) On the University of Miami campus, this renovated art house was launched in memory of the Miami Herald film critic.

## 2 CORAL GABLES ART CINEMA
(www.gablescinema.com; 260 Aragon Ave, Coral Gables) Indie and foreign films in a 144-seat cinema.

## 3 TOWER THEATER
(Mawww.mdc.edu/culture /tower; 1508 SW 8th St) In a gem of a deco building, managed by Miami Dade College.

## 4 O CINEMA
(Map p208; www.o-cinema.org; 90 NW 29th St) Indie screenings in Wynwood.

books, cigar-box purses and authentic clothing.

**SWEAT RECORDS** Records
(Map p208; ☎786-693-9309; 5505 NE 2nd Ave; ⏰noon-10pm Tue-Sat, to 5pm Sun) Sweat's almost a stereotypical indie record store – there's funky art and graffiti on the walls, it has big purple couches, it sells weird Japanese toys and there are skinny guys with thick glasses arguing over LPs and EPs you've never heard of, and of course, there are coffee and vegan snacks.

## ⓘ Information

### Dangers & Annoyances
At night, avoid Liberty City, in northwest Miami; Overtown, from 14th St to 20th St; Little Haiti and stretches of the Miami riverfront.

## Emergency

Ambulance (☎911)

Beach Patrol (☎305-673-7714)

Hurricane Hotline (☎305-468-5400)

Poison Information Center (☎305-585-5250)

Rape Hotline (☎305-585-7273)

Suicide Intervention (☎305-358-4357)

## Medical Services

**Miami Beach Community Health Center** (☎305-538-8835; 710 Alton Rd, South Beach) Walk-in clinic with long lines.

**Mount Sinai Medical Center** (☎305-674-2121; 4300 Alton Rd, Miami Beach) The area's best emergency room. Beware that you must eventually pay, and fees are high.

**Visitor's Medical Line** (☎305-674-2222; ⏰24hr) For physician.

## Tourist Information

**Art Deco Welcome Center** (Map p194; ☎305-672-2014; www.mdpl.org; 1001 Ocean Dr, South Beach; ⏰10am-7:30pm Mon-Sat, to 6pm Sun) Run by the Miami Design Preservation League (MDPL), has tons of art-deco district information and organizes excellent walking tours.

## Websites

**Art Circuits** (www.artcircuits.com) The best insider info on art events; includes excellent neighborhood-by-neighborhood gallery maps.

**Mango & Lime** (www.mangoandlime.net) The best local food blog is always ahead of the curve on eating events in the Magic City.

**Meatless Miami** (www.meatlessmiami.com) Vegetarians in need of an eating guide, look no further.

**Miami Beach 411** (www.miamibeach411.com) A great guide for Miami Beach visitors, covering just about all concerns.

Miami Nights (www.miaminights.com) Get a good, opinionated lowdown on Miami's ever-shifting after-dark scene.

Beached Miami (www.beachedmiami.com) The best independent arts website in Miami.

## Getting There & Away

### Air

Miami is served by all major carriers via two main airports: Miami International Airport (MIA) and the Fort Lauderdale-Hollywood International Airport (FLL), half an hour north of MIA. MIA (305-876-7000; www.miami-airport.com) is the third-busiest airport in the country. Just 6 miles west of downtown Miami, the airport is open 24 hours and is laid out in a horseshoe design. There are left-luggage facilities on two concourses at MIA, between B and C, and on G; prices vary according to bag size.

## Getting Around

### To/From the Airport

MIAMI INTERNATIONAL AIRPORT If you're driving, follow Rte 112 from the airport, then head east on the Julia Tuttle Causeway or the I-195 to get to South Beach. Other options

The Colony Theatre (p193) along Lincoln Road Mall.

include free shuttles offered by most hotels or a taxi ($38 flat rate from the airport to South Beach). Alternatively, catch the Airport Owl night-only public bus, or the **SuperShuttle** (305-871-8210; www.supershuttle.com) shared-van service, which will cost about $26 to South Beach.

### Bicycle

The city of Miami Beach offers the DecoBike (305-532-9494; www.decobike.com; 1-/3-day access $14/30) bike-share program. Bike stations are located in dozens of spots around Miami Beach (there's a map on the website, plus an iPhone app that tells you where the nearest station is).

Places that rent bicycles:

BikeAndRoll (Map p204; www.bikeandroll.com; 305-604-0001; www.bikeandroll.com; 401 Biscayne Blvd; 10am-6pm; per hr/day from $5/15) Also does bike tours.

Mangrove Cycles (305-361-5555; 260 Crandon Blvd, Key Biscayne; 10am-6pm Tue-Sun; per 2hr/day/week from $20/25/75)

Highgear Cycling (305-444-2175; www.highgearcycling.com; 3423 Main Hwy, Coconut Grove; 10am-7pm Mon-Fri, to 6pm Sat, noon-5pm Sun; per hr/day from $12/35)

ALAMY/ALEX SEGRE ©

**229**

### Bus

The local bus system is called Metrobus (☎305-891-3131; www.miamidade.gov/transit/routes.asp; tickets $2). An easy-to-read route map is available online. You may spend more time waiting for a bus than riding on one.

In South Beach, an excellent option is the South Beach Local Circulator (☎305-891-3131; $0.25), a looping shuttle bus with disabled-rider access that operates along Washington between South Pointe Dr and 17th St and loops back around on Alton Rd on the west side of the beach. Rides come along every 10 to 15 minutes.

### Taxi

Central Cabs (☎305-532-5555)
Dispatch Service (☎305-525-2455)
Flamingo Taxis (☎305-759-8100)
Metro (☎305-888-8888)
Sunshine (☎305-445-3333)
Yellow (☎305-400-0000)

# FLORIDA KEYS

The Keys are physically and culturally separate from the mainland. They march to the beat of their own drum, or Alabama country band, or Jimmy Buffet single, or Bahamanian steel calypso set...whatever. The point is, this is a place where those who reject everyday life in the Lower 48 escape to. What do they find? About 113 mangrove-and-sandbar islands where the white sun melts over tight fists of deep-green mangroves, long, gloriously soft mudflats and tidal bars and water as teal as Arizona turquoise.

## Upper Keys

No, really, you're in the islands!

It's a bit hard to tell when you first arrive, as the huge, rooty blanket of mangrove forest that forms the South Florida coastline spreads like a woody morass into Key Largo. In fact, the mangroves become Key Largo, which is more famous

**Left:** Fishing at Islamorada (p233); **Below:** Brown pelican at the Florida Keys Wild Bird Rehabilitation Center (p232).

(LEFT) ALAMY/MICHAEL VENTURA ©; (BELOW) ALAMY/AMERICA ©

for its underwater than above-ground views. If you want to avoid traffic on US Hwy 1, you can try the less trafficked FL 997 and Card Sound Rd to FL 905 (toll $1), which passes Alabama Jack's.

## Key Largo & Tavernier

### ◎ Sights & Activities

**JOHN PENNEKAMP CORAL REEF STATE PARK**          Park
(www.pennekamppark.com, www.florida
stateparks.org/pennekamp; MM 102.5 oceanside;
car/motorcycle/cyclist or pedestrian $8/4/2;
☯8am-sunset; ♿) John Pennekamp has
the singular distinction of being the first
underwater park in the USA. There are
170 acres of dry parkland here and over
48,000 acres (ie 75 sq miles) of wet: the
vast majority of the protected area is the
ocean.

To really get beneath the surface of this park (pun intended), you should take a 2½-hour **glass-bottom boat tour** (✆305-451-6300; adult/child $24/17; ☯tours 9:15am, 12:15pm & 3pm). You won't be ferried around in some rinky-dink fishing boat; you're brought out in a safe, modern 38ft catamaran from which you'll ooh and aah at filigreed flaps of soft coral, technicolor schools of fish, dangerous-looking barracudas and massive, yet ballerina-graceful sea turtles.

If you want to go even deeper, try straight-up **snorkeling trips** (✆305-451-6300; adult/child $29.95/24.95) or **diving excursions** (✆305-451-6322, 877-727-5348; dive excursions with/without own gear $60/90). DIYers may want to take out a canoe ($12 per hour) or kayak (single per hour $12, double $17), to journey through a 3-mile network of trails. Call ✆305-451-6300 for boat-rental information.

To learn more about the reef in this area, go to www.southeastfloridareefs.net.

## FLORIDA KEYS WILD BIRD REHABILITATION
**CENTER**  Animal Sanctuary

(www.fkwbc.org; 93600 Overseas Hwy, MM 93.6; $5 donation suggested; ☉sunrise-sunset) This sanctuary is the first of many animal hospitals you'll come across built by critter-loving Samaritans throughout the Keys. You'll find an alfresco bird hospital that cares for birds that have swallowed fish hooks, had wings clipped in accidents, been shot by BB pellets etc. A pretty trail leads back to a nice vista of Florida Bay and a wading bird pond. Just be warned, it does smell like bird doo back here.

 **Eating**

## KEY LARGO CONCH HOUSE   Fusion $$
(📞305-453-4844; MM 100.2 oceanside; lunch $8-14, dinner $13-25; ☉7am-9:30pm Sun-Thu, to 10pm Fri & Sat; 🛜) A wi-fi hotspot, coffee-house and innovative kitchen that likes to sex up local classics (conch in a lime and white-wine sauce, or in a vinegar sauce with capers), set in a restored old-school Keys mansion wrapped in a *Gone with the Wind* veranda? Yes please, and more of it. It's hard not to love the way the period architecture blends in seamlessly with the local tropical fauna. A justifiably popular spot with tourists and locals. The fish tacos are intensely good.

 **Drinking**

## ALABAMA JACK'S   Bar
(58000 Crad Sound Rd; ☉11am-7pm) Welcome to your first taste of the Keys: zonked-out fishermen, exiles from the mainland, and Harley heads getting drunk on a man-grove bay. This is the line where Miami-esque South Florida gives way to the country-fried American South. Wildlife lovers: you may spot the rare mulleted version of *Jacksonvillia Redneckus*! But seriously, everyone raves about the conch fritters, and the fact they have to close because of nightly onslaughts of mosqui-toes means this place is as authentically Florida as they come. Country bands take the stage on weekends from 2pm to 5pm.

A jetty in Islamorada at sunset.

ALAMY/ROD MCLEAN ©

# Keys for Children

Check out some of the following options to entertain the kids:

○ **Florida Keys Eco-Discovery Center** (p240) Get an understanding of the region's environment.

○ **Glass-bottom boat tours at John Pennekamp Coral Reef State Park** (p231) Your own window to the underwater world.

○ **Turtle Hospital** (p234) Save (or watch) the turtles.

○ **Conch Tour Train** (p244) Kitschy, corny, enjoyable tour.

○ **Robbie's Marina** (p233) All sorts of activities, including the ever-popular tarpon (giant fish) feeding frenzy.

## ℹ Information

Mariner Hospital ( ☎ 305-434-3000; www.
baptisthealth.net; Tavernier, MM 91.5 bayside)

## ℹ Getting There & Away

The Greyhound bus stops at MM 99.6 oceanside.

## Islamorada

Islamorada (eye-luh-murr-*ah*-da) is also known as 'the Village of Islands.' Doesn't that sound pretty? Well, it really is. This little string of pearls (well, keys) – Plantation, Upper and Lower Matecumbe, Shell and Lignumvitae (lignum-*vite*-ee) – shimmers as one of the prettiest stretches of the islands.

### ◉ Sights & Activities

**ROBBIE'S MARINA**                           Marina
( ☎ 800-979-3370, 305-664-9814; www.rob
bies.com; MM 77.5 bayside; tours from $35;
⊗ 8am-6pm; 🚸 ) Robbie's really may be the happiest dock on Earth. More than a boat launch, Robbie's is a local flea market, tacky tourist shop (all the shells you ever wanted), sea pen for tarpons (very big-ass fish) and jump-off for excellent fishing expeditions all wrapped into one driftwood-laced compound. There's a glut of boat-rental and tour options here.

The party boat (half-day/night/full-day trips $35/40/60) is just that: a chance to drink, fish and basically achieve Keys Zen. Or, for real Zen (ie the tranquil kind as opposed to drunken kind), take an ecotour ($35) on an electrically propelled silent boat deep into the mangroves, hammocks and lagoons. Snorkeling trips are a good deal; for adult/child $35/20 you get a few hours on a very smooth-riding Happy Cat vessel and a chance to bob amidst some of the USA's only coral reefs. If you don't want to get on the water, at least feed the freakishly large tarpons from the dock ($2.79 per bucket, $1 to watch).

**INDIAN KEY STATE**
**HISTORIC SITE**                           Island
(http://floridastateparks.org/indiankey;
⊗ 8am-sunset) You may have encountered spooky abandoned houses, mansions, even towns in your travels – but how about a derelict island? In 1831, renegade wrecker (shipwreck salvager) Jacob Housman turned this quiet island into a thriving city, complete with a warehouse, docks, streets, hotel and about 40 to 50 permanent residents. By 1836, Indian Key was the first seat of Dade County, but four years later the inhabitants of the island were killed or scattered by a Native American attack during the Second Seminole War. Robbie's used to bring boats this way, and still does boat rental

(single/double/glass-bottom kayak/canoe per hour $20/27.50/30/30). You can also see the island from the water on an ecotour with Robbie's ($35).

### ✖ Eating

**MIDWAY CAFE** Cafe $
( 305-664-2622; 80499 Overseas Hwy; mains under $5; ◷7am-3pm Thu-Tue, to 2pm Sun) The lovely folks who run this cafe – stuffed with every variety of heart-warming art the coffee shop trope can muster – roast their own beans, make baked goods that we would swim across the Gulf for and are friendly as hell. You're almost in the Middle Keys: celebrate making it this far with a cup of joe.

### ⓘ Information

Islamorada Chamber of Commerce
( 305-664-4503, 800-322-5397; www.islamoradachamber.com; MM 83.2 bayside; ◷9am-5pm Mon-Fri, 10am-3pm Sat & Sun) Located in an old caboose.

### ⓘ Getting There & Away

The Greyhound bus stops at the Burger King at MM 82.5 oceanside.

# MIDDLE KEYS

# Marathon

Marathon is at the halfway point between Key Largo and Key West, and is a good place to stop on a road trip across the islands.

### ◉ Sights & Activities

**CRANE POINT MUSEUM** Park
(www.cranepoint.net; MM 50.5 bayside; adult/child over 5yr/senior $12.50/8.50/11; ◷9am-5pm Mon-Sat, noon-5pm Sun; 👪) This is one of the nicest spots on the island to stop and smell the roses. And the pinelands. And the palm hammock – a sort of palm jungle (imagine walking under giant, organic Japanese fans) that only grows between MM 47 and MM 60. There's also Adderly House, a preserved example of a Bahamian immigrant cabin (which must have *baked* in summer) and 63 acres of green goodness to stomp through. This is a great spot for the kids, who'll love the pirate exhibits in an on-site museum and yet another bird hospital.

**TURTLE HOSPITAL** Animal Sanctuary
( 305-743-2552; www.theturtlehospital.org; 2396 Overseas Hwy; adult/child $15/7.50; ◷9am-6pm 👪)
Be they victims of disease, boat propeller strikes, flipper entanglements with fishing lines – whatever, really – any injured sea turtle in the Keys will hopefully end up in this motel-cum-sanctuary. We know we shouldn't anthropomorphize animals, but these turtles just seem so sweet, so it's sad but heartening to

Shrimp boats in Key West (p237).
ALAMY/WATER FRAME ©

ALAMY/AMAR AND ISABELLE QUILLEN - QUILLEN PHOTOGRAPHY ©

## Don't Miss **The Caribbean Club Bar**

Here's one for the movie fans, particularly Bogie buffs: the Caribbean Club Bar (open 7am to 4am), located at MM 104 bayside is, in fact, the only place in Key Largo where *Key Largo*, starring Humphrey Bogart and Lauren Bacall, was filmed (the rest of the island was a Hollywood soundstage). If that's not enough, the original *African Queen*, of the same-titled movie, is docked in a channel at the Holiday Inn at MM 100 – just walk around the back and there she is.

see the injured and sick ones well looked after. The whole setup is a labor of love by Richard Moretti, who's quite the Keys character himself. Tours are educational and fun, and offered at 10am, 1pm and 4pm. It's recommended you call ahead before visiting, as hospital staff may be away 'on call' at any moment.

###  Eating

**KEYS FISHERIES**     Seafood **$**
(3502 Gulf View Ave; mains $7-16; ⏱11am-9pm)
The lobster reuben is the stuff of legend here. Sweet, chunky, creamy, and so good it's making us leave unsightly drool all over our keyboard. But you can't go wrong with any of the excellent seafood

here, all served with sass (to order you have to identify your favorite car, color, etc; a question that depends on the mood of the guy behind the counter). Expect pleasant levels of seagull harassment as you dine on a working waterfront.

###  Drinking

**HURRICANE**     Bar
(📞305-743-2200; MM 49.5 bayside) The staff is sassy, sarcastic and warm. The drinks will kick your ass out the door and have you back begging for more. The ambience: locals, tourists, mad fishermen, rednecks and the odd journalist saddling up for endless Jägerbombs before

GETTY IMAGES/DANITA DELIMONT ©

# Don't Miss Florida Keys Overseas Heritage Trail

One of the best ways to see the Keys is by bicycle. The flat elevation and ocean breezes are perfect for cycling, and the **Florida Keys Overseas Heritage Trail** (FKOHT; www.dep.state.fl.us/gwt/state/keystrail) will connect all the islands from Key Largo to Key West. At the time of writing about 70 miles of the trail were paved, but there have been significant delays to its completion.

If you are keen to ride, it's currently possible to bike through the Keys by shoulder riding (it takes three days at a good clip). There are particularly pleasant rides around Islamorada, and if you're uncomfortable riding on the shoulder, you can contact the FKOHT through their website for recommended bike excursions.

dancing the night away to any number of consistently good live acts. It's the best bar before Key West, and it deserves a visit from you.

### ⓘ Information

**Fisherman's Hospital** ( ☏ 305-743-5533; www.fishermanshospital.com; 3301 Overseas Hwy) Has a major emergency room.

# LOWER KEYS

The Lower Keys are fierce bastions of conch culture. Some local families have

been Keys castaways for generations, and there are bits of Big Pine that feel more Florida Panhandle than Overseas Hwy.

## Big Pine, Bahia Honda & Looe Key

Big Pine is home to stretches of quiet roads, Key West employees who found a way around astronomical real-estate rates, and packs of wandering Key deer.

### ◎ Sights & Activities

**BAHIA HONDA STATE PARK**          Park
( ☏ 305-872-3210; www.bahiahondapark.com; MM 36.8; per car/motorcycle/bicycle $5/4/2;

⊘8am-sunset; 🚹) This park, with its long, white-sand (and seaweed-strewn) beach, named Sandspur Beach by locals, is the big attraction in these parts. As Keys beaches go, this one is probably the best natural stretch of sand in the island chain, but we wouldn't vote it best beach in the continental USA (although Condé Nast did...in 1992). As a tourist, the more novel experience is walking a stretch of the **old Bahia Honda Rail Bridge**, which offers nice views of the surrounding islands. Or check out the nature trails (ooh, butter-flies!) and science center, where helpful park employees help you identify stone crabs, fireworms, horseshoe crabs and comb jellies.

The **park concession** (☎305-872-3210; **MM 36.8 oceanside**) offers daily 1½-hour snorkeling trips at 9:30am and 1:30pm (adult $30, child $25). Reservations are a good idea in high season.

**NATIONAL KEY DEER REFUGE HEADQUARTERS**          Wildlife Reserve
(☎305-872-2239; www.fws.gov/nationalkey-deer; Big Pine Shopping Center, MM 30.5 bayside; ⊘8am-5pm Mon-Fri; 🚹) What would make Bambi cuter? Mini Bambi. Introducing: the Key deer, an endangered subspecies of white-tailed deer that prance about primarily on Big Pine and No Name Keys. The folks here are an incredibly helpful source of information on the deer and all things Keys. The refuge sprawls over several islands, but the sections open to the public are on Big Pine and No Name. The headquarters also administers the Great White Heron National Wildlife Refuge, 200,000 acres of open water and mangrove islands north of the main Keys that is only accessible by boat; there is no tourism infrastructure in place to get out here, but you can enquire about nautical charts and the heron themselves at the office.

##  Sleeping

**DEER RUN BED & BREAKFAST** B&B $$$
(☎305-872-2015; www.deerrunfloridabb.com; 1997 Long Beach Dr, Big Pine Key, off MM 33 oceanside; r $235-355; 🅿🐕) This state-certified green lodge and vegetarian B&B

is isolated on a lonely, lovely stretch of Long Beach Dr. It's a garden of quirky delights, complemented by assorted love-the-earth paraphernalia, street signs and four simple but cozily scrumptious rooms with names such as Eden, Heaven and Utopia. The helpful owners will get you out on a boat or into the heated pool for some chillaxation, while they whip up organic, vegetarian meals. We should add: the vibe is decidedly not self-righteous hippie. You could take home a steak-and-bacon sandwich and the staff wouldn't mind.

##  Eating

**NO NAME PUB**          Pizza $
(☎305-872-9115; N Watson Blvd, Big Pine Key, off MM 30.5 bayside; mains $7-18; ⊘11am-11pm) The No Name's one of those off-the-track places that everyone seems to know about. It feels isolated, it looks isolated, yet somehow, the tourists are all here – and this doesn't detract in the slightest from the kooky ambience, friendly service, excellent locally brewed beer and primo pizzas served up at this colorful semidive. Note, the name of this place implies that it is located on No Name Key, but it is on Big Pine Key, just over the causeway.

# Key West

Key West is still defined by its motto, which we love – One Human Family – an ideal that equals a tolerant, accepting ethos where anything goes and life is always a party (or at least a hangover the day after). The color scheme: watercolor pastels cooled by breezes on a sunset-kissed Bahamian porch. Welcome to the End of the USA.

##  Sights

**MALLORY SQUARE**          Square
(⊘sunset; 🚹) Take all those energies, subcultures and oddities of Keys life – the hippies, the rednecks, the foreigners and, of course, the tourists – and focus them into one torchlit, family-friendly (but playfully edgy), sunset-enriched street

# Should You Swim with Dolphins?

There are four swim-with-the-dolphin (SWTD) centers in the Keys, and many more arguments for and against the practice.

### FOR

◦ While SWTD sites are commercial, they are also research entities devoted to learning more about their charges.

◦ The dolphins raised on-site are legally obtained and have not been not captured from the wild.

◦ The dolphins are used to humans and pose a negligible danger to swimmers, especially when overseen by expert trainers.

◦ Dolphin-swim programs increase our knowledge of dolphins and promote conservation.

◦ At places such as the **Dolphin Research Center** (see below), the dolphins can actually swim out of their pens into the open water, but choose not to.

### AGAINST

◦ Dolphins are social creatures that require interaction, which is impossible to provide in captivity.

◦ SWTD tourism encourages the capture of wild dolphins in other parts of the world.

◦ Dolphin behavior is never 100% predictable. Dolphins can seriously injure a human, even while playing.

◦ SWTD centers encourage customers to think of dolphins as anthro-pomorphized 'friends,' rather than wild animals.

◦ Dolphins never appreciate captivity. Those that voluntarily remain in SWTD sites do so to remain close to food.

### SWTD CENTERS

If you decide to swim or see dolphins in the Keys, you can contact one of the following:

**Theater of the Sea** (☎305-664-2431; www.theaterofthesea.com; Islamorada, MM 84.5 bayside; swim programs $175; ☺9:30am-4pm) Has been here since 1946. Structured dolphin-swims and sea-lion programs ($135) include 30 minutes of instruction and a 30-minute supervised swim. You can also swim with stingrays ($55).

**Dolphins Plus** (☎305-451-1993, 866-860-7946; www.dolphinsplus.com, off MM 99.5 bayside; swim programs $135-220) Key Largo center that specializes in recreational and educational unstructured swims. They expect you know a good deal before embarking upon the swim, even though a classroom session is included.

**Dolphin Research Centre** (☎305-289-1121; www.dolphins.org; MM 59 bayside; adult/child under 4yr/child 4-12yr/senior $20/free/15/17.50, swim program $180-650; ☺9am-4pm) Here the dolphins are free to leave the grounds and a lot of marine-biology research goes on behind the (still pretty commercial) tourist activities, such as getting a dolphin to paint your T-shirt or playing 'trainer for a day' ($650).

party. The child of all these raucous forces is Mallory Sq, one of the greatest shows on Earth. It all begins as the sun starts to set, a sign for the madness that it's OK to break out. Watch a dog walk a tightrope, a man swallow fire, British acrobats tumble and sass each other. Have a beer. And a conch fritter. And wait for the sun to dip behind the ocean and for the carnival to really get going.

## DUVAL STREET                    Street

Key West locals have a love-hate relationship with the most famous road in Key West (if not the Keys). Duval, Old Town Key West's main drag, is a miracle mile of booze, tacky everything and awful behavior (and not awful in an awfully good way either). It's more like awful in a loud, belligerently drunk, omigodthatshirtsays 'Put some lipstick on my dipstick' *really*? kinda way). But it's fun. The 'Duval Crawl' is one of the best pub crawls in the country. The mix of live music drink-o-ramas, T-shirt kitsch, local theaters, art studios and boutiques is more charming than jarring. And the experience is quintessentially Key West ('Keezy'). Have some perspective, have a laugh, and appreciate Duval for her pimples and all, to see why this street continues to be the island's tipsy heart.

## HEMINGWAY HOME    Historical Home

(www.hemingwayhome.com; 907 Whitehead St; adult/child 6-12yr $12.50/6; ⌚9am-5pm) Key West's biggest darling, Ernest Hemingway, lived in this gorgeous Spanish colonial house from 1931 to 1940. Poppa moved here in his early 30s with wife No 2, a *Vogue* fashion editor and (former) friend of wife No 1. *The Short Happy Life of Francis Macomber* and *The Green Hills of Africa* were produced here, but Hemingway didn't just work; like all writers he wasted a lot of time, specifically by installing Key West's first saltwater swimming pool. The construction project set him back so badly he pressed his 'last penny' into the cement on the pool's deck. It's still there today, along with the evil descendants of his famous six-toed cat, who basically rule the house and grounds. The author's old studio is preserved as he left it – when he ran off in 1940 with wife No 3.

A bottlenose dolphin.

ALAMY/CORBIS PREMIUM RF ©

### FLORIDA KEYS ECO-DISCOVERY CENTER — Museum

(eco-discovery.com/ecokw.html; 35 East Quay Rd, Truman Annex; ⊙9am-4pm Tue-Sat; P i) So, you've been making your way down the Keys, visiting all these lovely state parks and nature reserves, thinking, 'Gosh, could there be a place that ties all the knowledge of this unique ecological phenomenon into one fun, well-put-together educational exhibit?' OK, maybe those weren't your exact thoughts, but this is exactly what you get at this excellent center. This place does a marvelous job of filling in all the wild details of the natural Keys. The kids love it, and by the way, it's free *and* has free parking, an abnormality around here.

### KEY WEST CEMETERY — Cemetery

(Margaret & Angela St; ⊙sunrise-sunset; i) A darkly alluring Gothic labyrinth beckons (rather incongruously) at the center of this pastel town. Built in 1847, the cemetery crowns Solares Hill, the highest point on the island (with an elevation of all of 16ft). Some of the oldest families in the Keys rest in peace – and close proximity – here. With body space at a premium, the mausoleums stand practically shoulder to shoulder. Island quirkiness penetrates the gloom: seashells and green macramé adorn headstones with inscriptions like 'I told you I was sick.' Get chaperoned by a guide from the **Historic Florida Keys Foundation** ( ☎305-292-6718), with guided tours for $10 per person at 9:30am on Tuesday and Thursday; departs from the main gate at Margaret and Angela Sts.

### STUDIOS OF KEY WEST — Gallery

(TSKW; ☎305-296-0458; www.tskw.org; 600 White St; ⊙10am-6pm) This nonprofit show-cases about a dozen artists' studios in a gallery space located in the old Armory building, which includes a lovely sculpture garden. Besides its public visual-arts displays, TSKW hosts readings by local authors like Robert Stone, literary and visual workshops, concerts, lectures and community discussion groups.

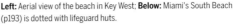

**Left:** Aerial view of the beach in Key West; **Below:** Miami's South Beach (p193) is dotted with lifeguard huts.

(LEFT) CRISTIAN LAZZARI ©; (BELOW) WITOLD SKRYPCZAK/LONELY PLANET IMAGES ©

10 ST

# Activities

## Beach Going
Beaches

Key West is *not* about beach going. In fact, for true sun 'n' surf, locals go to Bahia Honda (p236) whenever possible. Still, the three city beaches on the southern side of the island are lovely and narrow, with calm and clear water. **South Beach** is at the end of Simonton St. **Higgs Beach**, at the end of Reynolds St and Casa Marina Ct, has barbecue grills, picnic tables, and a big crowd of gay sunbathers and Key West's Eastern European seasonal workforce. **Smathers Beach**, further east off S Roosevelt Blvd, is more popular with jet-skiers, parasailers, teens and college students. The best local beach, though, is at Fort Zachary Taylor; it's worth the admission to enjoy the white sand and relative calm.

## Boating

Check www.charterboatkeywest.com for a directory of the many fishing and cruising charters offered in Key West.

**JOLLY II ROVER**
Boat Tour

( ☎ 305-304-2235; www.schoonerjollyrover. com; cnr Greene & Elizabeth Sts, Schooner Wharf; cruise $39) This outfit has a gorgeous tan-bark (reddish-brown) 80ft schooner that embarks on daily sunset cruises under sail. It looks like a pirate ship and has the cannons to back the image up.

**Dolphin Watch**
Dolphins

( ☎ 800-979-3370; dolphinwatchusa.com; 201 William Street; cruise $85) Head out with captain John Baltzell on the *Patty C* catamaran to find Keys dolphins. For our money, this is the most environmentally friendly way of spotting the marine mammals in the islands.

# Key West

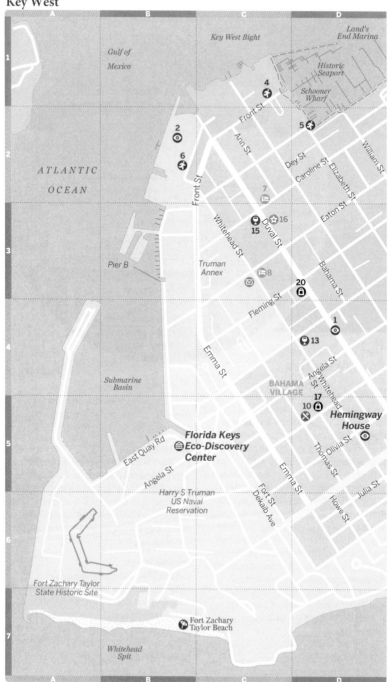

Gulf of
Mexico

Key West Bight

Land's
End Marina

Historic
Seaport

Schooner
Wharf

ATLANTIC
OCEAN

Pier B

Truman
Annex

Submarine
Basin

Florida Keys
Eco-Discovery
Center

BAHAMA
VILLAGE

Hemingway
House

Harry S Truman
US Naval
Reservation

Fort Zachary Taylor
State Historic Site

Fort Zachary
Taylor Beach

Whitehead
Spit

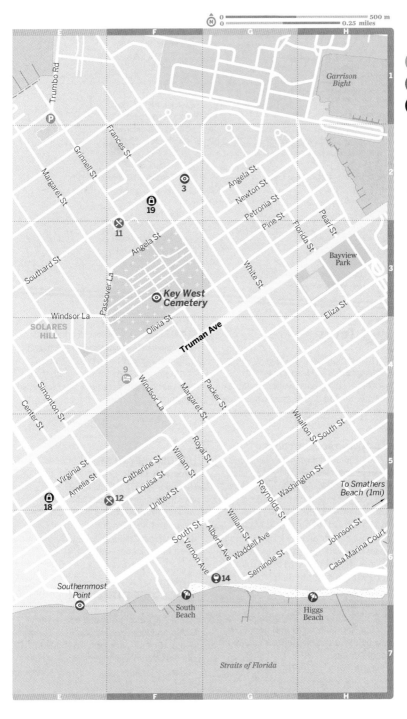

Garrison
Bight

Trumbo Rd

Frances St

Grinnell St

Margaret St

Angela St

Newton St

Petronia St

Pine St

Florida St

Pearl St

Southard St

White St

Bayview
Park

Angela St

Passover La

**Key West
Cemetery**

Eliza St

Windsor La

SOLARES
HILL

Olivia St

**Truman Ave**

Windsor La

Simonton St

Center St

Margaret St

Packer St

Whalton St

South St

Virginia St

Amelia St

Catherine St

Louisa St

William St

Royal St

United St

Reynolds St

Washington St

To Smathers
Beach (1mi)

South St

Alberta Ave

Vernon Ave

William St

Waddell Ave

Seminole St

Johnson St

Casa Marina Court

**Southernmost
Point**

South
Beach

Higgs
Beach

Straits of Florida

3

19

11

9

18

12

14

# Key West

 **Tours**

Worth noting is *Sharon Wells' Walking & Biking Guide to Historic Key West*, a booklet of self-guided walks available for free at inns and businesses around town, written by a local. See www.seekeywest.com.

**OLD TOWN TROLLEY TOURS**  Trolley
( ☎305-296-6688; www.trolleytours.com/key-west; adult/seniors/children 12 & under $29/26/free; ☺9am-4:30pm; ♿) These tours are a fantastic introduction to the city. The 90-minute, hop-on, hop-off narrated tram tour starts at Mallory Sq and makes a large, lazy loop around the whole city, with 12 stops along the way. Trolleys depart every 15 to 30 minutes from 9am to 4:30pm daily. You can hop on and off at any of the stops. The narration is hokey, but you'll get a good overview of Key West, its history, and gossipy dirt about local issues and people in the news. Save a couple of bucks if you book tickets online.

**CONCH TOUR TRAIN**  Train
( ☎305-294-5161; www.conchtourtrain.com; adult/children 12 & under/senior/$29/free/26; ☺9am-4:30pm; ♿) Run by the same company as trolley tours, though this one seats you in breezier linked train cars with no on/off option. Offers discounted admission to sights like the Hemingway House.

**HISTORIC KEY WEST
WALKING TOUR**  Walking
( ☎800-844-7601; 1 Whitehead St; www.trustedtours.com; adult/child $18/9) A walking tour that takes in some of the major architecture and historical sights of the island. Takes about two hours. You need to book in advance.

 **Sleeping**

There's a glut of boutique hotels, cozy B&Bs and four-star resorts here at the end of the USA. Any hotel in Old Town will put you within walking distance of all the action.

### CURRY MANSION INN    Hotel $$$

( ✆800-253-3466, 305-294-5349; http://curry
mansion.com; 511 Caroline St; r low season $195-
285, high season $240-365; P ❄ 🛜 ⛵ ) In a
city full of stately 19th-century homes,
the Curry Mansion is especially hand-
some. All the elements of an aristocratic
American home come together here,
from plantation-era Southern colonnades
to a New England–style widow's walk and,
of course, bright Floridian rooms with
canopied beds. Enjoy bougainvillea and
breezes on the veranda.

### MERMAID & ALLIGATOR  Guesthouse $$

( ✆305-294-1894, 800-773-1894; www.
kwmermaid.com; 729 Truman Ave; r low season
$148-198, high season $218-298; P ❄ @ ⛵ )
It takes a real gem to stand out amid
the jewelry store of Keys hotels, but this
place, located in a 1904 mansion, more
than pulls off the job. Each of the nine
rooms is individually designed with a
great mix of modern comfort, Keys Colonial ambience and playful laughs. The
treetop suite, with its exposed beams and
alcoved bed and bathroom, is our pick of
this idiosyncratic litter.

### L'HABITATION    Guesthouse $$

( ✆800-697-1766, 305-293-9203 www.lhabita
tion.com; 408 Eaton St; r $109-179; ❄ 🛜 ) A
beautiful classical Keys cottage with cute
rooms kitted out in light tropical shades,
with lamps that look like contemporary
art pieces and skittles-bright quilts. The
friendly bilingual owner welcomes guests
in English or French. The front porch,
shaded by palms, is a perfect place to
post and engage in Keys people watching.

 # Eating

Key West has delicious neighborhood
joints-in-the-wall to top end purveyors of
haute cuisine that could easily compete
with the best restaurants in Miami.

### CAFÉ SOLÉ    French $$$

( ✆305-294-0230; www.cafesole.com; 1029
Southard St; lunch $5-11, dinner $25-32; ⏰5:30-
10pm) Conch carpaccio with capers?
Yellowtail fillet and foie gras? Oh yes. This
locally and critically acclaimed venue is
known for its cozy back-porch ambience
and innovative menus, cobbled together
by a chef trained in southern French techniques who works with island ingredients.
The memory of the anchovies on crostini
makes us smile as we type. It's simple –
fish on toast! – but it's the sort of simple
yet delicious that makes you feel like
mom's whipped up something special for
Sunday dinner.

### CAMILLE'S    Fusion $$

(1202 Simonton St; breakfast $3-13, lunch $4-13,
dinner $14-25; ⏰8am-10pm; 🖉) This healthy
and tasty neighborhood joint is the kind
of place where players on the Key West
High School softball team are served by
friends from their science class, and the
hostess is the pitcher's mom – when
Conchs (Keys natives) head out for a
casual meal, they often come here. For 20
years the homey facade of Camille's has
concealed a sharp kitchen that makes a
mean chicken-salad sandwich, stone crab
claws with Dijon mayo and a macadamia-
crusted yellowtail we shudder (with pleasure) to recall.

### BLUE HEAVEN    American $$

( ✆305-296-8666; http://blueheavenkw.home
stead.com; 729 Thomas St; dinner mains $19-38;
⏰8am-10:30pm Mon-Sat, from 9am Sun) Proof
that location is *nearly* everything, this is
one of the quirkiest venues on an island of
oddities. Customers and a local chicken
flock dine in the spacious courtyard
where Hemingway once officiated boxing
matches; restrooms are in the adjacent
former brothel. This place gets packed
with customers who wolf down Southern-
fried takes on Keys cuisine – the barbe-
qued shrimp, drunk in a spicy sauce, are
gorgeous.

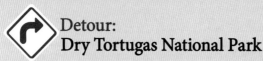

## Detour:
# Dry Tortugas National Park

Ponce de León named these islands Las Tortugas (The Turtles) for the sea turtles that roamed here. A lack of fresh water led sailors to add a 'dry.' Today the Dry Tortugas are a national park under the control of the **National Park Service** (☎305-242-7700; www.nps.gov/drto; admission $5) and are accessible by boat or plane.

The park is open for day trips and overnight camping. Garden Key has 13 campsites ($3 per person, per night), which are given out on a first-come, first-served basis. Reserve early by calling the National Park office. There are toilets, but no freshwater showers or drinking water; bring everything you'll need. The sparkling waters offer excellent snorkeling and diving opportunities. A **visitor center** is located within fascinating Fort Jefferson.

If you're hungry, watch for Cuban-American fishing boats trolling the waters. They'll happily trade for lobster, crab and shrimp; you'll have the most leverage trading beverages. Just paddle up and bargain for your supper. In March and April, there is stupendous bird-watching, including aerial fighting. Star-gazing is mind-blowing any time of the year.

### GETTING THERE

The **Yankee Freedom II** (☎305-294-7009, 800-634-0939; www.yankeefreedom.com; Historic Seaport) operates a fast ferry between Garden Key and the Historic Seaport (at the northern end of Margaret St). Round-trip fares cost $165/120 per adult/child. Reservations are recommended. Continental breakfast, a picnic lunch, snorkeling gear and a 45-minute tour of the fort are all included.

**Key West Seaplanes** (☎305-294-0709; www.seaplanesofkeywest.com) can take up to 10 passengers (flight time 40 minutes each way). A four-hour trip costs per adult/child under two years/child two to six years/child under 12 years $250/ free/160/190; an eight-hour trip costs $515/free/320/365. Again, reserve at least a week in advance.

The $5 park admission fees are included in the above prices.

 **Drinking**

Make your memories (or lack thereof) at one of the following.

**GREEN PARROT**                                    Bar
(601 Whitehead St) The oldest bar on an island of bars, this rogue's cantina opened in the late 19th century and hasn't closed yet. The owner tells you the parachute on the ceiling is 'weighed down with termite turds,' while a blues band howls through clouds of smoke. Defunct business signs and local artwork litter the walls and, yes, that's the city attorney showing off her new tattoo at the pool table. Men: check out the Hieronymus Bosch–like painting *Proverbidioms* in the restroom, surely the most entertaining urinal talk-piece on the island.

**PORCH**                                              Bar
(429 Caroline St) If you're getting tired of the frat boy bars on the Duval St strip, head to the Porch. It's a friendly little artisan beer bar that's more laid back (but hardly civilized) than your average Keys watering hole. The knowledgeable bartenders will trade jokes with you and point you in the right direction for some truly excellent brew. Then sit on the porch of the Porch and watch the Keys stumble on by.

**LOUIE'S BACKYARD** Bar
(700 Waddell Ave) With big windows that look out unto the street and classy music, Louie's is a refreshing break from the kegger attitude of most Duval bars, while still filled with the eccentric sense of fun that Key West is famous for.

 **Entertainment**

**Red Barn Theatre** Theater
(305-296-9911; www.redbarntheatre.org; 319 Duval St) An occasionally edgy and always fun, cozy little local playhouse.

**Tropic Cinema** Cinema
(877-761-3456; www.tropiccinema.org; 416 Eaton St) Great art-house movie theater with deco frontage.

 **Shopping**

Bright and breezy art galleries, excellent cigars, leather fetish gear and offensive T-shirts – Key West, what don't you sell?

**MONTAGE** Signs
(512 Duval St; 9am-10pm) Had a great meal or wild night at some bar or restaurant in the Keys? Well, this store probably sells the sign of the place (along with lots of Conch Republic tat), which makes for a nice souvenir.

**Bésame Mucho** Gifts
(315 Petronia St; 10am-6pm, till 4pm Sun) This place is well stocked with high-end beauty products, eclectic jewelry, clothing and housewares.

**Frangipani Gallery** Arts & Crafts
(1102 Duval St; 10am-6pm) One of the best galleries of local artists' work.

**Haitian Art Co** Arts & Crafts
(600 Frances St; 9am-5pm Mon-Fri) Haitian arts and crafts.

 **Information**

## Medical Services

The following are Key West's most accessible medical services:

**Lower Keys Medical Center** (305-294-5531, 800-233-3119; www.lkmc.com; 5900 College Rd, Stock Island, MM 5) Has a 24-hour emergency room.

**South Med** (305-295-3838; www.southmed.us; 3138 Northside Dr) Dr Scott Hall caters especially to the gay community, but serves all visitors.

## Tourist Information

**Key West Chamber of Commerce** (305-294-2587; www.keywestchamber.org; 510 Greene St; 8:30am-6:30pm Mon-Sat, to 6pm Sun) An excellent source of information.

## Getting There & Around

Key West International Airport (EYW) is off S Roosevelt Blvd on the east side of the island. You can fly into Key West from some major US cities such as Miami or New York.

# The Everglades

**More than Miami, the Everglades make South Florida truly unique.** Called the 'River of Grass' by Native Americans, this is not just a wetland, or a swamp, or a lake, or a river or a prairie – it is all of the above, twisted together into a series of soft horizons, long vistas, sunsets that stretch across your entire field of vision and the creeping grin of a large population of dinosaur-era reptiles.

When you watch anhinga flex their wings before breaking into corkscrew dives, or the slow, Jurassic flap of a great blue heron gliding over its domain, or the sun kissing miles of unbroken sawgrass as it sets behind humps of skeletal cypress domes, you'll have an idea of what we're speaking of. In a nation where natural beauty is measured by its capacity for drama, the Everglades subtly, contentedly flows on.

Aerial view of the Everglades National Park (p260).
JIM WARK/LONELY PLANET IMAGES ©

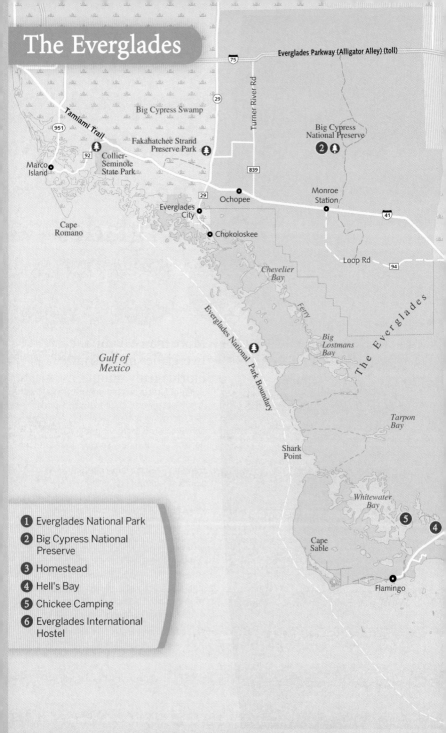

# The Everglades

Everglades Parkway (Alligator Alley) (toll)

75

Tamiami Trail

951

Big Cypress Swamp

29

Turner River Rd

Big Cypress
National Preserve

2

92

Fakahatchee Strand
Preserve Park

Collier-
Seminole
State Park

Marco
Island

839

29

Ochopee

Monroe
Station

41

Everglades
City

Cape
Romano

Chokoloskee

Loop Rd

94

Chevelier
Bay

Everglades National Park Boundary

Ferry

Big
Lostmans
Bay

The Everglades

Gulf of
Mexico

Tarpon
Bay

Shark
Point

Whitewater
Bay

5

4

Cape
Sable

Flamingo

1 Everglades National Park

2 Big Cypress National
Preserve

3 Homestead

4 Hell's Bay

5 Chickee Camping

6 Everglades International
Hostel

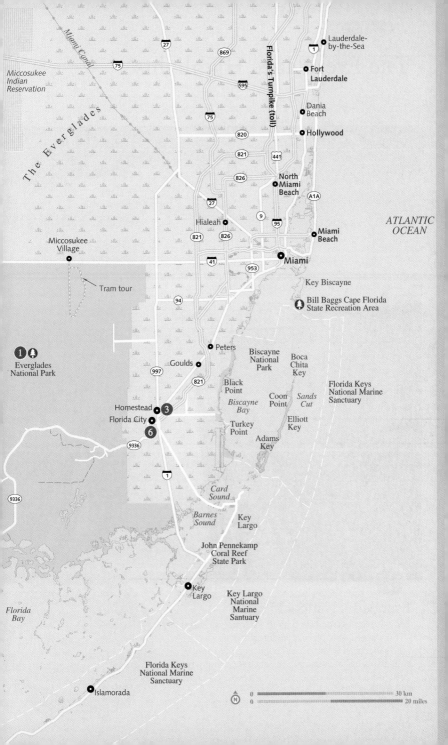

# The Everglades Highlights

## ① Everglades National Park

The third-largest national park in the lower 48 states is an odd, compelling place, a wilderness where elevation is recorded in inches and beauty is measured by subtlety rather than showy majesty. Yet beautiful the Everglades are, and visiting them is a highlight of many Florida trips. Pa-hay-okee Overlook (p265)

**Need to Know**
ALLIGATORS They'll ignore you if you don't get too close. MOSQUITOES In spring and summer. WHEN Winter is the dry season, best for wildlife viewing. For more see p261.

# Everglades National Park's Don't Miss List

LINDA FRIAR, A PARK RANGER IN EVERGLADES NATIONAL PARK

### 1 HIKING PINE ISLANDS
Go on the Anhinga Amble at **Royal Palm** (p263) where you'll see wading birds, alligators, and maybe a few turtles, otters, and different fish. From Anhinga head to Mahogany Hammock, where you'll experience one of the most beautiful tree islands in the Everglades! End with a hike to Pa-Hay-Okee, one of the highest points in the Everglades that offers sweeping views of the river of grass.

### 2 SLOUGH SLOG/WET WALK INTO CYPRESS DOMES
A **wet walk (or slough slog)** (p263) should be done the first time with a ranger guide. Once you're ready to go – you will get wet – either ankle- or hip-deep, the deeper the more exciting! Wading through the river of grass into the shadows of a 'gator hole' or cypress dome just can't be beat.

### 3 SHARK VALLEY TRAM TOUR
The **tram road** (p261), a remnant of oil exploration days, is a 15-mile loop through Everglades habitats. A naturalist provides an interpretive tour during the ride. There are opportunities to hop off the tram along the way to take photos and get a better look at the wildlife.

### 4 SHARK VALLEY SUNSET BIKE TOUR
Enjoy the kaleidoscope of colors and the movement of wildlife as the sun sets over the sawgrass prairie. Join a ranger for a 15-mile **bike ride** (p261). Bring your own bike or rent one. Explore the subtleness of this landscape. Listen to the Everglades symphony under the full moon. Climb to the observation tower to enjoy the mystery of the Everglades at night.

### 5 CANOE/KAYAK, GULF COAST
Paddle through the **Ten Thousand Islands** (p263) with a ranger as your guide. You'll look for wildlife, paddle through mangroves and learn about the park's natural and cultural history. If tide and weather allow, trips may include a walk on an island. Bring your own canoe/kayak or rent one. Reservations are required.

# Big Cypress National Preserve

This preserve both abuts and is partially encompassed by Everglades National Park. The portion of the Florida Scenic Trail that runs through the Big Cypress Preserve (p265) is a muddy yet absolutely gorgeous slog across the flooded forests and plains that spread across Florida's interior shelf. Hiking out here is not for novices, but if you have the experience, don't pass Big Cypress up.

## 4 Hell's Bay

The Everglades is truly the Wet Wild, and as such, to appreciate this landscape you need to get into the water. And not just any water, but the water that flows into and becomes a part of the land. There are countless creeks, streams and watercourses here, but our favorite is Hell's Bay (p265), a bracken tunnel that snakes through the dense vegetation of the River of Grass.

ALAMY/JAMES CALDWELL ©

## Homestead

ALAMY/TRAVEL DIVISION IMAGES ©

**3**

Homestead (p266) isn't exactly our favorite city in the world. It's a bit chaotically laid out and difficult to get your head around. But it houses some of the most charming sites in the Everglades area, including the fantastically weird Coral Castle, the fresh produce and quirky charm of the Robert is Here fruit stand, and the blessed, rescued wildlife of the Everglades Outpost. Coral Castle (p268)

EVERGLADES HOSTEL & TOURS PRESS PHOTO ©

**5**

## Chickee Camping

Just as you should get on the water via a boat to explore the far reaches of the Everglades, you may want to consider sleeping on the water via a chickee to get a sense of living in the Everglades. What's a chickee (p267)? Essentially, a raised, shaded platform. Chickee camping down here is incredibly romantic and serene, but you best bring some bug spray.

**6**

## Everglades International Hostel

This spot deserves a shout out for being one of the best hostels (p266) in America, bar none. How can you not love a lodging that collects travelers from every country, of every age group and every race, and unites them under one funky roof? Take excellent guided tours of the park with local staff, or chill out in the wonderfully weird backyard garden.

# The Everglades' Best...

## Wildlife

○ **Shark Valley Tram Tour**
(p261) This asphalt path
goes past loads of wading
birds and sunbathing
alligators.

○ **Royal Palm Visitor
Center** (p263) The
boardwalk trails lead over
literally dozens of alligators.

○ **Pa-hay-okee Overlook**
(p265) From this 'elevation'
you can see plenty of birds at
dawn and dusk.

○ **Wilderness Waterway**
(p265) Paddle and spot
jumping dolphins and fish-
eating raptors.

## Hiking

○ **West Lake Trail** (p265)
A boardwalk trail that
goes through a protected
mangrove forest.

○ **Florida National Scenic
Trail** (p264) A long slog, but
you'll see the best of the
Everglades.

○ **Christian Point** (p265)
This winding path leads
through forest and fields to
Florida Bay.

○ **Mahogany Hammock**
(p265) 'Island-hop' across
the Sea of Grass to copses of
hardwood trees.

## Boating

○ **Hell's Bay** (p265) Take a
canoe or kayak through this
overgrown watery labyrinth.

○ **10,000 Islands** (p265)
Can you count them all as
you paddle across the teal
Gulf?

○ **Biscayne National Park**
(p268) Practically the entire
park is protected waters!

○ **Graveyard Creek** (p265) A
beautiful series of tidal flats
and exposed mangroves.

# Need to Know

## Only in the Everglades

◦ **Robert is Here** (p267) Fun food stand and farmer's market.

◦ **Coral Castle** (p268) An oddly appealing monument to unrequited love and idiosyncrasy.

◦ **Skunk Ape Research Center** (p262) Reptile petting zoo meets 'research' outpost into Florida's Bigfoot.

◦ **Everglades Outpost** (p268) This preserve for abandoned and abused wild animals is fighting the good fight. Sadly closed till further notice.

◦ **Camping** If you're planning on camping within the park, contact the National Park Service (www.nops.gov/ever) and consult about what is the best campsite for your needs.

◦ **Weather** It's very important to check up on weather conditions before hiking or boating; the wind and rain here can be furious.

◦ **Maps** Again, contact the National Park Service to request the best maps if you intend to get into the bush.

◦ **Bug Spray** Bring it. Lots of it.

### GETTING AROUND

◦ **Car** You need a car to explore the three main areas of this enormous park in under a week.

◦ **Boat** Kayaking and canoeing is a great means of exploring interior waterways, while any kind of boat can be used to shoot up and down the gorgeous Gulf Coast.

◦ **Bicycle** The flat roads of the Everglades, especially in the Ernest Coe section, are great for cycling, but bring lots of food and water.

◦ **Foot** Hikes here are great; make sure to contact the National Park Service with your contact details and itineraries.

### BE FOREWARNED

◦ **Storms** From July to September is prime hurricane season, and bad thunderstorms can strike anytime.

◦ **Tides** If camping on the beach, pitch in designated, signed areas. Tides can wash in with no warning.

◦ **Wildlife** The main annoyance is bugs, but avoid snakes and, please, don't be foolish and feed the alligators.

◦ **Speed Limits** Obey them! It's tempting to speed, especially on US 41, but this is panther territory, and the endangered cats' biggest threat is cars.

**Left:** Alligator in the Everglades;
**Above:** Air boat cruising in the Everglades.

(LEFT) SHUTTERSTOCK IMAGES/CASTKA ©;
(ABOVE) ISTOCK IMAGES/ROBERTO A SANCHEZ ©

# The Everglades Itineraries

*While the Everglades have shrunk considerably since the beginning of the 20th century, they still take up a sizable chunk of South Florida. Everglades National Park is divided into three areas; we will explore all of them in these itineraries.*

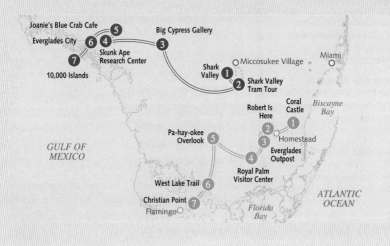

**MIAMI TO EVERGLADES CITY**

## 2 DAYS Tamiami Trail & the Gulf Coast

We will assume you'll be coming from Miami when you start this itinerary, but if you come from Fort Myers you can take this entire trip in reverse.

From Miami, head west on US 41/ Tamiami Trail, and feel free to stop for an airboat tour along the way. Our first mandatory stop is **(1) Shark Valley**, where you can embark down some quick walking paths. Just don't forget to either rent a bicycle or book a ticket onto the **(2) Shark Valley Tram Tour**, which winds its way past Everglades wildlife to a watchtower where you can look over the low horizon.

Head out of Shark Valley and continue west, making sure to peep in on the photographic exhibits on display in the **(3) Big Cypress Gallery** and the reptiles, weirdness and general eccentricity of the **(4) Skunk Ape Research Center**. You may also want to grab a bite to eat at **(5) Joanie's Blue Crab Cafe**, which fries up seafood like no other. In Everglades City, stop by the **(6) Gulf Coast Visitor Center** and either take a guided boat tour, or rent a boat and paddle along the **(7) 10,000 Islands**.

**3 DAYS**

**HOMESTEAD TO FLAMINGO POINT**
## Creeks & Prairies

In the southeast corner of the park, you'll explore the Ernest Coe section, rich in long grasslands and spidery waterways. You'll have to come through Homestead to get here, where you need to stop by a triumvirate of roadside attractions: **(1) Coral Castle**, a ruin of blocks of stone made by a lovestruck Latvian; **(2) Robert is Here**, a farmer's stand that sells fresh produce and is a family favorite; and the **(3) Everglades Outpost**, a volunteer-run refuge for rescued animals.

At Homestead, head to the **(4) Royal Palm Visitor Center**, where boardwalks stretch over what is likely the most alligators you'll ever spot in your life. We recommend waiting for night to fall and doing a guided tour of the boardwalks with a ranger; the nocturnal experience at Royal Palm is something special. Head from here to the **(5) Pa-hay-okee Overlook**, which affords fantastic views over the long surrounding grasslands and 'domes' of hardwood trees that characterize this part of the park. As you proceed to Flamingo Point, stop for side hikes down the boardwalk on the **(6) West Lake Trail** or wind your way to Florida Bay via beautiful **(7) Christian Point**.

Visitors along the picturesque Pa-hay-okee Overlook (p265).
ALAMY/ROB CRANDALL ©

# Discover the Everglades

## THE EVERGLADES NATIONAL PARK

The Everglades National Park was formed in the mid-20th century to protect the largest subtropical wilderness in the USA. The actual park boundaries cover some 25% of the fragile Everglades ecosystem, which ranges from mangrove islands to blackwater cypress forests to cyclically inundated grasslands. There are three primary 'regions' in the park: Shark Valley, Gulf Coast and Ernest Coe, all detailed below.

### History

It's tempting to think of the Everglades as a swamp, but 'prairie' may be a more apt description. The Glades (Colonial cartographer Gerard de Brahm named the region 'River Glades,' which became Everglades on later English maps) are grasslands that are flooded for most of the year. Run-off water from central Florida flows down the peninsula via streams and rivers, over and through the Glades, and into Florida Bay. Small wonder the Calusa Indians called the area Pa-hay-okee (grassy water). Conservationist Marjory Stoneman Douglas called the Everglades the River of Grass.

Starting in 1905, Floridians cut hundreds of canals to separate the Glades from the state's natural flow of water. The idea was to 'reclaim' the land and turn it into farmland. Unfortunately, this effort has actually upset the natural water cycle and replenishment of the Florida aquifer (the state's freshwater supply).

Boats moored along the inlets at Boca Chita Key (p269).
ALAMY/NATIONAL GEOGRAPHIC IMAGE COLLECTION ©

In 2011, the water levels in Okeechobee were almost 2.7 inches below normal levels. The number of wading birds nesting has declined by 90% to 95% since the 1930s. Currently, there are 67 threatened and endangered plant and animal species in the park. At this stage, scientists estimate the wetlands have been reduced by 50 to 75% of their original size.

The **Comprehensive Everglades Restoration Project** (CERP; www.evergladesplan.org), a partnership between several federal, state and local government agencies, is designed to address the root issue of water, but political battles over funding have intensified. Opponents of CERP say the program is low-priority during an economic recession. Old anti-Everglades arguments – that CERP curtails agriculture and development – have significantly slowed CERP's implementation.

### When to Go

December to March Dry season means optimum wildlife viewing along watercourses, but some kayaking will be difficult.

April to June Although the weather gets pretty hot, there's a good mix of water and wildlife.

July to November Lots of heat, lots of bugs and (except October and November) chances of hurricanes.

### Orientation

There are three main entrances and three main areas of the park: one along the southeast edge near Homestead and Florida City (Ernest Coe section); at the central-north side on the Tamiami Trail (Shark Valley section); and a third at the northwest shore (Gulf Coast section), past Everglades City.

 **Sights**

## Shark Valley Section

The northern and western portion of the park hugs the Tamiami Trail/US 41. Here you'll find flooded forests and swampy bottomlands.

**SHARK VALLEY**                              Park

(☎305-221-8776; www.nps.gov/ever/plan-yourvisit/svdirections; car/bicycle $10/5; ⊙8:30am-6pm) Shark Valley sounds like it should be the headquarters for the villain in a James Bond movie, but it is in fact a slice of National Park Service grounds heavy with informative signs and knowledgeable rangers. Shark Valley is located in the cypress-and-hardwood-and-riverine section of the Everglades, a more traditionally jungly section of the park than the grassy fields and forest domes surrounding the Ernest Coe visitor center. A 15-mile/24km paved trail takes you past small creeks, tropical forest and 'borrow pits' – manmade holes that are now basking spots for gators, turtles and birdlife. The pancake-flat trail is perfect for bicycles, which can be rented at the entrance for $7.50 per hour. Bring water with you.

**TRAM TOUR**                                 Tour

(☎305-221-8455; www.sharkvalleytram-tours.com; adult/child under 12yr/senior $18.25/11.50/17.25; ⊙departures 9:30am, 11am, 1pm, 3pm May-Dec, 9am-4pm every hour on the hour Jan-Apr) If you don't feel like exerting yourself, the most popular and painless way to immerse yourself in the Everglades is via the two-hour tram trip that runs along Shark Valley's entire 15-mile trail. If you only have time for one Everglades activity, this should be it, as guides are informative and witty, and you'll likely see gators sunning themselves on the road. Halfway along the trail is the 50ft-high **Shark Valley Observation Tower**, an ugly concrete tower that offers dramatically beautiful views of the park.

MARK NEWMAN/LONELY PLANET IMAGES ©

## Don't Miss **Skunk Ape Research Headquarters**

Ah, Florida. You can't make this stuff up. To whit: the Skunk Ape Research Center, topped by a giant panther statue, dedicated to tracking down southeastern USA's version of Bigfoot, the eponymous Skunk Ape (a large gorilla-man who supposedly stinks to high heaven). We never saw a Skunk Ape here, but you can see a corny gift shop and, in the back, a reptile and bird zoo run by a true Florida eccentric, the sort of guy who wraps albino pythons around his neck for fun. Donate a few bucks at the entrance.

### THINGS YOU NEED TO KNOW

🕿 239-695-2275; www.skunkape.info; 40904 Tamiami Trail E; 🕑 7am-7pm, 'zoo' closes around 4pm

**BIG CYPRESS GALLERY**     Gallery
( 🕿 941-695-2428; www.clydebutcher.com; Tamiami Trail; 🕑 10am-5pm Wed-Mon) The highlight of many Everglades trips, this gallery showcases the work of Clyde Butcher, an American photographer who follows in the great tradition of Ansel Adams. His large-format black-and-white images elevate the swamps to a higher level. Butcher has found a quiet spirituality in the brackish waters and you might, too, with the help of his eyes. Every Labor Day (first weekend in September) the gallery holds a gala event, which includes a fun $20 swamp walk onto his 30-acre property; the party attracts swamp-stompers from across the state. At the time of writing, the gallery was setting up two homes located in the cypress woods as guesthouses – the properties look pretty nice, can sleep from 4 to 6 people and will cost around $200 per night.

## Gulf Coast Section

The northwest corner of the park rubs up against Everglades City, an old Florida fishing village of raised houses, turquoise water and scattershot emerald-green mangrove islands.

## GULF COAST VISITOR CENTER  Park

(☎239-695-3311; Hwy 29, Everglades City, 815 Oyster Bar Ln; ⏰9am-4:30pm May-Oct, from 8am Nov-Apr; tours from $25, boat rentals from $13 per hr) This is the northwestern-most ranger station for Everglades National Park, and provides access to the 10,000 Islands area. Boat tours depart from the downstairs marina into the mangrove flats and green islands – if you're lucky you may see dolphins springing up beside your craft. This tangled offshore archipelago was a major smuggling point for drugs into the mainland USA during the late 1970s and early '80s; bales of marijuana were nicknamed 'square grouper' by local fishermen. It's great fun to go kayaking and canoeing around here; boats can be rented from the marina, but make sure to take a map with you (they're available for free in the Visitor Center).

## Ernest Coe Section

The southern and eastern portions of the park can be accessed from Homestead, an hour south of Miami. This part of the park consists of grassy prairies, small creeks and small wooded copses.

## ERNEST COE VISITOR CENTER  Park

(☎305-242-7700; www.nps.gov/ever; 40001 State Rd 9336; ⏰8am-5pm) You'll enter Everglades National Park at this friendly visitor center. Have a look at the excellent exhibits, including a diorama of 'typical' Floridians.

## ROYAL PALM VISITOR CENTER  Park

(☎305-242-7700; State Rd 9336; ⏰8am-4:15pm) Four miles past Ernest Coe Visitor Center, Royal Palm offers the easiest access to the Glades in these parts. Two trails, the **Anhinga** and **Gumbo Limbo** (the latter named for the gumbo-limbo tree, also known as the 'tourist tree' because its bark peels like a sunburned Brit), take all of an hour to walk, and put you face to face with a panoply of Everglades wildlife. Gators sun on the shoreline, anhinga spear their prey and wading birds stalk haughtily through the reeds. Come at night for a ranger walk on the boardwalk and shine a flashlight into the water to see one of the coolest sights of your life: the glittering eyes of dozens of alligators prowling the waterways.

The boardwalk at the Pa-hay-okee Overlook (p265).

ALAMY/WITOLD SKRYPCZAK©

**FLAMINGO VISITOR CENTER** Park
(☎ 239-695-2945; State Rd 9336; ⊙8am-
4:15pm) The most isolated portion of the
park is a squat **marina** (☎239-696-3101,
239-695-2591) where you can rent boats or
go on a backcountry boat tour, but facilities were shut down for renovations during our visit. In the past, boat tours have
run for around $20/10 for adult/child,
while canoes (one hour/half-day/full day
$8/22/32) and sea kayaks (half/full day
$35/45) were available for rental. You're
largely left to explore the channels and
islands of Florida Bay on your own. Be
careful in coastal areas here during rough
weather, as storm surges can turn an
attractive spread of beach into a watery
stretch of danger fairly quickly.

## 🏃 Activities

Be it by boat, bicycle or your own feet,
there are plenty of ways to explore the
wet wild of the Everglades. We have split
this section according to the park's geographic divisions.

# Shark Valley

## Hiking

At the park entrance, the easy **Bobcat
Boardwalk** makes a loop through a thick
copse of tropical hardwoods before
emptying you out right back into the
Shark Valley parking lot. A little ways
past is the **Otter Cave Trail**, which heads
over a limestone shelf that has been
Swiss-cheesed into a porous sponge by
rainwater. Animals now live in the eroded
holes (although it's not likely you'll spot
any) and Native Americans used to live on
top of the shelf.

There are some 31 miles of the **Florida
National Scenic Trail** (www.nps.gov/
bicy/planyourvisit/florida-trail.htm) within
Big Cypress National Preserve. From
the southern terminus, which can be
accessed via Loop Rd, the trail runs 8.3
miles north to US 41. The way is flat, but
it's hard going: you'll almost certainly
be wading through water, and you'll
have to pick your way through a series
of solution holes (small sinkholes) and
thick hardwood hammocks. There is
often no shelter from the sun, and the
bugs are...*plentiful*. There are (free)

Tourists taking photos of alligators.

ALAMY/IRENE ABDOU ©

# Detour:
## Big Cypress National Preserve

The 1139-sq-mile Big Cypress Preserve (named for the size of the park, not its trees) is the result of a compromise between environmentalists, cattle ranchers and oil-and-gas explorers. The rains that flood the Preserve's prairies and wetlands slowly filter down through the Glades. About 45% of the cypress swamp (actually a group of mangrove islands, hardwood hammocks, slash pine, prairies and marshes) is protected. Great bald cypress trees are nearly gone, thanks to pre-Preserve lumbering, but dwarf pond cypress trees are plentiful. The Oasis Visitor Center (☏239-695-4758, ☏941-695-1201; 33000 Tamiami Trail E; ☻8am-4:30pm Mon-Fri), about 20 miles west of Shark Valley, has great exhibits for the kids and an outdoor, water-filled ditch popular with alligators.

primitive campsites with water wells along the trail; pick up a map at the visitor center. **Monument Lake** (May-Dec 14 free, Dec 15-Apr $16) has water and toilets.

## Ernest Coe to Flamingo Point

State Rd 9336 cuts through the soft heart of the park; all of the following are half a mile (800m) long. **Mahogany Hammock** leads into an 'island' of hardwood forest floating on the waterlogged prairie, while the **Pinelands** takes you through a copse of rare spindly swamp pine and palmetto forest. Further on, **Pa-hay-okee Overlook** is a raised platform that peeks over one of the prettiest bends in the River of Grass. The **West Lake Trail** runs through the largest protected mangrove forest in the Northern Hemisphere. Further down you can take a good two-hour, 1.8-mile (2.9km) hike to **Christian Point**, which ends with a dramatic view of the wind-swept shores of Florida Bay

## Gulf Coast

### Kayaking & Canoeing

The **10,000 Islands** consist of many (but not really 10,000) tiny islands and a mangrove swamp that hugs the southwestern-most border of Florida. The **Wilderness Waterway**, a 99-mile path

between Everglades City and Flamingo, is the longest canoe trail in the area, but there are shorter trails near Flamingo.

Adhere to National Oceanic & Atmospheric Administration (NOAA) tide and nautical charts. Going against the tides is the fastest way to make a miserable trip. The Gulf Coast Visitor Center (p263) sells nautical charts and gives out free tidal charts.

## Ernest Coe to Flamingo Point

There are plenty of push-off points in the southeast part of the park, all with names that sound like they were read off Frodo's map to Mordor, including **Hell's Bay**, the **Nightmare**, **Snake Bight** and **Graveyard Creek**. The guys at **North American Canoe Tours** (NACT; ☏941-695-3299/4666; www.evergladesadventures.com; Ivey House Bed & Breakfast, 107 Camellia St; ☻Nov–mid-Apr) rent out camping equipment and canoes for full/half days ($35/$25) and touring kayaks ($45 to $65).

 **Sleeping**

If you don't feel like camping in the park, there are good hotels in Everglades City (near the Gulf Coast section of the park) and Homestead (near the Homestead section of the park).

Double-crested cormorants roosting in mangrove trees in the Everglades National Park.

ALAMY/KENNY WILLIAMS ©

## Inside the Park

**NATIONAL PARK SERVICE CAMPSITES**  Campground $

(NPS; ☏800-365-2267; www.nps.gov/ever/planyourvisit/camping; sites May-Oct free, Nov-Apr $16) There are campgrounds run by the NPS located throughout the park. Most sites are primitive and do not have hookups. NPS visitor centers can provide a map of campsites, as does the park website. **Long Pine Key** (☏305-242-7873; May-Oct free, Nov-Apr $16) is a good bet for car campers, while the **Flamingo Campground** (☏877-444-6777; May-Oct free, Nov-Apr $30) has electrical hookups.

## Homestead

**EVERGLADES INTERNATIONAL HOSTEL**  Hostel $

(☏305-248-1122, 800-372-3874; www.evergladeshostel.com; 20 SW 2nd Ave, Florida City; camping $18, dm $28, d $61-75; P ❄ 🤍 🐾) Located in a cluttered, comfy 1930s boarding house, this friendly hostel has good value dorms, private rooms and 'semiprivates' (you have an enclosed room within the dorms and share a bathroom with dorm residents). But what they've done with their back yard – wow.

It's a serious garden of earthly delights. There's a tree house; a natural rock-cut pool with a waterfall; a Bedouin pavilion that doubles as a dancehall; a gazebo; an open-air tented 'bed room'; an oven built to resemble a tail-molting tadpole. It all needs to be seen to be believed, and best of all you can sleep anywhere in the backyard for $18.

 **Eating**

Old Florida fare, rich produce, fresh seafood and Southern cuisine are the name of the game.

## Everglades City

**JOANIE'S BLUE CRAB CAFE**  American $

(joaniesbluecrabcafe.com; Tamiami Trail; mains $9-17; ⊙9am-5pm) This rather quintessential shack, east of Ochopee, with open rafters, shellacked picnic tables and alligator kitsch serves delicious food of the 'fried everything' variety on paper plates. There's live music most days.

## Everglades City

**EVERGLADES CITY MOTEL**     Motel $$
( 📞 239-695-4244, 877-567-0679; www.everg
ladescitymotel.com; 310 Collier Ave; r from $80;
❄ 🛜 🛗 ) With large renovated rooms that
have flat-screen TVs, arctic air-
conditioning and a fantastically friendly
staff that will hook you up with what-
ever tours your heart desires, this is an
exceptionally good value lodge for those
looking to spend some time near the
10,000 Islands.

**IVEY HOUSE BED &
BREAKFAST**                    B&B $$
( 📞 239-695-3299, 877-567-0679; www.ivey
house.com; 107 Camellia St; lodge $74-120, inn
$99-209; ❄ 🛜 🛗 ) This family-run tropical
inn serves good breakfasts in its small
Ghost Orchid Grill. Plus it operates some
of the best nature trips around (p265).

## Homestead

**ROBERT IS HERE**            Market $
(www.robertishere.com; 19200 SW 344th St,
Homestead; ⏲8am-7pm Nov-Aug) More than a
farmer's stand, Robert's is an institution.
This is Old Florida at its kitschy best, in
love with the Glades and the agriculture
that surrounds it. There's a petting zoo
for the kids, live music at night, plenty of
homemade preserves and sauces, and
while everyone goes crazy for the milk-
shakes – as they should – do not leave
without having the fresh orange juice. It's
the best in the world. What's up with the
funny name? Well, back in the day the
namesake of the pavilion was selling his
daddy's cucumbers on this very spot,
but no traffic was slowing down for the
produce. So a sign was constructed that
announced, in big red letters, that Robert
was, in fact, here. He has been ever since,
too.

### ℹ Information

**Everglades National Park** ( 📞 305-242-7700;
www.nps.gov/ever; car/bicycle & pedestrian
$10/5 for 7 days) The park is open 365 days a
year.

---

# Wilderness Camping

Three types of backcountry campsites are available: beach sites, on coastal
shell beaches and in the 10,000 Islands; ground sites (mounds of dirt built up
above the mangroves) and 'chickees,' wooden platforms built above the water
line where you can pitch a free-standing (no spikes) tent. Chickees, which have
toilets, are the most civilized – there's a serenity found in sleeping on what feels
like a raft levitating above the water.

Warning: if you're paddling around and see an island that looks pleasant for
camping but isn't a designated campsite, beware – you may end up submerged
when tides change.

From November to April, camping permits cost $10, plus $2 per person per
night; from May to October sites are free, but you must still self-register at
Flamingo and Gulf Coast Visitor Centers or call 📞239-695-2945.

Some backcountry tips:

◉ Store food in a hand-sized, raccoon-proof container (available at gear stores).

◉ Bury your waste at least 10 inches below ground, but keep in mind some
ground sites have hard turf.

◉ Use a backcountry stove to cook. Ground fires are only permitted at beach sites,
and you can only burn dead or drowned wood.

## If You Like...
# Roadside Attractions

Homestead, for all her sprawl, houses two great attractions of the Florida roadside.

### 1 CORAL CASTLE
(www.coralcastle.com; 28655 S Dixie Hwy; adult/child 7-18yr $12/7; ⊘8am-6pm, to 8pm Sat & Sun) One Latvian immigrant's monument to unrequited love is this rough-hewn rock compound which includes a 'throne room', a sun dial and stone stockade (his intended's 'timeout area').

### 2 EVERGLADES OUTPOST
(www.evergladesoutpost.org; 35601 SW 192nd Ave; recommended donation $20; ⊘10am-4pm Sat & Sun, by appointment Mon-Fri) Volunteers house, feed and care for wild animals that have been seized from illegal traders, abused, neglected or donated by people who could not care for them. Residents include gibbons, a lemur, wolves, cobras, alligators and a pair of tigers. During the week, call ahead to visit.

### ⓘ Getting There & Away
8th St SW in Miami becomes US 41/Tamiami Trail. Shark Valley is about an hour west of Miami. The Ernest Coe entrance is an hour south of Miami. There are no buses into the park.

# BISCAYNE NATIONAL PARK

Just to the east of the Everglades is Biscayne National Park, or the 5% of it that isn't underwater. A portion of the world's third-largest reef sits here off the coast of Florida, along with mangrove forests and the northernmost Florida Keys. Fortunately this unique 300-sq-mile park is easy to explore independently with a canoe, via a glass-bottom boat tour or a snorkeling or diving trip.

# Sights

**BISCAYNE NATIONAL PARK**  Park
(✆305-230-7275, 305-230-1100; www.nps.gov/bisc, www.biscayneunderwater.com; 9700 SW 328th St) The park itself offers canoe rentals, transportation to the offshore keys, snorkeling and scuba-diving trips, and glass-bottom-boat viewing of the exceptional reefs. All tours require a minimum of six people, so call to make reservations. Three-hour glass-bottom-boat trips ($45) depart at 10am and are very popular; if you're lucky you may spot some dolphins or manatees. Canoe rentals cost $12 per hour and kayaks $16; they're rented from 9am to 3pm. Three-hour snorkeling trips ($45) depart at 1:15pm daily; you'll have about 1½ hours in the water. Scuba trips depart at 8:30am Friday to Sunday ($99). You can also arrange a private charter boat tour around the park for $300.

**MARITIME HERITAGE TRAIL**  Trail
One of the only trails of its kind in the USA, the Maritime Heritage Trail was still technically under development at the time of research, but already taking 'hikers.' If you've ever wanted to explore a sunken ship, this may well be the best opportunity in the country. Six are located within the park grounds; the trail experience involves taking visitors out, by boat, to the site of the wrecks where they can swim and explore among derelict vessels and clouds of fish – there are even waterproof information site cards placed among the ships. Five of the vessels are suited for scuba divers, but one, the *Mandalay,* a lovely two-masted schooner that sank in 1966, can be accessed by snorkelers.

# Activities

**Boating** and **fishing** are naturally popular and often go hand in hand, but to do either you'll need to get some paperwork in order. Boaters will want to get tide charts from the park (or from www.nps. gov/bisc/planyourvisit/tide-predictions. htm). And make sure you comply with local slow-speed zones, designed to protect the endangered manatee.

The slow zones currently extend 1000ft out from the mainland, from Black Point south to Turkey Point, and include the marinas at Black Point and Homestead Bayfront Parks. Another slow zone extends from Sands Cut to Coon Point; maps of all of the above can be obtained from rangers, and are needed for navigation purposes in any case.

For information on boat tours and rental, contact **Biscayne Underwater** (www.biscayneunderwater.com), which can help arrange logistics.

##  Sleeping

Primitive camping on Elliott and Boca Chita Keys costs $15 per tent, per night; you pay on a trust system with exact change on the harbor (rangers cruise the Keys to check your receipt). There is potable water on the island, but it always pays to be prepared. It costs $20 to moor your boat overnight at Elliott or Boca Chita harbors, but that fee covers the use of one campsite for up to six people and two tents.

##  Information

**Dante Fascell Visitor Center** ( ☏ 305-230-7275; www.nps.gov/bisc; 9700 SW 328th St; ⏱ 8:30am-5pm) Located at Convoy Point, the grounds around the center are popular picnic grounds. Also showcases local artwork.

##  Getting There & Away

To get here, you'll have to drive about 9 miles east of Homestead (the way is pretty well signposted) on SW 328th St (North Canal Dr) into a long series of green-and-gold flat fields and marsh.

# Tampa Bay & the Gulf Coast

**The Gulf Coast is muddled color.** Slow tides. Soft wind. To drive along the water in southwest Florida is to enter an impressionistic watercolor painting. First, there is the dazzling white-quartz sand of its barrier-island beaches, whose illuminated turquoise waters darken to silver-mantled indigo as the fiery sun lowers to the horizon. Later, seen from the causeways, those same islands become a phosphorescent smear beneath the inky black, star-flecked night sky.

The Gulf Coast's beauty is surely its main attraction, but variety is a close second: from Tampa to St Petersburg to Sarasota to Naples, there is urban sophistication, passionate artistry and exquisite cuisine. There are secluded islands, family-friendly resorts and Spring Break–style parties.

Here, Ringling's circus and Salvador Dalí's melting canvases fit perfectly – both are bright, bold, surreal entertainments to match manatees, roseate spoonbills, open-mouthed alligators and earthy Ybor City cigars.

Brown pelicans in the Gulf Coast.
GETTY IMAGES/PAUL E TESSIER ©

Pensacola Beach (p352) in the Gulf Coast.
SHUTTERSTOCK/CHERYL CASEY ©

# Tampa Bay & The Gulf Coast

1 Sanibel & Captiva Island
2 Weeki Wachee Springs
3 Fort DeSoto Park & Beach
4 Mote Marine Laboratory
5 Salvador Dalí Museum
6 Ringling Museum Complex

Cedar Key
To Gainesville (34.5mi); I-10 (57.5mi)
Ocala National Park
Withlacoochee River
Tsala Apopka Lake
Crystal River
Homosassa Springs State Wildlife Park
Homosassa Springs
Inverness
Weeki Wachee
Brooksville
Hudson
Land O' Lakes
Dade City
To Orlando (20mi)
Hillsborough River State Park
Honeymoon Island State Park
Tarpon Springs
Tampa International Airport
Lakeland
Caladesi Island
Dunedin
Clearwater
Clearwater Beach
Tampa
St Petersburg-Clearwater International Airport
St Petersburg
Alafia River
St Pete Beach
Tampa Bay
Fort DeSoto Park & Beach
Anna Maria
Bradenton
Manatee River
Zolfo Springs
Longboat Key
Sarasota
Lido Key
Siesta Key
Myakka River
Myakka River State Park
Arcadia
Peace River
Venice
Port Charlotte
Punta Gorda
Charlotte Harbour
Lee County Manatee Park
Cayo Costa State Park
North Fort Myers
Fort Myers
Pine Island
Captiva Island
Matlacha
Southwest Florida International Airport
Sanibel Island
Fort Myers Beach
Bonita Springs
Corkscrew Swamp Sanctuary
To Everglades (50mi)
Naples

GULF OF MEXICO

50 km
30 miles

# Tampa Bay & the Gulf Coast Highlights

**1**

## Sanibel & Captiva Islands

This pair of barrier islands, connected to Fort Myers by a long causeway, is a prime example of Florida development done right. Businesses and residences are built low to the ground so as to minimize their visual presence, and the gentle physical beauty of the islands constantly shines through.

**Need to Know**

**TOLLS** It costs $6 to cross the causeway from Fort Myers to Sanibel. **BIKE** Flat Sanibel is perfect for biking. **For further coverage, see p305.**

# Sanibel & Captiva Island's Don't Miss List

RICHARD & SARAH FORTUNE ARE PHOTOGRAPHERS WITH THROUGH THE LENS NATURE PHOTOGRAPHY (WWW .THROUGHTHELENSGALLERY.COM)

## 1 JN 'DING' DARLING NATIONAL WILDLIFE REFUGE

High on the list for any birders and nature-lovers. The best time to visit is at low tide and early morning to see a feeding frenzy of bird species along **Wildlife Drive** (p306), especially Lagoons 2 and 3.

## 2 CAPTIVA CRUISES

Explore **barrier islands** on the pristine Gulf Coast (p307). The *Lady Chadwick* takes in Cabbage Key (promoted by Jimmy Buffett in *Cheeseburger in Paradise*), while Useppa Key has natural beauty not found anywhere else. No cars are allowed on this private island; footpaths are the main arteries. An added bonus is bottlenose dolphins that follow the boat during its one-hour cruise.

## 3 CIP'S PLACE

**Cip's Place** (p308) ranks way high on our list of local restaurants/pubs that have a Sanibel feel without being too commercial. The attentive service is fabulous and the garden atmosphere is true Sanibel style.

## 4 SUNSETS IN SANIBEL

A Gulf of Mexico **sunset** is second to none. The anticipation for that mystical moment is what vacationers and locals set their clocks for. The best viewing areas are Blind Pass (the beach between Sanibel and Captiva), and the Mucky Duck off Sandy Ross Lane in Captiva. Also very popular is the Causeway between Fort Myers and Sanibel.

## 5 SANIBEL THRILLER

A high-speed 50ft twin-diesel-powered **catamaran** (p307) departs Sanibel Marina daily to circumnavigate Sanibel and Captiva Islands. The highly educational narration covers the island's history and uniqueness in protecting and preserving the barrier island's ecological environment.

## Weeki Wachee Springs

Seriously, God bless Weeki Wachee Springs (p309) for keeping the greatest in Old Florida nostalgia alive and well. Grandparents take grandchildren here and the parents in the middle get teary, remembering their own first time marveling at beautiful mermaids dancing their graceful underwater acrobatics. Weeki Wachee is more than ballet. It's our memories of what makes Florida fun.

## Mote Marine Laboratory

We're tempted to say the Mote Marine Laboratory (p297) is the best aquarium in Florida, but it's not just an aquarium. It's a respected research facility that regularly breaks new ground in marine biological research. At the same time the Mote is very much open to visitors, who can marvel at stingrays, sharks, sea turtles and manatees. OK: it's the best aquarium in Florida.

ALAMY/INDEPENDENT PICTURE SERVICE ©

## Fort DeSoto Park & Beach

There are so many beaches stretching south of St Petersburg we're hard pressed to elevate any one above the others. But then along comes Fort DeSoto beach (p294). The sand and sea alone don't make this place great (although they are great). It's the mix of the beach and the accompanying park, with its canoe trails, nature trails, dog park and complex interplay of Gulf Coast ecosystems.

ALAMY/ALEX GORE ©

## Salvador Dalí Museum

Salvador Dalí was an exciting artist who should be known for more than pictures of clocks melting in the desert. If you want to know more about the man and his genius, visit this museum (p295) in St Petersburg. It's not just an art gallery; it's a building whose layout, design and exhibits all lead you into an exploration of the psyche behind surrealism.

## Ringling Museum Complex

The Ringling Museum (p301) is...well, where to start? It's an art museum, yes. A monument to John Ringling, father of the modern American circus? Sure. Yet it's also a house of whimsy and luxury, the sort of mansion you'd expect the Mad Hatter to own if he could afford it. Plus: the on-site Circus Museum really is an entertaining peek into the greatest show on Earth.

# Tampa Bay & the Gulf Coast's Best...

## Beach Bumming

○ **Fort DeSoto Park & Beach** (p294) Natural beauty and a sense of comfortable isolation south of St Petersburg.

○ **Bowman's Beach** (p305) White sand and long horizons on Sanibel Island.

○ **St Pete Beach** (p296) Not just beautiful; stacked with food and drinking options.

○ **Caladesi Island State Park** (p310) Practically pristine barrier island beach north of Tampa.

## Arts & Culture

○ **Straz Center for the Performing Arts** (p288) This enormous Tampa concert hall hosts symphonies, Broadway, ballet and opera.

○ **Salvador Dalí Museum** (p295) The finest modern-art museum in Florida.

○ **Arcade Theatre** (p303) Home base for the fantastic Florida Repertory Theatre.

○ **Ringling Museum Complex** (p301) Encompasses arts, local history and the institution of the American circus.

## Quirky Delights

○ **Weeki Wachee Springs** (p309) Mermaids performing underwater ballet? Sing us up!

○ **Sanibel Shelling** (p305) Pluck a huge assortment of enamel off these shell-studded beaches.

○ **Coffee Pot Bayou & Old Northeast** (p290) St Petersburg's most attractive neighborhood is her oldest one.

○ **Mote Marine Laboratory** (p297) Part research center, part amazing Gulf Coast aquarium.

# Need to Know

## Wildlife-Watching

○ **Myakka River State Park** (p302) Hundreds of alligators call these wetlands home.

○ **Homosassa Springs Wildlife State Park** (p308) See all the great birds, reptiles and mammals of the Florida menagerie.

○ **Crystal River National Wildlife Refuge** (p310) Excellent area for manatee sightings.

○ **JN 'Ding' Darling National Wildlife Refuge** (p306) A drive-through 'safari' takes you past clouds of birdlife.

## ADVANCE PLANNING

○ **Rentals** The Gulf Coast is studded with vacation properties; see www .gulfcoastrentals.com for a directory on short-term rentals.

○ **Events** There's a packed cultural calendar out here; see www.artstampabay .com for more information.

○ **Restaurants** Dining is pretty casual here, but it's still best to make reservations in cities like Tampa Bay and St Petersburg.

○ **Shelling** Beaches here (especially in Sanibel) are studded with shells; print this guide before you visit: www.sanibel-captiva.org /play/shelling_center

## RESOURCES

○ **Lee County Visitor & Convention Bureau** Information and resources for Fort Myers, Sanibel Island and the surrounding area; www .leevcb.com.

○ **Visit St Petersburg & Clearwater** Tourism website for St Pete and her beaches; www .visitstpeteclearwater.com.

○ **Ybor.org** Ybor City Chamber of Commerce, with information on galleries, nightlife and food; www.ybor.org.

○ **Visit Tampa Bay** Clearing house on tourism information for Tampa Bay; www.visittampabay .com.

## GETTING AROUND

○ **Car** I-75 is the main highway that connects the area of the Gulf Coast covered in this chapter.

○ **Bus** Greyhound buses connect Tampa Bay, St Petersburg, Bradenton (Sarasota) and Fort Myers.

○ **Air** Major airlines fly directly to St Petersburg, Tampa Bay, Sarasota and Fort Myers.

○ **Boat** Make sure to check out ferry schedules for information on services to various barrier islands; see relevant sections in the chapter for more information.

**Left:** Lifeguard shack along beach in St Pete (p296);
**Above:** White sand and emerald sea in the Gulf Coast
(LEFT) DREAMSTIME/JK3291 ©; (ABOVE) ALAMY/ZEREGA ©

# Tampa Bay & the Gulf Coast Itineraries

*The Gulf Coast is Florida's quiet, family-friendly alternative to the glamour and Spring Break partying of the Atlantic Coast. We'll explore gentle nature preserves, cerebral art museums and miles of soft beach.*

**4 DAYS**

**WEEKI WACHEE TO ST PETERSBURG,**

## Tampa Bay Blitz

**(1) Weeki Wachee Springs**, where mermaids dance underwater and kids and their grandparents laugh at the un-ironic joy of it all, is a slice of Old Florida that's a bit of a rarity these days. You'll see what we mean when you head from here to **(2) Busch Gardens**, an African-themed amusement park that improves its rides and attractions every day. From here you'll head down to **(3) Tampa Bay**, where you can get cultured by visiting the **(4) Museum of Art** and seeing a show at the **(5) Straz Center for the Performing Arts**.

Head to **(6) St Petersburg** the next day and take in the **(7) Salvador Dalí Museum**. In the historical neighborhood of **(8) Coffee Pot Bayou** walk the cobbled streets for their atmosphere, or inject your day with some greenery at the **(9) Gizella Kopsick Palm Arboretum**. Day four, take advantage of some of the beaches south of St Petersburg; we recommend **(10) Fort DeSoto Park**. Once you've gotten your fill of all the sun, sand and calm surf that is the Gulf Coast, get dinner in the artsy enclave/village of **(11) Gulfport**.

---

**Top Left:** Rollercoaster ride at Busch Gardens (p291);
**Top Right:** Sunset scene at Pier, Fort Myers (p300).
(TOP LEFT) DREAMSTIME/MARTIN BENNETT ©; (TOP RIGHT) ALAMY/TYPHOONSKI ©

**SARASOTA TO FORT MYERS**

# Best of Florida's Southwest

Sarasota is the home of some of Florida's quirkier attractions, including the **(1) Mote Marine Laboratory**, one of the nation's foremost marine research centers and a highly recommended aquarium that is open to the public. You'll want to spend a part of your day (and night) wandering around **(2) St Armand's Circle**, partaking of the shopping and nightlife in this tiny alfresco mall. Also visit the **(3) Ringling Museum Complex**, a sort of museum that has a hard time figuring out if it wants to showcase art, historical design and architecture or the history of the circus. To be honest, it does all three quite well.

Spend the next day driving down to Fort Myers; if it's anytime between November and March, head to the **(4) Lee County Manatee Park** and see if you can spot one of these gentle, cute 'sea cows.' Otherwise go to **(5) Six Mile Slough Cypress Preserve** and walk along the boardwalk into the heart of Florida's remaining wild wetlands. On your third day, grab breakfast in the historic downtown district of Ft Myers, then drive out to **(6) Sanibel Island**, for a 'safari' drive through the **(7) JN 'Ding Darling National Wildlife Refuge**.

# Discover Tampa Bay & the Gulf Coast

## TAMPA BAY AREA

## Tampa Bay

♪813 / POP 335,700

Tampa may be sprawling and business-like, but it's also more fun than meets the eye. New museums, parks and gourmet restaurants are popping up on a monthly basis, so much so we'd happily say the Gulf Coast capital is finally a bit stylish.

 **Sights**

Downtown, the attractive **Tampa River-walk** (www.thetampariverwalk.com) connects most sights. The Franklin St Mall is a pedestrian-only corridor between Kennedy Blvd and Zack St that's lined with food carts and lunchtime eateries.

**LOWRY PARK ZOO** Zoo
( ♪813-935-8552; www.lowrypark-zoo.com; 1101 W Sligh Ave; adult/child 3-11yr $24/19; ⊙9:30am-5pm; P ⚦) When it comes to animal encounters, Florida sets the bar high, and Tampa's AZA-accredited zoo clears it with room to spare. The well-designed exhibits emphasize getting as close to the animals as possible, with several free-flight aviaries, a camel ride, giraffe feeding, a wallaby enclosure, and a rhino 'encounter.' Not only does Lowry contain all the big-ticket African animals you'll find at Busch Gardens, but it highlights Florida's home-grown menagerie: scores of American alligators, roseate spoonbills, panthers, pink flamingos, manatees and more.

Willet on the beach at JN 'Ding' Darling National Wildlife Refuge (p306).

RICHARD MILLS/LONELY PLANET IMAGES ©

### FLORIDA AQUARIUM — Aquarium

(☎ 813-273-4000; www.flaquarium.org; 701 Channelside Dr; adult/child $20/15; ⏰ 9:30am-5pm; ⬥) Tampa's excellent aquarium makes a worthy complement to its zoo. It's cleverly and immersively designed: cutaway windows peek into exhibits on other floors, and a recreated swamp lets you walk among herons and ibis as they prowl the mangroves with fish swimming past their legs. Stroke enormous manta rays, and wonder at giant grouper, tarpon, sea turtles and sharks gliding through coral reefs. But don't just watch. Two dive programs let you swim with the fishes: anyone aged six and up can plunge into the Coral Reef Gallery ($75), and certified divers aged 15 and up can join the sharks ($175). For details and reservations, call ☎ 813-239-4015.

### GLAZER CHILDREN'S MUSEUM — Museum

(☎ 813-443-3861; www.glazermuseum.org; 110 W Gasparilla Pl; adult/child 1-12yr $15/9.50; ⏰ 10am-5pm Mon-Fri, to 6pm Sat, 1-6pm Sun; ⬥) Oh, to be eight again. Creative play spaces for kids don't get any better than this bright, brand-new museum. Eager staff help children engage their limbs and imaginations among the plethora of interactive exhibits: the watery port of Tampa, a TV station with hidden cameras throughout the museum, a working theater stage, art lab, Lego building station, paper-airplane tester, supermarket, vet clinic and more. Best of all: it's adjacent to Curtis Hixon Park, a scenic grassy swath with its own playground.

### TAMPA MUSEUM OF ART — Museum

(☎ 813-274-8130; www.tampamuseum.org; 120 W Gasparilla Plaza; adult/child 7-18yr $10/5, 4-8pm Fri free; ⏰ 11am-7pm Mon-Thu, to 8pm Fri, to 5pm Sat & Sun) Reopened in February 2010 on Curtis Hixon Park in a glorious, dramatically cantilevered building sheathed in a silver-mesh skin, the Tampa Museum of Art now commands attention among the bay area's crowded art world. Six cavernous galleries balance their permanent collection—an unusual mix of Greek and Roman antiquities, contemporary photography, and new media—with major traveling exhibitions. Enjoy a sandwich in the slow-food café, and no, no one has counted the number of holes.

### MANATEE VIEWING CENTER — Wildlife

(☎ 813-228-4289; www.tampaelectric.com/manatee; Big Bend Rd, Apollo Beach; ⏰ 10am-5pm Nov 1-Apr 15) One of Florida's more surreal wildlife encounters is spotting manatees in the warm-water discharge canals of coal-fired power plants. Yet these placid mammals show up here so reliably from November through April that this is now a protected sanctuary. Look for tarpon, rays and sharks, too. A snack bar, small exhibit, bathrooms and picnic tables round out the sight. It's half an hour from downtown Tampa; take I-75 south to exit 246 and follow signs.

### YBOR CITY — Neighbourhood

Like the illicit love child of Key West and Miami's Little Havana, Ybor City is a multiethnic, nostalgia-rich neighborhood that hosts the Tampa Bay area's hippest party scene. The cobblestone 19th-century historic district is a redolent mix of wrought-iron balconies and rustling palm trees, of globe streetlamps and brick buildings, that preserves a strong Cuban, Spanish and Italian heritage.

For a guided, 90-minute walking tour, reserve ahead with **Ybor City Historic Walking Tours** (☎ 813-505-6779; www.yborwalkingtours.com; adult/child $15/5); they typically run twice daily.

# Sleeping

Travelers are best situated in Ybor City or downtown. An abundance of midrange chains are also north of downtown, close to Busch Gardens and the University of South Florida.

### GRAM'S PLACE — Hostel $

(☎ 813-221 0596; www.grams-inn-tampa.com; 3109 N Ola Ave; dm $23, r $25-70; @) Named for Gram Parsons, this low-key hostel

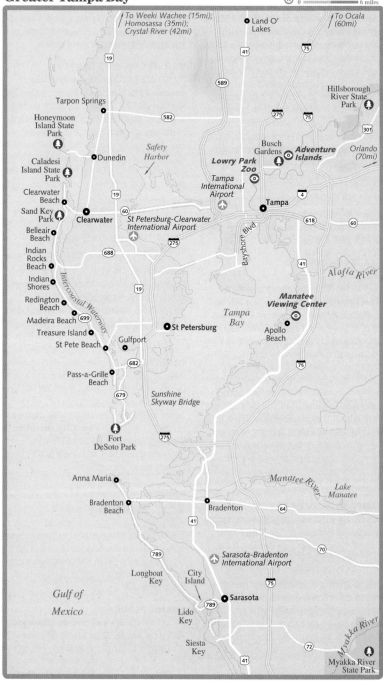

is as ramshackle as an aging rock star, and as charismatic. Genuine love infuses the music-themed rooms (the train-car dorm was inspired by Jimmy Rogers), and the owner, Bruce, creates a welcoming vibe for travelers of all ages, whether you're a middle-aged hippie or a Danish backpacker. Hostels aren't for everyone, but if you prefer personality over perfect linens, come here: relax around the in-ground hot tub, hang out for the Saturday-night jam session. Those songs about Key West life? This is what they're about.

**TAHITIAN INN**   Hotel $$
( ☎ 813-877-6721; www.tahitianinn.com; 601 S Dale Mabry Hwy; r $100-170; P ❋ @ ☎ ≋ 🏋 )
The highly recommended, family-owned Tahitian Inn performs a really neat trick: it offers classy full-service, boutique-hotel aspirations at (gasp!) midrange chain prices. The 81 rooms all sport fresh-feeling Tommy Bahama-style decor – think plush white sheets, soft lighting and brown hues. In addition to the attractive pool, spa, fitness center, lounge, a Latin-fusion cafe-restaurant, a poolside bar, it also offers airport transportation.

**DON VICENTE DE YBOR HISTORIC INN**   Historic Hotel $$
( ☎ 813-241-4545; www.donvicenteinn.com; 1915 Av República de Cuba; r $130-200; P ❋ ☎ )
Though slightly faded, the 1895 Don Vicente is the most atmospheric stay in Tampa, harkening back to Ybor City's glory days—especially the elegant, old-world public rooms with their rose-tinted chandeliers, oil paintings and grand staircase. The 16 rooms are less dramatic and warm, but they feature antiques, sleigh beds, velvet drapes and Persian rugs. Balcony rooms facing Av República de Cuba are best situated. Hot breakfast is included. In Ybor City.

 **Eating**

Tampa has an excellent restaurant scene, though precious little is downtown.

## Ybor City

**COLUMBIA RESTAURANT**   Spanish $$$
( ☎ 813-248-4961; www.columbiarestaurant.com; 2117 E 7th Ave; mains $17-28; ⏱ 11am-10pm Mon-Thu, to 11pm Fri & Sat, noon-9pm Sun) The Spanish atmosphere is so

Atmospheric Ybor City (p283) has plenty of shops, bars and restaurants.

CORBIS/JOHN COLETTI ©

# If You Like...
## Cigars

The old Tampa Sweethearts factory still stands (at 1301 N 22nd St), but the most personalized experience for cigar fanatics is the **Ybor City Museum walking tour** (☎813-428-0854; per person $8), run by PhD Wallace Reyes, who currently holds the world record for rolling the longest cigar (196ft ⅜in!).

The most knowledgeable (and legitimate) places to buy cigars in Ybor City are:

**1 METROPOLITAN CIGARS**
(2014 E 7th Ave; ⊙9:30am-8pm Mon-Fri, ⊙10:30am-5:30pm Sat) The store itself is actually a humidor; perhaps the best cigar shop in Tampa Bay.

**2 KING CORONA CIGAR FACTORY**
(www.kingcoronacigars.com; 1523 E 7th Ave; ⊙10am-6pm Mon, to 10:30pm Tue-Wed, to 1am Thu-Sat, noon-6pm Sun) The city's largest cigar emporium, with an old-fashioned cigar bar.

**3 EL SOL**
(www.elsolcigars.com; 1728 E 7th Ave; ⊙10:30am-5:30pm Mon-Sat) Established in 1929, the oldest cigar store in Ybor City.

**4 GONZALES Y MARTINEZ CIGAR COMPANY**
(2025 E 7th Ave; ⊙10am-9pm Mon-Thu, to 11pm Fri & Sat, noon-6pm Sun) Within the Columbia Restaurant gift store.

thick it feels like a schtick, but the Columbia's historic, original location is laudably authentic and truly memorable. Reserve ahead for the main dining room's 45-minute flamenco show (twice nightly): it's an exuberant performance, with red dresses swishing beneath dusty iron chandeliers. The Spanish cooking is robust and traditional, rather than refined. Stick to the classics that made them famous: *arroz con pollo,* paella, *ropa vieja,* and the 1905 salad, spun tableside. At minimum hit the burnished bar for a mojito and garlicky tapa.

**LA SEGUNDA BAKERY**   Bakery $
(2512 N 15th St; items $1-8; ⊙6:30am-5pm Mon-Fri, 7am-3pm Sat, 7am-1pm Sun) At 15th Ave and 15th St, just outside Ybor's main drag, this authentic Spanish bakery cranks out delicious breads and pastries, rich Cuban coffee and maybe Tampa's best Cuban sandwich. Here since 1915, it bustles every AM with a cross-section of Tampa society.

## South Tampa

**BERN'S STEAKHOUSE**   Steakhouse $$$
(☎813-251-2421; www.bernssteakhouse .com; 1208 S Howard Ave; steaks $25-60; ⊙from 5pm) Bern's is legendary, a nationally renowned steakhouse that offers far more than a meal: dining here is an unforgettable event. The menu is an education in steaks and beef (dry-aged on premises, naturally); sides are generous and often organic. There are dozens of caviars, and dessert is so overwhelming you relocate to a separate dining room; many reserve solely for dessert. Merely ask, and you may tour the kitchens and epic wine cellar. Jackets aren't required but won't feel out of place in this paean to old-world moneyed elegance.

**RESTAURANT BT**   Fusion $$$
(☎813-258-1916; www.restaurantbt.com; 2507 S MacDill Ave; lunch $10-13, dinner $23-34; ⊙11:30am-2:30pm & 5:30-10pm Mon-Sat, to 11pm Fri & Sat) Chef Trina Nyugan-Batley has combined her high-fashion background and Vietnamese upbringing to create this ultrachic temple to sustainable, locavore gourmet cuisine. While it freely raids the international cupboard, the backbone of BT's inventive menu is its distinctive French-Vietnamese hybrid. Lunch is a more low-key affair of *pho,* green-papaya salads and baguette sandwiches.

## Seminole Heights & Around

**REFINERY**   Fusion $$
(☎813-237-2000; www.thetamparefinery.com; 5137 N Florida Ave; mains $12-18; ⊙5-10pm Tue-Thu, 5-11pm Fri & Sat, 11am-3pm Sun; ✍)

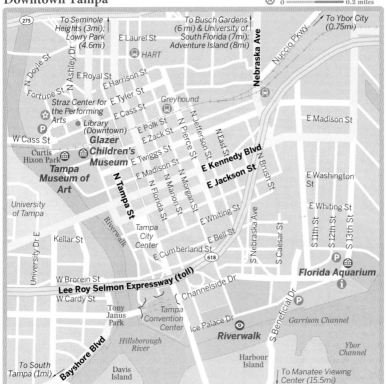

A semifinalist for the 2011 James Beard award for best new restaurant, the Refinery marries a sustainability ethic with a punk attitude. The hyperlocal changing menu features small plates (and 'more than a small plate'), allowing chef Greg Baker extreme latitude for his clever creativity. At this blue-collar gourmet joint, they promise chipped plates, mismatched cutlery and no pretentions, just playful, delicious cuisine 'for folks like us.'

# 🍷 Drinking & Entertainment

For nightlife, Ybor City is party central, though SoHo and Seminole Heights are also hip and happening.

Ybor City is also the center of Tampa's GLBT life; to connect with it, check out the **GaYbor District Coalition** (www.gaybor.com) and **Gay Tampa** (www.gaytampa.com).

**SKIPPER'S SMOKEHOUSE**   Live Music
( ☎813-971-0666; www.skipperssmokehouse.com; cnr Skipper Rd & Nebraska Ave; cover $5-25; ⊙11am-midnight Tue-Sun) Did this place blow in from the Keys on a hurricane? No, for over 30 years Skipper's has been an unpretentious, beloved Old Florida institution and Tampa's best open-air venue for blues, funk, folk, reggae and gator-swamp rockabilly. Hell, it's so damn friendly you can bring the kids. The attached seafood restaurant is nothing special, but Skipper's certainly is. Take I-275 N to exit 52/Fletcher Ave.

**INDEPENDENT** Bar

(www.independenttampa.com; 5016 N Florida Ave; ⊙from 4pm Mon-Fri, from 1pm Sat & Sun) If you appreciate craft brews, roll in to this converted gas station, now a low-key hip bar in Seminole Heights. You can count on one or more local Cigar City Brews, and they serve some mean pub grub.

**CINEBISTRO** Cinema

( ☎813-514-8300; www.cobbcinebistro.com; 1609 W Swann Ave, Hyde Park Village, South Tampa; mains $10-20) Cross a trendy South Beach nightclub with a plush arthouse cinema, and you get this: a snazzy, lobby cocktail bar, and upscale munchies to nosh at your seat while you watch. It's moviegoing... with style.

**STRAZ CENTER FOR THE PERFORMING ARTS** Performing Arts

( ☎813-229-7827; www.strazcenter.org; 1010 MacInnes Pl; tickets $10-80) Beautifully sited on a riverside park, this is the largest performing-arts center south of the Kennedy Center in Washington, DC. With five venues, ranging from the 2600-seat Carol Morsani Hall to a 130-seat black box stage, it hosts the full gamut of fine-arts performances: major pops concerts, the Florida Orchestra, touring Broadway productions, cutting-edge dramas, the Tampa Ballet, Opera Tampa and more.

 **Shopping**

On 8th Ave between 15th and 17th Sts, **Centro Ybor** (www.centroybor.com) is an attractive shopping, dining and entertainment complex. In addition, the **Ybor City Farmers Market** (Centennial Park, 8th Ave & 18th St; ⊙9am-3pm Sat) emphasizes arts and crafts.

**INKWOOD BOOKS** Books

(www.inkwoodbooks.com; 216 S Armenia at Platt; ⊙10am-6pm Mon-Sat, to 9pm Thu, 1-5pm Sun) In a small house close to Hyde Park, you'll find Tampa's best independent bookstore. Inkwood stocks a fantastic selection of

**Left:** The beach at Honeymoon Island State Park (p310);
**Below:** Art on display in Tampa Bay (p282).

(LEFT) CORBIS/JOHN COLETTI/JAI ©; (BELOW) CORBIS/EDMUND D. FOUNTAIN ZUMA PRESS ©

new Florida titles, both nonfiction and mysteries, and wonderful children's books.

# ⓘ Information

## Medical Services

**Tampa General Hospital** (☎ 813-844-7000; www.tgh.org; 1 Tampa General Circle, Davis Island; ⏰ 24hr) South of downtown on Davis Island.

## Tourist Information

**Tampa Bay Convention & Visitors Bureau** (☎ 813-223-1111, 800-826-8358; www .visittampabay.com; 615 Channelside Dr; ⏰ 9:30am-5:30pm Mon-Sat, 11am-5pm Sun) Has good free maps and lots of information. The website links directly to hotels for booking.

# ⓘ Getting There & Around

## Air

The region's major airport, and the state's third-busiest airport, is **Tampa International**

**Airport** (TPA; www.tampaairport.com; 5503 W Spruce St; 🔊), about 13 miles west of downtown, off Hwy 589. It's an easy, pleasant airport to negotiate.

All major car agencies have desks at the airport. By car, take the I-275 to N Ashley Dr, turn right and you're in downtown.

## Trolley & Streetcar

**In-Town Trolley** (fare 25¢; ⏰ 6-9am & 3-6pm Mon-Fri, also 6pm-2am Fri & Sat) Within downtown, HART's inexpensive trolley runs up and down Florida Ave, Tampa St and Franklin St every 10 minutes.

**TECO Line Streetcars** (www.tecolinestreetcar .org; tickets $2.50; ⏰ 11am-10pm Mon-Thu, 11am-2am Fri, 9am-2am Sat, noon-8pm Sun) HART's old-fashioned electric streetcars connect downtown's Marion Transit Center with Ybor City.

# St Petersburg

☎727 / POP 244,700

St Petersburg has a bawdy reputation as a party town, but in fact, the bay area's two cities are more alike than they are different. Both are working hard to revitalize and restore their historic neighborhoods and waterfront districts. Both are succeeding admirably and are well worth visiting.

## Sights & Activities

When taking in the sights, visitors can confine themselves to a walkable, T-shaped route: along Central Ave, mainly from 8th St to Bayshore Dr, and along Bayshore Dr from the Dalí Museum to the bayfront parks in the Old Northeast neighborhood.

### ST PETERSBURG MUSEUM
### OF FINE ARTS                    Museum

(☎727-896-2667; www.fine-arts.org; 255 Beach Dr NE; adult/child 7-18yr $17/10; ⊙10am-5pm Mon-Sat, noon-5pm Sun) The Museum of Fine Arts collection is as broad as the Dalí's is deep, and the two make satisfyingly complementary experiences. Here, traverse the world's antiquities and follow art's progression with examples from nearly every era. Monet, O'Keeffe and George Inness highlight the Impressionists, and intriguing galleries are devoted to pewter, silver, Steuben glass and Wedgwood vases.

### COFFEE POT BAYOU &
### THE OLD NORTHEAST     Neighborhood

North of downtown are the brick-lined streets of St Pete's most historic neighborhood, as well as a string of parks, recreation facilities, and a paved waterfront path that's perfect for **walking**, **jogging** or **biking** on one of St Pete's 361 sunny days. The visitor center has a **driving-tour** brochure and map.

The Old Northeast, or Coffee Pot Bayou, begins around 9th Ave NE and goes to 30th Ave NE; it extends inland from the bay to about 4th St. Simply follow North Shore Dr NE from 5th Ave NE. At about 10th Ave NE is the **North Shore Aquatic Complex** (visitors $5; ⊙9am-4pm Mon-Fri, 10am-4pm Sat, 1-4pm Sun), with three gorgeous swimming

Hindu statue at the St Petersburg Museum of Fine Arts (p290).

ALAMY/JEFF GREENBERG ©

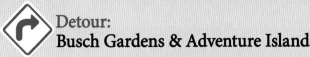

# Detour:
## Busch Gardens & Adventure Island

Orlando doesn't hold a monopoly on Florida theme parks. In Tampa, Busch Gardens presents two enormous thrill-seeker destinations: the Africa-themed Busch Gardens, with some of the country's best roller coasters, and the adjacent Adventure Island water park. If you'll be visiting both, get combo tickets.

Both parks are about 7 miles north of downtown Tampa; take I-275 north to exit 50/Busch Blvd and follow signs.

### BUSCH GARDENS

This **theme park** (☏813-987-5082, 866-353-8622; www.buschgardens.com; 10000 McKinley Dr; adult/child 3-9yr $80/70; ⌚varies by day & season) has nine named African regions, but these flow together without much fuss. The entire park is walkable. In **Egypt**, Busch Gardens has unveiled its newest coaster: Cheetah Hunt, an epic, low-to-the-ground scream-fest meant to mimic a cheetah's acceleration. The 80-acre **Serengeti Plain** recreates African plains, with hundreds of free-roaming animals. Other attractions include the formidable Kumba roller coaster and kid-friendly **Safari of Fun & Bird Gardens.**

### ADVENTURE ISLAND

This 30-acre **water park** (☏813-987-5600; www.adventureisland.com; 10001 McKinley Dr; adult/child 3-9yr $43/39; ⌚daily mid-Mar–Aug, weekends only Sep–Oct, hr vary by day & season) has everything a modern, top-flight water park requires: long, lazy river, huge wave pool, bucket-dumping splash zones, swimming pool, sandy lounge areas, and enough twisting, plunging, adrenaline-fueled waterslides to keep teens lining up till closing.

pools, including a kids' pool with a waterslide. Adjacent are grassy public parks, which include the **Gizella Kopsick Palm Arboretum** (admission free; ⌚sunrise-sunset), essentially an open, two-acre garden of over 500 palms, all signed and lovingly landscaped. Also here are large parking lots, restrooms, and a long, white-sand **swimming beach**. Or, keep going along the paved trail, past pretty homes and private docks, all the way to small **Coffee Pot Park**, where manatees are occasionally spotted.

## Sleeping

For southwest Florida, St Petersburg has a notable selection of nice B&Bs; contact the local **Association of Bed & Breakfast Inns** (www.spaabbi.com).

**DICKENS HOUSE**  B&B **$$**
(☏727-822-8622; www.dickenshouse.com; 335 8th Ave NE at Beach Dr NE; r $130-230; ✴@☏) Once a decrepit rooming house and now passionately restored into a Craftsman-style dream, this charming B&B in the historic Coffee Pot Bayou district has it all. The five lushly designed rooms are cozy romantic getaways that perfectly blend modern comforts and idiosyncratic personality. Book the humorous Cracker Suite for a headboard of raw tree limbs and your TV on an ironing board. The gregarious, gay-friendly owner knows St Pete well and whips up a gourmet breakfast.

**PONCE DE LEON**  Boutique Hotel **$$**
(☏727-550-9300; www.poncedeleonhotel.com; 95 Central Ave; r $110-150; P✴@☏) For a boutique hotel with Spanish flair in the heart of downtown, there is one option,

DISCOVER TAMPA BAY & THE GULF COAST  ST PETERSBURG

To Dickens House
(0.3mi)

5th Ave NE

4th Ave N

4th St

3rd St N

2nd St N

1st St N

3

Beach Dr NE

Bayshore Dr NE

To I-275
(0.25mi)

5

3rd Ave N

Mirror
Lake

Mirror
Lake Park

St Petersburg
Museum of
Fine Arts

2nd Ave N

4

1st Ave N

6

St Petersburg
Municipal
Marina

2

Central Ave

To Haslam's Book
Store (0.95mi)

7

8

1st Ave S

1

Demens
Landing
Park

8th St S

7th St S

6th St S

5th St S

2nd Ave S

To Tropicana Field
(0.1mi)

3rd Ave S

Progress
Energy Park

4th Ave S

4th St

3rd St S

2nd St S

1st St S

Looper Trolley

Bayshore Dr

Salvador
Dalí
Museum

5th Ave S

Dali Blvd

and it's a good one: the Ponce. Hallways have splashy murals of flamenco dancers, and rooms mix blood-red chairs, glass sinks, teal walls and hardwood floors; a few enjoy water views. It's not perfect: some bathrooms await renovations, wall-mounted TVs are small and parking is off-site. But for style, location and its hot restaurant (Ceviche), it's hard to beat.

## Eating

Beach Dr along the waterfront is a warm, friendly scene lined with attractive mid-range restaurants; stroll at sunset and let your palate guide you.

**CEVICHE** Tapas $$
( 727-209-2299; www.ceviche.com/1828; 95 Central Ave; tapas $5-13, mains $15-23; 11am-10pm Sun-Mon, to midnight Tue-Thu, to 1am Fri & Sat) Panache counts, and Ceviche has it in spades, with its upbeat atmosphere, colorful tiled tables and wrought-iron railings. While you won't think you've stumbled into Madrid, order a pitcher of sangria and a handful of the flavorful, generously portioned tapas and you'll definitely have a good time. This is virtually guaranteed if you end the evening in the Flamenco Room, a sexy, cavern-like bar below with live flamenco music and dancing Thursday and Saturday nights. Every morning (from 8am), the attached café Pincho y Pincho dishes up tasty Spanish-influenced breakfasts and espresso coffees.

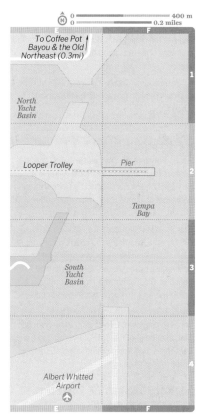

To Coffee Pot Bayou & the Old Northeast (0.3mi)

North Yacht Basin

Looper Trolley

Pier

Tampa Bay

South Yacht Basin

Albert Whitted Airport

0 — 400 m
0 — 0.2 miles

## St Petersburg

⊙ **Top Sights**

Salvador Dalí Museum .......................D4
St Petersburg Museum of Fine
Arts ..........................................D2

🛏 **Sleeping**
1 Ponce de Leon ..................................D3

🍴 **Eating**
2 Cassis .................................................D2
   Ceviche/Pincho y Pincho.............(see 1)
3 Moon Under Water ...........................D1

🎭 **Entertainment**
4 American Stage ................................C2
5 Coliseum Ballroom ...........................B1
6 Jannus Live .......................................C2
7 State Theatre ....................................A3

🛍 **Shopping**
8 Florida Craftsmen Gallery.................B3

heat to your palate. The British side of the menu specializes in fish and chips, shepherd's pie and bangers and mash. Both imported British and local Cigar City brews on tap.

 **Drinking & Entertainment**

Kicking off each month, 'First Friday' is an evening block party and giant pub crawl with live music on Central Ave.

**JANNUS LIVE**      Concert Venue
(☏727-565-0551; www.jannuslive.com; 16 2nd St N; tickets $15-30) The Tampa Bay area's most beloved concert venue received a welcome facelift in 2009, improving the bathrooms and bar areas. Unchanged is the intimate stage hidden in a cozy open-air courtyard in the middle of the block, where national and local bands reverberate downtown.

**STATE THEATRE**      Concert Venue
(☏727-895-3045; www.statetheatreconcerts.com; 687 Central Ave; tickets $8-20) Up-and-coming bands of all stripes, and occasional national acts, play at this restored art-deco theater (built in 1927).

**CASSIS**      French $$$
(☏727-827-2927; www.cassisab.com; 170 Beach Dr NE; lunch $10-20, dinner $18-28; ⊙8-11am Mon-Fri, 11am-10pm daily) Doing its best imitation of a Parisian brasserie, with globe lights and banquettes inside, and sidewalk tables outside, Cassis draws crowds for its affordable and well-executed French menu and for its perfect waterfront location. It runs its own bakery next door. Service suffers when it gets hopping.

**MOON UNDER WATER**      Indian $$
(☏727-896-6160; www.themoonunderwater.com; 332 Beach Dr NE; mains $9-17; ⊙11am-11pm, to midnight Fri & Sat) Sporting an upbeat, 19th-century British-colonial atmosphere, Moon Under Water serves admirably flavorful Indian curries; ask for a capsicum 'enhancer' to adjust the

DISCOVER TAMPA BAY & THE GULF COAST ST PETERSBURG

**COLISEUM BALLROOM** Dance
(www.stpete.org/coliseum; 535 4th Ave N; tea dances $7-10) This old-fashioned, beautiful 1924 ballroom hosts occasional events and has regular 'Tea Dances' on the first and third Wednesday every month. Sessions run from 1pm to 3:30pm; dance lessons start at 11:30am. The classic ballroom was featured in the 1985 film *Cocoon*.

**AMERICAN STAGE** Theatre
( ☎727-823-7529; www.americanstage.org; 163 3rd St N; tickets $25-47) One of the Tampa Bay area's most highly regarded regional theaters presents American classics and recent Tony winners (like *Red*). Its 'in the park' series presents Broadway musicals.

#  Shopping

The main shopping corridor is along Central Ave between 5th and 8th Sts and also between 10th and 13th Sts.

**HASLAM'S BOOK STORE** Books
(www.haslams.com; 2025 Central Ave; ⊘10am-6:30pm Mon-Sat, noon-5pm Sun) This bookstore is a bona fide attraction. A half-block long, with a tremendous selection of new and used books and a fantastic Florida section, Haslam's claims to be the largest independent bookstore in the US southeast. Many beach days have been lost perusing its shelves.

**FLORIDA CRAFTSMEN GALLERY** Arts & Crafts
( ☎727-821-7391; www.floridacraftsmen.net; 501 Central Ave; ⊘10am-5:30pm Mon-Sat) A nonprofit association runs this gallery-store dedicated to Florida craftspeople. Find unusual, unique, high-quality ceramics, jewelry, glass, clothing and art.

## ⓘ Information

All Children's Hospital ( ☎727-898-7451; www.allkids.org; 6th St S btwn 8th & 9th Aves; ⊘24hr)

Bayfront Medical Center ( ☎727-823-1234; www.bayfront.org; 701 6th St S; ⊘24hr)

St Pete Downtown Arts Association (www.stpetearts.org)

St Petersburg Area Chamber of Commerce ( ☎727-821-4069; www.pleasure.stpete.com; 100 2nd Ave N; ⊘9am-5pm Mon-Fri) Helpful, staffed chamber office has good maps and a driving guide.

St Petersburg/Clearwater Area Convention & Visitors Bureau (www.visitstpeteclearwater.com)

## ⓘ Getting There & Around

**Air** St Petersburg-Clearwater International Airport (www.fly2pie.com; Roosevelt Blvd & Hwy 686, Clearwater) Served by several major carriers, but Tampa is the main international airport.

**Bus** Pinellas Suncoast Transit Authority (PSTA; www.psta.net; 340 2nd Ave N; fare $2; ⊘5am-9pm Mon-Sat, 7am-5pm Sun) St Petersburg buses serve the barrier-island beaches, Clearwater and Tarpon Springs; unlimited-ride Go Cards are $4.50 per day.

**Trolley Car** Downtown Looper (www.loopertrolley.com; fare 25¢; ⊘10am-5pm Sun-Thu, to midnight Fri & Sat) Old-fashioned trolley cars run a downtown circuit every 15 minutes; great for sightseeing.

# St Pete Beach & Barrier Island Beaches
☎727 / POP 9,300

In just 20 minutes from downtown St Petersburg, you can reach the legendary barrier-island beaches that are the sandy soul of the peninsula. This 30-mile-long stretch of sun-faded towns, soft-sand beaches, and sun-kissed azure waters is the perfect antidote to city life and the primary destination of most vacationers.

## ◉ Sights & Activities

**FORT DESOTO PARK & BEACH** Beach
(www.pinellascounty.org/park; 3500 Pinellas Bayway S; ⊘sunrise-sunset) Fort DeSoto's North Beach is unquestionably one of the Gulf Coast's, and even Florida's, top beaches – with the accolades to prove it. This long, silky stretch of dune-cradled white sand is accessed by huge parking

CORBIS/JOHN COLETTI ©

# Don't Miss **Salvador Dalí Museum**

Unveiled in 2011, the theatrical exterior of the new **Salvador Dalí Museum** augurs great things: out of a wound in the towering white shoebox oozes the 75ft geodesic atrium Glass Enigma. Even better, what unfolds inside is like a blueprint of what a modern art museum should be, or at least, one devoted to understanding the life, art and impact of a single revolutionary artist.

The Dalí's 20,000 sq ft of gallery space is designed specifically to display all 96 oil paintings in the collection, along with 'key works from every moment and in every medium': drawings, prints, sculptures, photos, manuscripts, even movies, everything arranged chronologically and explained in context. The museum is so sharp it includes a 'contemplation area' with nothing but white walls and a window. Another great breather is the garden, which is small but, like everything, shot through with cleverness.

Excellent, free docent tours occur hourly (on the half hour); these are highly recommended to help crack open the rich symbolism in Dalí's monumental works. Topping this off, the Spanish cafe is first rate, and the gift store is the region's best, hands down.

### THINGS YOU NEED TO KNOW

📞727-823-3767; www.thedali.org; 1 Dali Blvd; adult/child 6-12yr $21/7, after 5pm Thu $10; ⏱10am-5pm Mon-Wed, to 8pm Thu, to 5:30pm Fri & Sat, noon-5:30pm Sun

lots and has excellent facilities, including grassy picnic areas and a **cafe and gift store** (⏱10am-4pm Mon-Fri, to 5pm Sat & Sun) with bike rentals. East Beach, meanwhile, is smaller and coarser, and consequently less crowded.

Fort DeSoto also offers terrific camping, two fishing piers (with bait shops and rentals) from where you can spot dolphins, kayak rentals, and its namesake historic fort, which dates to 1898 and the Spanish-American War.

ALAMY/ PATTI MCCONVILLE ©

# Don't Miss Gulfport

Gulfport is the cutest, quirkiest little beach town not on the barrier islands. Beach Blvd is a four-block stretch of funky boutiques, friendly locals, little cafes and surprisingly good restaurants. Get the full dose of wry local sensibilities during the twice-monthly art walk, essentially a low-key street party, every first Friday and third Saturday from 6pm to 10pm.

**Peg's Cantina** (727-328-2720; www.pegscantina.com; 3038 Beach Blvd; mains $10-16; 5-10pm Tue-Fri, noon-9pm Sat & Sun) is ripe with Gulfport mojo. This brewpub in a woodsy bungalow perfectly pairs fanciful Mexican dishes with creamy handcrafted beers, ideally enjoyed in the wonderful gardens.

If you're tempted to spend the night, the historic **Peninsula Inn** (727-346-9800; www .innspa.net; 2937 Beach Blvd; r $130-180; ✳ @ ) has been renovated into a pretty romantic choice. It also has a recommended restaurant with jazz music on weekends.

Fort DeSoto Park is signed off US 682/ Pinellas Bayway (exit 17 off I-275).

### BEACHES
Beach

The epic sliver of sand that is **Pass-a-Grille Beach** is almost idyllic, as it's backed only by beach houses and has by far the longest stretch of public parking. At the southernmost end, a cute, laid-back village center the size of a sand dollar provides T-shirts, eats and ice cream.

**St Pete Beach** is a long, double-wide strand with parasail booths and chair rentals seemingly every 50ft; big

public parking lots. Incredibly crowded with families and Spring Breakers, who appreciate all the restaurants, bars and motels just steps away.

### SUNCOAST SEABIRD SANCTUARY
Wildlife Sanctuary

(www.seabirdsanctuary.com; 18328 Gulf Blvd, Indian Shores; admission by donation; 9am-sunset) The largest wild-bird hospital in North America, this sanctuary has up to 600 sea and land birds available for public viewing at any one time, including a resident population of permanently injured birds. Thousands of birds are treated and released back to the wild annually.

 **Sleeping**

**POSTCARD INN**     Boutique Motel **$$$**
( ☎ 727-367-2711; www.postcardinn.com; 6300 Gulf Blvd, near 64th Ave; r $160-260; P ❄ @ ☎ ) For its vintage 1950s hang-10 style alone, the Postcard Inn leads the pack in St Pete Beach. The long, double-armed shell of a 1957 Colonial Gateway has been transformed into a designer-chic surf shack: rooms are amusing concoctions of woven mats, wood-slat shutters, mod couches, standing surfboards and wall-size murals of wave riders in the curl. Some have outdoor hammocks, and all surround the spacious courtyard and sizable pool, with ping-pong tables, tiki bar and direct access to the beach.

 **Eating**

**TED PETER'S FAMOUS SMOKED FISH**     Seafood **$$**
(1350 Pasadena Ave; mains $6.50-19; ☺ 11:30am-7:30pm Wed-Mon) Ted Peter's is an only-in-St-Pete-Beach experience you gotta try once. Since the 1950s, they've been smoking fresh salmon, mackerel, mahimahi and mullet in a little smokehouse, then dishing it up whole or in sandwich spreads. You eat at outdoor picnic tables. The salmon is awesome; the mullet intense. Cash only. Pasadena Ave is actually on the mainland side of the Corey Causeway.

 **Information**

Tampa Bay Beaches Chamber of Commerce ( ☎ 727-360-6957; www.tampabaybeaches.com; 6990 Gulf Blvd at 70th Ave; ☺ 9am-5pm Mon-Fri) Helpful VC, excellent maps and advice.

# SOUTH OF TAMPA

People who prefer Florida's Gulf side over its Atlantic one generally fall in love with this stretch of sun-kissed coastline.

# Sarasota

☎ 941 / POP 51,900

Entire vacations can be spent soaking up the sights and culture, and the egregiously pretty beaches, of sophisticated Sarasota. In fact, base your stay here, and the majority of the Tampa Bay area's highlights are within easy reach.

 **Sights & Activities**

**MOTE MARINE LABORATORY**   Aquarium
( ☎ 941-388-4441; www.mote.org; 1600 Ken Thompson Pkwy, City Island; adult/child $17/12; ☺ 10am-5pm) A research facility first and an aquarium second, the Mote is one of the world's leading organizations for shark study, and glimpsing its work is a highlight: marvel at seahorse 'fry' born that very day, and time your visit for **shark training** ( ☺ 11am Mon, Wed & Fri). Exhibits include a preserved giant squid (37ft long when caught), a stingray touch tank, a dramatic shark tank, and a separate building with intimate encounters with sea turtles, manatees and dolphins. An interactive immersion theater is perfect for kids. Also don't miss **Save Our Seabirds** (suggested donation $5; ☺ 10am-5pm); adjacent to Mote, it displays a wide range of rescued seabirds in outdoor cages. Finally, Sarasota Bay Explorers (see p298) is based here. To get there, go to St Armands Circle, take John Ringling Blvd north to Ken Thompson Parkway and follow to the end.

**ST ARMAND'S CIRCLE**     Square
(www.starmandscircleassoc.com) Conceived and initially developed by John Ringling in the 1920s, St Armand's Circle is essentially an upscale outdoor shopping mall surrounded by posh residences. Yet even more than downtown, this traffic circle is Sarasota's social center; it's where everyone strolls in the early evening, window shopping and buying souvenir T-shirts while enjoying a Kilwin's waffle cone. Numerous restaurants, from diners to fine dining, serve all day. The circle is also an unavoidable traffic chokepoint; midmorning and late-afternoon beach commutes are worst.

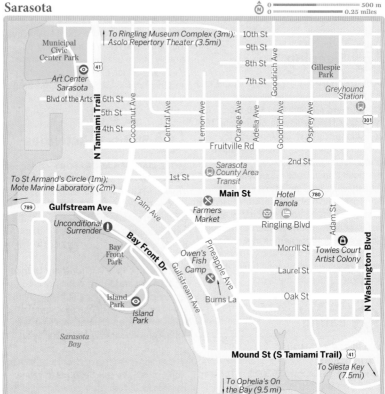

Sarasota

0          500 m
0          0.25 miles

To Ringling Museum Complex (3mi);
Asolo Repertory Theater (3.5mi)

Municipal
Civic
Center Park

Art Center
Sarasota
Blvd of the Arts

10th St
9th St
8th St
7th St
6th St
5th St
4th St

Gillespie
Park

Greyhound
Station

Fruitville Rd

To St Armand's Circle (1mi);
Mote Marine Laboratory (2mi)

Sarasota
County Area
Transit

Gulfstream Ave

Unconditional
Surrender

Bay
Front
Park

Farmers
Market

Main St

Hotel
Ranola

Ringling Blvd

Owen's
Fish
Camp

Morrill St

Towles Court
Artist Colony

Island
Park

Island
Park

Laurel St

Burns La

Oak St

Sarasota
Bay

Mound St (S Tamiami Trail)

To Siesta Key
(7.5mi)

To Ophelia's On
the Bay (9.5mi)

 **Tours**

**SARASOTA BAY EXPLORERS**   Boat tour
( ☎ 941-388-4200; www.sarasotabayexplorers
.com; 1600 Ken Thompson Parkway, Mote
Marine Laboratory) Under the supervision
of marine biologists, boat cruises trawl
a net and then examine the sponges,
sea horses and various fish you catch.
You also inspect rookeries and stop on
an uninhabited island for a short nature
walk; you may spot manatees and dolphins. The 1¾-hour ecotours (adult/child
$26/22) depart from the Mote aquarium
daily at 11am, 1:30pm and 4pm. They
also offer guided kayak tours (adult/child
$55/45).

 **Sleeping & Eating**

## Sarasota

**HOTEL RANOLA**   Boutique Hotel $$
( ☎ 941-951-0111; www.hotelranola.com; 118 Indian
Pl, No 6; r $180-190; P ❄ @ ) For urban funk
and livability, there's nothing like Hotel
Ranola in the Tampa Bay area. It is the only
hotel walkable to Sarasota's historic down-
town. The nine rooms feel like a designer's
actual brownstone apartment: free-spirit-
ed and comfortable, with hardwood floors,
royal grape accent walls, glass-topped
desks, bright paintings, leather armchairs,
and real working kitchens. Indeed, half of
the 1926 building is occupied by tenants,
so don't expect lots of amenities, just a
big-city home away from home.

## OWEN'S FISH CAMP
Southern $$

(☎941-951-6936; www.owensfishcamp.com; 516 Burns Lane; mains $9-20; ⏱4-10pm, to 11pm Fri & Sat) The actual house of Sarasota's founder has been turned into an ironic swamp shack serving upscale inter-pretations of Florida-style Southern cuisine. Order cornmeal-crusted catfish, chicken-fried steak, smooth cheesy grits and pecan pie. The delicious succotash is edamame, corn, chickpeas and peppers. The emphasis is on seafood, and the energy is high.

## Siesta Key

### BROKEN EGG
Breakfast $

(www.thebrokenegg.com; 140 Avenida Messina; mains $7-14; ⏱7:30am-2:30pm; 👪) Each morning, it feels like all of Siesta Key gathers on the outdoor patio of this diner-style restaurant for delicious skillet eggs, blintzes, cheddary home fries and pancakes as big as hubcaps. Yet service is unfailingly upbeat and efficient, and the wait goes fast.

## OPHELIA'S ON THE BAY
Fusion $$$

(☎941-349-2212; www.opheliasonthebay.net; 9105 Midnight Pass Rd; mains $27-34; ⏱5-10pm) On the harbor-side at the southern end of Siesta Key, Ophelia's is the island's top romantic spot. The water lapping the dock at your feet and the distant mangroves is balm to the soul. The menu is all over the map, reaching around the globe for influ-ences, but everything is finely prepared and stylishly presented. Reserve ahead.

 **Entertainment**

### ASOLO REPERTORY THEATRE
Theatre

(☎941-351-8000; www.asolorep.org; 5555 N Tamiami Trail; tickets $15-50; ⏱Nov-Jul) Adja-cent to the Ringling Estate, this lauded re-gional theater company is also an acting conservatory (in partnership with Florida State University). It presents a vibrant mix of commissioned works, classics and current Tony-winning dramas on two main stages. The **Sarasota Ballet** (www .sarasotaballet.org) also performs here.

Sea turtle in the Mote Marine Laboratory (p297).

ALAMY/JEFF GREENBERG ©

# 🔒 Shopping

**TOWLES COURT ARTIST COLONY**  Art
(www.towlescourt.com; cnr Morrill & Adam Sts;
⊙noon-4pm Tue-Sat) A dozen or so hip
galleries occupy quirky, parrot-colored
bungalows in this artist colony. The most
lively time to be here is the evening stroll
on the third Friday of each month (6pm to
10pm). Otherwise, individual gallery hours
can be, mmm, whimsical.

## ℹ️ Information

**MEDICAL SERVICES Sarasota Memorial
Hospital** (☎941-917-9000; www.smh.com; 1700
S Tamiami Trail; ⊙24hr) The area's biggest
hospital.

## ℹ️ Getting There & Around

Sarasota is roughly 60 miles south of Tampa
and 75 miles north of Fort Myers. Main roads are
Tamiami Trail/US 41 and I-75.

**Sarasota-Bradenton International Airport**
(SRQ; www.srq-airport.com; 6000 Airport Circle)
Served by major airlines. Go north on Hwy 41,
right on University Ave.

## Fort Myers
☎239 / POP 62,300

Nestled inland along the Caloosahatchee
River, Fort Myers is a family-friendly town
within striking distance of the region's top
beaches.

# 👁️ Sights & Activities

The historic district is a tidy, six-block grid
of streets along 1st St between Broadway
and Lee St.

**EDISON & FORD WINTER
ESTATES**  Museum
(☎239-334-7419; www.edisonfordwinterestates
.org; 2350 McGregor Blvd; adult/child $20/11;
⊙9am-5:30pm) Florida's snowbirds can be
easy to mock, but not this pair. Thomas
Edison built his winter home in 1885 and
lived in Florida seasonally until his death
in 1931. Edison's friend Henry Ford built

his adjacent bungalow in 1916. Together,
and sometimes side by side in **Edison's
lab**, these two inventors, businessmen
and neighbors changed our world.

The **museum** does a good job of
presenting the overwhelming scope of
Edison's achievements, which included
1093 patents for things like the lightbulb,
the phonograph, wafflemakers, talking
dolls, concrete and sprocketed celluloid
film.

While it's possible to buy discounted
tickets only for the museum and lab,
don't forgo a self-guided audio tour of
the estates, which won a 2008 national
preservation award (guided tours are $5
extra). The rich botanical gardens and
genteel homes very nearly glow, and are
decked out with more historical goodies
and period furniture. Grounds also
include one of the largest banyan trees in
the US.

**SIX MILE CYPRESS SLOUGH
PRESERVE**  Swamp
(☎239-533-7550; www.leeparks.org/sixmile,
www.sloughpreserve.org; 7791 Penzance Blvd;
parking per hr/day $1/5; ⊙dawn-dusk) A
2000-acre woodland and wetland, or
slough (pronounced 'slew'), this park is a
great, easily accessible place to experience southwest Florida's flora and fauna.
A 1.2-mile boardwalk trail is staffed by
volunteers who help point out and explain
the epiphytes, cypress knees, migrating
birds, turtles and nesting alligators you'll
find. Wildlife watchers should target the
winter dry season, when animals con
centrate around smaller ponds. However,
the wet summer season is also dramatic:
at its peak, the entire slough becomes a
forested stream up to 3ft deep. The small
**nature center** (⊙10am-4pm Tue-Sat, to 2pm
Sun) has excellent displays; from December to April, free guided walks are 9:30am
and 1:30pm daily.

**IMAGINARIUM HANDS
ON MUSEUM**  Museum
(☎239-337-3332; www.imaginariumfortmyers
.com; 2000 Cranford Ave; adult/child $12/8;
⊙10am-5pm Mon-Sat, noon-5pm Sun; 🚻)
Principally for the 10-and-under set, this

# Don't Miss **Ringling Museum Complex**

The 66-acre winter estate of railroad, real-estate and circus baron John Ringling and his wife, Mable, is one of the Gulf Coast's most eclectic attractions. There's a lot to see, and several ways to see it. For the complete experience, plan a full day or several shorter visits. For instance, the landscaped grounds and rose gardens are free to the public during open hours. The art museum (alone) is free Monday, while 5pm till 8pm Thursday both the art and circus museums are discounted (adult/child $10/5).

In addition to the sights below, the historic **Asolo Theater** shows a highly recommended, 30-minute PBS-produced film on Ringling's life (included with admission). The theater is itself an attraction – its ornate Italian interior dating to 1798 – and at night hosts a Hollywood film series and special events.

○ **John & Mable Ringling Museum of Art** The Ringlings amassed a vast, impressive collection of European tapestries and paintings ranging from the 14th to the 18th centuries. One wing, though, presents rotating exhibits of contemporary art. In 2012, the Searing Wing plans to open a new atrium, a stunning James Turrell-designed 'Sky Space.'

○ **Cá d'Zan** Ringling was a showman, and his winter home Cá d'Zan (1924–26), or 'House of John,' displays an unmistakable theatrical flair. Even the patio's zigzag marble fronting Sarasota Bay dazzles.

○ **Circus Museum** This is actually several museums in one, all as delightful as the circus itself. One building preserves the hand-carved animal wagons, calliopes, silver cannons and artifacts from Ringling Bros' original traveling show.

### THINGS YOU NEED TO KNOW

☎ 941-359-5700; www.ringling.org; 5401 Bayshore Rd; adult/child 6-17yr $25/10, Mon free; ⊙ 10am-5pm, to 8pm Thu

SHUTTERSTOCK/GRACIOUS_TIGER ©

# Don't Miss Myakka River State Park

Florida's oldest resident – the 200-million-year-old American alligator – is the star of this 57-sq-mile wildlife preserve. Between 500 and 1000 alligators make their home in Myakka's slow-moving river and its shallow, lily-filled lakes, and you can get up close and personal with these toothsome beasts via canoe, kayak and pontoon-style airboat. During mating season in April and May, the guttural love songs of males rings out across the waters and some 38 miles of trails.

## THINGS YOU NEED TO KNOW

📞 941-361-6511; www.myakkariver.org; 13207 State Rd 72; per car $6; 🕑 8am-sunset
**Myakka Oupost** 📞 941-923-1120; rental canoes/bikes from $20/15; 🕑 9:30am-5pm Mon-Fri, 8:30am-5pm Sat & Sun

above-average interactive play space stands out for its reptile-rich animal lab (including baby gators and a bufo toad), an outdoor pond with gigantic carp and turtles to feed, and 3-D movies (included with admission). Along with the more typical hands-on activities, it books first-rate traveling exhibits that make this worthy of an afternoon. It's on the corner of Cranford and Martin Luther King Jr Blvd.

**LEE COUNTY**
**MANATEE PARK**     Wildlife Sanctuary
( 📞 239-432-2038; www.leeparks.org; 10901 State Rd 80; parking per hr/day $1/5; 🕑 park 8am-sunset year-round, visitor center 9am-4pm Nov-Mar, closed summer) November through March, manatees flock up the Orange River to this warm-water discharge canal from the nearby power plant. The waterway is now a protected sanctuary, with a landscaped park and playground in addition to viewing platforms at water's edge,

where manatees swim almost at arm's reach. **Calusa Blueway Outfitters** (☎239-481-4600; www.calusabluewayoutfitters.com) rents kayaks; reserve ahead whenever the VC is closed. The park is signed off Hwy 80, about 6.5 miles from downtown Fort Myers, and 1.5 miles east of I-75.

## Eating

The historic downtown has attractive choices, and more are hidden within strip malls further out.

**CANTINA LAREDO** Mexican **$$**
(☎239-415-4424; www.cantinalaredo.com; 5200 Big Pine Way, Bell Tower Shops; mains $12-23; ☯11am-10pm Sun-Thu, noon-11pm Fri & Sat) Maybe it's the margarita talking, but this atmospheric Mexican spot does everything right, with sharp service, low, romantic lighting, top-shelf tequila, Mexican beer on tap, and guacamole made fresh tableside. Contemporary updates of standard Mexican entrees are well executed and delicious: the *camarones con Tocino* (bacon-wrapped, cheese-stuffed shrimp) and *poblano asado* (steak-wrapped poblano pepper) are superb.

**SPIRITS OF BACCHUS**
Tapas **$$**
(www.spiritsofbacchus.com; 1406 Hendry St; small plates $7-12; ☯from 4pm Mon-Fri, 6pm Sat, 1pm Sun) This stylish exposed-brick saloon is a favorite Fort Myers watering hole serving a range of fancy tapas, sandwiches and bar food, along with wine and cocktails. Nosh and slosh your way through an evening on the vine-wrapped patio.

## Drinking & Entertainment

The historic district becomes a veritable street party twice monthly: for the first-Friday **Art Walk** (www.fortmyersartwalk.com) and the third-Saturday **Music Walk** (www.fortmyersmusicwalk.com).

**ARCADE THEATRE** Theatre
(☎239-332-4488; www.floridarep.org; 2267 1st St; tickets $17-38; ☯Oct-May) The beautifully renovated 1908 Arcade Theatre is home to the **Florida Repertory Theatre**, one of the best theaters in Florida. It produces popular comedies, musicals and recent Tony winners, like *God of Carnage.*

**DAVIS ART CENTER** Performing Arts
(☎239-333-1933; www.sbdac.com; 2301 1st St; ☯Oct-Jun) This performance space downtown produces an eclectic slate of drama, children's theater, dance, music and film. At night, a sculpture splashes the old bank facade with illuminated words.

Dining setting on Naples Beach (p352).
DREAMSTIME/S_KELSEY ©

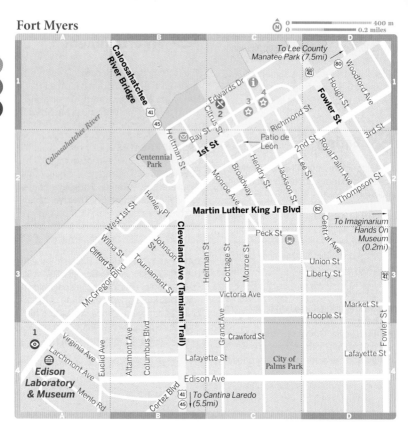

## Fort Myers

◉ **Top Sights**

Edison Laboratory & Museum............A4

◉ **Sights**

1 Edison & Ford Winter Estates.............A4

🍴 **Eating**

2 Spirits of Bacchus .............................. C1

🎭 **Entertainment**

3 Arcade Theatre....................................C1

4 Davis Art Center ................................. C1

Florida Repertory Theatre .......... (see 3)

**PRO BASEBALL**                    Sports

March in Fort Myers means major-league baseball's spring training. **City of Palms Park** (2201 Edison Ave) is the spring-training field for baseball's hallowed **Boston Red Sox** (www.redsox.com). The **Minnesota Twins** (www.mntwins.com) play in Hammond Stadium at **Lee County Sports Complex (14100 Six Mile Cypress Pkwy)**, just southwest of the intersection of Daniels Parkway and Six Mile Cypress Parkway.

ℹ️ **Information**

**Greater Fort Myers Chamber of Commerce** (📞239-332-3624; www.fortmyers.org; cnr Lee St & Edwards Dr; 🕑9am-4:30pm Mon-Fri) Lots of info, good maps, and they'll help you find a room.

**Lee Memorial Hospital** (📞239-343-2000; www.leememorial.org; 2776 Cleveland Ave; 🕑24hr)

# Detour: Cabbage Key

As all Parrotheads know, Jimmy Buffett's famous song 'Cheeseburger in Paradise' was allegedly inspired by a meal at the **Cabbage Key Inn** ( 239-283-2278; www. cabbagekey.com; r $100-140, cottages $160-415; 7:30-9am, 11:30am-3pm & 6-8:30pm). Truth be told, the burger is only average, and it wouldn't be worth writing a song about if it weren't served on this 100-acre, mangrove-fringed key in the Gulf of Mexico. Built atop a Calusa shell mound, and originally the 1938 home of writer Mary Roberts Rinehart, the inn has the romantic air of a secluded semitropical port for global wayfarers, one that receives ferry loads of tourists every lunchtime. The bar is certainly a sight: the walls are matted and spongy with perhaps $80,000 in signed $1 bills, including framed bills from ex-president Jimmy Carter and of course Mr Buffett. Bills flutter to the floor daily, which the inn collects, annually donating $10,000 to charity. Staying in the inn, which lacks TVs, pools and a swimming beach but drips with character, is a worthwhile choice.

To get here, contact Tropic Star (p306) and Captiva Cruises (p307).

## ⓘ Getting There & Around

US 41/S Cleveland Ave is the main north–south artery. From downtown, both Summerlin Rd/Hwy 869 and McGregor Blvd/Hwy 867 eventually merge and lead to Sanibel Island; they also connect with San Carlos Blvd/Hwy 865 to Fort Myers Beach.

**Southwest Florida International Airport** (RSW; http://flylcpa.com; 16000 Chamberlin Pkwy) I-75 exit 131/Daniels Parkway. It's also the main airport for nearby Naples.

## Sanibel & Captiva Islands

239 / SANIBEL POP 6,500 / CAPTIVA POP 580

The beautiful barrier islands of Sanibel and Captiva may largely be inhabited by the wealthy, yet by preference and design, island life is informal and egalitarian. Whether for a few days or few weeks, the islands make a genteel escape from balance sheets, status and traffic lights, of which there are none.

## ◎ Sights & Activities

The quality of **shelling** on Sanibel is so high dedicated hunters are identified by their hunchbacked 'Sanibel stoop.' However, if you're serious, buy a scoop net, get a shell guide from the visitor center, and peruse the blog www.iloveshelling.com.

**BEACHES**                    Beach

What you gain in shelling you lose in powdery white sand: beaches are excellent but the sand isn't as purely fine as it is elsewhere (like Siesta Key). Public-access beaches are located away from hotels, meaning that staying overnight allows private access to even less-crowded stretches.

**Bowman's Beach** is far and away the most popular beach; extremely long, with an enormous parking lot, sparkling sand and facilities and a playground. Modest-size parking lot limits access at **Tarpon Bay Beach**; the sand not quite as good as Bowman. The same can be said for **Gulfside City Park**.

**Lighthouse Beach** is a modest lot, narrow beach. The historic metal lighthouse can't be entered; short nature trails lead around the point. **Turner Beach & Blind Pass** are very small lots on either side of Captiva Island bridge. Shellers favor these short stretches.

Captiva's main beach at its northern end, **Alison Hagerup Beach** has a frustratingly small lot; arrive *very* early. Nice sand ideally positioned for sunset.

GETTY IMAGES/PURESTOCK ©

## Don't Miss Cayo Costa State Park

Unspoiled and all natural, as slim as a supermodel and just as lovely, Cayo Costa Island is almost entirely preserved as a 2500-acre state park. Bring a snorkel mask to help scour sandbars for shells and huge conchs – delightfully, many still house colorful occupants (who, by law, must be left there). Bike dirt roads to more-distant beaches, hike interior island trails, kayak mangroves. The ranger station near the dock sells water and firewood, and rents bikes and kayaks, but otherwise bring everything you need. There's a 30-site campground plus 12 cabins, or you can sleep on the beach, although by May, heat and no-see-ums get unpleasant.

The only access is by boat, which doubles as a scenic nature-and-dolphin cruise operated by the park's official concessionaire, Tropic Star. Day-trip ferries ($25) take an hour one-way; a range of other options include stops at Cabbage Key for lunch (see p305). It also offers private water taxis ($150 per hour), which are much faster.

**THINGS YOU NEED TO KNOW**
**Cayo Costa State Park** ☏941-964-0375; www.floridastateparks.org/cayocosta; entrance $2, campsites $22, 4-person cabins $40; ☉8am-sunset)
**Tropic Star** ☏239-283-0015; www.tropicstarcruises.com; Jug Creek Marina, Bokeelia

**JN 'DING' DARLING NATIONAL WILDLIFE REFUGE**  Wildlife Reserve
(☏239-472-1100; www.fws.gov/dingdarling; Sanibel-Captiva Rd at MM 2; per car/cyclist $5/1; ☉visitor center 9am-5pm, refuge 7am-7pm Sun-Thu) Named for cartoonist Jay Norwood 'Ding' Darling, an environmentalist who helped establish more than 300 sanctuaries across the USA, this 6300-acre refuge across northern Sanibel is home to an abundance of seabirds and wildlife, including alligators, night herons, red-shouldered hawks, spotted sandpipers, roseate spoonbills, pelicans and anhinga. The refuge's 5-mile Wildlife Drive provides

easy access, but bring binoculars; flocks sometimes sit at expansive distances. Only a few very short walks lead into the mangroves. For the best, most intimate experience, canoe or kayak Tarpon Bay (see p307).

Don't miss the free educational center, with excellent exhibits on refuge life and Darling himself. Naturalist-narrated **Wildlife Drive tram tours** (☎239-472-8900; www.tarponbaytours.com; 900 Tarpon Bay; adult/child $13/8; ☺Sat-Thu) depart from the visitor-center parking lot, usually on the hour from 10am to 4pm.

### BAILEY MATTHEWS SHELL MUSEUM
Museum

(☎239-395-2233; www.shellmuseum.org; 3075 Sanibel-Captiva Rd, Sanibel; adult/child 5-16yr $7/4; ☺10am-5pm) Like a mermaid's jewelry box, this museum is dedicated to shells, yet it's much more than a covetous display of treasures. It's a crisply presented natural history of the sea, detailing the life and times of the bivalves, mollusks and creatures who reside inside their calcium homes, as well as the role of these animals and shells in human culture, medicine and cuisine. Fascinating videos show living creatures. It's nearly a must after a day spent combing the beaches.

### TARPON BAY EXPLORERS
Kayaking

(☎239-472-8900; www.tarponbayexplorers .com; 900 Tarpon Bay Rd, Sanibel; ☺8am-6pm) Within the Darling refuge, this outfitter rents canoes and kayaks ($25 for two hours) for easy, self-guided paddles in Tarpon Bay, a perfect place for young paddlers. Guided kayak trips (adult/child $40/25) are also excellent, and they have a range of other trips. Reserve ahead or come early, as they book up.

 **Tours**

Boats and cruises are nearly as ubiquitous as shells on the islands. **Sanibel Marina** (☎239-472-2723; www.sanibel marina.com; 634 N Yachtsman Dr) is the main small-boat harbor with a ton of boat rentals (from $125) and charters (from $350). On Captiva, **McCarthy's Marina** (www.mccarthysmarina.com; 11401 Andy Rosse Lane, Captiva) is where **Captiva Cruises** (☎239-472-5300; www.captivacruises.com) departs from. It offers everything from dolphin and sunset cruises (from $25) to various island excursions (from $35), like Cayo Costa, Cabbage Key and Useppa Key. The **Sanibel Thriller** (☎239-472-2328; www.sanibelthriller.com; adult/child $42/28) does tours that circumnavigate Sanibel and Captiva; on the way you'll get great lessons on the islands' ecology and conservation.

 **Sleeping**

If you're interested in a one-week vacation rental, contact **Sanibel & Captiva Accommodations** (☎800-237-6004; www .sanibelaccom.com).

### 'TWEEN WATERS INN
Resort $$$

(☎239-472-5161; www.tween-waters.com; 15951 Captiva Dr, Captiva; r $160-215, ste $220-405, cottages $265-445; ✻@☎☎♦) For great resort value and an ideal getaway location on Captiva, choose 'Tween Waters Inn. Building exteriors are sun-faded, and you should request one of the recently renovated rooms, which are pristine, attractive roosts with rattan furnishings, granite counters, rainfall showerheads and Tommy Bahama-style decor. Kitchenettes are up-to-date, and tidy little cottages are romantic. All hotel rooms have view balconies; those directly facing the Gulf are splendid. Families make good use of the big pool, tennis courts, full-service marina and spa. Multinight discounts are attractive.

### TARPON TALE INN
Motel $$

(☎239-472-0939; www.tarpontale. com; 367 Periwinkle Way, Sanibel; r $150-260; ✻@☎♦) The five charming, tile-floored rooms evoke a bright, blue-and-white seaside mood; each has its own shady porch and tree-strung hammock.

Two rooms have efficiencies and three have full kitchens. With communal hot tub and loaner bikes, it does a nice imitation of a B&B without the breakfast.

##  Eating & Drinking

### MAD HATTER RESTAURANT
American $$$

(📞239-472-0033; www.madhatterrestaurant.com; 6467 Sanibel-Captiva Rd, Sanibel; mains $29-45; ⏰6-8:45pm) Vacationing Manhattan and Miami urbanites flock to what is widely regarded as Sanibel's best locavore gourmet restaurant. Contemporary seafood is the central focus, with creative appetizers like truffled oysters and a seafood martini, while mains emphasize bouillabaisse, crab cakes, pan-seared grouper and so on. As the name suggests, it's not stuffy, but it's for culinary mavens whose concern is quality, whatever the price.

### CIP'S PLACE
American $

(📞239-472-0223; www.cipsplace.com; 2055 Periwinkle Way, Sanibel; mains $10-25; ⏰11am-9:30pm) Cip's isn't an obviously good option, but get past the shopping center location and through the doors and you'll discover a locals' favorite, where solid mains like burgers, strip teak and fresh local fish are done with an enviable eye for attention and detail. Friendly, delicious and understatedly so.

### BUBBLE ROOM
American $$$

(www.bubbleroomrestaurant.com; 15001 Captiva Dr, Captiva; lunch $10-15, dinner $20-30; ⏰11:30am-3pm & 4:30-9pm; 👪) All the creativity is on the walls at this Captiva classic; if you have kids, it's almost required. Unbelievable decor is a blender-ized, overwhelming riot of 1930s to 1950s memorabilia, a pastiche of superheroes, cartoon characters, movie stars, toy trains, bric-a-brac and Christmas. Entertaining servers in scout uniforms bring meals and desserts that, if nothing else, don't lack for size. No reservations, so expect waits.

### ℹ Information

**Sanibel & Captiva Islands Chamber of Commerce** (📞239-472-1080; www.sanibel-captiva.org; 1159 Causeway Rd, Sanibel; ⏰9am-5pm; 📶)

### ℹ Getting There & Around

Driving is the only way to come. The Sanibel Causeway (Hwy 867) charges an entrance toll (cars/motorcycles $6/2).

## Corkscrew Swamp Sanctuary

The crown jewel in the **National Audubon Society's** (📞239-348-9151; www.corkscrew.audubon.org; adult/child 6-18yr $10/4; ⏰7am-5:30pm Oct–mid-Apr, 7am-7:30pm mid-Apr–Sep) sanctuary collection, this property provides an intimate exploration of six pristine native habitats, including sawgrass, slash pine and marsh, along a shady, 2.25-mile boardwalk trail. The centerpiece is North America's oldest virgin bald-cypress forest, with majestic specimens over 600 years old and 130ft tall.

## NORTH OF TAMPA

The Gulf Coast north of Tampa (and south of the Panhandle) is relatively quiet and often bypassed. As such, it preserves more of that oft-promised, hard-to-find 'Old Florida' atmosphere.

## Homosassa Springs
📞352 / POP 13,800

Signed along US 19, **Homosassa Springs Wildlife State Park** (📞352-628-5343; www.floridastateparks.org/homosassasprings; adult/child 6-12yr $13/5; ⏰9am-5:30pm, last entrance 4pm) is essentially an old-school outdoor Florida animal encounter – aka, zoo – that features Florida's wealth of headliner species: American alligators, black bears, bobcats, whooping cranes, Florida panthers, tiny Key deer, eagles, hawks and – especially – manatees. Homosassa's highlight is an underwater observatory directly over the springs, where through

CORBIS/RAYMOND GEHMAN ©

## Don't Miss Weeki Wachee Springs

Were the 'City of Mermaids' ever to close up shop, a bit of Florida's soul would wink out forever. The 'city' of Weeki Wachee is almost entirely constituted by this **state park**, and the park is almost entirely dedicated to the underwater mermaid show that has entertained families and the famous since 1947. Esther Williams, Danny Thomas and Elvis Presley have all sat in the glass-paneled underwater theater and watched as graceful mermaids perform pirouettes and adagios in the all-natural spring while turtles and fish swim past. The three daily half-hour shows (at 11am, 12:30pm and 2:30pm) remain celebrations of nostalgic kitsch.

The park also offers animal shows, a riverboat cruise, and a modest, weekend-only **waterpark (combined admission adult/child $26/12)**, that make for an afternoon's entertainment. Parking is free.

The spring itself is actually the headwater of the crystal-clear Weeki Wachee River. Kayaking or canoeing this river is one of the region's best paddles; at the back of the Weeki Wachee parking lot, follow signs to **Paddling Adventure**s ( ☎ 352-592-5666; kayak rentals $30-35; ⏱9am-3pm, last launch noon). The 7-mile route includes beach areas with good swimming and rope swings, plus you'll see lots of fish and even manatees in winter and spring. It's about 45 minutes from Tampa via I-75 north to Hwy 50 west.

### THINGS YOU NEED TO KNOW

☎ 352-592-5656; www.weekiwachee.com; 6131 Commercial Way/US 19 at Hwy 50; adult/child 6-12yr $13/5; ⏱10am-3pm Mar, to 4pm Apr-Aug

glass windows you can gawk eyeball to eyeball with enormous schools of some 10,000 fish and ponderous manatees nibbling lettuce. Various animal presenta-tions happen daily, but time your visit for the manatee program (11:30am, 1:30pm and 3:30pm). The park itself is a short, narrated boat ride from the visitor center.

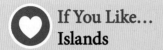

# If You Like…
# Islands

Two of the best beaches in Florida are just north of Greater Tampa: Honeymoon Island, which you can drive to, and ferry-only Caladesi Island.

**1 HONEYMOON ISLAND STATE PARK**
(www.floridastateparks.org/honeymoonisland; 1 Dunedin Causeway; per car $8; ☺8am-sunset)
Graced with the Gulf Coast's legendary white sand and warm aquamarine waters, and Honeymoon has the state park system's only dog-friendly beach. On the beach, the **Island Cafe** (www.romantic honeymoonisland.com; ☺9am-5pm) serves sandwiches, snacks and beer, and offers bike, kayak and umbrella rentals. Best of all, the island is blissfully undeveloped.

**2 CALADESI ISLAND STATE PARK**
(www.floridastateparks.org/caladesiisland; admission free; ☺8am-sunset) Just south of Honeymoon. Caladesi is today virtually as nature made it (and as hurricanes have reshaped it): unspoiled and pristine. Consequently, it often tops national beach polls, and its three palm-lined miles of sparkling, sugar-sand beaches should make the top of your list, too.

**3 CALADESI ISLAND ADVENTURE**
( ☎727-734-1501; www.caladesiferry.org; adult/child $12/6) Runs 20-minute ferries (longer if you spot dolphins) from Honeymoon every hour on the hour beginning at 10am and generally ending around 4pm.

The park is about 20 miles north of Weeki Wachee and 75 miles north of Tampa; US 19 north leads to the park entrance.

## Crystal River
☎352 / POP 3,100

Every winter, about 20% of Florida's Gulf Coast manatee population meanders into the 72°F, spring-fed waters of Kings Bay, near the town of Crystal River, and for this reason the bay is almost entirely protected within the **Crystal River National Wildlife Refuge** ( ☎352-563-2088; www.fws .gov/crystalriver; 1502 SE Kings Bay Dr; ☺visitor center 8am-4pm Mon-Fri). Up to 560 of these gentle, endangered sea creatures have been counted in a single January day, and like any wildlife spectacle, this draws crowds of onlookers. Nearly 40 commercial operators offer rentals and guided tours of Kings Bay, via every type of nautical convey-ance, and the chance to swim with wild manatees is a truly wondrous opportunity not to miss. However, whether visitors should be allowed to actively touch manatees is an ongoing controversy.

There is no public viewing area on land to view manatees; the only access to the refuge is by boat. However, a new boardwalk is in the works.

# Best of
# the Rest

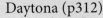

### Daytona (p312)
Fast cars, Spring Break, hot tans and sea turtles.

### St Augustine &
### Amelia Island (p313)
St Augustine is North America's oldest European settlement. Amelia Island meshes the historic with beaches.

### Tallahassee &
### Apalachicola (p315)
Experience the rustic beauty of North Florida and Tallahassee's history.

### Destin (p317)
Gulf Coast beauty on the Southern-fried Florida panhandle.

**Left:** Elevated bridge at Fort Clinch State Park (p314);
**Above:** Colorful chairlifts at Daytona Beach (p312).
(LEFT) LOU JONES/LONELY PLANET IMAGES ©; (ABOVE) SHUTTERSTOCK
IMAGES/ARKORN ©

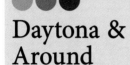

# Daytona & Around

## HIGHLIGHTS

**1** **Daytona Speedway (p312)** Fabled racing track of the South.

**2** **Daytona Beach (p312)** Prime swathe of sand for car or bicycle cruising.

**3** **Marine Science Center (p312)** Cares for injured turtles and seabirds.

Action at the Daytona International Speedway.
DREAMSTIME IMAGES/ACTION SPORTS (WALTER ARCE) ©

## Sights & Activities

**DAYTONA INTERNATIONAL SPEEDWAY** Racetrack, Tours
( ☎ 800-748-7467; www.daytonaintlspeedway.com; 1801 W International Speedway Blvd; tickets from $15) This legendary 480-acre speedway boasts a more diverse race schedule than any other track in the world. Event ticket prices accelerate sharply for big races, but if nothing is going on, you can wander through the gift shop and into the grandstands for free.

Tram tours take you behind the scenes at the track and pits. The standard 30-minute **Speedway Tour** (adult/child $15/10; ☉11:30am, 1:30pm, 3:30pm & 4pm) hits the main highlights, while the hour-long **All-Access Tour** (adult/child $17/22; ☉hourly 10am-3pm) is a lot more in-depth.

**DAYTONA BEACH** Beach
(per car $5; ☉8am-7pm May-Oct, sunrise-sunset Nov-Apr) One look at this perfectly planar stretch of sand and you can see why it served as the city's raceway. Today you can drive sections of the beach, tide permitting, to a strictly enforced top speed of 10mph. There are six well-signed beach entrances from Ormond Beach (Granada Blvd) to Ponce Inlet (Beach St); between Seabreeze Blvd and International Speedway Blvd it's traffic-free. Rent anything from a '58 'Vette convertible to fat-tired two-wheeled beach cruisers to recumbent trikes. If you're tired of wheels, beach-based vendors rent slick-bottomed boogie boards ($5 per hour), 8ft surfboards ($10 per hour), and offer banana-boat rides and other types of splashy fun.

**MARINE SCIENCE CENTER** Aquarium
(www.marinesciencecenter.com; 100 Lighthouse Dr; adult/child $5/2; ☉10am-4pm Tue-Sat, noon-4pm Sun; ⛹) Despite the built-up environs at Daytona Beach, loggerheads, green turtles, Kemp Ridleys and leatherbacks are found in the area. A rehab center for injured sea turtles and birds, the Marine Science Center has a wet/dry lab, some great kid-friendly exhibits and a guided tour of the on-site turtle and seabird rehabilitation facilities (call ahead).

# Sights & Activities

## St Augustine

### SPANISH QUARTER MUSEUM
*Historic Buildings*

(entry via 53 St George St; adult/child $7/4; ⊙9am-4:45pm) Spanning 2 acres, this multibuilding complex is a re-creation of 1740 St Augustine. Walled off from the street, you're encouraged to wander the garrison's restored buildings and speak to the craftspeople (re-enactors) who use 18th-century technology to operate re-created 'storefronts': a blacksmith, a leather shop and a carpentry studio. Craftspeople live out their period roles, often camping for weeks in nearby wilderness areas using only materials available in the 1700s, road-testing the clothing and tools you see them make here.

### LIGHTNER MUSEUM
*Museum*

(www.lightnermuseum.org; 75 King St; adult/child $10/5; ⊙9am-5pm) This brilliantly eclectic museum is in the restored Alcazar Hotel, one of Henry Flagler's two St Augustine resorts, which housed (at the time) the world's largest indoor pool. Expect everything from antique musical instruments (played at 11am and 2pm; amazing acoustics make this a must-hear), to a shrunken head, to Egyptian-themed art-deco sculpture and Renaissance art

### HOTEL PONCE DE LEÓN
*Historic Building*

(adult/child $7/1; 74 King St; ⊙tours hourly 10am-3pm summer) An 80ft domed rotunda and stained glass crafted by Louis Comfort Tiffany are the hallmarks of the Spanish Renaissance Revival hotel, Henry Flagler's flagship resort. This architectural wonder, the first wmajor poured-concrete structure in the US, quickly became the country's most exclusive winter resort, before succumbing to a lack of guests in the 1960s, which then led it to become part of the private Flagler College.

# St Augustine & Amelia Island

## HIGHLIGHTS

**1** **Spanish Quarter Museum (p313)** Living history in the USA's oldest city.

**2** **Lightner Museum (p313)** Crazy palace with diverse collection of artifacts.

**3** **Hotel Ponce de León (p313)** Spanish-style grand hotel – one of Florida's finest historical buildings

**4** **Amelia Island (p314)** Take a stroll into the past or hunt for Augustine's ghosts.

Statue of Pedro Menéndez de Avilés, founder of St Augustine.
DENNIS JOHNSON/LONELY PLANET IMAGES©

### CASTILLO DE SAN MARCOS
### NATIONAL MONUMENT
Fort

(www.nps.gov/casa; adult/child $6/free; ⏱8:45am-5:15pm, grounds closed midnight-5:30am; 👫) Wandering from the clogged downtown streets onto the headland where this incredibly photogenic fort stands guard really amplifies its imposing scale. In 1672, after the British had burned the city around them one too many times, the Spanish began constructing this coquina citadel. Completed 23 years later, it's the oldest masonry fort in the continental US. Rangers wearing Spanish colonial-era uniforms add to the medieval ambience and can answer questions as you take the fort's excellent self-guided tour. Cannons can be heard all over town when they're fired on the half-hour (10:30am to 3:30pm Friday to Sunday; fired when more than four visitors are at the monument). The fort is located between San Marco Ave and Matanzas River.

### ST AUGUSTINE CITY
### WALKS
History Tour

(☎904-540-3476; www.staugustinecitywalks .com; tours $14-45) Super-popular and extremely fun, these walking tours range from the Haunted Pub Crawl to the Savory Faire Food Tour (exploring the culture and history behind the city's cuisine) to the History, Mystery, Mayhem and Murder tour of the city's cemeteries, pirate hangouts and other dark spots.

## Amelia Island

13 miles from the Georgia border, this glorious sea island combines the moss-draped charm of the Deep South with the sun 'n' fun beach culture of Florida.

### FORT CLINCH STATE PARK
Park

(2601 Atlantic Ave; park pedestrian/car $2/6; ⏱park 8am-sunset, fort 9am-5pm) The US government began constructing Fort Clinch in 1847. State of the art at the time, rapid advancements in military technology rendered its masonry walls obsolete by the Civil War. A Confederate militia occupied the almost-complete fort early in the conflict but evacuated soon after. Federal troops again occupied the fort during WWII, when it served as a surveillance and communications station for the US Coast Guard. Today, the park offers a variety of activities. In addition to a 0.5-mile-long fishing pier, there are also serene beaches for shelling and 6 miles of peaceful, unpaved trails for hiking and biking.

### AMELIA ISLAND MUSEUM
### OF HISTORY
Museum

(www.ameliamuseum.org; 233 S 3rd St; adult/ student $7/4; ⏱10am-4pm Mon-Sat, 1-4pm Sun) Housed in the former city jail (1879–1975), Florida's only oral-history museum has tiny but informative exhibits exploring Native American history, the Spanish-mission period, the Civil War and historic preservation. There's also a good overview of the history of water, timber and tourism in the county. Most fun of all is the eight-flags tour, every day at 11am and 2pm, when guides provide lively interpretations of the island's intricate history: eight flags have flown over the island, starting with the French flag in 1562, followed by the Spanish, the English, the Spanish again, the Patriots, the Green Cross of Florida, the Mexican Rebels, the US, the Confederates, then the US again (1821 onward).

 **Eating**

## St Augustine

### FLORIDIAN
Modern American $$

(☎904-829-0655; www.thefloridianstaug.com; 39 Cordova St; mains $12-20; ⏱11am-3pm & 5-9pm Mon & Wed-Fri, to 10pm Sat & Sun, closed Tue) Though it oozes hipster-locavore earnestness, this new farm-to-table restaurant is so fabulous you won't even roll your eyes. The chef-owners scour every corner of North Florida for produce, meat and fish, which they turn into whimsical neo-Southern creations – fried-green-tomato bruschetta with local goat cheese, Vietnamese *bahn mi* sandwiches with acorn-fed pork, catch-of-the-day with Florida citrus–sweet potato salsa.

# Tallahassee & Apalachicola

## HIGHLIGHTS

① **Museum of Florida History (p315)** An extensive, family-fun peek into the story of Florida.

② **Apalachicola National Forest (p315)** The best wilderness area in North Florida.

③ **Mission San Luis (p315)** Beautifully restored Spanish mission settlement.

Shrimp boats in Apalachicola Bay.
CORBIS/RICHARD BICKEL ©

 **Sights & Activities**

**MUSEUM OF FLORIDA HISTORY** Museum
(www.museumoffloridahistory.com; 500 S Bronough St, Tallahassee; admission free; 9am-4:30pm Mon-Fri, 10am-4:30pm Sat, noon-4:30pm Sun) This museum is filled with wonderful exhibits, tackling everything from Florida's Paleo-Indians to Civil War times, Spanish shipwrecks in the Atlantic and the rise of 'Tin-Can Tourism,' when the middle-class traveler began hitting Florida in droves.

**APALACHICOLA NATIONAL FOREST** Forest
(day-use areas $5; 8am-sunset) The largest of Florida's three national forests, Apalachicola occupies almost 938 sq miles – more than half a million acres – of the Panhandle from just west of Tallahassee to the Apalachicola River. Made up of lowlands, pine, cypress hammocks and oaks, dozens of species call the area home including mink, gray and red foxes, coyotes, six bat species, beavers, red cockaded woodpeckers, alligators, Florida black bears and the elusive Florida panther. A total of 68.7 miles of the Florida National Scenic Trail extends through the forest as well.

**MISSION SAN LUIS** Historic Site
(www.missionsanluis.org; 2020 W Mission Rd, Tallahassee; adult/child $5/2; 10am-4pm Tue-Sun) In a lofty hilltop setting spanning 60 acres, the Mission San Luis was site of a Spanish and Native American mission settlement from 1656 to 1704. The entire mission has been wonderfully reconstructed – look out for the dramatic, soaring council house of the Apalachee village, which stands like a towering, light-filled teepee on the bucolic land.

**MARY BROGAN MUSEUM OF ART & SCIENCE** Museum
(www.thebrogan.org; 350 S Duval St, Tallahassee; adult/child $7.50/5; 10am-5pm Mon-Sat, 1-5pm Sun; 🚹) Affiliated with the Smithsonian, this museum is a hit with kids. It houses both a science center on the 1st and 2nd floors, and the Tallahassee art

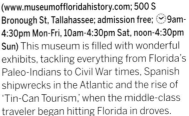

museum, mounting international exhibits, on the 3rd. It may seem like a strange marriage at first, but the museum does a great job of pointing out connections between left- and right-brained creations, with highlights including a living sea eco-lab and a TV weather station where kids can try their hands at forecasting.

### HISTORIC CAPITOL     Historic Building
(www.flhistoriccapitol.gov; Tallahassee) Next door to the current state capitol is its far more charming 1902 predecessor, adorned by candy-striped awnings and topped with a reproduction of the original glass dome as grand as its successor is uninviting. It now houses the **Florida Legislative Research Center & Museum** (www.flrcm.com; 400 S Monroe St; Tallahassee; admission free; ⊙9am-4:30pm Mon-Fri, 10am-4:30pm Sat, noon-4:30pm Sun & holidays), including a restored House of Representatives chamber and governors' reception area, plenty of governors' portraits, and exhibits on immigration, state development and the infamous 2000 US presidential election, with displays such as the equally infamous butterfly ballot, now enclosed in glass.

### FLORIDA STATE
### CAPITOL     Government Building
(New Capitol; cnr Pensacola St & Duval St, Tallahassee; ⊙8am-5pm Mon-Fri) It's stark, ugly and massively imposing, but the 22-story Florida State Capitol still deserves your visit. That's mainly because of its top floor

observation deck, which affords wonderful 360-degree views of the city and its edge of rolling green hills that stretch to the horizons. In session, the Capitol is a hive of activity, with politicians, staffers and lobby groups buzzing in and around its honeycombed corridors.

# Eating

### KOOL BEANZ CAFÉ     Eclectic $$
( ☎850-224-2466; www.koolbeanz-café.com; 921 Thomasville Rd, Tallahassee; mains $16-23; ⊙11am-2pm Mon-Fri, 5:30-10pm Mon-Sat, 10:30am-2pm Sun) It's got a corny name but a wonderfully eclectic and homey vibe – plus great, creative fare. The menu changes daily, but you can count on finding anything from hummus plates to jerk-spiced scallops to duck in blueberry-ginger sauce.

### ANDREW'S
### DOWNTOWN     American, Italian $$
( ☎850-222-3444; www.andrewsdowntown .com; 228 S Adams St, Tallahassee; downstairs mains $9-13, upstairs mains $14-36; ⊙downstairs 11:30am-10pm, upstairs 6-10pm Mon-Sat) Downtown's see-and-be-seen spot, politicians love this two-level restaurant – Capital Grill & Bar is a casual burgers-and-beer spot with indoor and outdoor seating, while Andrew's 228 (upstairs) is an upscale neo-Tuscan restaurant serving creative fare like pork chops with butternut squash orzo.

## Destin

### HIGHLIGHTS

**①** **Indian Temple Mound & Museum (p317)** A major site for Florida's Native Americans.

**②** **Southern Star (p317)** Excellent dolphin tours on calm Gulf waters.

**③** **Grayton Beach State Park (p317)** One of the state's most beautiful beach parks.

Soft morning light at one of Destin's beaches.
ISTOCK IMAGES/RICARDO REITMEYER ©

## ◉ Sights & Activities

**INDIAN TEMPLE MOUND & MUSEUM** Archeological Site **(admission free)** One of the most sacred sites for local Native American culture to this day, the 17ft tall, 223ft wide ceremonial and political **temple mound**, built with 500,000 basket loads of earth and representing what is probably the largest prehistoric earthwork on the Gulf Coast, dates back to somewhere between AD 800 and 1500. On top of the mound you'll find a recreated temple housing a small exhibition center. Next door, the **museum (139 Miracle Strip Parkway; adult/child $5/3; ⏰12-4:30pm Mon-Sat, from 10am Sun)** offers an extensive overview of 12,000 years of Native American history.

**SOUTHERN STAR** Dolphin Cruise **( ☏850-837-7741; www.dolphin-sstar.com; Harborwalk Marina; adult/child $29/15.50; ⏰4 tours per day Mon-Sat Jun-Aug)** Bottlenose dolphins live year-round in the temperate waters of these parts; Southern Star is one of several companies offering dolphin cruises in hopes of spotting a few. The welcoming owner-operators will take you out on a two-hour cruise in a 76ft glass-bottom boat. Call for schedules in other months.

**GRAYTON BEACH STATE PARK** Park **(357 Main Park Rd, Santa Rosa Beach; vehicle $5)** A 1133-acre stretch of marble-colored dunes 25 miles west of Destin, this state park's beauty is genuinely mind-blowing. The park sits nestled against the wealthy but down-to-earth community of Grayton Beach, and also contains **Grayton Beach Nature Trail**, which runs from the east side of the parking lot through the dunes, magnolias and pine flatwoods and onto a boardwalk to a return trail along the beach.

# Florida
# In Focus

Signboard in Key West (p237).
ISTOCK PHOTOS/CRISTIAN LAZZARI ©

# Florida Today

Art deco hotels along Ocean Drive (p196) in Miami's South Beach.

❝

*a new boom...just around the corner, ready to spark another frenzy of immigration, real estate and tourism*

❞

## belief systems
(% of population)

**40** Protestant  **26** Roman Catholic  **16** Non-Religious  **15** Other  **3** Jewish

## if Florida were 100 people

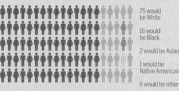

75 would be White
16 would be Black
2 would be Asian
1 would be Native American
6 would be other

## population per sq miles

👤 = 90 people

USA    FLORIDA    MIAMI

## House for Sale

Florida is a boom-and-bust sort of place. People find something they can get rich with – oranges, real estate, tourism – and they ride it into the sky until nature, the stock market or their own exuberance sends them tumbling back to earth.

This truism is being keenly felt today as Florida tries to recover from a double whammy. First, there was the national real-estate-market collapse, which began in 2007 (sparked by banking's home-mortgage crisis). Among US states, Florida felt the effects first and hardest. As home prices tumbled, the construction industry tanked and growth essentially flatlined to its lowest point in 30 years. Foreclosures flooded the state, so that by 2010, 18% of Florida homes were vacant. Median home prices, meanwhile, tumbled to virtually half their 2006 value.

Without real estate, construction, and population growth, Florida's economy has only one other main pillar: tourism. Yet this suffered a major blow following the April

ISTOCK PHOTOS /CRISTIAN LAZZARI ©

# A State Divided

Ever since the controversial 2000 Bush-Gore presidential election, Florida politics has been almost evenly divided between Republicans and Democrats. This held true in 2010, when the Tea Party–backed Republican Rick Scott won the governorship by a razor-thin margin of 1.15%, or 61,550 votes out of over 5.3 million cast.

Then within months of taking office, Governor Scott's statewide approval ratings sank to 35% due to a series of actions: he refused to join a federal lawsuit to recover oil-spill-related losses; he scuttled a high-speed-rail initiative between Orlando and Tampa; he enacted sweeping education reform that ended teacher tenure and tied pay to student test scores; and he vowed to balance the state budget through cuts alone.

Florida's mercurial political landscape has nationwide implications. Once again, most observers anticipate that the coming 2012 presidential election will be decided by Florida, which voted for President Obama by 50.9% in the 2008 election. However, the national Republican party, which is holding its 2012 nominating convention in Tampa, fervently hopes Governor Scott rallies, rather than alienates, state voters.

Other important issues continue to galvanize residents – particularly the uncertain future of environmental programs like Florida Forever and Everglades restoration. Everything likely hinges on how fast Florida can sweep away the economic gray clouds. If history is a guide, a new boom must be just around the corner, ready to spark another frenzy of immigration, real estate and tourism, and once again brightening the outlook of the Sunshine State.

2010 Deepwater Horizon oil spill in the Gulf of Mexico (the worst in US history). Even though only Panhandle beaches were touched by any oil, bad press and fear kept visitors away from Florida's entire Gulf Coast. Though impossible to calculate exactly, it's estimated Florida lost well over $3 billion in tourism-related spending.

By 2011, all Florida's Gulf beaches were clean of tar balls, and the state was sending out an urgent message to you, dear reader: Please come back!

Also while real estate, construction, tourism and growth were again showing a pulse by 2011, it was insufficient to make up the estimated $3.6 billion shortfall in the state's $70 billion 2011 budget. How to bridge that gap – whether solely through budget cuts or by a combination of cuts and tax hikes – was dividing Florida's politics along now-predictable lines.

# History

A palatial mansion in Florida's Palm Beach (p152).

ISTOCK PHOTO/MELISSA MADIA

*Florida has the oldest recorded history of any US state. Native Americans were here thousands of years before the first Europeans planted a flag at St Augustine. The state has switched hands between three European and two American flags, and evolved from an agricultural citrus and sugar basket into the tourism capital and international center of commerce it is today.*

## From Tycoons to Disney

Florida's history isn't just extensive; it's always been a little bizarre too. Spanish explorers chased golden cities, antiaging water and mermaids, but if they found none of those, only a funhouse mirror separates them from us: in Florida, mermaids perform daily, aging snowbirds flock for rejuvenation, Disney World prom-

### 10,000 BC
After crossing the Bering Strait from Siberia, humans arrive in Florida.

ises a Magic Kingdom and real-estate developers long ago discovered how to get gold from a swamp. Simply drain it.

Florida's modern history truly begins with the late-19th-century tycoons who dried the marshes, built railroads and resorts, and then ceaselessly promoted Florida as an 'emerald kingdom by southern seas.' Since then, each era has been marked by wild-eyed speculation inspiring great tides of immigration – from the 1920s real-estate mania to the 1950s orange boom to the 1960s Cuban exodus to the 1980s influx of Latin Americans – each inevitably followed by a crash: the Great Depression, race riots, cartel cocaine wars, 1992's Hurricane Andrew, and so on.

Today, Florida's boom-and-bust cycle continues. Whatever else, it makes for great storytelling.

## First Inhabitants & Seminoles

Florida's original inhabitants never organized into large, cohesive tribes. For some 11,500 years, they remained split into numerous small chiefdoms or villages, becoming more settled and agricultural in the north and remaining more nomadic and warlike in the south.

The Apalachee in Florida's Panhandle developed the most complex agriculture-based society, but other tribes included the Timucua in northern Florida, the Tequesta along the central Atlantic Coast, and the fierce Calusa in southern Florida. Legends say it was a poison-tipped Calusa arrow that killed Ponce de León.

The most striking evidence of these early cultures are shell mounds or middens. Florida's ancestral peoples ate well, and their discarded shells reached 30ft high and themselves became the foundations of villages, as at Mound Key.

When the Spanish arrived in the 1500s, the indigenous population numbered perhaps 250,000. Over the next 200 years, European diseases, war and slavery killed 80% of them. As the 18th century unfolded, Creeks and other tribes fleeing European colonies (and later, the new USA) migrated into Florida. These tribes intermingled and intermarried, and in the late 1700s they were joined by numerous runaway black slaves.

At some point, these uncooperative, fugitive, mixed peoples occupying Florida's interior were dubbed 'Seminoles,' a corruption of the Spanish word *cimarrones,* meaning 'free people' or 'wild ones.' Defying European rule and ethnic category, they were soon considered too free for the newly independent United States, who brought war to them (see p324).

**1513**

Ponce de León lands near Cape Canaveral and names it La Florida, 'Feast of Flowers.'

**1565**

Pedro Menéndez de Aviles founds St Augustine, the first permanent European settlement in the New World.

**1702**

The British burn St Augustine; two years later they destroy 13 Spanish missions.

## The Unconquered Seminoles

From 1817 to 1858, the US waged war on Florida's Seminoles three times, always to conquer territory and punish the tribe for sheltering escaped slaves. Of the three conflicts, the Second Seminole War is the most well-known. The war was fought guerrilla-style by 2000 or so Seminoles in swamps and hammocks, led by the famous Osceola, eventually captured under a flag of truce. After the Third Seminole War, 200 to 300 Seminoles refused to sign a peace treaty and slipped away into the Everglades. Technically, these Seminoles never surrendered and remain the only 'unconquered' American Indian tribe. In 1957, the US officially recognized the **Seminole Tribe** (www.semtribe.com), and in 1962, the **Miccosukee Tribe** (www.miccosukee.com). For more history, visit the **Ah-Tah-Thi-Ki Museum** (www.ahtahthiki.com).

## Five Flags: Florida Gets Passed Around

Spain claimed Florida in 1513 – when explorer Ponce de León arrived. Five more Spanish expeditions followed (and one French), and nothing bore fruit until 1565, when St Augustine was settled. A malarial, easily pillaged outpost, St Augustine truly succeeded at only one thing: spreading the Catholic religion. Spanish missionaries founded 31 missions across Florida, converting and educating Indians, occasionally with notable civility.

In 1698 Spain established a permanent military fort at Pensacola, which was then variously captured and recaptured by the Spanish, French, English and North Americans for a century. Pensacola set the trend for Florida as a state: as a piece of real estate to be fought over. From now till 1865 Florida would be ruled by five flags: Spain, France, Britain, the US and the Confederacy.

## From Civil War To Civil Rights

In 1838 the Florida territory was home to about 48,000 people, of whom 21,000 were black slaves. By 1860, 15 years after statehood, Florida's population was 140,000, of whom 40% were slaves, most of them working on highly profitable cotton plantations. Thus, unsurprisingly, when Abraham Lincoln was elected president on an antislavery platform, Florida joined the confederacy of Southern states that seceded from the Union in 1861. During the ensuing Civil War, which lasted until 1865, only moderate fighting occurred in Florida.

After Southern surrender the US government imposed 'Reconstruction' on all ex-Confederate states. Reconstruction protected the rights of freed blacks, and led to

**1823**
Tallahassee is established as Florida's capital because it's halfway between Pensacola and St Augustine.

**1845**
Florida is admitted to the Union as the 27th state.

ISTOCK PHOTO/RUSKPP ©

19 blacks becoming elected to Florida's state congress. Yet this radical social and political upheaval led to a furious backlash. When federal troops finally left, Florida 'unreconstructed' in a hurry, adopting a series of Jim Crow laws that segregated and disenfranchised blacks in every sphere of life – in restaurants and parks, on beaches and buses – while a poll tax kept blacks and the poor from voting. From then until the 1950s, black field hands in turpentine camps and cane fields worked under a forced-labor 'peonage' system, in which they couldn't leave till their wages paid off their debts, which of course never happened.

The Ku Klux Klan thrived, its popularity peaking in the 1920s, when Florida led the country in lynchings. Racial hysteria and violence were commonplace; most infamously, a white mob razed the entire town of Rosewood in 1923.

In 1954 the US Supreme Court ended legal segregation in the US with Brown vs Board of Education, but in 1957 Florida's Supreme Court rejected this decision, declaring it 'null and void.' This sparked protests but little change until 1964, when a series of race riots and demonstrations, some led by Martin Luther King Jr, rocked St Augustine and helped spur passage of the national Civil Rights Act of 1964. More race riots blazed across Florida cities in 1967 and 1968, after which racial conflict eased as Florida belatedly and begrudgingly desegregated itself.

Florida's racial wounds healed equally slowly – as evidenced by more race riots in the early 1980s. Today, despite much progress and the fact that Florida is one of the nation's most ethnically diverse states, these wounds still haven't completely healed.

**The Best...
Historical
Homes**

1 Flagler Museum (p152)

2 Vizcaya Museum & Gardens (p201)

3 Edison & Ford Winter Estates (p300)

4 Hemingway House (p239)

## Draining Swamps & Laying Rail

By the middle of the 19th century, the top half of Florida was reasonably well explored, but South Florida was still a swamp. So, in the 1870s, Florida inaugurated its first building boom by adopting laissez-faire economic policies centered on three things: unrestricted private development, minimal taxes, and land grants for railroads.

In 10 years, from 1881 to 1891, Florida's railroad miles quintupled, from 550 to 2566. Most of the track crisscrossed northern and central Florida, but one rail line went south to nowhere. In 1886, railroad magnate Henry Flagler started building a railroad down the coast on the spectacular gamble that once he built it, people would come.

**1861**

Voting 62–7, Florida secedes from the USA, raising the stars-and-bars of the Confederacy.

**1912**

'Flagler's Folly,' Henry Flagler's 128-mile overseas railroad connecting the Florida Keys, reaches Key West.

**1926–28**

Hurricanes take a toll of some 2400 lives across the state.

## The Best... Florida Histories

In 1896 Flagler's line stopped at muddy Fort Dallas, which incorporated as the city of Miami that same year. Then, people came, and kept coming, and Flagler is largely credited with founding every town from West Palm Beach to Miami.

In 1900 Governor Napoleon Bonaparte Broward, envisioning an 'Empire of the Everglades,' set in motion a frenzy of canal building. Some 1800 miles of canals and levees were etched across Florida's limestone. These earthworks successfully drained about half the Everglades (about 1.5 million acres) below Lake Okeechobee, replacing it with farms, cattle ranches, orange groves, sugarcane and suburbs.

From 1920 to 1925, the South Florida land boom swept the nation. In 1915, Miami Beach was a sandbar; by 1925, it had 56 hotels, 178 apartment buildings, and three golf courses. In 1920, Miami had one skyscraper; by 1925, 30 were under construction. In 1925 alone, 2.5 million people moved to Florida. Real-estate speculators sold undeveloped land, undredged land, and then just promises of land.

Then, two hurricanes struck, in 1926 and 1928, and the party ended. The coup de grâce was the October 1929 stock-market crash. Florida plunged into depression, though the state rode it relatively well due to New Deal public works, tourism, and a highly profitable foray into rum running – smuggling being a popular illicit means of income in a state intersected by thousands of miles of tiny waterways.

## Tin Can Tourists, Retirees & A Big-Eared Mouse

For the record, tourism is Florida's number-one industry, and this doesn't count retirees – the tourists who never leave.

Tourism didn't become a force in Florida until the 1890s, when Flagler built his coastal railroad and hoity-toity Miami Beach resorts. In the 1920s, middle-class 'tin can tourists' arrived via the new Dixie Hwy – driving Model Ts, sleeping in campers and cooking their own food.

In the 1930s, savvy promoters created the first 'theme parks': Cypress Gardens and Silver Springs. But it wasn't until after WWII that Florida tourism exploded. During

**1933–40**
New Deal public-works projects employ 40,000 Floridians and build the Overseas Highway, replacing Flagler's railroad.

**1935**
Dick Pope opens Cypress Gardens, the USA's first theme park.

**1946**
Frozen concentrated orange juice is invented, leading to Florida's orange boom.

the war, Miami was a major military training ground, and afterward, many of those GIs returned with their families.

In addition, after the war, Social Security kicked in, and the nation's aging middle class migrated south to enjoy a new concept: retirement. Many came from the East Coast, and quite a few were Jewish: by 1960, Miami Beach was 80% Jewish.

Then one day in 1963, so the story goes, Walt Disney flew over central Florida, spotted the intersection of I-4 and the Florida Turnpike, and said, 'That's it.' In secret, he bought 43 sq miles of Orlando-area wetlands. Exempt from a host of state laws and building codes, largely self-governing, Disney World opened in 1971. How big did it become? In 1950, Florida received 4.5 million tourists, not quite twice its population. By the 1980s, Disney alone drew 40 million visitors a year, or four times the state population.

Disney had the Midas touch. In the shadow of the Magic Kingdom, Florida's old-school attractions – Weeki Wachee, Seminole Village, Busch Gardens; all the places made famous through billboards and postcards – seemed hokey, small-time. The rules of tourism had changed forever.

Cigars (p286) on sale in Little Havana, Miami.
ALAMY/PETER TITMUSS ©

**1947**

Everglades National Park is established, successfully culminating a 19-year effort to protect the Everglades.

**1961**

Brigade 2506, a Miami-based 1300-strong volunteer army, invades Cuba but is defeated by Castro.

**1969**

*Apollo 11* lifts off from Cape Canaveral and lands on the moon.

## The Best...
# Historical Hotels

1 Curry Mansion Inn (p245)

2 Hotel Ponce de León (p313)

3 Breakers (p153)

4 Biltmore Hotel (p202)

5 Cardozo Hotel (p211)

# Viva Cuba Libre!

South Florida has an intimate relationship with Cuba. In the 20th century, so many Cuban exiles sought refuge in Miami, they dubbed it the 'Exile Capital.' Later, as immigration expanded, Miami simply became the 'Capital of Latin America.'

From 1868 to 1902, during Cuba's long struggle for independence from Spain, Cuban exiles settled in Key West and Tampa, giving birth to Ybor City. Then, in 1959, Fidel Castro's revolution (plotted partly in Miami hotels) overthrew the Batista dictatorship. This triggered a several-year exodus of over 600,000 Cubans to Miami, most of them white, wealthy, educated professionals.

In April 1961, Castro declared Cuba communist, setting the future course for US–Cuban relations. The next day, President Kennedy approved the ill-fated Bay of Pigs invasion, which failed to overthrow Castro, and in October 1962, Kennedy blockaded Cuba to protest the presence of Russian nuclear missiles. Khrushchev famously 'blinked' and removed the missiles, but not before the US secretly agreed never to invade Cuba again.

None of this sat well with Miami's Cuban exiles, who agitated for the USA to free Cuba (chanting 'Viva Cuba libre': long live free Cuba). Between 1960 and 1980, a million Cubans, or 10% of the island's population, emigrated; by 1980, 60% of Miami was Cuban.

In the 1980s and '90s, poorer immigrants flooded Miami from all over Latin America and the Caribbean – particularly El Salvador, Nicaragua, Mexico, Colombia, Venezuela, the Dominican Republic and Haiti. These groups did not always mix easily, but they found success in a city that already conducted business in Spanish. By the mid-1990s, South Florida was exporting $25 billion in goods to Latin America, and Miami's Cubans were more economically powerful than Cuba itself.

Today, Miami's Cubans are firmly entrenched, and the younger generation no longer consider themselves exiles, but residents. Although younger Cubans remain firmly anti-Castro, some call for more moderate dealings with the motherland, arguing for limited trade and engagement.

# Hurricanes, Politics & the Everglades

Florida has a habit of selling itself too well. The precarious foundation of its paradise was driven home in 1992, when Hurricane Andrew ripped across South Florida, leaving a wake of destruction that stunned the state and the nation. Plus, mounting evidence

## 1971
Walt Disney World opens and around 10,000 people arrive on the first day.

## 1984
*Miami Vice* debuts. The glamorous but gritty show raises South Beach's international profile.

ALAMY/PICTORIAL PRESS LTD ©

of rampant pollution – fish kills, dying mangroves, murky bays – appeared like a bill for a century of unchecked sprawl and population growth.

Newcomers were trampling what they came for. From 1930 to 1980, Florida's population growth rate was 564%. Florida had gone from the least-populated to the fourth-most-populated state, and its infrastructure struggled to keep up with the strain.

In particular, saving the Everglades became a moral, as well as environmental, crusade. Would one of the Earth's wonders become a subdivision? The Florida Forever Act and the Comprehensive Everglades Restoration Plan were both signed into law in 2000, but state funding for the latter has dropped from $200 million to $17 million at the time of writing.

As the 21st century dawned, Florida's historic tensions – between its mantra of growth and development and the demands that places on society and nature, between its white Southern north and its multiethnic immigrant-rich south – seemed as entrenched as ever. At the same time, the state continues to attract millions of visitors and immigrants, domestic and international, seeking the better life the 'Feast of Flowers' has promised for over 400 years.

**1999**
Despite wild protests in Miami, the US returns refugee Elián Gonzalez to Cuba.

**2000**
The US presidential election is determined by 537 votes in Florida.

**2010**
The Deepwater Horizon oil spill cost Florida tourism an estimated $3 billion dollars.

# Family Travel

Seuss Landing ride (p123) at Universal Studios.

UNIVERSAL STUDIOS ©

*Florida does two things better than just about any place in America — beaches and theme parks. If you're traveling with kids, you may want to stop reading right now, because that's pretty much your itinerary. Indeed, a Florida family trip can easily achieve legendary status with just a few well-placed phone calls. That's why so many families return year after sandy, sun-burned year.*

## Florida for Kids

Every tourist town in Florida has already anticipated the needs of every age demographic in your family. With increasing skill and refinement, nearly every Florida museum, zoo, attraction, restaurant and hotel aims to please traveling families of all stripes.

Your only real trouble is deciding what to do. Florida offers so much for kids and families that planning can be tough. That simple beach-and-theme-park itinerary can suddenly become a frantic dawn-to-dusk race to pack it all in. We can't help you there. In fact, we can't even fit everything in this book.

### Eating Out

Most midrange Florida restaurants have a dedicated kid's menu, along with high chairs, crayons for coloring, and changing tables in restrooms. And nearly every restaurant, even high-end ones, is happy to make a kid's meal on request. As a rule, families with infants or toddlers will get better service earlier in the dinner hour (by 6pm). Only a few truly snooty big-city gourmet temples will look askance at young diners; if you're unsure, simply ask when making reservations.

## Theme Parks

Walt Disney World, Universal Studios, SeaWorld, Discovery Cove, Busch Gardens: Florida's biggest theme parks are verily worlds unto themselves. You can visit for a day, or make them your sole destination for a week, even two.

### Beaches

The prototypical Florida family beach is fronted by or near very active, crowded commercial centers with lots of watersports and activities, tourist shops, grocery stores and midrange eats and sleeps. Some may be known for Spring Break–style party scenes, but all have family-friendly stretches and usually only get rowdy in the late evening.

### Zoos, Museums & Attractions

Up-close animal encounters have long been a Florida tourist staple, and the state has some of the best zoos and aquariums in the country. Florida's native wildlife is truly stunning, and it's easy to see. Florida's cities also have an extremely high number of top-quality hands-on children's museums, and there's a wealth of smaller roadside attractions and oddities designed for, or that appeal to, kids.

## Getting into Nature

Don't overlook unpackaged nature. Florida is exceedingly flat, so rivers and trails are frequently ideal for short legs and little arms. Raised boardwalks through alligator-filled swamps make perfect pint-size adventures. Placid rivers and intercoastal bays are custom-made for first-time paddlers, adult or child. Never snorkeled a coral reef or surfed? Florida has gentle places to learn. Book a sea-life cruise, a manatee swim or nesting sea-turtle watch.

# The Best... Family Friendly Wildlife Encounters

1 Shark Valley, Everglades National Park (p261)

2 National Key Deer Refuge (p237)

3 Bill Baggs Cape Florida State Recreation Area (p200)

4 Lee County Manatee Park (p302)

## Rules of the Road

Florida carseat laws require that children under three must be in a carseat, and children under five in at least a booster seat (unless they are over 80lb and 4'9" tall, allowing seat belts to be positioned properly). Rental-car companies are legally required to provide child seats, but only if you reserve them in advance; they typically charge $10 to $15 extra. Avoid surprises by bringing your own.

# Best Regions for Kids

**Orlando** (p93) Two words: theme parks. No, seven words: the theme park capital of the world.

**Miami** (p192) Kid-focused zoos and museums, plus amazing beaches, but also Miami itself, one of the USA's great multicultural cities.

**Florida Keys** (p191) Active families with older kids will adore the snorkeling, diving, fishing, boating and all-around no-worries vibe.

**Tampa Bay & Gulf Coast** (p282) Top-flight zoos, aquariums and museums, plus some of Florida's prettiest, most family-friendly beaches.

**Daytona & Space Coast** (p312) Surfing, sandcastles, four-wheeling on the beach, kayaking mangroves: all ages love this stretch of Atlantic coastline.

**Panhandle Beaches** (317) Frenetic boardwalk amusements, family-friendly resorts, stunningly white sand: Panama City and Pensacola beaches aim to please everyone.

# Planning

If you're a parent, you already know that luck favors the prepared. But in Florida's crazy-crowded, overbooked high-season tourist spots, planning can make all the difference. Before you come, plot your trip like a four-star general: pack everything you might need, make reservations for every place you might go, schedule every hour. Then, arrive, relax and go with the flow.

## Accommodations

The vast majority of Florida hotels stand ready to aid families: they have cribs and rollaway beds (perhaps charging extra); they have refrigerators and microwaves (but ask to confirm); and they have adjoining rooms and suites. Particularly in beach towns, large hotels and resorts can go toe-to-toe with condos for amenities: including partial or full kitchens, laundry facilities, pools and barbecues, and various activities. Properties catering specifically to families are marked by a family icon ( ).

The only places that discourage young kids (they aren't allowed to discriminate) are certain romantic B&Bs and high-end boutique hotels. If you're unsure, ask, and they'll tell you what minimum age they prefer.

# Need to Know

- **Change Facilities** Found in most towns, theme parks, malls and many chain restaurants
- **Cots** Available in midrange and top-end establishments
- **Health** See the general health section (p358)
- **Highchairs** Widely available in restaurants, as are booster seats
- **Nappies** (diapers) Widely available
- **Strollers** Can be rented at many theme parks and hotels, and folks on public transport will give you a helping hand
- **Transport** All public transport caters for young passengers

## Date Night

Traveling with kids doesn't necessarily mean doing everything as a family. Want a romantic night on the town? Several child-care services offer in-hotel babysitting by certified sitters; a few run their own drop-off centers. For more resources while staying at Walt Disney World resorts, see p91

- **Kid's Nite Out** (www.kidsniteout.com)
- **Sittercity** (www.sittercity.com)
- **Sunshine Babysitting** (www.sunshinebabysitting.com) Statewide.

### Travel Advice & Baby Gear

If you prefer to pack light, several services offer baby gear rental (high chairs, strollers, car seats, etc), while others sell infant supplies (diapers, wipes, formula, baby food, etc), all delivered to your hotel; book one to two weeks in advance. These and other websites also provide family-centered travel advice. Most focus on Orlando, Miami and Tampa, but a few are statewide.

**Baby's Away** (www.babysawayrentals.com) Rents baby gear.

**Traveling Baby Company** (www.travelingbabyco.com) Rents baby gear.

**Babies Travel Lite** (www.babiestravellite.com) Sells baby supplies for delivery; also offers general and Florida-specific family travel advice.

**Jet Set Babies** (www.jetsetbabies.com) Sells baby supplies, plus general infant travel advice.

**Travel For Kids** (www.travelforkids.com) Florida-specific family travel; helpful planning advice.

**Family Vacation Critics** (www.familyvacationcritics.com) Trip Advisor-owned, parent-reviewed hotels, sights and travel.

**Go City Kids** (http://gocitykids.parentsconnect.com) Nickelodeon-sponsored family travel in Miami, Orlando and Tampa.

## Florida-themed Books for Kids

We're big fans of getting reading-age kids in a Florida mood. Try these great books.

*Hoot* (2002) by Carl Hiaasen: Hiaasen's same zany characters, snappy plot twists and environmental message, but PG-rated. If you like it, pick up *Flush* (2005) and *Scat* (2009).

*Because of Winn-Dixie* (2000) by Kate DiCamillo: Heart-warming coming-of-age tale about a 10-year-old girl adjusting to her new life in Florida.

*The Yearling* (1938) by Marjorie Kinnan Rawlings: Pulitzer-prize-winning literary classic about a boy who adopts an orphaned fawn in Florida's backwoods.

*The Treasure of Amelia Island* (2008) by MC Finotti: Historical fiction that re-creates Spanish-ruled Florida through the eyes of an 11-year-old.

*Bad Latitude* (2008) by David Ebright: Pirate adventure for tween boys, with a dash of historical realism.

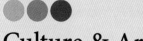

RICHARD L'ANSON/LONELY PLANET IMAGES ©

*Florida's peoples and culture are a compelling mix of accents and rhythms, pastel hues and Caribbean spices, rebel yells and Latin hip-hop, Jewish retirees and Miami millionaires. Florida is, in a word, diverse. Like the prehistoric swamp at its heart, it is both fascinatingly complex and too watery to pin down, making for a very intriguing place to explore.*

## Portrait of a Peninsula

Pessimists say Florida is so socially and culturally fractured that it will never have a coherent identity. Optimists, strangely enough, embrace the diversity and say nearly the same thing.

In terms of geography, Florida is a Southern state. Yet culturally, only Florida's northern half is truly Southern. In the Panhandle, Jacksonville and the rural north, folks speak with that distinctive Southern drawl, serve sweet tea as a matter of course, and still remember the Civil War.

Central Florida and the Tampa Bay area were favoured by Midwesterners, and here you often find a plainspoken, Protestant worker-bee sobriety. East Coast Yankees have carved a definable presence in South Florida – such as the Atlantic Coast's Jewish retirement communities, in Miami and the southern Gulf Coast.

Rural Florida, north or south, can still evoke America's western frontier. In the 19th century, after the West was won, Florida became one of the last places where pioneers could simply plant stakes and make a life. Today, even if they live in cookie-cutter suburbs, many Floridians like to feel they share that same streak of fierce, undomesticated self-reliance.

In parts of Miami and Tampa you won't feel like you're in the US at all. The air is filled with Spanish, the majority of people are Roman Catholic, and the politics of Cuba, Haiti or Colombia animate conversations.

Ultimately, Florida satisfies and defies expectations. You might find Cuban lawyers more politically conservative than Confederate flag-waving construction workers, and fixed-income retirees more liberal than gay South Beach restaurateurs. This is one reason why it's so hard to predict Florida elections, and why sometimes they turn on a handful of votes.

## The Capital of Latin America

Modern Florida has been redefined by successive waves of Hispanic immigrants from Latin America. What sets Florida apart is the teeming diversity of its Latinos and their self-sufficient, economically powerful, politicized, Spanish-speaking presence.

How pervasive is Spanish? One in four Floridians speak a language other than English at home, and three-quarters of these speak Spanish (many of the rest speak Haitian Creole). Spanish is the first language for over 90% of the population of Hialeah, a suburb of Miami.

Today, every Latin American country is represented in South Florida. Argentines can be found in North Miami Beach, Colombians in Coral Gables and Downtown, and Cubans, of course, are everywhere. The children of Cuban exiles are now called YUCAs, 'young urban Cuban Americans,' while the next generation of Latinos has been dubbed Generation Ñ (pronounced enyey).

With each other, young Latinos slip seamlessly between English and Spanish, typically within the same sentence, reverting to English in front of Anglos and Spanish in front of relatives.

## Immigration by Numbers

Before WWII, Florida was the least populated state (with under two million people); today it's the fourth most populated, with 18.8 million in 2010.

Florida's growth rate was an astonishing 44% during the 1970s. While that rate has declined since, it was still over 17% for the 21st century's first decade, twice the national average.

Florida ranks fourth in the nation for the largest minority population (7.9 million), and the largest number and percentage of foreign-born residents (3.5 million people, who make up 18%). In Miami, the foreign-born population exceeds 60% – easily tops among large US cities.

**IN FOCUS   CULTURE & ARTS**

# Floridians at Play

Floridians are passionate about sports. For the majority of Floridians, college football is the true religion. Florida has three of the country's best collegiate teams – the University of Miami Hurricanes, the University of Florida Gators (in Gainesville), and the Florida State University Seminoles (in Tallahassee).

Florida boasts three pro football teams (Miami Dolphins, Tampa Bay Buccaneers and Jacksonville Jaguars) and two pro basketball teams (Orlando Magic and Miami Heat). The Stanley Cup–winning Tampa Bay Lightning is one of several pro and semipro hockey teams in the state, including the Miami-based Florida Panthers.

Major-league baseball's spring training creates a frenzy of excitement in March, when 13 pro teams practice across southern Florida. These stadiums then host minor-league teams, while two pro teams are based here: the Florida Marlins (in Miami) and Tampa Bay Rays (in St Petersburg).

Nascar originated among liquor bootleggers who needed fast cars to escape the law. Fast outgrowing its Southern roots, Nascar is near and dear to Floridians and hosts regular events in Daytona.

Imported sports also flourish in South Florida. One is the dangerous Basque game of jai alai, popular with Miami's wagering types (betting is still legal at jai alai matches). Cricket, surprisingly enough, is popular in South Florida thanks to large Jamaican and West Indian populations.

# Literature

Beginning in the 1930s, Florida developed its own bona-fide literary voice, courtesy mainly of three writers. The most famous was Ernest Hemingway, who settled in Key West in 1928. 'Papa' wrote For Whom the Bell Tolls and A Farewell to Arms here, but he only set one novel in Florida, To Have and Have Not (1937).

The honor of 'most Floridian writer' is generally bestowed on Marjorie Kinnan Rawlings, who lived in Cross Creek between Gainesville and Ocala. She turned her sympathetic eye on Florida's pioneers and the elemental beauty of the state's swampy wilderness. Her novel The Yearling (1938) won the Pulitzer Prize, while Cross Creek (1942) is a much-lauded autobiographical novel.

Zora Neale Hurston, an African-American writer who was born in all-black Eatonville, near Orlando, became a major figure in New York's Harlem renaissance of the 1930s. Her most famous novel, Their Eyes Were Watching God (1937), evokes the suffering of Florida's rural blacks, particularly women.

Florida writing is perhaps most famous for its eccentric take on hard-boiled crime fiction. Carl Hiaasen almost singlehandedly defines the genre; his stories are hilarious gumbos of misfits and murderers, who collide in plots of thinly disguised environmentalism, in which bad guys are developers and the true crimes are against nature. Other popular names are Randy Wayne White, John D MacDonald, James Hall, and Tim Dorsey.

## Painting & Visual Arts

Florida has an affinity for modern art, and modern artists find Florida allows them to indulge their inner pink. In 1983, Bulgarian artist Christo 'wrapped' 11 islands in Biscayne Bay in flamingo-colored fabric, so they floated in the water like giant discarded flowers, dwarfing the urban skyline.

Everyone loved it; it was so Miami.

Cartoon-hued grandeur and exhibitionism seem Miami's calling cards. That certainly applies to Brazilian émigré Romero Britto, whose art graces several buildings, such as the Miami Children's Museum (p206). Miami's prominence in the contemporary art world was cemented in 2002, when the Art Basel festival arrived, and Miami's gallery scene is arguably unmatched outside of LA and Manhattan.

The rest of the state does not lack for high-quality art museums. In addition to Miami, other notable cities are Fort Lauderdale, West Palm Beach, St Petersburg, Tampa, Sarasota, Naples and Orlando.

## Music

Tom Petty, Lynyrd Skynyrd and the Allman Brothers form Florida's holy rock trio, while Matchbox Twenty and Dashboard Confessional also got their start in Florida. Tampa is the home to both punk and 'death metal.' And yet, the popular musician who most often defines Florida is Jimmy Buffett, whose heart lives in Key West, wherever his band may roam.

Rap and hip-hop have flourished in Tampa and Miami, most notoriously with 2 Live Crew, while Orlando (by way of mogul and now jailbird Lou Pearlman) bestowed to the world the boy bands N Sync and Backstreet Boys.

Miami is a tasty mélange of Cuban salsa, Jamaican reggae, Dominican merengue, and Spanish flamenco, plus mambo, rumba, cha-cha, calypso and more. Gloria Estefan and the Miami Sound Machine launched a revival of Cuban music in the 1970s, when they mixed Latin beats with disco with 'Conga.'

## Cinema & Television

Some of the more notable popular films filmed in Florida include the Marx Bros farce *Cocoanuts*, *Creature from the Black Lagoo*n (filmed at Wakulla Springs), T*he Truman Show* (filmed at Seaside), *Ulee's Gold, Donnie Brasco, Get Shorty, Hoot* and *Miami Blues*.

Florida, as setting, has been a main character in a number of TV shows. In the 1960s, the most famous were *Flipper,* about a boy and his dolphin, and *I Dream of Jeannie,* about an astronaut and his one-woman harem.

In the 1980s, Miami was never the same after *Miami Vice* hit the air: a groundbreaking drama that made it OK to wear sport coats over T-shirts and helped inspire the renovation of South Beach's then-dilapidated historic district. Today's popular *CSI: Miami* owes a debt to Don Johnson and *Miami Vice* it can never repay.

## The Best...
## Art
## Museums

1 Morikami Museum & Japanese Gardens (p162)

2 Salvador Dalí Museum (p295)

3 Bass Museum of Art (p198)

4 Lowe Art Museum (p202)

5 Orlando Museum of Art (p94)

IN FOCUS CULTURE & ARTS

# Floridian Food

Grilled shrimp at a restaurant in Florida's Key West (p245).

SHUTTERSTOCK IMAGES/MEZZOTINT ©

*Florida offers as much culinary excellence and adventure as you'd like. The state draws from sublime fresh bounty from land and sea, and menus playfully nick influences from a hemisphere's worth of cultures: Southern, Creole, Cuban, Caribbean, and Central and South American, but also Jewish, Asian, Spanish, and more. Gourmets can genuflect before celebrity chefs, while gourmands hunt Florida's bizarre delicacies, like boiled peanuts, frog's legs, snake, and gator.*

## Destination Dining

Florida has a rich culinary heritage, but the state wasn't known as a place for good restaurants until the 1990s, when a wave of gourmet chefs transformed the Miami dining scene. They dedicated themselves to pleasing sophisticated urban palates by spicing up menus with South Florida's unique combination of Cuban, Caribbean and Latin American influences, which came to be dubbed Floribbean cuisine.

Today, Miami remains the epicenter of all things gourmet, and has the greatest selection of ethnic cuisines, but the ripples have spread statewide. In big cities and anywhere moneyed tourists and snowbirds land, you will find upscale restaurants and skilled chefs plying their trade, often in contemporary dining rooms framing ocean views.

North of Miami and Miami Beach, Fort Lauderdale, Palm Beach and West Palm Beach offer the well-heeled foodie oodles of fun. Key West is, as in all things, more laid-back, but its dining scene is notably stocked with creative-fusion cool.

The southern Gulf Coast is similarly satisfying: Tampa is riding the cusp of a culinary renaissance, with everything from Old World Iberian to locavore-inspired modern gastronomy. Skip south through the rich beach towns of Sarasota, Sanibel Island and Naples, and a memorable meal is a reservation away.

As you go north, robust Southern cuisine comes to dominate, and high-end dining favors classic Italian, French and seafood. Though lacking gourmet 'scenes,' great choices are sprinkled around Orlando and its theme parks. Along the Atlantic Coast, Amelia Island and St Augustine are foodie havens.

## Bounty of the Sea

Florida has always fed itself from the sea, which lies within arm's reach from nearly every point. If it swims or crawls in the ocean, you can bet some enterprising local has shelled or scaled it, battered it, dropped it in a fryer and put it on a menu.

Grouper is far and away the most popular fish. Grouper sandwiches are to Florida what the cheesesteak is to Philadelphia or pizza to Manhattan – a defining, iconic dish, and the standard by which many places are measured. Hunting the perfect grilled or fried grouper sandwich is an obsessive Floridian quest, as is finding the creamiest bowl of chowder.

Of course, a huge range of other fish is offered. Popular species include snapper (with dozens of varieties), mahimahi and catfish.

Florida shines when it comes to crustaceans: try pink shrimp and rock shrimp, and don't miss soft-shell blue crab – Florida is the only place with blue-crab hatcheries, making them available fresh year-round. Winter (October to April) is the season for Florida spiny lobster and stone crab (out of season, both will be frozen). Florida lobster is all tail, without the large claws of its Maine cousin, and stone crab is heavenly sweet, served steamed with butter or the ubiquitous mustard sauce.

Finally, the Keys popularized conch (a giant sea snail); now fished out, most conch is from the Bahamas. It's best served 'cracked,' or fried, with a variety of dipping sauces, or curried in a spicy gravy and served with rice; the latter dish is popular in many Caribbean restaurants.

## Cuban & Latin American Cuisine

Cuban food, once considered 'exotic,' is itself a mix of Caribbean, African and Latin American influences, and in Tampa and Miami, it's a staple of everyday life. Sidle up to a Cuban *loncheria* (snack bar) and order a *pan cubano:* a buttered, grilled baguette stuffed with ham, roast pork, cheese, mustard and pickles.

Integral to many Cuban dishes are *mojo* (a garlicky vinaigrette, sprinkled on sandwiches), *adobo* (a meat marinade of garlic, salt, cumin, oregano and sour orange juice) and *sofrito* (a stew-starter mix of garlic, onion and chili peppers). Main-course meats are typically accompanied by rice and beans and fried plantains.

With its large number of Central and Latin American immigrants, the Miami area offers plenty of authentic ethnic eateries. Seek out Haitian griots (marinated fried pork), Jamaican jerk chicken, Brazilian BBQ, Central American gallo pinto (red beans and rice) and Nicaraguan *tres leches* ('three milks' cake).

In the morning, try a Cuban coffee, also known as *café cubano* or *cortadito.* This hot shot of liquid gold is essentially sweetened espresso, while *café con leche* is just *café au lait* with a different accent: equal parts coffee and hot milk.

**339**

## The Best...
## Cuban Restaurants

Another Cuban treat is *guarapo*, or fresh-squeezed sugarcane juice. Cuban snack bars serve the greenish liquid straight or poured over crushed ice, and it's essential to an authentic mojito. It also sometimes finds its way into *batidos*, a milky, refreshing Latin American fruit smoothie.

## Southern Cooking

The further north you travel, the more Southern the cooking, which makes up in fat what it may lack in refinement. 'Meat and three' is Southern restaurant lingo for a main meat – like fried chicken, catfish, barbecued ribs, chicken-fried steak or even chitlins (hog's intestines) – and three sides: perhaps some combination of hush puppies, cheese grits, cornbread, coleslaw, mashed potatoes, black-eyed peas, collard greens or buttery corn. End with pecan pie, and that's living. Po' boys are merely Southern hoagies, usually filled with fried nuggets of goodness.

Cracker cooking is Florida's rough-and-tumble variation on Southern cuisine, but with more reptiles and amphibians. And you'll find a good deal of Cajun and Creole as well, which mix in spicy gumbos and bisques from Louisiana's neighboring swamps. Southern Floridian cooking is epitomized by writer Marjorie Kinnan Rawlings' famous cookbook *Cross Creek Cookery.*

Ice tea is so ubiquitous it's called the 'wine of the South,' but watch out for 'sweet tea,' which is an almost entirely different Southern drink – tea so sugary your eyes will cross.

## Florida Specialities

From north to south, here are dishes strange and sublime, but 100% Florida; try not to leave without trying them at least once.

**Boiled peanuts** In rural north Florida, they take green or immature peanuts and boil them until they're nice and mushy, sometimes spicing them up with Cajun or other seasonings. Sure, they feel weird in the mouth, but they're surprisingly addictive.

**Alligator** Alligator tastes like a cross between fish and pork. The meat comes from the tail, and is usually served as deep-fried nuggets, which overwhelms the delicate flavor and can make it chewy. Try it grilled. Most alligator is legally harvested on farms and is often sold in grocery stores. It's also healthier than chicken, with as much protein but half the fat, fewer calories and less cholesterol.

**Frog's legs** Those who know say the 'best' legs come from the Everglades; definitely ask, since you want to avoid imported ones from India, which are smaller and disparaged as 'flavorless.'

**Stone crabs** The first recycled crustacean: only one claw is taken from a stone crab – the rest is tossed back in the sea (the claw regrows in 12 to 18 months, and crabs plucked again are called 'retreads'). The claws are so perishable that they're always cooked before selling. October through April is less a 'season' than a stone-crab frenzy. Joe Weiss of Miami Beach is credited with starting it all.

**Key lime pie** Key limes are yellow, and that's the color of an authentic Key lime pie, which is a custard of Key lime juice, sweetened condensed milk and egg yolks in a cracker crust, then topped with meringue. Avoid any slice that's green or stands ramrod straight. The combination of extra-tart Key lime with oversweet milk nicely captures the personality of Key West Conchs.

## Libations

Is it the heat or the humidity? With the exception of the occasional teetotaling dry town, Florida's embrace of liquor is prodigious, even epic. And as you ponder this legacy – from Prohibition-era rumrunners, Spring Break hedonists and drive-thru liquor stores to Ernest Hemingway and Jimmy Buffett – it can seem that quantity trumps quality most of the time.

Yet as with Florida's cuisine, so with its bars. Surely, Anheuser-Busch's Jacksonville brewery will never go out of business, but Tampa also boasts several handcrafted local microbreweries. Daytona's beaches may be littered with gallon-size hurricane glasses, but Miami mixologists hone their reputations with their designer takes on martinis and mojitos.

Indeed, Cuban bartenders became celebrities in the 1920s for what they did with all that sugarcane and citrus: the two classics are the *Cuba libre* (rum, lime and cola) and the mojito (rum, sugar, mint, lemon and club soda), traditionally served with *chicharrónes* (deep-fried pork rinds).

As for Hemingway, he favored piña coladas, lots of them. Jimmy Buffett memorialized the margarita – so that now every sweaty beach bar along the peninsula claims to make the 'best.' Welcome, good friends, to Margaritaville.

## The Best... Florida Food Blogs

1 Jan Norris (www .jannorris.com)

2 Mango & Lime (http://mangoandlime .net)

3 Meatless Miami (www.meatlessmiami .com)

4 Florida Food Hound (www.flfoodhound .com)

5 Pure Florida Food (http://pure floridafood.com)

IN FOCUS FLORIDIAN FOOD

# The Outdoors

Man kayaking in Florida.

ALAMY/AURORA PHOTOS ©

*Florida's beaches are justifiably her claim to fame, and we explore them in-depth later. But the state's waters do more than frame a coastline. Under the ocean is the largest coral reef system in North America, while the peninsula is crisscrossed with 11,000 miles of rivers and streams. The flat topography is perfect for cycling and conceals a trove of hiking trails.*

## Hiking

One thing Florida hikers never have to worry about is elevation gain. But the weather more than makes up for it. Particularly if your destination is South Florida, hike and camp from November through March. This is Florida's 'dry season,' when rain, temperature, humidity and mosquitos decrease to tolerable levels. In summer, make sure to hike first thing, before noon, to avoid the midday heat and afternoon thundershowers.

**Florida National Scenic Trail** (FSNT; www.floridatrail.org) is one of 11 national scenic trails and covers 1400 not-yet-contiguous miles. It runs north from the swamps of **Big Cypress National Preserve** (p265); around Lake Okeechobee; through the **Ocala National Forest** (fs.usda.gov/ocala); and then west to the **Gulf Islands National Seashore** (www.nps.gov/guis) near Pensacola. All the parks above are rife with great hikes.

Other prime hiking areas include the remote pine wilderness, karst terrain and limestone sinkholes of **Apalachicola National Forest** (p315), while **Wekiwa Springs State Park** (p97) rewards hikers, paddlers and snorkelers.

South Florida swamps tend to favor 1- to 2-mile boardwalk trails; these are excellent, and almost always wheelchair accessible. But to really explore the swamps, get in a kayak.

For reservations, hiking organizations and statewide trail information, see p357.

## Canoeing & Kayaking

To really experience Florida's swamps and rivers, its estuaries and inlets, its lagoons and barrier islands, you need watercraft, preferably the kind you paddle. The intimate quiet of dipping among mangroves, startling alligators and ibis, stirs wonder in the soul.

As with hiking, the winter 'dry' season is best for paddling. If it's summer, canoe near cool freshwater springs and swimming beaches.

Some unforgettable rivers include: Orlando's 'Wild and Scenic' **Wekiva River** (p97); and the Tampa region's alligator-packed **Myakka River** (p302).

You'll tell your grandchildren about kayaking **Everglades National Park** (p260); **Hell's Bay paddling trail** (p265) is heavenly. The nearby **10,000 Islands** (p267) are just as amazing, and nothing beats sleeping in the Everglades in a chickee (wooden platform above the waterline; p267).

And don't forget the coasts. You'll kick yourself if you don't kayak Miami's **Bill Baggs Cape Florida State Recreation Area** (p200); Tampa Bay's **Caladesi Island** (p310) and Sanibel Island's **JN 'Ding' Darling National Wildlife Refuge** (p306). Plus, on Florida's Atlantic Coast, more mangroves, waterbirds, dolphins and manatees await in the **Canaveral National Seashore** (www.nps.gov/cana), particularly Mosquito Lagoon. Also seek out **Indian River Lagoon** (www.indianriverlagoon.org). **Big and Little Talbot Islands** (☎904-251-2320; www.floridastateparks.org/bigtalbotisland) provide more intercoastal magic.

For paddling organizations, see p356.

## Surfing

Ten-time world champion surfer Kelly Slater is from Cocoa Beach, and four-time women's champion Lisa Anderson is from Ormond Beach. Both first learned how to carve in Space Coast waves, in the shadow of rockets, and Slater honed his aerials at Sebastian Inlet.

All of which is to say that while Florida's surf may be considered 'small' by Californian and Hawaiian standards, Florida's surfing community and history are not. Plus, Florida makes up in wave quantity what it may lack in wave size.

Nearly the entire Atlantic Coast has rideable waves, but the best spots are gathered along the Space Coast: shoot for **Cocoa Beach** (p106). You'll also find tiny,

# The Best... Canoeing & Kayaking

1 Hell's Bay (p265)

2 JN 'Ding' Darling National Wildlife Refuge (p306)

3 Bill Baggs Cape Florida State Recreation Area (p200)

4 Indian Key State Historic Site (p233)

5 10,000 Islands (p267)

**IN FOCUS THE OUTDOORS**

# The Best...
# Diving & Snorkeling

1 John Pennekamp
Coral Reef State Park
(p231)

2 Biscayne National
Park (p268)

3 Dry Tortugas (p246)

longboard-friendly peelers from **Fort Lauderdale** (p168)
down to Miami's **South Beach** (p193).

Florida's northern Atlantic Coast is less attractive,
partly due to chilly winter water, but consistent, 2ft
to 3ft surf can be had at **Daytona Beach** (p312); at **St
Augustine** (p313), and around **Amelia Island** (p314).

## Diving & Snorkeling

For diving and snorkeling, most already know about
Florida's superlative coral reefs and wreck diving,
but northern Florida is also the 'Cave Diving Capital
of the US.' The peninsula's limestone has more holes
than Swiss cheese, and most are burbling goblets of
diamond-clear water.

If you prefer coral reefs teeming with rainbow-bright
tropical fish, you're in luck...Florida has the continent's
largest coral reef system. The two best spots are
**John Pennekamp Coral Reef State Park** (p231) and
**Biscayne National Park** (p268, but you won't be
disappointed at **Bahia Honda State Park** (p236). Named for their abundant sea
turtles, the **Dry Tortugas** (p246) islands are well worth the effort to reach them.

Wreck diving in Florida is also epic, and some are even accessible to snorkelers;
check out **Fort Lauderdale** (p168) and **Biscayne National Park** (p268).

Many spots line the Suwannee River: try **Peacock Springs State Park** (www
.floridastateparks.org/peacocksprings), one of the continent's largest underwater cave
systems or **Troy Springs State Park** (www.floridastateparks.org/troyspring). Another fun
dive is **Blue Spring State Park** ( ☏386-775-3663; www.floridastateparks.org/bluespring),
near Orlando. Note you need to be cavern certified to dive springs (open-water
certification won't do), and solo diving is usually not allowed. But local dive shops
help with both (for dive organizations and resources, see p356).

## Biking

Florida is too flat for mountain biking, but there are plenty of off-road opportunities,
along with hundreds of miles of paved trails for those who prefer to keep their ride
clean. As with hiking, avoid biking in summer, unless you like getting hot and sweaty.

Top off-roading spots include **Big Shoals State Park** (www.floridastateparks.org
/bigshoals), with 25 miles of trails along the Suwannee River. Also recommended are the
**Ocala National Forest** (fs.udsa.gov/ocala) and the **Apalachicola National Forest** (p315),
particularly the sandy Munson Hills Loop.

With so many paved cycling trails, it's hard to choose. Two of the most
unforgettable? Palm Beach's **Lake Trail** ( ☏561-966-6600; www.pbcgov.com/parks), aka the
'Trail of Conspicuous Consumption' for all the mansions and yachts, and the 15-mile
**Shark Valley Tram Road Trail** (p261), which pierces the Everglades' gator-infested
sawgrass river.

For more-involved overland adventures, do the **Florida Keys Overland Heritage Trail**
(p236), which mirrors the Keys Hwy for 70 noncontiguous miles, and the urban-and-
coastal **Pinellas Trail** ( ☏727-549-6099; www.pinellascounty.org/trailgd), which goes 43 miles
from St Petersburg to Tarpon Springs. For more biking advice, see p355.

# Tread Lightly, Explore Safely

These days, it should go without saying that any wilderness, even a swamp, is a fragile place. Whether hiking, biking, paddling, or snorkeling, always practice 'Leave No Trace' ethics (see www.lnt.org for comprehensive advice). In short, this boils down to staying on the trail, cleaning up your own mess, and observing nature rather than plucking or feeding it.

As you enjoy Florida's natural bounty, take care of yourself, too. In particular, carry lots of water, up to a gallon per person per day, and always be prepared for rain. Line backpacks with plastic bags, and carry rain gear and extra clothes for when (not if) you get soaked. Reid Tillery's *Surviving the Wilds of Florida* will help you do just that, while Tillery's website **Florida Adventuring** (www.floridaadventuring.com) covers backcountry essentials.

## Fishing

The world may contain seven seas, but there's only one Fishing Capital of the World: Florida. No, this isn't typically overwrought Floridian hype. Fishing here is the best the US offers, and for variety and abundance, nowhere else on Earth can claim an indisputable advantage.

In Florida's abundant rivers and lakes, largemouth bass are the main prize. Prime spots, with good access and facilities, are **Lake Manatee State Park** (www.floridastateparks.org/lakemanatee), south of St Peterburg; fly-fishing at **Myakka River State Park** (p302); and **Jacksonville** (www.jacksonvillefishing.com), which has charters to the St Johns River and Lake George for freshwater fishing, to the bay for ocean fishing, plus kayak fishing.

Near-shore saltwater fishing means redfish and mighty tarpon, snook, spotted seatrout and much more, up and down both coasts. In the Keys, **Bahia Honda** (p236) offers shore-fishing highlights.

However, as 'Papa' Hemingway would tell you, the real fishing is offshore, where majestic sailfish leap and thrash. Bluefish and mahimahi are other popular deep-water fish. For offshore charters, aim for **Fort Lauderdale** (p170), **Lauderdale-by-the-Sea** (p166), **Destin** (p317), and **Key West** (p241). The best strategy is to walk the harbor, talking with captains, till you find one who speaks to your experience and interests.

Note that you usually need a license to fish, and there are a slew of regulations about what you can catch; see p356 for fishing organizations and details.

## Sailing

If you prefer the wind in your sails, Florida is your place. **Miami** is a sailing sweet spot, with plenty of marinas for renting or berthing your own boat – **Key Biscayne** (p199) is a particular gem. **Fort Lauderdale** (p170) is chock full of boating options. In **Key West** (p241), sail on a schooner with real cannons, though tour operators are plentiful throughout the Keys.

# Wildlife

A flamingo, native to South Florida.

ISTOCK PHOTO/MAREK GAHURA ©

*With swamps full of gators, rivers full of snakes, manatees in mangroves, sea turtles on beaches, and giant flocks of seabirds taking wing at once, how is it that a squeaky-voiced mouse became Florida's headliner (especially when one of the state's flagship species is a hunting cat)? Dinosaurs, diving birds and the wild heart of a tropical wilderness await you...*

## Birds

Nearly 500 avian species have been documented in the state, including some of the world's most magnificent migratory waterbirds: ibis, egrets, great blue herons, white pelicans and whooping cranes.

Nearly 350 species spend time in the Everglades, the prime birding spot in Florida. But you don't have to brave the swamp. Completed in 2006, the **Great Florida Birding Trail** (http://floridabirdingtrail .com) runs 2000 miles and includes nearly 500 bird-watching sites. Nine of these are 'gateway' sites, with staffed visitor centers and free 'loaner' binoculars; see the website for downloadable guides, and when driving, look for brown road signs.

Among the largest birds, white pelicans arrive in winter (October to April), while brown pelicans, the only pelicans to dive for their food, live here year-round. To see the striking pale-pink roseate spoonbill, a member of the ibis family, visit **JN 'Ding' Darling National Wildlife Refuge** (p306), the wintering site for a third of the US population.

About 5000 nonmigratory sandhill cranes are joined by 25,000 migratory cousins each winter. White whooping cranes, at up to 5ft the tallest bird in North America, are nearly extinct; about 100 winter on Florida's Gulf Coast near Homosassa.

Songbirds and raptors fill Florida skies, too. The state has over 1000 mated pairs of bald eagles, the most in the southern US, and peregrine falcons migrate through in spring and fall.

## Land Mammals

Florida's most endangered mammal is the Florida panther. Though hunting was stopped in 1958, it was too late for panthers to survive on their own. Without a captive breeding program, begun in 1991, the Florida panther would now be extinct, and with only some 120 known to exist, they're not out of the swamp yet.

You're not likely to see a panther, but black bears have recovered to around 3000; as their forests diminish, bears are occasionally seen traipsing through suburbs in northern Florida.

White-tailed deer are an all-too-common species that troubles landscaping everywhere. Endemic to the Keys are Key deer, a Honey-I-Shrunk-the-Ungulate subspecies: less than 3ft tall and lighter than a 10-year-old boy, they live mostly on **Big Pine Key** (p237).

## Marine Mammals

Florida's coastal waters are home to 21 species of dolphins and whales. By far the most common is the bottlenose dolphin, which is frequently encountered around the entire peninsula. Bottlenose dolphins are the species most often seen in captivity.

Winter is the manatee season; they seek out Florida's warm-water springs and power-plant discharge canals beginning in November. These lovable, lumbering creatures are another iconic Florida species whose conservation both galvanizes and divides state residents.

## Reptiles & Amphibians

Boasting an estimated 184 species, Florida has the nation's largest collection of reptiles and amphibians. Uninvited guests add to the total, many after being released by pet owners. Some of the more problematic invasive species include Burmese pythons, black and green iguanas and Nile monitor lizards.

The American alligator is Florida's poster species, and they are ubiquitous in Central and South Florida. South Florida is also home to the only North American population of American crocodile. Florida's crocs number around 1500; they prefer saltwater, and to distinguish them from gators, check their smile – a croc's snout is more tapered and its teeth stick out.

Turtles, frogs and snakes love Florida, and nothing is cuter than watching bright skinks, lizards and anoles skittering over porches and sidewalks. Of 44 species

## The Best...
## Wildlife
## Sanctuaries

1 Suncoast Seabird Sanctuary (p296)

2 Everglades Outpost (p268)

3 Turtle Hospital (p234)

4 Florida Keys Wild Bird Rehabilitation Center (p232)

# The Best...
# State Parks

of snakes, six are poisonous, and only four of those are common. Of the baddies, three are rattlesnakes (diamondback, pygmy, canebrake), plus copperheads, cottonmouths, and coral snakes. While cottonmouths live in and around water, *most* Florida water snakes are not cottonmouths.

## Sea Turtles

Predominantly three species create over 80,000 nests in Florida annually, mostly on southern Atlantic Coast beaches but extending to all Gulf Coast beaches. Most are loggerhead, then far-fewer green and leatherback, and historically hawksbill and Kemp's ridley as well; all five species are endangered or threatened.

During the May-to-October nesting season, sea turtles deposit 80 to 120 eggs in each nest. Infants can become confused by artificial lights and noisy human audiences. For the best, least-disruptive experience, join a sanctioned turtle watch; for a list, visit http://myfwc .com/seaturtle, then click on 'Educational Information' and 'Where to View Sea Turtles.'

## National, State & Regional Parks

About 26% of Florida's land lies in public hands, which breaks down to three national forests, 11 national parks, 28 national wildlife refuges (including the first, Pelican Island), and 160 state parks. Overall attendance is up, with over 20 million folks visiting state parks annually. Florida's state parks have twice been voted the nation's best.

For specific park information:

**Florida State Parks** (www.floridastateparks.org)

**National Forests, Florida** (www.fs.usda.gov/florida)

**National Park Service** (NPS; www.nps.gov)

**National Wildlife Refuges, Florida** (NWR; www.fws.gov/southeast/maps/fl.html)

**Recreation.gov** (www.recreation.gov) National lands campground reservations.

The **Florida Fish & Wildlife Commission** (http://myfwc.com) manages Florida's mostly undeveloped Wildlife Management Areas (WMA). The website is an excellent resource for wildlife viewing, as well as boating, hunting, fishing and permits.

## A Kinder, Gentler Wilderness Encounter

Everyone has an obligation to consider the best ways to experience nature without harming it in the process. For most activities, there isn't a single right answer; specific impacts are often debated. However, there *are* a few clear guidelines.

**Airboats and swamp buggies** While airboats have a much lighter 'footprint' than big-wheeled buggies, both are motorized (and loud) and have larger impacts than canoes for exploring wetlands. As a rule, nonmotorized activities are least damaging.

**Coral-reef etiquette** Never touch the coral reef. Coral polyps are living organisms. Touching or breaking coral creates openings for infection and disease.

**Dolphin encounters** Captive dolphins are typically rescued animals already acclimated to humans. For a consideration of dolphin swims, see p238. However, when encountering wild dolphins in the ocean, federal law makes it illegal to feed, pursue, or touch them. Habituating any wild animal to humans can lead to the animal's death, since approaching humans often leads to conflicts and accidents (as with boats).

**Feeding wild animals** Don't. Kind animals like deer and manatees may come to rely on human food (to their detriment), while feeding bears and alligators just encourages them to hunt you.

**Manatee swims** When swimming near manatees, a federally protected endangered species, look but don't touch. 'Passive observation' is the standard.

**Sea-turtle nesting sites** It's a federal crime to approach nesting sea turtles or hatchling runs. Most nesting beaches have warning signs and a nighttime 'lights out' policy. If you encounter turtles on the beach, keep your distance and no flash photography.

# Beaches

People relaxing on Clearwater Beach (p352) in St Petersburg.

DREAMSTIME IMAGES/GVICTORIA ©

*Here's a telling statistic: 80% of Florida's population lives along its coastline. So it's not just visitors who come to Florida for the beach; it's the natives too. The word 'coastline' is a loaded term, as Florida has two coasts, Atlantic and Gulf, and different beaches for each body of water. Whatever coast you choose to chill on, remember that in Florida, life is always a beach.*

Florida's beaches are the best in the country outside of Hawaii, and incredibly diverse, so let's start with two questions: Do you prefer sunrise or sunset? Do you prefer surfing and boogie boarding or sunbathing and sandcastles? For the former, hit the bigger, east-facing waves of the Atlantic Coast; for the latter, choose the soporific, west-facing waters of the Gulf Coast.

With few exceptions, Florida's beaches are uniformly safe places to swim; the most dangerous surf will occur just before and after a storm. Also, stingrays in summer and occasional jellyfish can trouble swimmers (look for posted warnings).

Be careful about driving down any old road and popping onto the sand in Florida; you may be on someone's property, and folks here can get prickly about that sort of thing. Parking lots for public beaches and public beaches themselves are always well signed. Expect to pay a dollar or two an hour to park at a public beach.

Florida's best beach? Aaw, why not ask us to choose a favorite child. But visitors do have to make decisions. Also consult Dr Beach (www.drbeach.org).

# The Atlantic Coast

The Atlantic Coast is the adult coast of Florida beaches. While there are family friendly options, the beaches here, in terms of their main marketing thrust, tend to cater to a more adult crowd. The Atlantic Ocean brings decent waves and occasionally unpredictable swells and riptides. The presence of the Bahamas means that most of the water that filters in below Jupiter is pretty uniformly calm.

## The Keys

The Keys are islands, but they're fringed more by mangroves than sand and as such aren't great for beaches. Exceptions include **Sombrero Beach** in Marathon and the **Bahia Honda State Park**.

## South Beach

Famed for celebrities, skin, parties, speedos and thongs. South Beach isn't all glam jetsetters, Latin American aristocrats and European fashionistas – there's plenty of Middle Americans out there too – but there's more than a grain of truth to that stereotype. The exception: **South Pointe Park**, at the bottom of South Beach, was specifically designed to be family-friendly.

## Other Miami Beaches

Further north you'll run into sedate **Mid-Beach** and **North Miami Beach**. Haulover Beach Park in North Miami Beach is clothing optional! Miami locals also like to party on the sand in North Miami Beach, but this tends to be a nighttime activity. The lovely beaches of **Key Biscayne** are popular with families and water-sports enthusiasts.

## Fort Lauderdale

The main beach is a magnificent stretch of sand, as is the **promenade** that accompanies it. The north end of Fort Lauderdale beach is gay-friendly, while the southern end caters more to families. **Hollywood Beach & Boardwalk** is aimed at all types, lacks pretension and is great.

## The Best...
## Atlantic Coast Beaches

1 Bahia Honda (p236)

2 Bill Baggs Cape Florida State Recreation Area (p200)

3 Fort Lauderdale (p168)

4 Lake Worth (p151)

5 Hollywood Beach & Broadwalk (p176)

## Come sail away

Miami is a sailing sweet spot, with plenty of marinas for renting or berthing your own boat – **Key Biscayne** (p199) is a particular gem. Fort Lauderdale is chock-full of boating options. In **Key West** (p237) you can sail on a schooner with real cannons, though tour operators are plentiful throughout the Keys. There are sailing schools in all of the major coastal cities in Florida, including Tampa, St Petersburg, Fort Lauderdale, Ft Myers and Sarasota.

## Gold Coast

As you head up to Palm Beach you'll find great beaches all along the coast. Some of the best include **Lake Worth Beach**, an extraordinarily pretty slice of seashore, any of the sand near **Delray Beach** and well-kept **Palm Beach Municipal Beach**.

## Space Coast

**Cocoa Beach** is popular with college students, surfers and water-sports enthusiasts, while **Apollo Beach** is a 6-mile coastline that draws in a family crowd. **Vero Beach** is the spot for those who want a bit of peace, quiet, pedestrian walkways and a cozy arts scene to complement their beach experience.

## Northeast Florida

**Amelia Island** is a quirky getaway for the family crowds and history buffs, while **Daytona Beach** is a bit more... down to earth (read: fun boardwalk with crass T-shirts).

# The Best... Gulf Coast Beaches

1 Fort DeSoto Park (p294)

2 Honeymoon Island State Park (p310)

3 Sanibel Island (p305)

4 Pass-a-Grille Beach (p296)

# The Gulf Coast

The Gulf Coast is warm and calm as bathwater. This is where you find a mom, dad and 2.5 children having the time of their lives. Spring Breakers make their way here too, but in general, the beach scene here is peaceful.

## Naples

We give Naples immense credit for keeping **Naples City Beach** entirely free of concession stands. It helps that this is a postcard-perfect snapshot of snowy white sand.

## Fort Myers

**Fort Myers Beach** is full of bars, restaurants and kids looking for a good time, but it's popular with parents and their little ones too. There's pretty, silky sand on **Sanibel** and **Captiva** islands, which also happen to be some of the best beaches in the world for shelling. Offshore **Cayo Costa State Park** is an all-natural, peaceful escape from reality.

## Sarasota

Sarasota is packed with beaches, including the immensely popular, family-oriented **Bradenton Beach**, beautiful **Lido Beach** and quiet **Turtle Beach**, a popular nesting spot for its namesake reptiles from May to November.

## St Petersburg

The beaches on 'St Pete' are some of the best on the Gulf Coast. Favorites include the natural beauty of family-friendly **Fort DeSoto Park & Beach**, the vintage charm of **Pass-a-Grille** and the bright lights and flash of **St Pete Beach**. Just 30 minutes north of St Petersburg is **Clearwater Beach**, a decidedly party-oriented locale; nearby **Sand Key Park** is tamer.

## The Panhandle

The 'Redneck Riviera' of **Destin** is actually a fantastic slice of old-school seaside Americana, while raucous **Panama City** is (in)famously Spring Break central. **Pensacola** and surrounding beaches are geared towards Southern families on weekend breaks.

# Survival Guide

Boulders along a beach in Florida.
SHUTTERSTOCK IMAGES/STEVE CAROLL ©

# Directory

## Accommodations

Our reviews (and rates) use the following room types:

- single occupancy (s)
- double occupancy (d)
- room (r), same rate for one or two people
- suite (ste)
- apartment (apt)

Unless otherwise noted, rates do not include breakfast, bathrooms are private and all lodging is open year-round.

Rates don't include taxes, which vary considerably between towns; in fact, hotels almost never include taxes and fees in their rate quotes, so always ask for the *total rate with tax*. Florida's sales tax is 6%, and some communities tack on more. States, cities and towns also usually levy taxes on hotel rooms, which can increase the final bill by 10% to 12%.

Throughout the book, quoted rates are usually 'high season' rates, unless rates are distinguished as winter/summer or high/low season. Note that 'high season' can mean summer *or* winter depending on the region; see destination chapters and p48 for general advice on seasons.

Our hotel price indicators refer to standard double rooms:

- $ less than $100
- $$ $100 to $200
- $$$ more than $200

These price indicators are guidelines only. Many places have certain rooms that cost above or below their standard rates, and seasonal/holiday fluctuations can see rates rise and fall dramatically, especially in Orlando and tourist beach towns. Specific advice for the best rates varies by region, and is included throughout: on the one hand, booking in advance for high-season tourist hotspots (like beaches and Orlando resorts) can be essential to ensure the room you want. On the other, inquiring at the last minute, or even same-day, can yield amazing discounts on any rooms still available.

For discounted rooms and last-minute deals, check the following websites:

- www.expedia.com
- www.hotels.com
- www.hotwire.com
- www.orbitz.com
- www.priceline.com
- www.travelocity.com

### B&BS & INNS

These accommodations vary from small, comfy houses with shared bathrooms (least expensive), to romantic, antique-filled historic homes and opulent mansions with private baths (most expensive). Those focusing on upscale romance may discourage children. Also, inns and B&Bs often require a minimum stay of two or three days on weekends and advance reservations. Always call ahead to confirm policies (regarding kids, pets, smoking) and bathroom arrangements.

### HOTELS

We have tried to highlight independently owned hotels in this guide, but in some towns, chain hotels are the best and sometimes the only option in places. The calling-card of chain hotels is reliability: acceptable cleanliness, unremarkable yet inoffensive decor, and a comfortable bed. TV, phone, air-conditioning, mini-refrigerator, microwave, hair dryer and safe are standard amenities in midrange chains. A recent trend, most evident in Miami and beach resorts, is chain-owned hotels striving for upscale

## Book Your Stay Online

For more accommodations reviews by Lonely Planet authors, check out hotels.lonelyplanet.com/Florida. You'll find independent reviews, as well as recommendations on the best places to stay. Best of all, you can book online..

boutique-style uniqueness in decor and feel.

High-end hotels – Ritz-Carlton in particular – overwhelm guests with services: valet parking, room service, newspaper delivery, dry cleaning, laundry, pools, health clubs, bars and other niceties. You'll find plenty of boutique and speciality hotels in places like Miami's South Beach and Palm Beach. While all large chain hotels have toll-free reservation numbers, you may find better savings by calling the hotel directly.

Chain-owned hotels include the following:

**Hilton** ( ☎ 800-445-8667; www.hilton.com)

**Holiday Inn** ( ☎ 888-465-4329; www.holidayinn.com)

**Marriott** ( ☎ 888-236-2427; www.marriott.com)

**Radisson** ( ☎ 888-201-1718; www.radisson.com)

**Ritz-Carlton** ( ☎ 800-542-8680; www.ritzcarlton.com)

**Sheraton** ( ☎ 800-325-3535; www.starwoodhotels.com /sheraton)

## MOTELS

Budget and midrange motels remain prevalent in Florida; these 'drive-up rooms' are often near highway exits and along a town's main road. Many are still independently owned, and thus quality varies tremendously; some are much better inside than their exteriors suggest: ask to see a room first if you're unsure. Most strive for the same level

# Practicalities

◦ Florida has three major daily newspapers: *Miami Herald* (in Spanish, *El Nuevo Herald*), *Orlando Sentinel* and *St Petersburg Times*.

◦ Florida receives all the major US TV and cable networks. **Florida Smart** (www.floridasmart.com/news) lists them all by region.

◦ Video systems use the NTSC color TV standard, not compatible with the PAL system.

◦ Electrical voltage is 110/120V, 60 cycles.

◦ Distances are measured in feet, yards and miles; weights are tallied in ounces, pounds and tons.

◦ Florida bans smoking in all enclosed workplaces, including restaurants and shops, but excluding 'stand-alone' bars (that don't emphasize food) and designated hotel smoking rooms.

◦ Most of Florida is in the US eastern time zone: noon in Miami equals 9am in San Francisco and 5pm in London. West of the Apalachicola River, the Panhandle is in the US central time zone, one hour behind the rest of the state. During daylight-saving time, clocks 'spring forward' one hour in March and 'fall back' one hour in November.

of amenities and cleanliness as a budget chain hotel.

A motel's 'rack rates' can be more open to haggling, but not always. Demand is the final arbiter, though simply asking about any specials can sometimes evoke a discount.

## RESORTS

Florida resorts, much like Disney World, aim to be so all-encompassing you'll never need, or want, to leave. Included are all manner of fitness and sports facilities, pools, spas, restaurants and bars, and so on. Many also have on-site babysitting services. However, some also tack an extra 'resort fee' onto rates, so always ask.

# Activities

For more information on Florida's national and state parks, visit www.floridastateparks.com or www.nps.org.

## BIKING

Note that the state organizations listed under Hiking also discuss biking trails. Florida law requires that all cyclists under 16 must wear a helmet (under 18 in national parks).

**Bike Florida** (www.bikeflorida.org) Nonprofit organization promoting safe cycling and organized rides, with good biking links.

# Climate

## Orlando

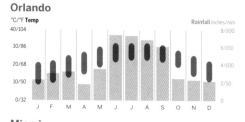

°C/°F **Temp**
40/104
30/86
20/68
10/50
0/32

Rainfall Inches/mm
8/200
6/150
4/100
2/50
0

J F M A M J J A S O N D

## Miami

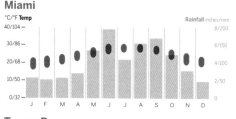

°C/°F **Temp**
40/104 —
30/86 —
20/68 —
10/50 —
0/32 —

Rainfall inches/mm
8/200
6/150
4/100
2/50
0

J F M A M J J A S O N D

## Tampa Bay

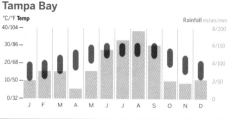

°C/°F **Temp**
40/104 —
30/86 —
20/68 —
10/50 —
0/32 —

Rainfall inches/mm
8/200
6/150
4/100
2/50
0

J F M A M J J A S O N D

**Florida Bicycle Association** (www.floridabicycle.org) Advocacy organization providing tons of advice, a statewide list of cycling clubs, and links to off-road cycling organizations, racing clubs, a touring calendar and more.

## CANOEING & KAYAKING

Water-trail and kayaking information is also provided by the Florida State Parks and the Greenways & Trails websites under Hiking & Camping. Here are more resources:

**American Canoe Association** (ACA; www.americancanoe.org) ACA publishes a newsletter, has a water-trails database and organizes courses.

**Florida Professional Paddlesports Association** (www.paddleflausa.com) Provides a list of affiliated member kayak outfitters.

**Kayak Online** (www.kayakonline.com) A good resource for kayak gear, with links to Florida outfitters.

## DIVING

Ocean diving in Florida requires an Open Water I certificate, and Florida has plenty of certification programs (with good weather, they take three days). To dive in freshwater springs, you need a separate cave-diving certification, and this is also offered throughout the state.

**National Association for Underwater Instruction** (NAUI; www.naui.org) Information on dive certifications and a list of NAUI-certified Florida dive instructors.

**Professional Diving Instructors Corporation** (PDIC; www.pdic-intl.com) Similar to NAUI, with its own list of PDIC-certified Florida dive instructors.

## FISHING

Note that all nonresidents 16 and over need a fishing license to fish, and Florida offers several short-term licenses. There are lots of regulations about what and how much you can catch where; locals can give you details, but it doesn't hurt to review the Florida Fish & Wildlife Conservation Commission (FWC) website.

**Florida Fish & Wildlife Conservation Commission** (FWC; www.myfwc.com) The official source for all fishing regulations and licenses (purchase online or by phone). Also has boating and hunting information.

**Florida Fishing Capital of the World** (www.visitflorida.com/fishing) State-run all-purpose fishing advice and information.

**Florida Sportsman** (www.floridasportsman.com) Get the lowdown on sport fishing, tournaments, charters, gear and detailed regional advice.

# Hiking & Camping

For advice on low-impact hiking and camping, visit **Leave No Trace** (www.lnt.org). For a rich introduction to Florida trails, see **Florida Hikes** (www.floridahikes.com).

**Florida Greenways & Trails** (www.visitflorida.com/trails) The Florida Department of Environmental Protection has downloadable hiking, biking and kayaking trail descriptions.

**Florida State Parks** (www.floridastateparks.org) Comprehensive state-park information and all cabin and camping reservations.

**Florida Trail Association** (www.floridatrail.org) Maintains the Florida National Scenic Trail (FNST); a wealth of online advice, descriptions and maps.

**Florida Trails Network** (www.floridatrailsnetwork.com) The state's main database of current and future trails.

**Rails-to-Trails Conservancy** (www.railstotrails.org) Converts abandoned railroad corridors into public biking and hiking trails; has a Florida chapter and reviews trails at www.traillink.com.

**Recreation.gov** (www.recreation.gov) Reserve camping at all national parks and forests.

For short hikes in national, state or regional parks, free park maps are perfectly adequate. Most outdoor stores and ranger stations sell good topographical (topo) maps. Or order them online:

**US Geological Survey** (USGS; ☎ 888-275-8747; www.store.usgs.gov)

**Trails.com** (www.trails.com) Create custom, downloadable topo maps.

**National Geographic** (www.nationalgeographic.com) Custom maps and GPS maps.

# Surfing

Looking for lessons, surf reports or competitions? Start here:

**Florida Surfing** (www.floridasurfing.com) Instructors, contests, webcams, weather, equipment, history.

**Florida Surfing Association** (FSA; www.floridasurfing.org) Manages Florida's surf competitions; also runs the surf school at Jacksonville Beach.

**Surfer** (www.surfermag.com) *Surfer*'s travel reports cover Florida and just about every break in the USA.

**Surf Guru** (www.surfguru.com) East Coast Florida surf reports.

# Business Hours

Unless otherwise noted the standard business hours in this guide are as follows:

**Banks** 8:30am to 4:30pm Monday to Thursday, to 5:30pm Friday; sometimes 9am to 12:30pm Saturday.

**Bars** most bars 5pm to midnight; to 2am Friday and Saturday.

**Businesses** 9am to 5pm Monday to Friday.

**Post offices** 9am to 5pm Monday to Friday; sometimes 9am to noon Saturday.

**Restaurants** Breakfast 7am to 10:30am Monday to Friday; brunch 9am to 2pm Saturday; lunch 11:30am to 2:30pm Monday to Friday; dinner 5pm to 9:30pm, later Friday and Saturday.

**Shops** 10am to 6pm Monday to Saturday, noon to 5pm Sunday; shopping malls keep extended hours.

# Electricity

120V/60Hz

120V/60Hz

# Food & Drink

In this book, price indicators apply to a typical main course dinner dish; they are:

- ○ $ less than $10
- ○ $$ $10 to $20
- ○ $$$ more than $20

For Miami and Orlando:

- ○ $ less than $15
- ○ $$ $15 to $30
- ○ $$$ more than $30

# Gay & Lesbian Travelers

Florida is not uniformly anything, and it's not uniformly embracing of gay life. The state is largely tolerant, particularly in major tourist destinations, beaches and cities, but this tolerance does not always extend into the more rural and Southern areas of northern Florida. However, where Florida does

embrace gay life, it does so with a big flamboyant bear hug. Miami (p192) and South Beach (p193) are as 'out' as it's possible to be, with some massive gay festivals. Fort Lauderdale (p168), West Palm Beach (p156), and Key West (p237) have long supported vibrant gay communities. But notable gay scenes and communities also exist in Orlando (p105), Jacksonville and Pensacola, and to far lesser degrees in Daytona Beach, Tampa, and Sarasota.

Good gay-and-lesbian resources include:

**Damron** (www.damron.com) Publishes popular national guidebooks, including *Women's Traveller, Men's Travel Guide,* and *Damron Accommodations.*

**Gay Yellow Network** (www.gayyellow.com) City-based yellow-page listings including six Florida cities.

**Out Traveler** (www.outtraveler.com)

**Purple Roofs** (www.purpleroofs.com) Lists queer accommodations, travel agencies and tours worldwide.

# Health

Florida, and the USA generally, has a high level of hygiene, so infectious diseases are not generally a significant concern for most travelers. There are no required vaccines, and tap water is safe to drink. Despite Florida's plethora of intimidating wildlife, the main concerns for travelers are sunburn and mosquito

bites – as well as arriving with adequate health insurance in case of accidents.

## ANIMAL & SPIDER BITES

Florida's critters can be cute, but they can also bite and sting. Here are a few to watch out for:

**Alligators and snakes** Neither attack humans unless startled or threatened. If you encounter them, simply back away. Florida has several venomous snakes. Seek immediate treatment if bitten.

**Jellyfish and stingrays** Florida beaches can see both; avoid swimming when present (lifeguards often post warnings). Treat stings immediately; they hurt but aren't dangerous.

**Spiders** Florida is home to two venomous spiders – the black widow and the brown recluse. Seek immediate treatment if bitten by any spider.

## HEALTH CARE

In general, if you have a medical emergency, go to the emergency room of the nearest hospital. If the problem isn't urgent, call a nearby hospital and ask for a referral to a local physician; this is usually cheaper than a trip to the emergency room. Stand-alone, for-profit urgent-care centers provide good service, but can be the most expensive option.

Pharmacies are abundantly supplied. However, some medications that are available over the counter in other countries require a prescription in the US. If you don't have insurance to cover the cost of prescriptions, these can be shockingly expensive.

## HEALTH INSURANCE

The United States offers some of the finest health care in the world. The problem is that it can be prohibitively expensive. It's essential to purchase travel health insurance if your policy doesn't cover you when you're abroad.

Bring any medications you may need in their original containers, clearly labeled. A signed, dated letter from your physician that describes all of your medical conditions and medications (including generic names) is also a good idea.

If your health insurance does not cover you for medical expenses abroad, consider obtaining supplemental health or travel insurance. Find out in advance whether your insurance plan will make payments directly to the providers or if they will reimburse you later for any overseas health expenditures.

## INTERNET RESOURCES

There is a wealth of travel health advice on the internet. Two good sources are:

**World Health Organization** (www.who .int/ith) The superb book *International Travel and Health* is available free online.

**MD Travel Health** (www .mdtravelhealth.com) Provides complete, updated and free travel health recommendations for every country.

Also, consult your government's travel health website before departure, if one is available:

**Australia** (www.smartraveller .gov.au)

**Canada** (www.hc-sc.gc.ca /index-eng.php)

**UK** (www.fco.gov.uk/en/travel -and-living-abroad)

**United States** (wwwnc.cdc .gov/travel)

# Insurance

It's expensive to get sick, crash a car or have things stolen from you in the US. Make sure to have adequate coverage before arriving. For car insurance see p368. To insure yourself for items that may be stolen from your car, consult your homeowner's (or renter's) insurance policy or consider investing in travel insurance.

Worldwide travel insurance is available at www.lonely planet.com/travel_services. You can buy, extend and claim online anytime – even if you're already on the road.

# Internet Access

The USA and Florida are wired. Nearly every hotel and many restaurants and businesses offer high-speed internet access. In hotel listings, @ indicates a guest internet terminal and 🛜 indicates in-room wi-fi. With few exceptions, all hotels offer in-room plug-in and wi-fi in the lobby. Always ask about connection rates.

Most cafes offer inexpensive internet access, and most transportation stations and city parks are wi-fi hotspots. Public libraries provide free internet terminals, though sometimes you must get a temporary nonresident library card ($10). See destination Information sections.

For a list of wi-fi hotspots (plus tech and access info), visit **Wi-Fi Alliance** (www.wi -fi.org) and **Wi-Fi Free Spot** (www.wififreespot.com). If you bring a laptop from outside the USA, invest in a universal AC and plug adapter. Also, confirm that your modem card will work.

# Legal Matters

In everyday matters, if you are stopped by the police, note that there is no system for paying traffic tickets or other fines on the spot. The patrol officer will explain your options to you; there is usually a 30-day period to pay fines by mail.

If you're arrested, you are allowed to remain silent, though never walk away from an officer; you are entitled to have access to an attorney. The legal system presumes you're innocent until proven guilty. All persons who are arrested have the right to make one phone call. If you don't have a lawyer or family member to help you, call your embassy or consulate. The police will give you the number on request.

# International Visitors

## ENTERING THE REGION

A passport is required for all foreign citizens. Unless eligible under the Visa Waiver Program (see below), foreign travelers must also have a tourist visa. To rent or drive a car, travelers from non-English-speaking countries should obtain an International Drivers Permit before arriving.

Travelers entering under the Visa Waiver Program must register with the US government's program **ESTA (https://esta.cbp.dhs.gov)** at least three days before arriving; earlier is better, since if denied, travelers must get a visa. Registration is valid for two years.

Upon arriving in the US, all foreign visitors must register in the US-Visit program, which entails having two index fingers scanned and a digital photo taken. For information on US-Visit, see the **Department of Homeland Security (www.dhs.gov/us-visit)**.

## VISAS

All visitors should reconfirm entry requirements and visa guidelines before arriving. You can get visa information through www.usa.gov, but the **US State Department (www.travel.state.gov)** maintains the most comprehensive visa information, with lists of consulates and downloadable application forms. **US Citizenship & Immigration Services (www.uscis.gov)** mainly serves immigrants, not temporary visitors.

The **Visa Waiver Program** allows citizens of three dozen countries to enter the USA for stays of 90 days or less without first obtaining a US visa. See the ESTA website above for a current list. Under this program you must have a nonrefundable return ticket and 'e-passport' with digital chip. Passports issued/ renewed before October 26, 2006, must be machine-readable.

Visitors who don't qualify for the Visa Waiver Program need a visa. Basic requirements are a valid passport, recent photo, travel details and often proof of financial stability. Students and adult males also must fill out supplemental travel documents.

The validity period for a US visitor visa depends on your home country. The length of time you'll be allowed to stay in the USA is determined by US officials at the port of entry. To stay longer than the date stamped on your passport, visit a local **USCIS** ( ☏ 800-375-5283; www.uscis.gov) office.

## CUSTOMS

For a complete, up-to-date list of customs regulations, visit the website of **US Customs and Border Protection (www.cbp.gov)**. Each visitor is allowed to bring into the US duty-free 1L of liquor (if you're 21 or older) and 200 cigarettes (if you're 18 or older) and up to $100 in gifts and purchases.

## EMBASSIES & CONSULATES

To find a US embassy in another country, visit the website of the **US Department of State (www.usembassy.gov)**. Most foreign embassies in the US have their main consulates in Washington, DC, but some have representation in Miami.

## DRINKING & DRIVING

Despite what you sometimes see, it's illegal to walk with an open alcoholic drink on the street. More importantly, don't drive with an 'open container'; any liquor in a car must be unopened or else stored in the trunk. If you're stopped while driving with an open container, police will treat you as if you were drinking and driving. Refusing a breathalyzer, urine or blood test is treated as if you'd taken the test and failed. A DUI (driving under the influence) conviction is a serious offense, subject to stiff fines and even imprisonment.

To purchase alcohol, you must be at least 21 and need photo ID to prove your age.

# Money

Prices quoted in this book are in US dollars ($). See Need to Know (p49) for exchange rates.

The ease and availability of ATMs have largely negated the need for traveler's checks. However, traveler's checks in US dollars are accepted like cash at most midrange and top-end businesses (but rarely at budget places). Personal checks not drawn on US banks are generally not accepted. Exchange foreign currency at international airports and most large banks in Miami, Orlando, Tampa and other Florida cities.

Major credit cards are widely accepted, and they are required for car rentals. Most ATM withdrawals using out-of-state cards incur surcharges of $2 or so.

## TIPPING

Tipping is standard practice across America. In restaurants, for satisfactory to excellent service, tipping 15% to 20% of the bill is expected; less is okay at informal diners. Bartenders expect $1 per drink; café baristas a little change in the jar. Taxi drivers and hairdressers expect 10% to 15%. Skycaps at airports and porters at nice hotels expect $1 a bag or so. If you spend several nights in a hotel, it's polite to leave a few dollars for the cleaning staff.

# Public Holidays

For festivals and events, see Month by Month (p42). On the following national public holidays, banks, schools and government offices (including post offices) are closed, and transportation, museums and other services operate on a Sunday schedule. Many stores, however, maintain regular business hours. Holidays falling on a weekend are usually observed the following Monday.

**New Year's Day** 1 January

**Martin Luther King Jr Day** Third Monday in January

**Presidents Day** Third Monday in February

**Easter** March or April

**Memorial Day** Last Monday in May

**Independence Day** 4 July

**Labor Day** First Monday in September

**Columbus Day** Second Monday in October

**Veterans Day** 11 November

**Thanksgiving** Fourth Thursday in November

**Christmas Day** 25 December

# Safe Travel

When it comes to crime, there is Miami, and there is the rest of Florida. As a rule, Miami suffers the same urban problems facing other major US cities such as New York and Los Angeles, but it is no worse than others. The rest of Florida tends to have lower crime rates than the rest of the nation, but any tourist town is a magnet for petty theft and car break-ins.

If you need any kind of emergency assistance, such as police, ambulance or firefighters, call ☎ 911. This is a free call from any phone. For health matters see p358.

## HURRICANES

Florida hurricane season extends from June through November, but the peak is September and October. Relatively speaking, very few Atlantic Ocean and Gulf of Mexico storms become hurricanes, and fewer still are accurate enough to hit Florida, but the devastation they wreak when they do can be enormous. Travelers should take all hurricane alerts, warnings and evacuation orders seriously.

Hurricanes are generally sighted well in advance, allowing time to prepare.

When a hurricane threatens, listen to radio and TV news reports. For more information on storms and preparedness, contact the following:

**National Weather Service** (www.nws.noaa.gov)

**Florida Emergency Hotline** ( 📞 800-342-3557) Updated storm warning information.

**Florida Division of Emergency Management** (www.floridadisaster.org) Hurricane preparedness.

# Telephone

Always dial '1' before toll-free ( 📞 800, 888 etc) and domestic long-distance numbers. Some toll-free numbers only work within the US. For local directory assistance, dial 📞 411.

To make international calls from the US, dial 📞 011 + country code + area code + number. For international operator assistance, dial 📞 0. To call the US from abroad, the international country code for the USA is 📞 1.

Pay phones are readily found in major cities, but are becoming rarer. Local calls cost 50¢. Private prepaid phone cards are available from convenience stores, supermarkets and drug stores.

Most of the USA's mobile-phone systems are incompatible with the GSM 900/1800 standard used throughout Europe and Asia. Check with your service provider about using your phone in the US. In terms of coverage, Verizon has the most extensive network, but AT&T, Sprint and T-Mobile are decent. Cellular coverage is generally excellent, except in the Everglades and parts of rural northern Florida.

# Tourist Information

Most Florida towns have some sort of tourist information center that provides local information; be aware that chambers of commerce typically only list chamber members, not all the town's hotels and businesses. This guide provides visitor center information throughout.

To order a packet of Florida information prior to coming, contact **Visit Florida** (www.visitflorida.com), and also see the list of websites in Get Inspired (p47).

# Travelers With Disabilities

Because of the high number of senior residents in Florida, most public buildings are wheelchair accessible and have appropriate restroom facilities. Transportation services are generally accessible to all, and telephone companies provide relay operators for the hearing impaired. Many banks provide ATM instructions in Braille, curb ramps are common and many busy intersections have audible crossing signals.

A number of organizations specialize in the needs of disabled travelers:

**Access-Able Travel Source** (www.access-able.com) An excellent website with many links.

**Flying Wheels Travel** ( 📞 507-451-5005; www.flyingwheelstravel.com) A full-service travel agency specializing in disabled travel.

**Mobility International USA** (www.miusa.org) Advises disabled travelers on mobility issues and runs an educational exchange program.

**Travelin' Talk Network** (www.travelintalk.net) Run by the same people as Access-Able Travel Source; a global network of service providers.

# Volunteering

Volunteering can be a great way to break up a long trip, and it provides memorable opportunities to interact with locals and the land in ways you never would when just passing through.

**Volunteer Florida** (www.volunteerflorida.org), the primary state-run organization, coordinates volunteer centers across the state. Though it's aimed at Floridians, casual visitors can find situations that match their time and interests.

Florida's state parks would not function without volunteers. Each park coordinates its own volunteers, and most also have the support of an all-volunteer 'friends' organization (officially called Citizen Support Organizations). Links and contact information are on the website of **Florida State Parks** (www.floridastateparks .org/getinvolved/volunteer.cfm).

Finally, **Habitat for Humanity** (www.habitat.org) does a ton of work in Florida, building homes and helping the homeless.

# Women Travelers

Women traveling by them-selves or in a group should encounter no particular problems unique to Florida. Indeed, there are a number of excellent resources to help traveling women.

The community resource **Journeywoman** (www .journeywoman.com) facilitates women exchanging travel tips, with links to resources. The Canadian government also publishes the useful, free, downloadable booklet *Her Own Way;* look under 'Publications' at www.voyage.gc.ca.

These two national advocacy groups might also be helpful:

**National Organization for Women** (NOW; ☏ 202-628-8669; www.now.org)

**Planned Parenthood** (☏ 800-230-7526; www .plannedparenthood.org) Offers referrals to medical clinics throughout the country. In terms of safety issues, single women need to exhibit the same street smarts as any solo traveler, but they are sometimes more often the target of unwanted attention or harassment. Some women like to carry a whistle, mace or cayenne-pepper spray in case of assault. These sprays are legal to carry and use in Florida, but only in self-defense. Federal law prohibits them being carried on planes.

If you are assaulted, it may be better to call a rape-crisis hotline before calling the **police** (☏ 911); telephone books have listings of local organizations, or contact the 24-hour **National Sexual Assault Hotline** (☏ 800-656-4673; www .rainn.org). Or, go straight to a hospital. Police can sometimes be insensitive with assault victims, while a rape-crisis center or hospital will advocate on behalf of victims and act as a link to other services, including the police.

## Transportation

# Getting There & Away

Nearly all international travel-ers to Florida arrive by air, while most US travelers prefer air or car. Getting to Florida by bus is a distant third option, and by train an even more distant fourth. Major regional

## Climate Change & Travel

Every form of transport that relies on carbon-based fuel generates CO2, the main cause of human-induced climate change. Modern travel is dependent on aeroplanes, which might use less fuel per kilometer per person than most cars but travel much greater distances. The altitude at which aircraft emit gases (including CO2) and particles also contributes to their climate-change impact. Many websites offer 'carbon calculators' that allow people to estimate the carbon emissions generated by their journey and, for those who wish to do so, to offset the impact of the greenhouse gases emitted with contributions to portfolios of climate-friendly initiatives throughout the world. Lonely Planet offsets the carbon footprint of all staff and author travel.

hubs in Florida include Miami (p229), Fort Lauderdale (p175), Orlando (p108) and Tampa (p289).

Flights, tours and rail tickets can be booked online at www.lonelyplanet.com /bookings.

 **AIR**

Unless you live in or near Florida, flying to the region and then renting a car is the most time-efficient option.

### Airports & Airlines

Whether you're coming from within the US or from abroad, the entire state is well-served by air.

Major airports:

**Fort Lauderdale-Hollywood International Airport** (FLL; www.broward.org/airport) Serves metro Fort Lauderdale and Broward County. It's about 30 miles north of Miami and is frequently a less-expensive alternative to Miami.

**Miami International Airport** (MIA; www.miami-airport.com) One of the state's two busiest international airports. It serves metro Miami, the Everglades and the Keys, and is a hub for American, Delta and US Airways.

**Orlando International Airport** (MCO; www.orlandoairports.net) Handles more passengers than any other airport in Florida. Serves WDW, the Space Coast and the Orlando area.

**Tampa International Airport** (TPA; www.tampaairport.com) Serves the Tampa Bay and St Petersburg metro area.

Other airports with increased international traffic include Daytona Beach (DAB) and Jacksonville (JAX).

Most cities have airports and offer services to other US cities; these include Palm Beach (PBI; actually in West Palm Beach), Sarasota (SRQ), Tallahassee (TLH), Gainesville (GNV), Fort Myers (RSW), Pensacola (PNS) and Key West (EYW).

The following international airlines service Florida:

**Aerolineas Argentinas** (AR; www.aerolineas.com)

**AeroMexico** (AM; www.aeromexico.com)

**Air Canada** (AC; www.aircanada.com)

**Air France** (AF; www.airfrance.com)

**Air Jamaica** (JM; www.airjamaica.com)

**Air New Zealand** (NZ; www.airnewzealand.com)

**Alitalia** (AZ; www.alitalia.com)

**Bahamas Air** (UP; www.bahamasair.com)

**British Airways** (BA; www.britishairways.com)

**Cayman Airways** (KX; www.caymanairways.com)

**El Al** (LY; www.elal.com)

**Iberia** (IB; www.iberia.com)

**KLM** (KL; www.klm.com)

**Lan** (LA; www.lan.com)

**Lufthansa** (LH; www.lufthansa.com)

**Qantas** (QF; www.qantas.com)

**Varig Brazilian Airlines** (RG; www.varig.com)

**Virgin Atlantic** (VS; www.virgin-atlantic.com)

## TICKETS

There are no ticket-buying strategies unique to Florida. However, compare flights among the handful of major international airports, as rates can sometimes fluctuate widely between them, depending on season and demand. As anywhere, the keys to bargains are research, reserving early – at least three to four weeks in advance – and flexible timing. Booking midweek and off-season can net savings.

For a good overview of online ticket agencies, visit **Airinfo** (www.airinfo.travel), which lists travel agencies worldwide. Then visit these:

**Cheap Tickets** (www.cheaptickets.com)

**Expedia** (www.expedia.com)

**Kayak** (www.kayak.com)

**Mobissimo** (www.mobissimo.com)

**Orbitz** (www.orbitz.com)

**Travelocity** (www.travelocity.com)

**Travelzoo** (www.travelzoo.com)

 ## BUS

Standard long-distance fares can be relatively high: bargain airfares can undercut buses on long-distance routes; on shorter routes, renting a car can be cheaper. Nonetheless, discounted (even half-price) long-distance bus trips are often available by purchasing tickets online seven to 14 days in advance. Then, once in Florida, you can rent a car to get around. Inquire about multiday passes.

 ## CAR & MOTORCYCLE

Driving to Florida is easy; there are no international

borders or entry issues. Incorporating Florida into a larger USA road trip is very common, and having a car while in Florida is often a necessity.

 **TRAIN**

If you're coming from the East Coast, **Amtrak** ( 📞 800-872-7245; www.amtrak.com) makes a comfortable, affordable option for getting to Florida. Amtrak's *Silver Service* (which includes *Silver Meteor* and *Silver Star* trains) runs between New York and Miami, with services that include Jacksonville, Orlando, Tampa, West Palm Beach and Fort Lauderdale, plus smaller Florida towns in between. Unfortunately, there is no longer any direct service to Florida from Los Angeles, New Orleans, Chicago or the Midwest. Trains from these destinations connect to the *Silver Service* route, but the transfer adds a day or so to your travel time.

Another option is Amtrak's *Auto Train,* which is designed to take you and your car from the Washington, DC area and to the Orlando area; this saves you gas, the drive, and having to pay for a rental car. The *Auto Train* leaves daily from Lorton, Virginia, and goes only to Sanford, Florida. It takes about 18 hours, leaving in the afternoon and arriving the next morning. On the *Auto Train,* you pay for your passage, cabin and car separately. Book tickets in advance. Children, seniors and military personnel receive discounts.

**SEA**

Florida is nearly completely surrounded by the ocean, and it's a major cruise-ship

## Car Travel Times

Sample distances and times from various points in the US to Miami:

| CITY | DISTANCE (MILES) | DURATION (HR) |
| --- | --- | --- |
| Atlanta | 660 | 10½ |
| Chicago | 1380 | 23 |
| Los Angeles | 2750 | 44 |
| New York City | 1280 | 22 |
| Washington, DC | 1050 | 17 |

## Bus Fares

Sample one-way fares (advance-purchase/standard fares) between Miami and some major US cities:

| CITY | FARE | DURATION (HR) | FREQUENCY (PER DAY) |
| --- | --- | --- | --- |
| Atlanta | $79/144 | 16–18 | 5–6 |
| New Orleans | $136/149 | 23–24 | 3–4 |
| New York City | $156/172 | 33–35 | 5–6 |
| Washington, DC | $149/164 | 27–29 | 5–6 |

## Train Fares

Sample one-way fares (from low to high season) and durations from NYC to points in Florida:

| FROM | TO | FARE | DURATION (HR) |
| --- | --- | --- | --- |
| New York City | Jacksonville | $125–210 | 18–20 |
| New York City | Miami | $125–215 | 28–31 |
| New York City | Orlando | $125–210 | 22–23 |
| New York City | Tampa | $125–210 | 26 |

port. For more on cruises, see Cruises (p367). Fort Lauderdale is the largest transatlantic harbor in the US, and adventurous types can always sign up as crew members for a chance to travel the high seas.

# Getting Around

Once you reach Florida, traveling by car is the best way of getting around – it allows you to reach areas not otherwise served by public transportation.

 **AIR**

The US airline industry is reliable, safe and serves Florida extremely well, both from the rest of the country and within Florida. However, the industry's continuing financial troubles have resulted in a series of high-profile mergers in recent years: Midwest joining Frontier; Orlando-based Air Tran merging into Southwest; and biggest of all, Continental merging with United.

In general, this has led to fewer flights, fuller airplanes, less perks, more fees and higher rates. Airport security screening procedures also keep evolving; allow extra time.

Air service between Florida's four main airports – Fort Lauderdale, Miami, Orlando, and Tampa – is frequent and direct. Smaller destinations such as Key West, Fort Myers, Pensacola, Jacksonville, Tallahassee and West Palm Beach are served, but sometimes less often or directly.

## Airlines in Florida

Domestic airlines operating in Florida include:

**American** (AA; ☎ 800-433-7300; www.aa.com) Miami hub; service to and between major Florida cities.

**Cape Air** (9K; ☎ 866-227-3247; www.flycapeair.com) Convenient between Fort Myers and Key West.

**Delta** (DL; ☎ 800-221-1212; www.delta.com) International carrier serving the main Florida cities, plus flights from Miami to Orlando and Tampa.

**Frontier** (F9; ☎ 800-432-1359; www.frontierairlines.com) Flies to Tampa, Orlando and Fort Lauderdale from Denver, Minneapolis and Midwest.

**JetBlue** (JB; ☎ 800-538-2583; www.jetblue.com) Serves Orlando, Fort Lauderdale and smaller Florida cities from the East and West Coast.

**Southwest** (SW; ☎ 800-435-9792; www.southwest.com) Major budget carrier flying to and between Fort Lauderdale, Tampa, Fort Myers, Orlando and Jacksonville.

**Spirit** (NK; ☎ 800-772-7117; www.spiritair.com) Florida-based discount carrier serving Florida cities from East Coast US, Caribbean, and Central and South America.

**United** (UA; ☎ 800-864-8331; www.united.com) International flights to Orlando and Miami, plus domestic flights to and between the main Florida cities.

**US Airways** (US; ☎ 800-428-4322; www.usairways.com) Serves Florida from most of US.

## Air Passes

International travelers who plan on doing a lot of flying, both in and out of the region, might consider buying an air pass. Air passes are available only to non-US citizens, and they must be purchased in conjunction with an international ticket. Conditions and cost structures can be complicated, but all include a certain number of domestic flights (from three to 10) that must be used within 60 days. Sometimes you must plan your itinerary in advance, but dates (and even destinations) can sometimes be left open. Talk with a travel agent to determine if an air pass would save you money based on your plans.

The two main airline alliances offering air passes are **Star Alliance** (www.staralliance.com) and **One World** (www.oneworld.com).

## BICYCLE

Regional bicycle touring is very popular. Flat countryside and scenic coastlines make for great itineraries. However, target winter to spring; summer is unbearably hot and humid for long-distance biking.

For Florida biking organizations, some of which organize bike tours, see the Directory (p355). Renting a bicycle is easy throughout Florida; see destination chapters.

Some other things to keep in mind:

**Helmet laws** Helmets are required for anyone aged 16 and younger. Adults are not required to wear helmets, but should.

**Road rules** Bikes must obey auto rules; ride on the right-hand side of the road, with traffic, not on sidewalks.

**Theft** Bring and use a sturdy lock (U-type is best). Theft is common, especially in Miami Beach.

**Transporting your bike to Florida** Bikes are considered checked luggage on airplanes, but often must be boxed and fees can be high (over $200).

For more information and assistance, visit these organizations:

**League of American Bicyclists** (www.bikeleague.org) General advice, plus lists of local bike clubs and repair shops.

**International Bicycle Fund** (www.ibike.org) Comprehensive overview of bike regulations by airline and lots of advice.

**Better World Club** (www.betterworldclub.com) Offers a bicycle roadside assistance program.

 **BOAT**

Florida is a world center for two major types of boat transport: crewing aboard privately owned yachts, and the fast-growing cruise-ship industry.

Each coastal city has sightseeing boats that cruise harbors and coastlines. It really pays (in memories)

to get out on the water. Water-taxi services along intracoastal waterways are a feature in Fort Lauderdale and around Sanibel Island and Pine Island on the Gulf.

## Cruises

Florida is a huge destination and departure point for cruises of all kinds. Miami likes to brag that it's the 'cruise capital of the world,' and Walt Disney World runs its own **Disney Cruise Line** (☏ 800-951-3532; www.disneycruise.disney.go.com), which has a number of three- to seven-night cruises throughout the Caribbean, including to Disney's own private island, Castaway Cay. In Fort Lauderdale, also see the boxed text on day trips to the Bahamas (p177).

For specials on other multinight and multiday cruises, see:

**Cruise.com** (www.cruise.com)

**CruiseWeb** (www.cruiseweb.com)

**Vacations To Go** (www.vacationstogo.com)

**CruisesOnly** (www.cruisesonly.com)

Florida's main ports:

**Port Canaveral** (www.portcanaveral.com) On the Atlantic Coast near the Kennedy Space Center and giving Miami a run for its money.

**Port Everglades** (www.porteverglades.net, www.fort-lauderdale-cruises.com)

Near Fort Lauderdale, and the third-busiest Florida port.

**Port of Miami** (www.miamidade.gov/portofmiami) At the world's largest cruise-ship port, the most common trips offered are to the Bahamas, the Caribbean, Key West and Mexico.

**Port of Tampa** (www.tampaport.com) On the Gulf Coast, and rapidly gaining a foothold in the market.

Major cruise companies:

**Carnival Cruise Lines** (☏ 800-764-7419; www.carnival.com)

**Norwegian Cruise Line** (☏ 866-234-7350; www.ncl.com)

**Royal Caribbean** (☏ 866-562-7625; www.royalcaribbean.com)

 **BUS**

The only statewide bus service is by **Greyhound** (☏ 800-231-2222; www.greyhound.com), which connects all major and midsize Florida cities, but not always smaller towns (even some popular beach towns). Regional or city-run buses cover their more limited areas much better; used together, these bus systems make travel by bus possible, but time-consuming.

Individual city sections in this book usually include the local bus and Greyhound station information. On Greyhound, it's always a bit cheaper to take the bus during the week than on the weekend. Fares for children are usually about half the adult fare.

# Greyhound Fares

To get you started, here are some round-trip Greyhound fares and travel times around Florida:

| FROM | TO | FARE | DURATION (HR) |
|------|-----|------|---------------|
| Daytona Beach | St Augustine | $25 | 1 |
| Fort Lauderdale | Melbourne | $54 | 4 |
| Jacksonville | Tallahassee | $51 | 3 |
| Melbourne | Daytona Beach | $34 | 3½ |
| Miami | Key West | $54 | 4½ |
| Miami | Naples | $41 | 3 |
| Panama City | Pensacola | $40 | 3 |
| St Augustine | Jacksonville | $18 | 1 |
| Naples | Tampa | $54 | 5 |
| Tampa | Orlando | $32 | 2 |
| Tallahassee | Panama City | $34 | 2½ |

## 🚗 CAR & MOTORCYCLE

The most convenient and popular way to travel around Florida is by car. While it's quite possible to avoid using a car on single-destination trips – to Miami, Orlando theme parks, or a self-contained beach resort – relying on public transit can be inconvenient for even limited regional touring. Even smaller tourist-friendly towns like Naples, Sarasota or St Augustine can be frustrating to negotiate without a car. Motorcycles are also popular in Florida, given the flat roads and warm weather (summer rain excepted).

### Automobile Associations

The **American Automobile Association** (AAA; ☎ 800-874-7532; www.aaa.com) has reciprocal agreements with several international auto clubs (check with AAA and bring your membership card). For members, AAA offers travel insurance, tour books, diagnostic centers for used-car buyers and a greater number of regional offices, and it advocates politically for the auto industry.

An alternative is the **Better World Club** (☎ 866-238-1137; www.betterworldclub .com), which donates 1% of earnings to assist environmental cleanup, offers ecologically sensitive choices for services and advocates politically for environmental causes. Better World also has a roadside assistance program for bicycles.

In both organizations, the central member benefit is 24-hour emergency roadside assistance anywhere in the USA. Both clubs also offer trip planning and free maps, travel agency services, car insurance and a range of discounts (car rentals, hotels etc).

## Driver's License

Foreign visitors can legally drive in the USA for up to 12 months with their home driver's license. However, getting an International Driving Permit (IDP) is highly recommended; this will have more credibility with US traffic police, especially if your home license doesn't have a photo or is printed in a foreign language. Your automobile association at home can issue an IDP, valid for one year, for a small fee. You must carry your home license together with the IDP. To drive a motorcycle, you need either a valid US state motorcycle license or an IDP specially endorsed for motorcycles.

## Insurance

Don't put the key into the ignition if you don't have insurance, which is legally required, or else you risk financial ruin if there's an accident. If you already have auto insurance (even overseas), or if you buy travel insurance, make sure that the policy has adequate liability coverage for a rental car in Florida; it probably does, but check.

Rental car companies will provide liability insurance, but most charge extra. Always ask. Rental companies almost never include collision damage insurance for the vehicle. Instead, they offer an optional Collision Damage Waiver (CDW) or Loss Damage Waiver (LDW), usually with an initial deductible of $100 to $500. For an extra premium, you can usually get this deductible covered as well. However, most credit cards now offer collision damage coverage for rental cars if you rent for 15 days or less and charge the total rental to your card. This is a good way to avoid paying extra fees to the rental company, but note that if there's an accident, you sometimes must pay the rental car company first and then seek reimbursement from the credit-card company. Check your credit-card policy. Paying extra for some or all of this insurance increases the cost of a rental car by as much as $10 to $30 a day.

## Rental

### CAR

Car rental is a very competitive business. Most rental companies require that you have a major credit card, that you be at least 25 years old and that you have a valid driver's license (your home license will do). Some national companies may rent to drivers between the ages of 21 and 24 for an additional charge. Those under 21 are usually not permitted to rent at all.

Good independent agencies are listed in this guide and by **Car Rental Express** (www.carrental express.com), which rates and compares independent agencies in US cities; it's particularly useful for searching out cheaper long-term rentals.

National car-rental companies include:

**Alamo** (www.alamo.com)

**Avis** (www.avis.com)

**Budget** (www.budget.com)

**Dollar** (www.dollar.com)

**Enterprise** (www.enterprise.com)

**Hertz** (www.hertz.com)

**National** (www.nationalcar.com)

**Rent-a-Wreck** (www.rentawreck.com)

**Thrifty** (www.thrifty.com) Rental cars are readily available at all airport locations and many downtown city locations. With advance reservations for a small car, the daily rate with unlimited mileage is about $35 to $55, while typical weekly rates are $200 to $400, plus myriad taxes and fees. If you rent from a nonairport location, you save the exorbitant airport fees.

An alternative in Miami is **Zipcar** (www.zipcar.com), a car-sharing service that charges hourly/daily rental fees with free gas, insurance and limited mileage included; prepayment is required.

### MOTORCYCLE

To straddle a Harley across Florida, contact **EagleRider** (☏ 888-900-9901; www.eaglerider.com), with offices in Daytona Beach, Fort Lauderdale, Miami, St Augustine and Orlando. They offer a wide range of models, which start at $150 a day, plus liability insurance. Adult riders (over 21) are not required by Florida law to wear a helmet, but you should.

### MOTORHOME (RV)

Forget hotels. Drive your own. Touring Florida by recreational vehicle can be as low-key or as over-the-top as you wish.

After settling on the vehicle's size, consider the impact of gas prices, gas mileage, additional mileage costs, insurance and refundable deposits; these can add up quickly. Typically, RVs don't come with unlimited mileage, so estimate your mileage up front to calculate the true rental cost.

**Cruise America** (☏ 800-671-8042; www.cruiseamerica.com) The largest national RV-rental firm has offices across Florida.

**Adventures on Wheels** (☏ 800-943-3579; www.adventuresonwheels.com) Office in Miami.

**Recreational Vehicle Rental Association** (☏ 703-591-7130; www.rvra.org) A good resource for RV information and advice, and helps find rental locations.

## Road Rules

If you're new to Florida or US roads, here are some basics:

○ The maximum speed limit on interstates is 75mph, but that drops to 65mph and 55mph in urban areas. Pay attention to the posted signs. City street speed limits vary between 15mph and 45mph.

○ Florida police officers are strict with speed-limit enforcement, and speeding tickets are expensive. If caught going over the speed limit by 10mph, the fine is $155.

○ All passengers in a car must wear seat belts; the fine for not wearing a seat belt is $30. All children under three must be in a child safety seat.

○ As in the rest of the US, drive on the right-hand side of

the road. On highways, pass in the left-hand lane (but anxious drivers often pass wherever space allows).

o Right turns on a red light are permitted after a full stop. At four-way stop signs, the car that reaches the intersection first has right of way. In a tie, the car on the right has right of way.

## HITCHHIKING

Hitchhiking is never entirely safe in any country, and we don't recommend it. Travelers who decide to hitch should understand that they are taking a small but serious risk. You may not be able to identify the local rapist or murderer before you get into the vehicle. People who do choose to hitch will be safer if they go in pairs and let someone know where they are planning to go. Be sure to ask the driver where he or she is going rather than telling the person where you want to go.

## LOCAL TRANSPORTATION

### 🚌 Bus

Local bus services are available in most cities;

along the coasts, service typically connects downtown to at least one or two beach communities. Some cities (like Tampa and Jacksonville) have high-frequency trolleys circling downtown, while some coastal stretches are linked by seasonal trolleys that ferry beachgoers among towns (like between St Pete Beach and Clearwater).

Fares are between $1 and $2. Exact change upon boarding is usually required, though some buses take $1 bills. Transfers – slips of paper that will allow you to change buses – range from free to 25¢. Hours of operation differ from city to city, but generally buses run from approximately 6am to 10pm.

### 🚇 Metro

Walt Disney World has a monorail, and Tampa has an old-fashioned, one-line streetcar, but the only real metro systems are in and near Miami. In Miami, a driverless Metromover circles downtown and connects with Metrorail, which connects downtown north to Hialeah and south to Kendall.

Meanwhile, north of Miami, Hollywood, Fort Lauderdale and West Palm Beach (and the towns between them) are well connected by Tri-Rail's double-decker commuter trains. Tri-Rail runs all the way to Miami, but the full trip takes longer than driving.

### 🚆 TRAIN

**Amtrak** (☎ 800-872-7245; www.amtrak.com) trains run between a number of Florida cities. As a way to get around Florida, Amtrak offers extremely limited service, and yet for certain specific trips their trains can be very easy and inexpensive. In essence, daily trains run between Jacksonville, Orlando and Miami, with one line branching off to Tampa. In addition, thruway motorcoach (or bus) service gets Amtrak passengers to Daytona Beach, St Petersburg and Fort Myers.

# Behind the Scenes

## Author Thanks

### ADAM KARLIN

Thanks: Anna Whitlow, Paula Nino, Jordan Melnick, Megan Harmon, the Paquet family, my Keys crew and every other Floridian who hooked it up. Big thanks to the Lonely Planet crew: Alison, Jennye Garibaldi, Jeff, Jennifer and Emily. Thanks to my grandmother, Rhoda Brickman, for getting me down to Florida in the first place, to my parents who always give me a place to write, and to Rachel for being Rachel.

## Acknowledgments

Climate map data adapted from Peel MC, Finlayson BL & McMahon TA (2007) 'Updated World Map of the Köppen-Geiger Climate Classification', *Hydrology and Earth System Sciences*, 11, 163344.

Cover photographs: Front: Dumbo the Flying Elephant Ride at Walt Disney World, Orlando, Florida; Blane Harrington III/Corbis

Back: People on beach near colorful lifeguard station, South Beach, Miami; Eddie Brady/Lonely Planet Images

Many of the images in this guide are available for licensing from Lonely Planet Images: www.lonelyplanetimages.com.

## This Book

This first edition of Lonely Planet's *Discover Florida* guidebook was written by Adam Karlin, Jeff Campbell, Jennifer Denniston and Emily Matchar. This guidebook was commissioned in Lonely Planet's Oakland office and produced by the following:

**Commissioning Editor** Jennye Garibaldi
**Coordinating Editor** Shawn Low
**Coordinating Cartographer** Valeska Cañas
**Coordinating Layout Designer** Joseph Spanti
**Managing Editors** Bruce Evans, Tasmin McNaughtan, Imogen Bannister
**Senior Editors** Susan Paterson, Angela Tinson
**Managing Cartographer** Alison Lyall
**Managing Layout Designers** Chris Girdler, Jane Hart
**Assisting Editors** Rebecca Chau, Jackey Coyle, Saralinda Turner
**Assisting Cartographers** Andy Rojas
**Cover Research** Naomi Parker
**Internal Image Research** Sabrina Dalbesio
**Thanks to** Trent Paton, Helen Christinis, Ryan Evans, Gerard Walker

## SEND US YOUR FEEDBACK

We love to hear from travelers – your comments keep us on our toes and help make our books better. Our well-traveled team reads every word on what you loved or loathed about this book. Although we cannot reply individually to postal submissions, we always guarantee that your feedback goes straight to the appropriate authors, in time for the next edition. Each person who sends us information is thanked in the next edition, and the most useful submissions are rewarded with a free book.

Visit **lonelyplanet.com/contact** to submit your updates and suggestions or to ask for help. Our award-winning website also features inspirational travel stories, news and discussions.

Note: We may edit, reproduce and incorporate your comments in Lonely Planet products such as guidebooks, websites and digital products, so let us know if you don't want your comments reproduced or your name acknowledged. For a copy of our privacy policy visit lonelyplanet.com/privacy.

**NOTES**

# Index

**000** Map pages

# Y

# Z

# How to Use
# This Book

**These symbols will help you find the listings you want:**

| | | | | | |
|---|---|---|---|---|---|
| 🏖 Beaches | 🎫 Tours | 🍷 Drinking |
| ⊙ Sights | 🎉 Festivals & Events | 🎭 Entertainment |
| 😊 Activities | 🛏 Sleeping | 🛍 Shopping |
| 😊 Courses | 🍴 Eating | ℹ Information/Transport |

**Look out for these icons:**

| FREE | No payment required |
|---|---|
| 🌿 | A green or sustainable option |

*Our authors have nominated these places as demonstrating a strong commitment to sustainability – for example by supporting local communities and producers, operating in an environmentally friendly way, or supporting conservation projects.*

**These symbols give you the vital information for each listing:**

| | | | | | |
|---|---|---|---|---|---|
| ☑ Telephone Numbers | 📶 Wi-Fi Access | 🚌 Bus |
| ⊙ Opening Hours | 🏊 Swimming Pool | 🚢 Ferry |
| P Parking | 🥗 Vegetarian Selection | Ⓜ Metro |
| ⊖ Nonsmoking | 🇬🇧 English-Language Menu | Ⓢ Subway |
| ✳ Air-Conditioning | 👪 Family-Friendly | ⊖ London Tube |
| @ Internet Access | 🐾 Pet-Friendly | 🚊 Tram |
| | | 🚆 Train |

**Reviews are organised by author preference.**

# Map Legend

## Sights
- 🏖 Beach
- ⚑ Buddhist
- 🏰 Castle
- ✝ Christian
- ☸ Hindu
- ☪ Islamic
- ✡ Jewish
- ❶ Monument
- 🏛 Museum/Gallery
- ⊗ Ruin
- 🍇 Winery/Vineyard
- 🐾 Zoo
- ⊙ Other Sight

## Activities, Courses & Tours
- ⊘ Diving/Snorkelling
- 🛶 Canoeing/Kayaking
- ⛷ Skiing
- 🏄 Surfing
- 🏊 Swimming/Pool
- 🚶 Walking
- 🏄 Windsurfing
- ⊕ Other Activity/Course/Tour

## Sleeping
- 🛏 Sleeping
- ⛺ Camping

## Eating
- 🍴 Eating

## Drinking
- 🍷 Drinking
- ☕ Cafe

## Entertainment
- 🎭 Entertainment

## Shopping
- 🛍 Shopping

## Information
- ✉ Post Office
- ℹ Tourist Information

## Transport
- ✈ Airport
- ⊗ Border Crossing
- 🚌 Bus
- ⊶ Cable Car/Funicular
- 🚲 Cycling
- ⛴ Ferry
- Ⓜ Metro
- 🚝 Monorail
- P Parking
- Ⓢ S-Bahn
- 🚕 Taxi
- 🚆 Train/Railway
- 🚊 Tram
- ⊖ Tube Station
- Ⓤ U-Bahn
- • Other Transport

## Routes
- Tollway
- Freeway
- Primary
- Secondary
- Tertiary
- Lane
- Unsealed Road
- Plaza/Mall
- Steps
- Tunnel
- Pedestrian Overpass
- Walking Tour
- Walking Tour Detour
- Path

## Boundaries
- International
- State/Province
- Disputed
- Regional/Suburb
- Marine Park
- Cliff
- Wall

## Population
- ❸ Capital (National)
- ◉ Capital (State/Province)
- ⊙ City/Large Town
- ⊙ Town/Village

## Geographic
- ⌂ Hut/Shelter
- 🏮 Lighthouse
- ⊙ Lookout
- ▲ Mountain/Volcano
- ⊙ Oasis
- ⊕ Park
- )( Pass
- ⊕ Picnic Area
- ⊙ Waterfall

## Hydrography
- River/Creek
- Intermittent River
- Swamp/Mangrove
- Reef
- Canal
- Water
- Dry/Salt/Intermittent Lake
- Glacier

## Areas
- Beach/Desert
- Cemetery (Christian)
- Cemetery (Other)
- Park/Forest
- Sportsground
- Sight (Building)
- Top Sight (Building)